REFLECTING WITH SOLOMON

Books by Roy B. Zuck

A Biblical Theology of the New Testament (editor)
A Biblical Theology of the Old Testament (editor)
Adult Education in the Church (coeditor)
Basic Bible Interpretation
Barb, Please Wake Up!
The Bib Sac Reader (coeditor)
The Bible Knowledge Commentary (coeditor)
Biblical Archaeology Leader's Guide
Childhood Education in the Church (coeditor)
Christian Youth: An In-Depth Survey (coauthor)
Church History Leader's Guide
Creation: Evidence from Scripture and Science
Communism and Christianity Leader's Guide
Devotions for Kindred Spirits (editor)
How to Be a Youth Sponsor
Integrity of Heart, Skillfulness of Hands: Biblical and Leadership Studies in Honor of Donald K. Campbell (coeditor)
Job
Reflecting with Solomon: Select Studies on the Book of Ecclesiastes (editor)
Sitting with Job: Select Studies on the Book of Job (editor)
Teaching as Jesus Taught
Teaching with Spiritual Power
The Life of Christ Commentary (coeditor)
Vital Biblical Issues (editor)
Vital Contemporary Issues (editor)
Vital Ministry Issues (editor)
Vital Theological Issues (editor)
Youth and the Church (coeditor)
Youth Education in the Church (coeditor)

REFLECTING WITH SOLOMON

SELECTED STUDIES ON THE BOOK OF ECCLESIASTES

EDITED BY

ROY B. ZUCK

Baker Books

A Division of Baker Book House Co
Grand Rapids, Michigan 49516

© 1994 by Roy B. Zuck
Published by Baker Books,
a division of Baker Book House Company
P.O. Box 6287
Grand Rapids, Michigan 49516–6287

Printed in the United States of America

Library of Congress Cataloging-in-Publication Data

Reflecting with Solomon : selected studies on the book of Ecclesiastes / edited by Roy B. Zuck.
    p. cm.
Includes bibliographical references and indexes.
ISBN 0-8010-9939-0
    1. Bible. O.T. Ecclesiastes—Criticism, interpretation, etc. I. Zuck, Roy B.
BS1475.2.R44 1994
223'.806—dc20   94-1703
                                                                          CIP

\# 29844649

CONTENTS

5

ABBREVIATIONS

AB	Anchor Bible
ANET	*Ancient Near Eastern Texts,* J. B. Pritchard, ed.
ASTI	*Annual of the Swedish Theological Institute*
ATD	Alte Testament Deutsche
AV	Authorized Version
BASOR	*Bulletin of the American Schools of Oriental Research*
BDB	Francis Brown, S. R. Driver, and Charles A. Briggs, *A Hebrew and English Lexicon of the Old Testament*
Bib	*Biblica*
BJ	*La Bible de Jérusalem*
BKAT	Biblischer Kommentar: Altes Testament
BZAW	Beihefte zur Zeitschrift für die alttestamentliche Wissenschaft
CBQ	*Catholic Biblical Commentary*
CCD	Confraternity of Christian Doctrine
CPIQ	Mitchell J. Dahood, "Canaanite-Phoenician Influence in Qoheleth," *Biblica* 33 (1952): 191–221
EBC	The Expositor's Bible Commentary
GK	Gesenius-Kautzsch, *Hebräische Grammatik*
GNB	Good News Bible
HAT	Handbuch zum Alten Testament
HUCA	*Hebrew Union College Annual*
IBD	*The Illustrated Bible Dictionary,* N. Hillyer, ed.
ICC	International Critical Commentary
Int	*Interpretation*
JAOS	*Journal of the American Oriental Society*

JB	Jerusalem Bible
JBC	Jerome Biblical Commentary
JBL	*Journal of Biblical Literature*
JDMGSup	Zeitschrift der deutschen morgenländischen Gellschaft Supplements
JE	Jewish Encyclopedia
JETS	*Journal of the Evangelical Theological Society*
JQR	*Jewish Quarterly Review*
JSOT	*Journal for the Study of the Old Testament*
JSS	*Journal of Semitic Studies*
JTS	*Journal of Theological Studies*
KAT	Kommentar zum Alten Testament
KB	L. Koehler and W. Baumgartner, *Lexicon in Veteris Testament libros*
KJV	King James Version
LXX	Septuagint
MS, MSS	manuscript(s)
MT	Masoretic Text
NAB	New American Bible
NASB	New American Standard Bible
NCB	New Century Bible Commentary
NEB	New English Bible
NIV	New International Version
NKJV	New King James Version
NT Studies	*New Testament Studies*
RHPR	*Revue d'histoire et philosophie religieuses*
RSV	Revised Standard Version
RV	Revised Version
SBT	Studies in Biblical Theology
SJT	*Scottish Journal of Theology*
SOTI	*A Survey of Old Testament Introduction*, Gleason Archer
Syr	Syriac
TEV	Today's English Version
THAT	*Theologische Handwörterbuch zum Alten Testament*
ThR	*Theologische Rundschau*
TI	Text and Interpretation
TOTC	Tyndale Old Testament Commentary

TWAT	*Theologische Wörterbuch zum Alten Testament,* G. J. Botterweck and H. Ringgren, eds.
TWNT	*Theological Wordbook of the New Testament*
VDBS	*Dictionnaire de la Bible Supplement*
VT	*Vetus Testamentum*
VT[S]	Vetus Testamentum Supplements
WTJ	*Westminster Theological Journal*
ZAW	*Zeitschrift für die alttestamentliche Wissenschaft*

CONTRIBUTORS

George A. Barton
Professor of Biblical Literature and Semitic Languages, Bryn Mawr College, Bryn Mawr, Pennsylvania. Deceased.

Wayne A. Brindle
Associate Professor of Biblical Studies, Liberty University, Lynchburg, Virginia

Ardel B. Caneday
Assistant Professor of Biblical Studies, Northwestern College, St. Paul, Minnesota

George R. Castellino
Pontificium Athenaeum Salesianum, Rome, Italy

James L. Crenshaw
Professor of Old Testament, Divinity School, Duke University, Durham, North Carolina

Barry C. Davis
Bible teacher and author, Palatine, Illinois

Michael A. Eaton
Lecturer in Old Testament, Baptist Theological College of Southern Africa, Johannesburg, South Africa

Kathleen A. Farmer
Professor of Old Testament, United Theological Seminary, Dayton, Ohio

Michael V. Fox
Professor of Hebrew and Semitic Studies, University of Wisconsin, Madison, Wisconsin

Duane A. Garrett
Professor of Hebrew and Old Testament, Canadian Southern Baptist Seminary, Cochrane, Alberta

Donald R. Glenn
Chairman and Senior Professor of Old Testament Studies, Dallas Theological Seminary, Dallas, Texas

Louis Goldberg
Professor of Theology and Jewish Studies, Moody Bible Institute, Chicago, Illinois

11

Robert Gordis
Rapaport Professor of the Philosophies of Religion and Professor of Bible, Jewish
    Theological Seminary of America, New York City, New York. Deceased.
David A. Hubbard
President Emeritus, Fuller Theological Seminary, Pasadena, California
Robert K. Johnston
Provost and Senior Vice President, Fuller Theological Seminary, Pasadena, California
Derek Kidner
Former Warden, Tyndale House, Cambridge, England
Michael Leahy
Professor of Sacred Scripture, St. Patrick's College, Maynooth, Ireland. De-
    ceased.
J. A. Loader
Professor of Semitics and Old Testament, University of Pretoria, Pretoria, South
    Africa
Roland E. Murphy
George Washington Ivey Emeritus Professor of Biblical Studies, Duke University,
    Durham, North Carolina
Graham S. Ogden
Translation Consultant, United Bible Societies, Wamboin, NSW, Australia
H. Carl Shank
Senior Pastor, Refton Brethren in Christ Church, Refton, Pennsylvania
C. Taylor
Fellow and Divinity Lecturer, St. John's College, Cambridge, England. Deceased.
R. N. Whybray
Professor Emeritus of Hebrew and Old Testament Studies, University of Hull,
    England
Warren W. Wiersbe
Author and speaker, and former General Director and Bible Teacher, Back to the
    Bible Broadcast, Lincoln, Nebraska
Addison G. Wright
Distinguished Lecturer in Biblical Studies, Marywood College, Scranton,
    Pennsylvania
J. Stafford Wright
Former Principal, Tyndale Hall, Bristol, and Canon Emeritus of Bristol Cathedral
Roy B. Zuck
Chairman and Senior Professor of Bible Exposition, and Editor, *Bibliotheca Sacra,*
    Dallas Theological Seminary, Dallas, Texas

INTRODUCTION

Perhaps no book of the Bible is more perplexing—and yet more majestic in its appeal—than the Book of Ecclesiastes. Its appraisal that much or all of life is meaningless or futile, its seeming contradictions with other portions of the Scriptures, its apparent pessimistic outlook, its supposed rejection of the value of wisdom and wealth—all these contribute to the puzzling nature of the book. No wonder J. Stafford Wright has called it "the black sheep of the Bible"[1] and R. B. Y. Scott has dubbed it "the strangest book in the Bible."[2]

In examining and exploring "all the things that are done under the sun" (Eccles. 1:14), the writer of Ecclesiastes probed wisdom and folly, life and death, pleasure and sorrow, youth and old age, work and laziness, wealth and poverty, good and evil. As with many people today, the writer was expending his energies and efforts on everything to discover why he should expend his energies and efforts on anything!

Yet the book is hardly a biblical misfit. Though despair seems to permeate its pages, much of what Ecclesiastes presents accords with the rest of Scripture. The fact of injustice, the futility of wealth, the fatigue and frustration of work, the fervor and force of evil, the fate of death—all of these themes coa-

1. J. Stafford Wright, "The Interpretation of Ecclesiastes," *Evangelical Quarterly* 18 (1946): 18.
2. R. B. Y. Scott, *Proverbs, Ecclesiastes,* Anchor Bible (Garden City, N.Y.: Doubleday, 1965), 191.

lesce with those in other Bible books. Nor is Ecclesiastes without its emphasis on God—his creative power, his sovereign control, his loving gifts, his testing of humanity.

Admitting the harsh realities of life and the blunt inescapable fact of death, the Book of Ecclesiastes repeatedly calls its readers to enjoy life (2:24–25, 3:12–13, 22; 5:18–20; 8:15; 9:7–9; 11:8–9) and to fear God (3:14; 5:7; 7:18; 8:12–13; 12:13).

Scholars differ widely on many aspects of the book, including its authorship, date of composition, structure, original language, purpose, and message. This array of views and the emphatic nature of the book have resulted in an extensive flood of writings on Ecclesiastes in books and journals. This anthology gathers what, in my estimation, is some of the better material on this perplexing but profitable book of the Bible. The chapters discuss introductory matters, such as the book's purpose, interpretation, structure, and authorship; specific issues in the book, such as the meaning of *hebel* (variously translated "vanity," "futility," "meaninglessness," "incomprehensibility"); and numerous problem passages. Other chapters were not included because of the limitation of space.

The anthology's title, *Reflecting with Solomon*, reveals my view of the book's author, the traditional view up to the seventeenth century. However, many scholars, including some conservatives, hold to a non-Solomonic authorship. Reasons for and against Solomon as the author are discussed in some of the introductory essays in the anthology.

Readers will note some variations in editorial style and format from chapter to chapter of these copyrighted materials. Also evident are differences in interpretation of various parts of Ecclesiastes. Those differing views give readers opportunity to draw their own conclusions regarding those passages of this enigmatic book.

I am grateful to the publishers for their kind permission to reprint from their works, and to the authors for their excellent contributions to the study of Ecclesiastes, a book not of gloom and doom, but of reality and responsibility. I trust these writings will give readers a new appreciation of Ecclesiastes—which recounts one man's search for satisfaction, his hunt for happiness—and will deepen their sense of their own dependence on God, the One who "has made everything beautiful in its time" (Eccles. 3:11) and who "will bring every deed into judgment" (12:14).

Part 1

Overviews of the Book of Ecclesiastes

1

THE INTERPRETATION
OF ECCLESIASTES

J. Stafford Wright

T he book of Ecclesiastes might be called the black sheep of the Bible. In olden days the Rabbinic schools of Hillel and Shammai disputed whether or not this Book "defiled the hands," that is, whether it was a canonical Book that conveyed holiness when it was handled. Today the examiner asks, "On what ground would you defend the inclusion of Ecclesiastes in the Canon?" In fact the history of the interpretation of the Book shows the profound suspicion with which it has always been regarded. It did, however, find its place in the Canon of Scripture, chiefly because of its Solomonic authorship and the orthodoxy of the final chapter. Yet today few of us would care to maintain that Solomon was the author, while many scholars reject the final chapter.

Ought the book then to remain in the Bible? Would it not be better to admit straight away that the contradictions and unorthodox statements, that have delighted skeptics and puzzled devout minds would have been far better

From *Evangelical Quarterly* 18 (1946): 18–34. Reprinted by permission.

employed in writing for the Rationalist Press Association than for the Library of the Holy Spirit? It is a question that must be faced. If there is no satisfactory interpretation of the book—satisfactory, that is, from the Christian standpoint—there is no logical reason for retaining it in the Bible.

I need not at this point enumerate the particular passages that have shocked the devout; we are familiar with the general tone of them. But it will be worthwhile to refer briefly to the methods of exegesis that Jews and Christians have employed to justify the retention of the book as part of the Word of God.

Jewish expositors made use of three methods. (1) Some of them read the so-called Epicurean passages with a question mark after them, thus; "Is there nothing better for a man than that he should eat and drink, . . . ?" (2) Others adopted a legend that Solomon was driven from his throne in consequence of his disobedience to God, and held that this book was the product of his period of estrangement from God. The origin of this legend appears to be 1:12 which says, "I the preacher *was* King over Israel," implying that now he is no longer king. (3) The unorthodox statements were paraphrased and explained away, as they are in the Targum on this book. Thus such a verse as 9:7, "Go thy way, eat thy bread with joy, and drink thy wine with a merry heart, for God hath already accepted thy works," becomes in the Targum, "Solomon said by the spirit of prophecy before Jehovah, 'The Lord of the world shall say to all the righteous one by one, Go taste with joy thy bread which has been given to thee on account of the bread which thou hast given to the poor and the unfortunate who were hungry, and drink with good heart thy wine, which is hidden for thee in the Garden of Eden, for the wine which thou hast mingled for the poor and needy who were thirsty, for already thy good work has been pleasing before Jehovah.'" Paraphrases along these lines could make even Wellhausen a fundamentalist!

Early Christian commentaries used similar methods of allegorizing, paraphrasing, and explaining away. Jerome wrote a commentary on the book to induce a Roman lady to adopt the monastic life. According to him, the purpose of the book is to show the utter vanity of every sublunary enjoyment, and hence the necessity of betaking oneself to an ascetic life, devoted entirely to the service of God.

Martin Luther was probably the first to deny the Solomonic authorship. He regarded the book as "a sort of Talmud, compiled from many books, probably from the library of King Ptolemy Euergetes of Egypt." Grotius in 1644 followed Luther in the idea that the book was a collection, and once the idea of the unity of the book was broken, it became possible to follow a fresh line of interpretation. Thus Herder and Eichhorn (c. 1780) regarded the book as a dialogue between a refined sensualist and a sensual worldling, or between a teacher and a pupil. The successor to this theory today is the commonly adopted one of three hands in the book. First, there is Koheleth himself. Koheleth is the title assumed by the main author. Our English versions translate it as "The Preacher." Probably this is near enough to the correct meaning, but the commentaries commonly transliterate the Hebrew, so we shall do the same. Koheleth states doubts and problems that arise in his mind as he examines life. Then there is the Pious Man who interjects orthodoxy when he finds a saying of Koheleth that shocks him. Finally a Wise Man sprinkles in a few maxims and proverbs. It is, of course, possible to have many more writers than these three if you wish. Siegfried has a pessimist, a Sadducee, a wise man, a pious man, a proverbial anthologist, a Redactor, an Epilogist, a second Epilogist, and a Pharisee.

On the other hand some commentators hold strongly to the unity of the book. Canon Lukyn Williams in the Cambridge Bible accepts it almost entirely, as previously did such commentators as Delitzsch, C. H. H. Wright and Cornill. What interpretation on this view will justify the retention of the book in the Bible? Without concerning ourselves with details, the interpretation generally adopted is that here we have the struggles of a thinking man to square his faith with the facts of life. In spite of all the difficulties, he fights his way through to a reverent submission to God. The book then is valuable, since it shows that even with the lesser light of the Old Testament it was possible for a thinking man to trust God; how much more is it possible for us with the fuller light of the New Testament! Cornill thus regards the book as marking one of the greatest triumphs of Old Testament piety.

Another type of interpretation is worth mentioning. This stresses the phrase "under the sun" and holds that the author deliberately concerns himself only with the things of this world. Revelation and the world to come are laid aside for the purpose of the argument. Experience of the world leads only to pessimism. Where then is satisfaction to be found? The author does no more than hint that there is something more to be found in God. His purpose in writing is primarily negative—to cause dissatisfaction, so that men will turn in search of something that will satisfy.

Among those commentators who hold to the full inspiration of the Bible there is a certain hesitancy in dealing with Ecclesiastes. The introductory note in the Scofield Bible may be taken as fairly representative. "This is the Book of man 'under the sun,' reasoning about life; it is the best man can do, with the knowledge that there is a Holy God, and that He will bring everything into judgment. The key phrases are 'under the sun'; 'I perceived'; 'I said in my heart.' Inspiration sets down accurately what passes, but the conclusions and reasonings are, after all, man's."

Without being concerned with minor details, we have now reviewed the main lines of interpretation of this fascinating book. I do not know how far any one of them has satisfied you, but none of them completely satisfies me.

This is not to say that there is no truth in them: obviously most of them contain some truth. But I do not feel that any of them has given a key that will unlock the book as a whole, though all assume that there must be a key somewhere. That is to say, Ecclesiastes cannot be treated as a string of texts, each of which may be interpreted in isolation. Even though we may conclude that the author jotted down different passages at different times, in the manner of a diary of his spiritual experiences, yet most of us will feel that there must be some underlying unity, some theme by which the whole is to be interpreted. At any rate I am proceeding on that assumption. So it is useless to take a text and ask "What does that mean?" unless we have in our minds some scheme for the whole book into which that text must fit. Most commentators have, of course, realized this. The point is, what is the scheme?

First of all there is one interpretation that I believe we must unhesitatingly reject. This is the conclusion that we have here the uninspired reasonings of the natural man or even of the skeptic. The theory of Scofield, and the theory of those who hold to several hands in the book, do not strike me as in the least likely. Koheleth is spoken of in the last chapter as a wise man. He evidently had a high reputation for wisdom. There is a proverbial saying that a fool can raise problems which a wise man cannot answer. If Koheleth was the skeptic whose doubts needed to be dealt with by the other two writers, I do not see that his wisdom is much greater than that of the modern tub-thumping objector to Christianity. Anyone who wants to fling doubts at religion has plenty of ammunition in the world around.

Moreover it does not seem to be worthy of God to occupy valuable space in the Bible with the arguments of the skeptic and of the natural man. We can buy those anywhere or have them for nothing. That is the difficulty with Scofield's theory. This objection, of course, does not hold good against those who, like Cornill, see in the book the triumph of piety over the arguments of skepticism. There is something very attractive in this view, but none the less I do not feel that it gives us the master key to the whole book.

Let us then turn to the book afresh, and try to examine it without prejudice. And let us see whether we can interpret it as a unity before cutting the Gordian Knot and dividing the book among three or more hands.

If you pick up a book and want to find the author's viewpoint, where do you turn? The preface is usually helpful—sometimes it saves you reading the book! The conclusion also in a well-written book generally sums up the point that the author has been trying to put over. When you look through the book, you may also be struck by something in the nature of a refrain, that by its continual recurrence tends to drive some point home. Suppose we apply these methods to Ecclesiastes.

The preface is a gaunt and stark announcement, "Vanity of vanities, saith the Preacher; vanity of vanities, all is vanity." That may be the grumblings of a pessimist. To me it is the trumpets sounding the opening theme of some co-lossal overture. "Vanity of vanities, saith the Preacher; vanity of vanities, all is vanity."

My opinion may be purely subjective; I do not ask you to accept it yet. But I do ask you not to dismiss the text as a sub-Christian verdict on life. It is sometimes said that Ecclesiastes is never quoted in the New Testament. But surely Paul has this verse in mind when he says in Romans 8:20, "The creation was subjected to vanity," and in the context he includes us Christians in the whole creation. In other words whatever may be the precise meaning of Ko-heleth's sentiment, there is a general agreement between him and Paul that everything is subject to vanity. Incidentally I wonder whether this text is a genuine utterance of Solomon's, handed down as his comment on life. Ko-heleth at a much later date is so struck by it that he proceeds to put himself in the position of Solomon, and examines life through Solomon's eyes, so as to see how far his verdict was justified. That, of course, is only an idea, and has no direct bearing upon the theme of the book.

From the preface we turn to the conclusion. Here again, not far from the end, we find the words of the preface recurring "Vanity of vanities, saith the Preacher; all is vanity" (12:8). But the final conclusion is definitely presented as the final conclusion: "This is the end of the matter; all hath been heard; fear God, and keep his commandments; for this is the whole duty of man. For God shall bring every work into judgment, with every hidden thing, whether it be good or whether it be evil" (12:13, 14). This conclusion is so orthodox that we hardly need any parallel quotations to support it, but we may notice the statement of Christ in Matthew 19:17, "If thou wouldest enter into life, keep the commandments," and that of Paul in 1 Corinthians 3:13, "The fire shall prove each man's work of what sort it is."

Now if this is the deliberate conclusion of Ecclesiastes, and if the book is a unity, it stands to reason that no statement elsewhere in the book can be in-terpreted as a final conclusion if it contradicts the statement at the end of the book. Or, to put it from another angle, if any statement in the course of the book is given as a final conclusion, it must be interpreted in the light of the ultimate conclusion at the end. This is not a matter of inspiration or non-inspiration; it is the treatment that we should give to any book written by a reasonable man.

The third way of finding an author's point of view is to see whether there is any statement that recurs as a kind of refrain. There are several of these in Ecclesiastes. The "Vanity" theme recurs a number of times: Koheleth keeps reminding us of his text. "Under the sun" is another theme. One might add also, as Scofield does, "I perceived," and "I said in my heart," and similar phrases that describe a personal experience. We can see how these refrains fit into the general argument.

But there is yet another refrain, and this is the one that causes most of the difficulty in the interpretation of the book. Six times over it comes, repeated in slightly different phraseology but reiterating the same sentiment. Its first occurrence in 2:24 is representative of all the six: "There is nothing better for a man than that he should eat and drink, and make his soul enjoy good in his labor." The other occurrences are in 3:12, 13; 3:22; 5:18, 19; 8:15; 9:7–9. In each case the statements appear to be made as final conclusions. So the solution to life is that of the Epicurean sensualist, "Let us eat, drink, and be merry, for tomorrow we die"!

Now something must have gone wrong with our deductions somewhere. For this is completely different from the ultimate conclusion of the book. We must face the contradiction and look at the alternatives which might resolve it. Koheleth may be a slipshod writer who does not worry about contradictions. But this is not a minor contradiction; the whole basis and argument of the book is at stake. Perhaps then the Epicurean sentiments represent a temporary mood, which described, only to be rejected. If this is so, it is strange that the mood keeps recurring, each time in a dogmatic form that suggests a reasoned conclusion. At this point we may grow faint-hearted and adopt the counsel of despair, and dismember poor Koheleth, sending him to join the noble army of martyrs, among which will be found most of the books of the Old Testament. This dismembering is an easy way out of many Bible difficulties, so easy that no one seems to have wondered why the Hebrews were so much more careless with their literature than any other people have been.

But let us have one more look and see whether we can save the unity of the book. Why do we read Epicureanism into this refrain? Because we are familiar with the Epicurean slogan. But suppose that Koheleth was not familiar with the slogan. Would he then necessarily mean by his statement precisely the same as the Epicureans meant by theirs? Could he possibly mean something that would be consistent with his ultimate conclusion? This line of thought is worth following up.

There may be something in it. For at the beginning of Chapter 2 Koheleth describes Solomon's adventures in what we may call Epicureanism—mirth, pleasure, laughter, wine, servants, silver, gold, music and love. What more could a good Epicurean want? But Koheleth's conclusion is that it is all vanity. He can hardly then be advocating a similar course of pleasure for all men, even on a lesser scale. What then does he mean? Let us return to the preface and to the conclusion.

"Vanity of vanities, all is vanity." "Fear God, and keep his commandments . . . God shall bring every work into judgment." The first is a verdict on all life. The second is counsel in view of the verdict. But is the verdict true? That is what Koheleth examines for us, turning life over and over in his hands so that we see it from every angle. And he forces us to admit that it is vanity, emptiness, futility; yet not in the sense that it is not worth living. Koheleth's use of the term "vanity" describes something vastly greater than that. All life is vanity in this sense, that it is unable to give us the key to itself. The book is the record of a search for the key to life. It is an endeavor to give a meaning to life, to see it as a whole. And there is no key under the sun. Life has lost the key to itself. "Vanity of vanities, all is vanity." If you want the key you must go to the locksmith who made the lock. "God holds the key of all unknown." *And He will not give it to you.* Since then you cannot get the key, you must trust the locksmith to open the doors.

Before we come back to the Epicurean refrain, I want us to be convinced that this really is the theme of the book and not just a fancy of my own. The statement in 3:10, 11 is instructive: "I have seen the travail which God hath given to the sons of men to be exercised therewith. He hath made everything beautiful in its time: also he hath set the world in their heart, yet so that man cannot find out the work that God hath done from the beginning even to the end." A number of commentators adopt the R.V. marginal rendering here, and translate the Hebrew *ha-'olam* as "eternity" instead of "the world," and, as this makes better sense, we may adopt it. The previous context deals with the occurrence of events at their right times. "To everything there is a season, and a time to every purpose under the heaven: a time to be born, and a time to die; a time to plant and a time to pluck up that which is planted." And a long list follows. Then come the two verses that I quoted just now. God has given us a sore travail. Events happen to us from time to time, but God has given us a longing to know the eternity of things, the whole scheme; but, try as we will, we cannot see it, though we can declare by faith that each event plays its part in the beauty of the plan.

This is not an isolated thought. It occurs again in 7:14: "In the day of prosperity be joyful, and in the day of adversity consider: God hath even made the one side by side with the other, to the end, that man should not find out anything that shall be after him." Again it comes in 8:17: "Then I beheld all the work of God, that man cannot find out the work that is done under the sun, because however much a man labor to seek it out, yet he shall not find it: yea moreover, though a wise man think to know it, yet shall he not be able to find it."

This is not pessimism. It is the solemn truth—just as true today in Christian times as it was in the days of Koheleth. That eternal WHY hangs over our lives. It meets us at every turn. Our fondest hopes are shattered. Why? The Nazi hordes overrun Europe. Why? God allows the War. Why? A brilliant young Christian life is swept away, while a good-for-nothing wastrel is miraculously delivered. Why? Why? Why? Where is the sense in it all? And yet we must go on looking for the sense. It is incredible that life should make no sense. Every man who thinks at all believes that there is sense somewhere, if only he could find it. He may not look very far; he may settle down to an un-worthy philosophy of life. Or he may plumb the depths of reason, of science, or of theology in an endeavor to find the plan. But he cannot find it. Joad has not found it. Huxley has not found it. Karl Barth has not found it. No one has. The moment we think we have it, something happens that does not fit into the scheme at all. But we go on looking. We must look. We cannot help it. "It is a sore travail which God hath given to the sons of men to be exercised therewith. . . . He hath set eternity in their heart, yet so that man cannot find out the work that God hath done from the beginning even to the end."

See how Koheleth develops his theme. We go through the world with him, looking for the solution to life, and at every turn he forces us to admit that here is only vanity, frustration, bewilderment. Life does not provide the key to itself.

Come with him in the first chapter, and study Nature, that great revelation of God. But Nature is a closed system, an endless round of sunshine, winds, rain, rivers, speaking of God, it is true, but not disclosing the plan of God. The key is not in Nature.

Then let us try Man. Perhaps the key will be found in the process of history or in the progress of science. But all we see is an endless chain of generation after generation, striving for this and for that, groping for something and find-ing no satisfaction, producing new inventions, which are but adaptations of what already exists in the closed system of Nature, and which never bring to light that new truth and solution to life that all men long for. The key is not in humanity.

But it may be in Wisdom. Surely the greatest minds have the solution, or what is Wisdom for? Does Wisdom satisfy? Koheleth faces the question in the second part of his first chapter. Even though you have the Wisdom of So-lomon, the verdict is: "In much wisdom is much grief; and he that increaseth knowledge increaseth sorrow." Why should it be so? Verse 15 suggests the answer, "That which is crooked cannot be made straight: and that which is deficient cannot be made up." If we may paraphrase the last clause, the world is bankrupt and can do nothing about it. It is only the really wise man who realizes the bankruptcy of life. Philosophy may easily lead to despair. It has been said that it is better to be a discontented Socrates than a contented pig. Certainly your Socrates will always be discontented, because he knows that he must forever search for the key that he will never find.

But is there such a thing as a contented human pig? If there is, perhaps he has found the key dropped after all in the mire of his sty. So Koheleth looks there. In Chapter 2 he becomes the complete human animal. He runs the whole course of sensual pleasure, and his verdict is: "Vanity and a striving after wind." You can no more grasp the solution to life's eternal discontent there than you can grasp the wind in your fist.

Koheleth's mind sways to and fro. The clue is not in wisdom, but perhaps it may be in folly, in an attitude that closes its mind to all ideas? Is a fool the ideal man? No, cries Koheleth, I cannot admit that. "Wisdom excelleth folly, as far as light excelleth darkness." "Yet I perceived that one event happeneth to them all. . . . How doth the wise man die even as the fool! So I hated life." Now for the first time Koheleth faces us with that supreme vanity death, death that beats at every man's door, death that comes when man least expects him, death that undoes man's finest plans. Death can make a man hate life, not because he wants to die, but because it renders life so futile, just as a child on the seashore may grow weary of the sand castles that he builds so patiently only to have them swallowed up by the inexorable sea. Koheleth gives an illustration in 2:18–23. A man gains wealth and power and makes an honored name for himself. If he could live forever, all would be well. But at his death all his possessions pass to another, and he may be a wastrel and a fool.

Pessimism of pessimisms: all is pessimism! God then has made us to dance like puppets, in a play that we must always be trying to understand but can never comprehend.

There seems to be no cure, but to cut the strings and end the play by suicide, or to dance to our own tune and call it God's. The last is the conclusion of Omar Khayyám, but neither of the two is the solution of Koheleth. And yet so nicely balanced are the ultimate conclusions of life and religion that there is in places only a hair's breadth between Koheleth and Omar Khayyám. Yet that hair's breadth puts Koheleth's book in heaven and leaves the Rubaiyat of Omar Khayyám tied to the earth.

Now at last we are ready to deal with the interpretation of the refrain to which we have already referred. But let us pause one moment more to ask ourselves what are the possible solutions to the problem of life that Koheleth raises, and what is the Christian solution? Suicide is a possible solution, we give life up in despair as a problem too great for us to understand. Few philosophers have accepted this solution, which is no solution at all. Popular Epicureanism is another solution which gives up the problem as insoluble. Some have believed this to be Koheleth's answer. But if it is, the closing verses of the book, and other passages in the course of the book, must be ascribed to another hand and Koheleth himself written off as a worldling. Fatalism may solve the problem. God is the arbitrary Judge, or maybe he is no more than impersonal Fate, working according to his whims and fancies. Omar Khayyám combines this Fatalism with Epicureanism. But what is this driving force that compels our minds to turn again and again to the problem of life? Is it no more than idle curiosity? Or is it part of our inheritance as those made in the image of God, so that we see that the universe has a wholeness, and that it must make sense if only we could find what the sense is?

The Christian answer is that the universe does make sense. There is a plan and a purpose that has its center and its climax in Christ. We as Christians have been predestinated to be an integral part of that plan. We have been "created in Christ Jesus for good works, which God afore prepared that we should walk in them" (Eph. 2:10). But not even to Christians has it been given to comprehend the plan. Not even a Christian can explain how everything that comes into his life takes its place in the plan. But, none the less, all the time he is trying to catch a glimpse of a certain wholeness that will link together all his individual experiences. But again and again he is driven back to the position of Romans 8:28: "We know that to them that love God all things work together for good, even to them that are called according to his purpose"; or, if *ho theos* is read in place of *ton theos,* "We know that God works all things for good with them that love him." The Christian attitude then is one of faith and confidence. The Christian says, "I know that all these things must play their part in God's total plan. I long to know what the plan is and to see it as a whole, and I shall always go on trying to see it. But in the meantime I will live my life one day at a time, believing that in the common round of life I am doing the will of God. I will be content with what God gives me and take my life from the hand of God."

If, as I believe, this is the Christian solution, it is also the solution of Koheleth. If his refrain is interpreted in the light of the rest of the book, it can only mean what the Christian means when he says, "I will take the things that make up my life, my food, my drink, my work from the hand of God. All things work together for my good." Thus Koheleth says in 2:24: "There is nothing better for a man than that he should eat and drink, and make his soul enjoy good in his labor. This also I saw, that it is from the hand of God." Or again in 3:11–13: "He hath made everything beautiful in its time; also he hath set eternity in their heart, yet so that man cannot find out the work that God hath done from the beginning even to the end. I know that there is nothing better for them, than to rejoice, and to get good so long as they live. And also that every man should eat and drink, and enjoy good in all his labor, is the gift of God."

Now this theme is worked out, not only in the refrains, but continually throughout the book. There is the thought of the certainty of a divine plan, even though individual steps in the plan remain a mystery, and must be accepted by faith. But man must never lose the realization that there is a plan, and he must never begin to treat the common things of life, his food and drink and work, as though they were not the gift of God. Hence man must learn to serve God from his youth and he must remember that there is to be judgment. Judgment, of course, implies a divine plan. If our sins were not a falling away from the divine plan, it would be difficult to vindicate God's justice in bringing us to judgment. But if we are brought up to realize that we owe a responsibility to God, it will help us to make our daily lives from the hand of God. This is Koheleth's thought in 11:9, 10: "Rejoice, O young man, in thy youth and let thy heart cheer thee in the days of thy youth, and walk in the ways of thine heart, and in the sight of thine eyes; but know thou, that for all these things God will bring thee into judgment. Therefore remove sorrow from thy heart and put away evil from thy flesh; for youth and the prime of life are vanity." In other words, Koheleth advises young men to enjoy their lives, but not to forget that their pleasures should be regulated by a sense of accountability to God. They should put away all that would harm mind or body, and remember that youth is not the whole of life; it will give place to middle age, old age, and death. Could even a C.S.S.M. leader say more?

But this question of death needs a little more consideration. Once again Koheleth's statements must be interpreted against the background of the whole Book. Death is a salutary and sobering thing to Koheleth. See how he deals with it in 3:18–22. Man commonly tends to live as though he had unlimited time for doing the plan of God. It is an extraordinary fact that most of us live as though this life were to be prolonged indefinitely. Or, looking at it from another point of view, we dwell upon the immortality of the soul, and forget that the vehicle for the service of God now is the body, and, if we fail to serve God in the body now, we shall never be able to make up in the future for what we have failed to do now. But the body is a frail thing. It links man with the animal world. Animals and men both possess that which the mineral and plant world lack—body and spirit. It may sound rather shocking to say that animals possess spirit, but, if you are shocked, I believe that shows that you have misinterpreted Koheleth. Some biblical psychology has failed to recognize different uses of the term "spirit" in Scripture. Hence Koheleth has been understood to teach in 3:21 that man perishes at death in the same way as the beasts perish; and in 12:7, when he says that the spirit shall return unto God who gave it, that man at death goes straight to heaven, and not to Sheol. But the fact is that Koheleth is not discussing the survival of the personal spirit in either of these passages. All animal life, which includes human life, has two features in common—a physical body and a life principle which animates the body. The thought is expressed again in Psalm 104:29, 30: "Thou takest away their breath, they die, and return to their dust. Thou sendest forth thy spirit, they are created." This life principle, or spirit is the gift of God, and when the body turns back to dust, the life principle goes back to the Author of all life.

Thus, to return to the interpretation of 3:18–22, this body that we share with the animal world is a frail thing, yet it is the instrument with which we serve God. When an animal dies where does it go? It goes to dust. What about its life principle? Can you assert that its destination is different from that of man? Are you, in other words, on a higher footing than an animal so far as the fact of physical death is concerned? Never mind about future opportunities of service. We are talking about service in the body. This life is the portion that God has given you. Here you must find your satisfaction and must realize yourself. For you will not come back again to this earth any more than an animal will.

I submit that that is a straightforward interpretation of the passage. And I should give a similar interpretation to 8:16–9:10. Here once again we find the longing to know the plan. "I beheld all the work of God, that man cannot find out the work that is done under the sun: because however much a man labor to seek it out, yet he shall not find it." Here too we have the acceptance of the plan by faith. "The righteous, and the wise, and their works, are in the hand of God." Here too is the bewilderment at individual events: "All things come alike to all." Those events that are beyond the individual's own control so often appear to happen in a haphazard way. The tower at Siloam falls on the good as well as on the bad. And then, looming ahead, is the one event for all mankind, the one event of death. And death closes all. "A living cur is better than a dead lion." "The living know that they shall die," and can make their plans accordingly. There is a sense in which it is never too late in this life to take up your part in God's plan. But the dead have run their course. They are waiting in Sheol for the judgment. They do not, like the living, know what is happening on the earth. They have no further opportunities of earning the Master's reward. Their bodies, the vehicles of the emotions of love and hatred and envy, have gone to dust, and no more can they share in life under the sun.

Now see how beautifully the refrain follows in verses 7–10. Take up the common things of life, and find your joy in the service of God there. Life is but vanity, but it is a vanity that may be turned to profit if only one grasps the opportunity while it is present. "Whatsoever thy hand findeth to do, do it with thy might; for there is no work, nor device, nor knowledge, nor wisdom in Sheol, whither thou goest." And if that last verse sounds sub-Christian, we may remind ourselves that Christ himself said, "I must work the works of him that sent me while it is day; the night cometh when no man can work" (John 9:4).

This emphasis upon doing our work with all our might is a necessary counterbalance to the thought of accepting our life as from the hand of God. We are not to live in a spirit of complete resignation to life, tamely submitting to the flow of events, saying about everything, "This is the will of God." This is not Koheleth's idea. The fact that he introduces the idea of moral responsibility, with his warning of the Judgment, shows that we are to live our life as free beings. Moreover the incidental pieces of proverbial wisdom are intended to be a guide for the practical side of life. We have reached the conclusion that the events of life by themselves do not furnish the clue to their own meaning. "The race is not to the swift, nor the battle to the strong, neither yet bread to the wise, nor yet riches to men of understanding, nor yet favor to men of skill; but time and chance happeneth to them all." So Koheleth says in 9:11 and, if we are honest, we must admit that this is the impression that life makes on us. No one can guarantee success, and no one can quite see how God will deal with him in the events of life. Therefore many things in life must be planned on this basis. As God's people we may sincerely desire to arrange our lives for His glory, but we find it very difficult to say for certain, "If I do such-and-such a thing, I know I shall be conforming with God's plan, and he will bless me in it." That is the point of Chapter 11. If you are a merchant or a farmer, it is no use waiting for infallible guidance so that you can invest all your possessions in one venture, or plant all your seed with the prospect of 100 per cent success. You must use your common sense, and make such provision as you can to meet the unknown quantities in life. If you are a merchant, distribute your ventures over seven or eight schemes. If you are a farmer, sow your seed at different times so as to make sure of one crop, if not of more than one. This all sounds rather banal, but it seems to me to be a true guide for life. Until such time as God gives us infallible guidance, and as long as events in the world continue to happen apparently indiscriminately, I do not see that we can do anything else. Let us remember, however, that belief in the Providence of God does allow us to hold that there are exceptions to the ordinary run of things. God can and does work miracles, which are none the less miracles because they are brought about through natural causes. His people are often miraculously delivered. But it is fair to hold, as Koheleth held, that the vindication of God's way in individual lives is the miracle, while the apparent chance—which to us, as to Koheleth, is no more than *apparent*—is the normal rule. But let us emphasize it once again, God has a plan, and at the end of it he will be vindicated. But until we have reached the ultimate end, we must not attempt to judge the plan from what we see by the way. Foolish men may try to do this and will be led to a false philosophy of life. Listen to Koheleth in 8:11–13: "Because sentence against an evil work is not executed speedily, therefore the heart of the sons of men is fully set in them to do evil. Though a sinner do evil an hundred times, and prolong his days, yet surely I know that it shall be well with them that fear God, which fear before him: but it shall not be well with the wicked, neither shall he prolong his days as a shadow [i.e., in quiet coolness after the fever of life]; because he feareth not before God."

Here then is the case for Koheleth. As counsel for the defense let me adopt a sentence of Cicero in his *Pro Archia* and say, I hope I have caused you to say, not only that Ecclesiastes ought not to be struck out of the Canon, since it finds a place there, but that, if it had not been placed in the Canon, it ought to have been placed there. It is a unique book, and its omission from the Bible would be a definite loss. Quite obviously it is not the last word on the problems of life, for it belongs to the Old Testament and not to the New. But its solution is along the consistent Bible lines that appear in both the Old and the New Testaments. Is it only by chance that Paul in Romans 8, after speaking of the vanity of the whole creation, goes on to speak of the sufferings that create a problem even for the Christian, and the confidence of the Christian in his daily life that all things work together for good for him? "All things" means those fortuitous events that we share in common with all mankind, where the race is not to the swift nor the battle to the strong. The world is not weighted in our favor. But the same things, which break the man of the world, can make the Christian, if he takes them from the hand of God. Go on looking for the key that will unify the whole of life.

You must look for it: God has made you like that, sore travail though it be. But you will not find it in the world; you will not find it in life; in revelation you will find the outskirts of God's ways; in Christ your finger tips touch the key, but no one has closed his fingers on it yet. No philosophy of life can satisfy if it leaves out Christ. Yet even the finest Christian philosophy must own itself baffled. But do not despair. There is a life to be lived day by day. And in the succession of apparently unrelated events God may be served and God may be glorified. And in this daily service of God, we may find pleasure, because we are fulfilling the purpose for which God made us.

That was Koheleth's philosophy of life. Was he wrong?

2

QOHELET
AND
HIS WISDOM

George R. Castellino

In the history of exegesis Qohelet has proved to be a baffling book.
The reading of it gives rise to many problems of textual criticism,
language, grammar and interpretation, not only of single passages, but of the
book as a whole. One meets with statements that in their obvious sense are
hard to harmonize with the general doctrine of OT man; for example, his activities in life, his position in the world are described in rather dark colors and
valued so low as to contrast with other better pages of the Scriptures. Some
scholars have even gone so far as to read in the book the systems of skepticism, agnosticism, pessimism, etc.; God himself has been seen represented as
acting in the world with principles and criteria difficult to understand from
the point of view of justice and equitable retribution, so that man is led to
fatalism and, out of despair, to a hedonistic way of life. These "errors" are
counterbalanced by more orthodox statements in the same book; nonetheless
one can not deny the presence of a series of "antitheses" that makes it difficult

From *Catholic Biblical Quarterly* 30 (1968): 15–28. Reprinted by permission.

to assess the true meaning of the book. Due to these "antitheses," exegetes are divided when called upon to judge what fundamental note Qohelet really strikes. Those who are impressed by the opening and concluding statements of Qohelet (1:2; 12:8, "Vanity of vanities . . .") see in the book an all pervading pessimistic outlook and therefore range Qohelet among the pessimistic productions of mankind. Others on the contrary, who direct their attention to the more positive and richer statements that are also found in the book, are inclined to credit Qohelet with the intention of conveying a message of truth and values for man and his activity, even while he presents [a] realistic consideration of life's distress and miseries. There is no denying that both sides could substantiate their judgment through an array of apposite quotations. A harmonization of the two opposing tendencies, that could be attempted by appealing to a synthesis on a higher level, as is done by Di Fonzo, would only result, in our opinion, either in denying a part of the facts, or in merging the contrasting colors into a nondescript hue that in no way can do justice to the book itself.

We believe that, without suppressing or blurring the antinomies or antilogies that are met with in the book, indeed acknowledging their full value, we can arrive at an assessment of Qohelet, showing it to be in keeping with the spirit of wisdom literature of the OT, although with characteristics of its own. To investigate what those characteristics may be and what kind of message we are entitled to read in the book is the purpose of the present paper.

Style and Vocabulary

Our first observation is this: after the prologue (1:1–11) Qohelet introduces himself, speaking in the first person singular: "I Qohelet have been king in Jerusalem. . . ." He continues, always in the same style, relating his personal experience or the experience gathered by investigation of the world. The tenses, as in narration of past events, are obviously in the preterit or in the present with waw consecutive. A few examples: "I have been king" (*hāyîtî melek*, 1:12); "And I gave my heart to investigate" (*wᵉnātattî ʾet-libbî . . .* 1:13); "I noticed" (*rāʾîtî*, 1:14); "I said" (*dibbartî*, 1:16); "I grew" (*higdaltî*), "I added wisdom" (*wᵉhôsaftî ḥokmāh*, 1:16); "And I gave my heart" (*wāʾettᵉnāh libbî*, 1:17); "And I said in my heart" (*ʾāmartî*, 2:1). And so on, through chapters 2 and 3 and 4. Here, "And I turned" (*wᵉšabtî*, 4:1, 7); "And I saw" (*wᵉrāʾîtî*, 4:4); "I saw" (*rāʾîtî*, 4:15). At this point, if we continue our reading, we are struck by the sudden change of the verbal forms: "*šᵉmōr raglêkā*, Watch your steps!" (4:17) and this is the first imperative we find in the book, addressed to the reader or listener. It is followed by another negative imperative: "*ʾal-tᵉahēl ʿal pîkā*, Do not be rash with your mouth" (5:1), and so on (5:3, 4, 5, 7, etc.).

We see that the style has suddenly and unexpectedly changed. Qohelet is no longer speaking about himself, but has turned to the reader, or listener, and is imparting to him admonitions and instructions. The direct speech in the second person, however, is not exclusive and consistent, and occasionally Qohelet falls back again into narrative style. This does not obscure the fact that from 4:17 on we observe a different kind of discourse. So that on the simple grammatical analysis of the verbs, we can establish a tentative division in the book as Part I (1:1–4:16) and Part II (4:17–12:12).

However, if we pass from grammar to vocabulary, here again we notice a few terms that occur with greater frequency. Besides, as they are more meaningful than others, they appear as key words. We shall point out just two or three, as a complete analysis is not our purpose. One of the most important words is undoubtedly the term "vanity" (*hebel*). Statistically, it occurs 36 times in the twelve chapters; but if we consider its rate of frequency in the single chapters we see at once that the greater majority of occurrences fall in chs. 1–4, while from chs. 5–12 the term occurs just a little over a dozen times (5:6, 9; 6:2, 4, 12; 7:6, 15; 8:10, 14; 9:9; 11:8, 10; 12:8). Together with *hebel* we could list the two expressions with practically the same meaning: *reʿût rûaḥ, raʿyôn rûaḥ,* "chasing of the wind" (Vg. "afflictio spiritus"). These occur ten times, seven and three respectively, but only one occurrence is found after ch. 5 (6:9).

Another relevant term is *ʿāmāl,* with the meanings: "labor, toil, striving, anxiety, frustration," according to the context; the verb from the same root *ʿāmal,* "to labor, to strive," etc. The substantive occurs about 20 times and the verb about 14 times, all together, substantive and verb, 34 times. Now in Part II (5–12) the substantive is met with only six times and the verb four times.

Quite the contrary is the case of another relevant term, *rāʿāh, raʿ,* "evil, bad," substantive and adjective. Of the total of occurrences, 27 times, more than 20 (21) are met with in Part II. Omitting other similar observations, we deem it sufficient to point out here, as regards these key words, that the frequency of the term "vanity," especially in Part I, is due to the fact that precisely in this part is contained Qohelet's appraisal about his experiences; there is a general repudiation of everything as being only "vanity," i.e., having at most but a flimsy reality and an utter inability lastingly to satisfy man. Similarly, the other word, *ʿāmāl* with its cognate verb, expresses the labor and toil that usually accompany the quest for riches and the enjoyment of pleasures. This labor, more often than not ending in frustration, is necessarily part of that experience and found together with *hebel.* Finally, as for *rāʿāh* and *raʿ,* it is to be observed that these bear an ethical connotation and could be the counterpart of "vanity"! While this last term points to irreality, unsubstantiality, non-entity, *rāʿāh* and *raʿ*

mark the impact of "non-reality" on man, who, as a consequence, finds evil and distress where he thought he would find satisfaction and pleasure. Or, temporal and local contingencies may bring about for man a situation of frustration or suffering (physical and moral) that can be called an "evil." We shall see that moral evaluations are more frequent in Part II, in accord with its fundamental characteristic.

Division of the Book

Keeping in mind these relatively small, but important findings, we can now proceed a step further and analyze the contents of the book in order to see whether the distinction we have been led to make between Part I and Part II can be validated or not.

In a broad outline we can distinguish the following sections: In 1:1–11 the introduction, or prologue, with title, general theme on the vanity of all things, the application to man, and (vv. 5–11) the general law of how events follow each other in a sequence that is always the same, without marking any progress ("nihil sub sole novi"!). In 1:12f. Qohelet presents himself and tells us about his investigations as regards human life and history, always concluding in the negative as to the value of wisdom itself in comparison with folly. In ch. 2 he starts from his personal experience and proceeds to the consideration that his is not a private and singular experience, but appears as the common lot of man, and then he proves his two points. He deals here with the results gleaned from several activities and quests of man and marks each one of them by means of the recurrent word "vanity" (*hebel*) or $r^e\hat{u}t\ r\hat{u}\check{a}\dot{h}$, "chasing of the wind," or $r\bar{a}\,\hat{a}h\ rabb\bar{a}h$, "great evil."

The following section (3:1–15) deals with man's activities as seen within the frame of the world as God's creation, stressing the uselessness of anxiety and strivings. Passing on to new experiences gathered from life (3:16–4:3), Qohelet urges man to take life and whatever it brings with an easy mind and forbearance, since nothing on man's part can change anything in it. As a kind of counter-demonstration, by means of three contrasts, Qohelet shows the uselessness of strivings and stress (4:4–16): (a) the contrast of the man who, urged on by envious rivalry, strives to acquire riches and goods, and of the man who almost allows himself to die of starvation out of sheer laziness; (b) the contrast of the man who works himself to death to no purpose, being all alone, as opposed to the man who can enjoy the companionship of others; (c) finally, the young man, poor but wise, who is contrasted with the man in authority and power, but a fool.

Looking more closely at the literary procedure followed by Qohelet in the presentation of his experience, we discover that generally a theoretical statement in the form of a thesis about some point is offered the reader, then the statement is validated or illustrated through experience (at times in terms of a proverb or a saying), and finally, a judgment is passed on the "non-value," "vanity," of the experience in question. The procedure is already apparent in the prologue. The thesis is stated directly and bluntly at the very beginning of the book: "All is vanity." The notion of vanity is shown to apply also to man (1:3–4) and is further developed (1:5–11) through the demonstration that all forms of life and happenings and activities of man in the world are subject to the same law of "eternal return," to use a modern expression, i.e., nothing really new ever happens "under the sun," or "the skies." In 1:13–15, the sequence is as follows: (a) consideration of reality (v. 13–14a); (b) judgment (v. 14b); (c) confirmation by means of a proverb (v. 15). This is followed by another triplet about wisdom, foolishness and folly, with (a) consideration (v. 16–17a); (b) judgment (v. 17b); (c) confirmation by means of a proverb (v. 18). Then 2:1–11 gives the development of the first triplet, and 2:12–16 the development of the second triplet, etc.

If now we turn to the second part we shall notice differences in the presentation of the contents, in addition to the literary and grammatical peculiarities previously noted.

As in Part I, in the opening of Part II also, we find a programmatic statement that clearly indicates the change in the trend of thought. It comes in the form of an admonition about how man must be careful in his dealings with God, not to be rash in speaking of God (venting criticism) or trying to oblige God through rash promises and vows. Here too the admonition is confirmed by means of a saying. Of relevance for us are the concluding words of this admonition: *kî ʾet-hā ʾĕlōhîm yᵉrā* (5:6) "Take care always to fear God!" This reminder about the "fear of God" sets the note to the music of the second part of the book. We anticipate at once that this shall also be the last note of the book (12:13): "The end of the discourse: all (of it) 'hears' (= sounds, means): 'Fear God!'" (*ʾet hā ʾĕlōhîm yᵉrā*). This is the clue to the second part; with these words it opens and closes. Can this also be the general conclusion to the whole book?

The chapters that follow the opening admonition (4:17–5:6, a kind of prologue) can be grouped as follows:

A) In 5:7–6:12, Qohelet takes up facts of experience touched upon in Part I, about injustice in the world, riches that cannot assuage man's thirst for pleasure, and about their perishable nature. The statement is illustrated with the contrasting figures of the anxiety of the rich versus acceptance by the poor (5:7–16). Qohelet's appraisal follows (5:17–19), stressing the fact that all goods are a gift of God and the truly wise should take them in the measure and circumstances they are given, without striving to force them from life. The opposite behavior is represented by the man who, for lack of wisdom, labors and toils after riches and is never satisfied (6:1–12).[1] The conclusion in v. 12 recalls the appraisal in 5:19!

B) Chapters 7–12 intend to describe wisdom and the wise at work. In 7:1–8:8, Qohelet offers suggestions for practical life, dictated by wisdom (7:1–10); he urges an intelligent use of wisdom, that is, putting together wisdom and prudence; he warns man not to be led astray by the "bad" woman[2] and to be prudent toward king and God(?). In the remaining chapters (8:9–11:6) three series of difficulties are brought forward that the wise may meet with in the practice of wisdom. Problems that had been presented in Part I (especially 3:16–4:3, about injustice and oppressions in the world) are answered here: (1) the "scandal" of irrational distribution of goods and sufferings; the good fortune of the evil man, contrasted with the sufferings of the pious[3]—in other words, the perplexing problem of retribution (8:9–15); (2) the inscrutability of God in his administration of justice (8:16–9:10), and (3) finally, the unpredictableness of God's providence in the allotment of goods to men, resulting in the "antinomies" of life (9:11–11:6); the prudence that is necessary to the wise, ending with rules of wisdom, together with an appraisal of youth and old age (the well-known allegory of 12:1–7).

The book is concluded by an epilogue (12:9–14) containing autobiographical indications about the person of Qohelet, here in the third person, and ending, as we remarked above, with the "moral lesson" to be gathered from the book.

The Relationship Between Part I and Part II

We can now proceed to determine in what lies the difference between Part I and Part II, and see what bearing this has on the assessment of Qohelet's doctrine. We saw that the fundamental note struck by Qohelet at the be-

1. In v. 7 the proverb states a thesis and in v. 8 *ḥākām* is used, not in the meaning of "wise," but in the more ordinary one of "able man," capable in commerce and business. The word is used for the general activities of life, Gen. 41:3, 39; Deut. 1:13–15; 16:19; 2 Sam. 14:20, etc., and for artistic abilities and technical skill in Isa. 3:3; Exod. 28:3; 31:6; 35:10; 36:1, 4, 8; Jer. 10:9, etc.—The curious expression in v. 9, *marᵓeh ʿênayim*, lit., vision of the eyes, or sight-power, in the context seems to mean "a positive, realistic, objective outlook," what the eyes (really) see. Translations differ. Our interpretation is in substantial agreement with Di Fonzo's.

2. The allurement of woman is a topos of wisdom literature: Prov. 7:6–27; Eccles. 9; in Mesopotamian literature, "The Dialogue of Pessimism," for which see *ANET* 437; W. G. Lambert, *Babylonian Wisdom Literature* (Oxford, 1960) 139–49.

3. 8:15 must not be understood to mean that man is entitled to give himself up to revelry; he is to enjoy life as it is given him by God, avoiding anxiety and speculation on the problems of his destiny. The terms for "eating, drinking and rejoicing," *ᵓākal, šātāh, śāmaḥ* can be used in a good as well as in a bad sense (ethically) *ᵓākal leḥem* "to eat bread," can be just "to live, or spend one's days." Religious feasts, as a matter of fact, were the proper times for eating, drinking and rejoicing.

ginning of the book and continued throughout all Part I is the "vanity" of all things. Going through his personal experience and the experience gathered from the world around himself, Qohelet constantly and inevitably comes to the same conclusion that everything is vanity. Each and every section ends with the same word, *hebel*. Also, the world goes through the same revolutions, phase following phase, without progress or novelties: what now exists has already been in existence and shall come again, repeating what was before. Turning to wisdom itself and considering its achievements, Qohelet concludes again that it does not pay to be wise (1:17–18). Neither do riches and pleasures of life really satisfy man (see the conclusion in 2:11); neither wisdom nor folly help him to shape his own life and future, as everything depends exclusively on God (2:24f.). Even accepting the fact that the world frequently appears to man in a topsy-turvy condition, one cannot explain the maladministration of justice (3:16–22) and an appeal to God does not really solve the problem. Giving vent to pessimism, Qohelet is led to put on the same level men and beasts (3:19–22); he even asks doubtingly whether the spirit (*rûaḥ*) of man and beast have a different destination.[4] The unborn is given an advantage in comparison with the living and the dead (4:1–3). One last negative answer is given as regards the man who has no one to succeed him in his possessions and nevertheless toils along to no purpose at all (4:8).

Summing up the impression one gains from Part I, we must say that Qohelet is consistent in his critical and negative appraisal of man and his activities in life. Having laid down his thesis at the opening of his discourse he proceeds to prove it forcibly and ruthlessly. It is no wonder that practically all difficulties for the interpretation of the book stem from Part I.

However, if we go on to analyze Part II, the negative impression is soon relieved by more positive and orthodox language that sounds more in tune with the other wisdom books (Prov., Sir.). Are we therefore entitled simply to discard the "unorthodox" Part I and rely on Part II in order to get Qohelet's doctrine, or should we try to harmonize the two parts by reading into the first part the spirit of the second? Both ways would be faulty in method and unsound in the conclusions. Therefore, given the differences between Part I and Part II, and given (or granted for the sake of argument) the unity of composition, a way to account for both these facts could be to view Part I, with its characteristics, in function of Part II. That is, the true meaning of Part I can only be discovered when we consider Part I as finding its explanation and evaluation in Part II. The two parts must be looked upon as being comple-

---

4. If one identifies *rûaḥ*, "vital breath," with *nefeš*, "soul," as a spiritual component of man, Qohelet seems to doubt the immortality of the soul. For the difference between *rûaḥ* and *nefeš* see Gen. 2:7 where the term corresponding to *rûaḥ* is *nᵉšāmāh*, compared with Ps. 104:29f. where the *rûaḥ* of beasts is recalled by God at their death, and see also Job 34:14f. where *nᵉšāmāh* and *rûaḥ* occur together, as also Qohelet 12:7 speaking in the same sense.

mentary to each other. The function of Part I is to bring forward clearly and forcibly the "case for the prosecution." But, as in every trial the advocate for the prosecution is answered by the defense, Part II will receive full meaning, we think, when read as "the brief for the defense."

Let us see whether Part II can rightfully be considered as the answer to Part I. The prologue that opens Part II (4:17–5:6) appears already as a basic and programmatic statement something like the "Sed contra" of the *Summa*. The admonition not to be rash with one's mouth seems for us to gain point if we read it as aimed at the "rash statements" of Part I. The attitude of mind to be substituted for the attitude dominant in Part I is given by the concluding sentence of the prologue: "Therefore, fear God!" (5:6). As this admonition is repeated further down and again appears at the end as the final conclusion (12:13) it is surely meant to give the background against which all problems are to be discussed and properly analyzed. The term (and the verb) "fear (of) God" never occurs in Part I. Further, taking up the problem of injustice in the world, Part II (5:7) answers the difficulty by saying that there is a kind of Nemesis even for extortions, as the lower extortioner is watched by a higher one and both by him who is above all.[5] If the interpretation of *gᵉbōhîm*, "(His) Highness" as an indication for God were accepted (it had been suggested by the Jewish commentators like Rashi and Ibn Ezra) the meaning of v. 7 would be clearer still. Proceeding in his analysis, Qohelet takes up another point, the inability of riches and pleasures to give full satisfaction. His answer (5:17–19) is that goods and pleasures are gifts of God and as such they must be viewed and enjoyed. To try to impose on the donor in order to have more and at will, would be to no purpose, as experience normally shows. Leaving aside, for the moment, the difficult passage of 7:16–18, to which we shall return presently, Qohelet next (7:26–29) points out that woman is not a "radical" evil. Borrowing Our Lord's words, we could say that "At the beginning it was not so" (Matt. 19:8); God had created man as a good and straightforward creature but it was through man's own fault that man devised

---

5. The passage 5:7–8 is a crux. The text seems critically sound, at least as regards v. 7, except for the last two words, but the interpretation is difficult. Two opposite interpretations have been suggested, according as he who "watches" can watch either for justice, or for a greater injustice. The interpretation of v. 7 depends also on the meaning of v. 8. As the text stands it is not easy to give it a satisfactory interpretation. The *nifal* participle at the end of the verse *neʿĕbad*, "made subservient," "enslaved," allows again of two interpretations: the king may be said to be interested in agriculture, or to exploit the ground for his own interest in a domineering manner. The connection with v. 7 would then be difficult to see.

We venture a suggestion that makes use of a slight textual correction, changing *neʿĕbad* into *yaʿăbíd*. Verse 8 could then be understood: The land yields for all (can yield itself to unlawful exploitation by the extortioners or officials) but the king (indicated in v. 7 by *gᵉbōhîm* "([His]) Highness"?) shall reduce the extortioners to labor in the fields. This interpretation could perhaps find some support in the *Babylonian Theodicy*, strophe VI, particularly lines 63–66: "The opulent *nouveau riche* who heaps up goods, will be burned at the stake by the king before his time," etc.

for himself many evils. The conclusion implicit in the solution is: "Try to follow God's plan for man and woman and you will avoid the allurement of the sinful woman." His words about authority can also be taken as a suggestion for avoiding griefs and troubles in life (8:2–7). Against the "scandal" of unjust retribution of good and evil (8:9–12) Qohelet recalls the programmatic doctrine that God surveys everything and shows his consideration towards those who fear him (8:12b–13); "Indeed I also know that it will be well with those who fear God!"

Besides being difficult in itself, 7:15–18 can be brought against our thesis. Qohelet takes up the difficulty arising from the experience of injustice (see 3:16–4:3), and he answers it in the spirit and language of wisdom (7:16–18): Do not be over-virtuous, nor too wise in order not to ruin yourself. This can be accepted, although it sounds already somewhat strange. But Qohelet goes on and says: Do not be wicked to excess! do not be a fool, in order not to die before your time. And this comes not only as a surprise, but as a shock. Finally, the finishing touch is the invitation which is appended: One should have a little of both—the one who fears God will succeed. The latest commentary (Di Fonzo, pp. 235–37) tries to solve the difficulty by considering v. 17 "un piccolo paradosso a tinta popolare e bonaria (a little paradox of a popular and accommodating character), and v. 18 is said to be 'più paradossale ancora' (yet more of a paradox); . . ." a new popular paradox by which Qohelet warns man: "non eccedere, per non accorciarsi la vita, nei vizi o col delitto poi punibile" (not to go to excess—so as not to shorten one's life—as regards vices or crime that shall call for punishment). His conclusion is: "E duro, ma meglio spiegabile alla pari del caso precedente [v. 17] come paradosso popolare" (It is a hard saying, but such that it can better be explained like the former case, as a popular paradox). Such an explanation is hardly acceptable. If this were the meaning intended by Qohelet we should confess that the religious spirit prompting such an ethical norm is at its lowest ebb! We are forced to look for some other explanation that does better justice to the text.

A clue may be found in the verbal form *hithakkam* (v. 16b). It is a *hitpael* that usually serves as a reflexive of *piel*, but among other particular values the form can also mean: "to show oneself such and such, to pass for," and reflexively "to esteem oneself furnished with such and such a quality."[6] The meaning, therefore, can be: do not consider yourself overwise, making high claims for your wisdom and criticizing God and his way of ruling the world. This be-

---

6. For this interpretation of the *hitpael* cf. Joüon, *Grammaire* § 54 *i* (p. 120). Analogical and similar values are also found in the second and tenth conjugation of Arabic: *istaḥsana* (from *ḥasu-na*), "to consider beautiful," etc. If a reference of our passage to 3:16ff. is admitted, there would be an analogy with the *Babylonian Theodicy*, strophe XXIV, lines 254–257, 264, where the "patient" is called wise, but is said to accuse the gods wrongly, to blaspheme, while the will of the gods is too remote and quite outside the reach of man.

gins to make sense. The admonition could be aimed at the statements in
3:16ff.; but even if a reference to that passage is denied and *al-hithakkam* is
given a more general interpretation, it will not cease to be valid. In this verse
al-tᵉhî ṣaddîq harbeh can be translated and interpreted: "Do not multiply
your justice" (i.e., in your own eyes), for which almost an exact parallel is
found in Prov. 3:7: "Be not wise in your own eyes," where the words we supply in parenthesis are actually given. Analogically v. 17 will be interpreted:
"Do not multiply your wickedness and do not be a downright fool, because
this will draw God's displeasure down on you and bring you to an untimely
death." To act foolishly (*sākal* in *nifal* or *hifîl*) and to be a fool (*sākāl*) is
mostly understood in a moral or spiritual sense (1 Sam. 15:31; 26:21; 2 Sam.
24:10 = 1 Chron. 21:8; 2 Chron. 16:9). Foolishness provokes God's anger
and punishment.

If our interpretation of v. 15–17 is correct, then also v. 18 can be given an
acceptable meaning: "You will fare well if you will take of this and not relax
your hand in that. Indeed he who fears God will succeed in both." "This" and
"that" in our interpretation are true wisdom and the avoidance of foolishness,
and both are achieved through the fear of God. Seen in this light, the passage
becomes understandable and acceptable in its religious and ethical contents,
perfectly in line with the ordinary teaching of the OT and especially of the wisdom books. This passage is central in Part II and its correct interpretation is
essential for a final appraisal of the whole doctrine of Qohelet.

The Teaching of Qohelet

Qohelet was a sage who has pondered on life's antinomies and has drawn
on his own experience, but also on the common experience of men and history. Like the Greek sage Theophrastus to whom we owe the well-known
treatise on "The moral characters of men," Qohelet also can say of himself:
"Having considered human nature for a long time, and having lived up to
ninety-nine years of age [this can hardly strike us as an exaggeration as we
know that Isocrates, for example, composed his Panegyric when he was 96
years of age] and having had familiar intercourse with many and different natures and having closely scrutinized the good and the bad. . . ."[7] Qohelet
therefore represents the sage and his wisdom, both taken on a human level (to
say an "international" level would sound too modern) and his purpose is to
lay down his "philosophy," first of all for himself, perhaps in order to reconcile
himself with life and the world he has to live in, and then for others as well,
in order to show them how to organize and direct their own life, especially
when it becomes hard and contradictory, or full of delusions and frustrations.

7. Theophrastus, *Characters*, Introduction.

The fundamental position and the over-all spirit of this wisdom is not a pe-
culiarity of Israel, but was something common to all the ancient world, not
only in the time of Qohelet (4th–3d cent. BC), but already centuries and millennia earlier, as we can see from the wisdom literature of ancient Sumer,
Egypt, and later in the classical world. Notes of similar ring and tone are
struck in many places, and, we would say, at all times, whenever and wherever
man comes across the troubles and trials of life. The literary expressions may
vary with time and place, characteristic movements and literary productions
may appear in determined epochs and exercise an influence beyond their own
geographical limits, but the subjects dealt with will always be the fundamental
problems of the human soul. In the mass of literary productions frequently it
is the darker side of human experience that comes to the fore as new pieces of
pessimistic literature appear. Side by side with the pessimistic documents we
find the pessimists themselves that openly rebel against God and life. On the
other side we have literary works that draw from the trials of life those teachings of practical philosophy which set the mind at peace.

In Israel only this second kind of wisdom could develop and enter the
Scriptures. As personal characters, it produced Job, as literary productions,
the books of Proverbs, Ecclesiasticus, the Book of Wisdom, besides Qohelet,
the most characteristic of all. In our opinion also the Song of Songs is to be
ranged among the wisdom books, but we cannot stop here to give the evidence for the assumption. Israel's wisdom viewed all problems within the
frame of the doctrine of a personal God who could not be capricious, or indifferent, or, worse still, unjust, as the gods of the nations could be.[8] This set
the sages in Israel on a vantage ground in comparison with the sages of Me-
sopotamia, Egypt and also Greece. Man's relations with God rested on the
"fear of God,"[9] which expressed all religion and its manifestations (see Prov.
1:7, 29; 2:5; 3:5, etc.; Sir. 1:9–18, 25; 2:7–11, etc.). On this same basis also
Qohelet's wisdom rests (4:17–5:6; 7:18; 8:12; 11:9; 12:1–13) and on it is
built his characteristic doctrine that makes the book so peculiar and distinct
from its colleagues in the canon. Prov. and Sir. enforce, in the language and
style of wisdom, the practical philosophy and theology that rests on the traditional theodicy: God is just, good and merciful. Everything and all depend on
him. Life may be hard at times, but for those who fear him, God's justice and
goodness will prevail in the end (cf. Job 34:10–12). Adhere therefore to him
and have confidence in him and be satisfied with what he gives, avoiding all
greediness and the pursuit of riches, honors, pleasures, etc.—all causes for
anxiety and frustration. But while Prov. and Sir. offer the results of experience
in simple and straightforward admonitions, sayings and proverbs, Qohelet

---

8. See G. R. Castellino, *Sapienza babilonese* [Torino, 1962] 8–36.

9. This was also a fundamental tenet of pagan wisdom, e.g., O Kyrnos, be in awe of the gods
and fear (them). (Theognis, 1179).

goes to the root of things, questions opinions and situations in order to discover the source of so many griefs and so much distress. His blunt presentations of the facts and accidents of life, the problems to which they give rise, the vivid description of the haphazards of everyday life, are what make the book so intriguing, so human. And to this philosophical and psychological character is due the ever-renewed interest in the book.

The fundamental aspect we have just sketched colors all the doctrine of Qohelet which we can try to sum up in a few points, as a general conclusion to our study.

1) Whatever man usually calls the "goods" of life: health, riches, possessions, material and sensual pleasures, honors, ambition, career, prestige, etc., are of their nature incapable of giving man full satisfaction to his craving for happiness (2:1–11, 17–19; 5:9–14).

2) Further, these values are not stable; man cannot rely on them, because they may easily be lost; and then man's frustration is greater, the greater had been his efforts to obtain them and the greater the enjoyment while they lasted (2:20–21; 5:12–16; 6:2–6, 12–16).

3) Another essential point of Qohelet's doctrine concerns man's activity in general and in its results. Experience shows that the pursuit of happiness at all costs does not bring with it necessarily either the goods or the happiness man was seeking in them. Man experiences that he is not the master of events. The world, on the contrary goes on its own way, carried on by its own laws, slipping off man's hands, so to speak, without allowing itself to be shaped or ruled by man. God alone is the full master of it and rules it at his own will, distributing what he pleases and to whom he pleases, independently of man's desires, and also (the grave problem of retribution) independently, at least apparently, of man's merits (2:22–26;[10] 3:13; 4:7–8; 8:16–17; 9:1–2, 11–12).

---

10. In this passage v. 25 presents difficulties. The Jerusalem Bible paraphrases thus: "since plenty and penury both come from God." Generally translations agree in giving the verb *ḥûš* the meaning, "to feel pleasure, to enjoy." But this would be the only occurrence of this meaning for *ḥûš*. In Semitic languages there is a cognate root meaning "to feel" (Arabic *ḥassa;* Ethiopic *ḥewas,* "perception"; Aramaic and Syriac, "to feel pain"). Even if we accept the meaning "to feel pleasure," for which no evidence can be found, the text is not very much clarified. It is possible to start from the ordinary meaning of the root, "to hasten, make haste," adopting for our passage the nuance "to worry, fuss, feel agitation," which is found quite clearly in Job 20:2, *ḥûšî bî,* "my *agitation* inside of me," where no physical motion is implied. Here we would have this same meaning, the agitation, the worrying and fuss in order to get one's livelihood. The two verbs, "to eat" and "to hasten," are found together as here in Hab. 1:8, *kᵉnešer ḥāš leᵉᵉkōl,* "like the eagle hastening to the prey." Another difficulty lies in the concluding expression *mimmenni,* "without me, outside of me," that is hardly fitting in the context. Therefore the correction has been suggested: *mimmennú,* "out of him, independently of him (God)." With this the text is perfectly clear: "Who can provide his own livelihood and worry, or fuss, about it independently of God?" The same thought is repeated below in 3:13 where it is said that for man eating and drinking is a *mattat ᵉᵉlōhîm,* a gift of God!

4) Against such an order of things man finds himself powerless. He can do nothing and he is absolutely unable to penetrate the laws of government and providence in the world. It is not for man to investigate. Job tried it in the discussion with his friends, but failed, and was obliged (and taught) to acquiesce to God's will, recalling at the same time his wisdom and justice (3:9–11, 15, 22; 6:10–12; 8:8–16).

Such an impossibility for man to penetrate the intentions, will and plans of the gods was common throughout the ancient East (and it will always be the ordinary experience of man everywhere).[11]

5) All things considered, what is man to do? Fall into despair and just grab at any cost at the goods of life within reach, in rebellion against the supernatural power that rules the world? Such a course was not taken even by Gilgamesh when utterly frustrated in his pursuit of fame, and of life eternal.[12] The only reasonable course will be to view life and man's lot in the world with a sober mind and a realistic consideration (6:9).

Therefore: a) set aside all anxious striving and labor (ʿāmāl); b) avoid all speculation on God's ruling of the world and c) be thankful to God for whatever satisfaction he gives you, valuing and measuring everything as a gift from him and enjoying it, never forgetting that you shall have to render strict account to God himself.

These are the points of doctrine that wisdom can teach man (for the advantages of wisdom see 7:11–24; 8:1 against 2:12–16; finally 12:9–12). Human experience contributes the negative element that could drive man to agnosticism and scepticism. Wisdom and religion contribute the background and framework of God's presence and justice that help man to accept the facts, transferring them onto a higher plane where a solution is believed to exist, although not clearly perceived by man. God, surely, will never forget the orderly life of the sage and he will deal with him at the proper time with all due consideration (5:17–19; 8:12–13).[13]

11. For the impenetrability of the divine will, see also the quotation of the *Babylonian Theodicy*, strophe XXIV in n. 6 above, and further Theognis, vv. 141–142.

12. See our *Sapienza babilonese*, 31–36, for presentation and discussion.

13. In order to have the full picture it would be necessary now to investigate the position of "wisdom" within the OT doctrine on man and God. This would require another and independent paper, that would be out of place here. Therefore we refer the reader of the Theologies of the OT, and only add that we have made a few observations on the subject lately when dealing with the contents of requests and prayers in the OT (see *Studi in onore di S. E. Card, Ottaviani*, Vol. I, Rome, 1967).

3

THE RIDDLE
OF THE SPHINX
THE STRUCTURE
OF THE BOOK OF QOHELETH

Addison G. Wright

Qoheleth is one of the most difficult books in the Bible, and it has long been an enigma and a source of fascination for its readers and students. In 1898 Plumptre wrote: "It comes before us as the sphinx of Hebrew literature, with its unsolved riddles of history and life,"[1] riddles such as the title "Qoheleth" which the author assumes, the date and place of composition, the language, the unity of authorship, the structure, genre, message and background of the book, indeed the reasons for its very presence in the biblical canon. In this century there has been a growing consensus of scholarly opinion on positions connected with a few of these issues (title, date, background, presence in the canon). Among recent commentators there has also been a trend away from the earlier assessments of Qoheleth as a hedonist or pessimist or skeptic or agnostic, and a trend toward a more balanced view which does justice to Qoheleth as a man of faith and which realizes that no single label expresses the complexity of his thought; but there is still a lack of

From *Catholic Biblical Quarterly* 30 (1968): 313–34. Reprinted by permission.

1. E. H. Plumptre, *Ecclesiastes* (Cambridge Bible; Cambridge, 1898) 7.

agreement on what the dominant note is that Qoheleth strikes. So we have advanced a certain distance since Plumptre, but the basic problem of the book remains: its seeming lack of order and of progression of thought, as well as its alternation of orthodox and of heterodox statements sometimes to the point of apparent contradiction. It is only when the principle underlying this maze can be established with evidence sufficiently objective to give some promise of a consensus, that we will have the requisite data to move ahead with confidence to attack the remaining and major problems (message, genre, and unity) and to solve the essential riddles.

The present writer believes that the principle underlying this maze is not to be sought in multiple authorship, or in an appeal to a "dialectic" mode of thought or to Qoheleth's supposed vacillating attitude toward tradition (now standing with it, now against it), but that the principle is to be sought in the area of structure. He believes that the book is in fact structured and that the key to that structure is to be found in three successive patterns of verbal repetition in 1:12–11:6. When these patterns are taken as indicating the framework of the book and when that framework is brought to the material as an overlay as it were, there emerges out of the apparent disorder a straightforward presentation of a very simple theme, albeit somewhat reduced in content from what has previously been seen as the message of the book. The following pages elaborate on these assertions and present the evidence upon which they are based.

Previous Views on the Structure

In the past, two positions, *grosso modo,* have been taken with regard to the structure of Qoheleth. One position is that there is no plan; one cannot make an outline. Impressed by the disorder, these commentators have concluded that it would be to force the material if one tried to show order and overall sequence of thought, and they have concluded that the respectful approach to the work is to isolate units or themes or even authors, and to view the book as a collection like Prov. or as assorted observations around the theme that all is vanity and other secondary ideas. The words of Delitzsch well represent this position: ". . . a gradual development, a progressive demonstration, is wanting, and even the grouping together of the parts is not fully carried out; the connection of the thoughts is more frequently determined by that which is external and accidental, and not infrequently an incongruous element is introduced into the connected course of kindred matters. . . . All attempts to show, in the whole, not only oneness of spirit but also a genetic progress, an all-embracing plan, and an organic connection, have hitherto failed, and must fail."[2] This

---

2. F. Delitzsch, *Commentary on the Song of Songs and Ecclesiastes,* trans. by M. G. Easton (Edinburgh, 1891) 188.

view is espoused in one form or another by a large number of commentators and is the prevailing opinion.[3]

Another position is represented by those who feel that the book must have some unity or progession of thought and who have attempted to offer an outline, e.g., Bea,[4] H. L. Ginsberg,[5] and some of the commentaries.[6] The results

3. Thus C. H. H. Wright, *The Book of Koheleth* (London, 1883); G. Wildeboer, *Der Prediger* (*Kurzer Handkommentar zum AT;* Frieburg, 1898); Plumptre, op. cit.; A. H. McNeile, *An Introduction to Ecclesiastes* (Cambridge, 1904); V. Zapletal, *Das Buch Kohelet* (Freiburg, 1905); G. A. Barton, *The Book of Ecclesiastes* (ICC; New York, 1908); G. C. Martin, *Proverbs, Ecclesiastes and Song of Songs* (Century Bible; Edinburgh, 1908); M. Jastrow, *A Gentle Cynic* (Philadelphia, 1919); A. L. Williams, *Ecclesiastes* (Cambridge Bible; Cambridge, 1922); A. Allgeier, *Das Buch des Predigers* (*Die Heilige Schrift des AT;* Bonn, 1925); G. Kuhn, *Erklärung des Buches Koheleth* (BZAW 43; Gressen, 1926); B. Gemser, *Prediker* (Groningen, 1931); K. Galling, "Kohelet-Studien," *ZAW* 50 (1932) 276–99; id., *Die fünf Megilloth* (HAT; Tübingen, 1940); A. D. Power, *Ecclesiastes* (London, 1952); R. H. Pfeiffer, *Introduction to the Old Testament* (London, 1952) 724; R. Gordis, *Qoheleth—The Man and His World* (New York,[2] 1955); E. Jones, *Proverbs and Ecclesiastes* (Torch Bible Commentaries; London, 1961); W. Zimmerli, *Das Buch des Predigers Salomo* (ATD; Göttingen, 1962); E. T. Ryder, "Ecclesiastes," *Peake's Commentary on the Bible,* eds. M. Black and H. H. Rowley (London, 1962); H. W. Hertzberg, *Der Prediger* (*Kommentar zum AT;* Gütersloh,[2] 1963); O. Eissfeldt, *The Old Testament: An Introduction,* trans. by P. R. Ackroyd (Oxford, 1965) 493–94; R. B. Y. Scott, *Proverbs. Ecclesiastes* (Anchor Bible; New York, 1965); A. Barucq, *Ecclésiaste* (*Verbum Salutis;* Paris, 1968).

4. A. Bea, *Liber Ecclesiastae* (Romae, 1950):

1:2–3	Theme
1:4–2:26	Neither the study of nature nor pleasure nor wisdom satisfies man
3:1–7:24	Wisdom cannot solve the enigmas of life
7:25–9:17	Study of the practical utility of wisdom
9:18–12:8	Practical advice
12:9–13	Epilogue

5. H. L. Ginsberg, *Studies in Koheleth* (*Texts and Studies of the Jewish Theological Seminary of America,* XVII; New York, 1950) 1–11; id., "Supplementary Studies in Koheleth," *Proceedings of the American Academy for Jewish Research* 21 (1952) 35–62; id., "The Structure and Contents of the Book of Koheleth," *Wisdom in Israel and in the Ancient Near East,* eds. M. Noth and D. W. Thomas (VT[S] 3; Leiden, 1955) 138–149:

A.	1:2–2:26	All is vanity and man's only profit is using his goods
B.	3:1–4:3	All happenings are foreordained but never fully foreseeable
A'.	4:4–6:9	} are complementary to A and B
B'.	6:10–12:8	

6. F. Hitzig, *Der Prediger Salomo's* (*Kurzgefasstes exegetisches Handbuch zum AT;* Leipzig, 1847) 125–26:

1:1–4:16	Theoretical foundation
4:17–8:15	Rejection of false advice
8:16–12:14	Qoheleth's advice

C. D. Ginsberg, *Coheleth* (London, 1861):

1:2–11	Prologue
1:12–2:26	Investigation of pleasure and wisdom
3:1–5:19	Investigation of toil
6:1–8:15	Investigation of riches and prudence
8:16–12:7	Résumé and conclusion
12:8–12	Epilogue

and similarly, O. Zöckler, *Ecclesiastes,* trans. W. Wells (New York, 1870).

J. F. Genung, *Words of Koheleth* (Boston, 1904):

1:2–11	The fact and the question
1:12–2:26	An induction of life
3:1–22	Times and seasons

have been quite disparate, and this lack of agreement has been viewed by many as the final and conclusive evidence, if more were needed, that there is indeed no plan in the book to begin with. These attempts at outlines with few

4–5	In a crooked world
6:1–7:18	Fate and the intrinsic man
7:19–9:10	Avails of wisdom
9:11–11:6	Wisdom encountering time
11:7–12:7	Rejoice and remember
12:8–14	The nail fastened

E. Podechard, *L'Ecclésiaste* (*Études Bibliques;* Paris, 1912):

1:2–3	Theme of the book
1:4–11	Preliminary consideration
1:12–2:26	Vanity of wisdom and of pleasures
3:1–22	Vanity of man's efforts
4:1–5:8	Diverse anomalies in human society
5:9–7:12	Vanity of riches
7:13–9:10	Virtue is unable to assure happiness
9:11–11:6	Effort and talent are unable to assure success
11:7–12:8	Conclusion
12:9–14	Epilogue

and similarly D. Buzy, *L'Ecclésiaste* (*La Sainte Bible,* Pirot-Clamer; Paris, 1946).

A. Vaccari, *Institutiones biblicae* (Romae, 1935) II, 77:

1:4–3:15	The vanity of the transitory effects of effort
3:16–5:19	The vanity of evil in society
6–7	The vanity of the insatiableness of desires
8:1–11:6	The vanity of the uncertainty of the future
11:7–12:8	Conclusion

A. Miller in H. Höpfl, *Introductionis in sacros utriusque testamenti libros compendium* (Romae,[5] 1946) II, 328:

1:4–2:26	
3:1–7:29	} Three series of reflections
8:1–10:20	
11:1–12:7	Conclusion

J. J. Weber, *L'Ecclésiaste* (Paris, 1947):

1:1–11	Introduction
1:12–2:26	Investigation of wisdom and pleasure
3:1–22	The powerless efforts of man
4:1–6:9	Diverse anomalies in society
6:10–9:10	Assorted reflections on life
9:11–11:8	The disproportion between effort and success
11:9–12:14	Conclusion

R. Pautrel, *L'Ecclésiaste* (*BJ;* Paris, 1948) sees eight vanities discussed in two parts:

Part I

1:4–11	Prologue on ennui
1:12–2:26	The good life
3:1–22	Death
4:1–5:8	The individual lost in the collectivity of society
5:9–6:12	Money

Part II

7:1–7	Prologue on laughter
7:8–8:15	Belief in a sanction during life
8:16–9:10	Love does not satisfy
9:11–11:6	Chance
11:7–12:8	Old age

exceptions,[7] have largely the "this is how I read Qoheleth" sort of thing with no evidence offered aside from the critic's assurance that he sees a sequence of thought. The writer has no desire to add one more attempt of that kind here; rather he is speaking out of another tradition of criticism, a sort of third approach to Qoheleth that is beginning to form.

In the field of literary criticism, the twentieth century has seen the development of a new school known as the New Stylistics or the New Criticism. It is a term which describes a great variety of literary critics, but the distinguishing features of all of them are: (1) a trend away from the psychological, historical, and biographical approaches to literature; (2) a placing of the point of departure for criticism in the work itself; and (3) a careful verbal and structural analysis.[8] The elements of the method are not new; but the emphasis is new, the explicit and singleminded manner in which the work is done is new, and the interest in structure is thoroughly modern and corresponds to structural preoccupations in many of the sciences today.

The New Criticism in its pure form is of course a reaction to other schools of criticism and needs to be balanced by them, especially (for our purposes) whenever it exhibits a tendency to view as secondary the meaning the author intended to give his work. In addition, many feel that its close analysis and dissection leave a piece of literature lifeless, and they heartily agree with T. S. Eliot's

---

H. Lamparter, *Das Buch der Weisheit: Prediger und Sprüche* (Stuttgart, 1955):

    1:3–2:26
    3:1–7:24 } Three series of sayings
    7:25–12:7
    12:8–14   Epilogue

O. S. Rankin, "Ecclesiastes," *The Interpreter's Bible,* 5 (New York, 1956):

    1:2–4:3   Qoheleth's world outlook
    4:4–9:16   A wise man's experiences
    9:17–12:7   Concluding advice

C. Siegfried (*Die Sprüche, Prediger und Hoheslied* [*Handkommentar zum AT*; Göttingen, 1898]), who considers the book in its present form to be the product of nine authors, provides a plan for the *Grundschrift*.

7. C. D. Ginsburg (op. cit., 17) constructs his plan on the basis of the recurrence of the advice to enjoy the fruits of one's labor in 2:26; 5:17–19 and 8:15, and interprets these as the conclusions of sections. Weber (op. cit., 222) views the repetitions of that same idea in 2:26; 3:22; 6:9; 9:7–10. Hitzig (op. cit., 125–26) based his plan on the change to an imperative in 4:17 (similarly Castellino below) and on the repetition of the enjoyment idea in 5:17–19; 8:15 and 9:7–10. None takes into account all of the occurrences of the idea, and each sees its appearance in 3:13 as not significant.

8. P. Guiraud, *La stylistique* (Paris, 1961) and G. Watson, *The Literary Critics* (Harmondsworth, 1962) briefly survey the school in its European and American forms. A handbook that synthesizes much of the trend is R. Wellek and A. Warren, *Theory of Literature* (New York,[3] 1962). Further bibliography can be found in each. Examples of work in the same spirit in biblical criticism are the studies of Muilenburg and Alonso-Schökel (on Hebrew poetic and prose selections), Galbiati (on Exod.), Lamarche (on Zech. 9–14), Vanhoye (on Heb.), Reese and the present writer (on Wis.), and much of the *redaktionsgeschichtlich* work on the Gospels.

sneer that it is "the lemon-squeezer school of criticism."[9] Here surely it is a question of judgment as to the suitability and potential of the method for the study of a given work, and undoubtedly it is also and ultimately a matter of taste. Of special value for the exegete, though, is the school's emphasis on structural analysis. Reading in context is universally recognized as the cardinal rule of objective exegesis, but the ascertaining of context in the past has been all too often something less than objective. The New Stylistics can shore up this weakness.

With regard to structural analysis in its restricted sense, i.e., the isolating of the plan of a work, the New Critics observe that there are two methods which can be used. One which they do not employ and which might be called the subjective method is to go immediately to the thought of a work and attempt to describe the sequence of ideas by translating them into an outline. The method has the advantage of being direct (one immediately produces that which is desired, the outline), but it has the disadvantage of being quite open to subjectivity in that the logical development seen by the critic may not be the logic of the author at all. One may well mistake topic sentence for development or development for topic sentence, and, of course, one such alteration and the thrust of the material of that particular section becomes different for the reader from what the author intended. Sometimes, too, our thought patterns may prevent us from seeing any plan at all in works that are indeed structured. This is generally the method that has been used on Qoheleth in the past (and on many other biblical books) and the variety of outlines that have been produced bears eloquent witness to the subjectivity of this approach.

The other procedure and the one pursued by the New Critics is what we might call an objective method.[10] It must remain vague in its formulation so as to be flexible, but essentially it is to put attention, first of all, not on the thought but on the form. The critic looks for repetitions of vocabulary and of grammatical forms and thus seeks to uncover whatever literary devices involving repetition the author may have used, such as inclusions, *mots crochets,* anaphora, chiasm, symmetry, refrains, announcement of topic and subsequent resumption, recapitulation, etc. In this way too he discovers indeliberate repetitions that might provide a key to the thought and its emphases, and he becomes aware of clusters of vocabulary which may indicate blocks of material. The critic also looks for changes: changes of genre, person, mood, etc., all of which are potential indicators of seams between units. He searches for numerical patterns which the author may have impressed upon his work for

9. T. S. Eliot, *On Poetry and Poets* (New York, 1957) 125.

10. For a discussion of this aspect of criticism see L. Alonso-Schökel, *Estudios de poética hebrea* (Barcelona, 1963) 309–336; "Poésie Hébraïque," *VDBS* 8 (Paris, 1967) 85–90 and the bibliography in each.

one reason or another and which can provide clues to the author's conception of the plan of the work. The critic then brings whatever patterns there are to the thought and evaluates as significant those patterns that coincide with breaks in the thought and with conceptual units, and in that way gradually develops an outline. The subjective element is by no means removed entirely, but it is considerably lessened in that one is dealing with objective indices of structure in the work itself. And where there is a multiple convergence of indices in conjunction with breaks in the thought, the conclusions can approach a certitude.[11]

There have been two studies of Qoheleth in the spirit of the New Stylistics. One is the work of Oswald Loretz, *Qohelet und der alte Orient*,[12] which is an analysis of the book's style and themes. With regard to the plan, Loretz seems to have started with a proneness to be easily convinced that the book is not structured and that the key to its understanding lies in a study of interwoven themes. This apparently has led him to utilize the data of his analysis[13] more as a microstylist concerned with vocabulary and motifs than as a macrostylist concerned with overall structure. In any event he does not see a plan in the book.

The second study in the spirit of the New Criticism is to be found in a recent article of George Castellino[14] which is addressed solely to the question of structure. The method that Castellino wished to apply is sound. He goes immediately to the external form of the book and subjects it to analysis. He looks to repetitions and changes of verb forms. He observes that the book starts out with reflections on human life in the first person singular and that this pattern obtains all the way to 4:16. At 4:17, however, there is the abrupt change to the imperative for eight verses and, while this is not sustained and Qoheleth falls back again occasionally into the I-narrative, Castellino (as did Hitzig a century ago)[15] sees a different kind of discourse from there on. He

---

11. For example, in Wis. (which is a virtual textbook case because of the multiple literary devices used by the author) the limits of sections are marked with inclusions and at the same time with *mots crochets*. Frequently the sections thus indicated are paralleled with others and this symmetry further confirms the division into units and also indicates their arrangement into larger groupings. Finally, the number of verses in each unit is proportioned to the number of verses in the neighboring unit on a fixed ratio obtained from additive series, and this proportioning is carried out in a pyramid fashion so that the same patterns are found ultimately in the major divisions of the book. The discovery of these interlocking patterns provides the final confirmation of the structure. Cf. "The Structure of the Book of Wisdom," *Bib* 48 (1967) 165–84; "Numerical Patterns in the Book of Wisdom," *CBQ* 29 (1967) 524–38.

12. Freiburg, 1964.

13. In a work as large as Qoheleth it is of course necessary to make a selection of the vocabulary to be analyzed. Unfortunately as it turned out Loretz overlooked one key word, *mṣ'*, and so its patterns did not figure in his study.

14. "Qohelet and His Wisdom," *CBQ* 30 (1968) 15–28.

15. See note 7 above.

thus divides the book into two parts: 1:1–4:16 and 4:17–12:12. As supporting evidence he offers the patterns of occurrence of five words and phrases in
parts one and two. He sees the first part of the book as a negative appraisal of
life upon which appraisal Qoheleth passes judgment in part two in a more positive and orthodox manner.

There are two problems with Castellino's proposal. First of all, the plan
does not match the thought. There is no major break at 4:17, because the
positive advice offered by Qoheleth in 5:17–19 has already been given in 2:24
and in 3:12–13, and the negative appraisal of life in 1:1–4:16 is continued in
5:12–6:9. Secondly, the objective data upon which the analysis is based are
meager. No evidence at all is offered for the analysis of 4:17–12:12; it is the
subjective method that is used. Statistics on vocabulary occurrence are difficult to interpret and need considerable reinforcement by other data before
anything approaching certitude can be reached. The only "other data" offered
are the changes of person in 4:17–5:7,[16] and these, viewed in complete isolation from all that follows, do not necessarily prove anything; as it turns out
the book is constructed on other patterns, and the change in person at 4:17
is in fact of secondary significance for overall structure. Despite its shortcom-
ings, however, the writer is deeply indebted to Castellino's article, because
through it he became interested in the problem and was alerted to a meaningful pattern of repetition in 1:12–6:9; once entry was gained to the plan in that
way, the solution of the rest of the riddle soon followed.

The Analysis

Let us remove from consideration for the moment 1:1 (the title of the
book) as well as 1:2–11 on the endless round of events, etc.; it is generally acknowledged that the book gets underway in 1:12. In 1:12–15 there is an introductory statement and it ends with "all is vanity and a chase after wind,"
plus a proverb. This is followed by a second and parallel introduction in 1:16–
18 and this ends with "a chase after wind," plus a proverb. Qoheleth then tells
in 2:1–11 how he tested pleasure-seeking, and this section ends with "all was
vanity and a chase after wind." He then takes up in 2:12–17 the "wisdom,
madness and folly" of 1:17 and tests them and finds no advantage to wisdom,
and this paragraph ends with "all was vanity and a chase after wind." So there
is a double introduction and then two paragraphs which are a development
on them. These four units are generally recognized, and it is generally recognized that there is a development of thought up to this point. It is generally
seen that these four paragraphs end with "(all is vanity and) a chase after
wind," but as far as the present writer knows no one has ever pursued the pat-

---

16. If 12:9–14 is from the hand of the editor, the repetition of "fear God" in 5:6 and 12:13
is not significant structurally.

tern further in seeking a plan. In the spirit of the New Criticism let us pursue it further. The phrase occurs five more times: 2:26; twice together in 4:4–6; once in 4:16 and again in 6:9, and there it ends, never to be repeated in the remaining six chapters of the book. If we follow the analogy of the first four sections and let these subsequent occurrences of the phrase mark the ends of units also, they mark off four additional sections in a short-long-short-long arrangement: 2:18–26; 3:1–4:6; 4:7–16; 4:17–6:9. (The two occurrences of the phrase in 4:4–6 are taken together as marking the end of one section.) Are these meaningful units? In these four sections and only in these four sections the author evaluates the results of man's toil (an idea taken up from 2:10–11), and 24 of the book's 35 occurrences of the stem ʿml are here. In this material he in fact makes four observations on the results[17] of man's toil (2:18–26; 3:1–15; 4:7–9; 5:12–6:9), and each of the four sections, marked out by the pattern, contains *one* of these observations plus digressionary remarks suggested by the discussion of toil (see below). Moreover, three of the four sections begin with the "toil" idea; only 4:17–6:9 inserts digressionary remarks at the outset. So the verbal pattern coincides with a thought pattern and alerts us to the fact that the main subject of 2:18–6:9 is "toil."

There is, then, a continuity of thought from 1:12–6:9. In these chapters Qoheleth is reporting the results of his investigation of life undertaken to "understand what is best for men to do under the heavens during the limited days of their life" (2:3). He begins with a double introduction (1:12–15; 1:16–18), and then evaluates pleasure-seeking (2:1–11), wisdom (2:12–17), and finally the results of toil in four sections (2:18–6:9). The evaluation repeated at the end of each section is that it is a vanity and a chase after wind. These eight units are tied together not only by the repetition of the evaluation but also by an interlocking arrangement whereby once the series begins, each section picks up an idea mentioned two units earlier. The "wisdom, madness and folly" of 2:12–17 resumes 1:17; "toil" in 2:18–26 picks up that idea from 2:10–11; "one fate" in 3:19 resumes 2:14; the problem of a man having no one with whom he can share the fruits of his toil in 4:7–16 picks up the idea of leaving the fruits of one's toil to another in 2:18–26; "oppression" in 5:7 resumes the same idea in 4:1; 5:11 recalls 2:23; and the idea of the non-satisfaction of riches in 5:9 resumes 4:8 (from the immediately preceding section in this final instance).

Running through these four sections on the vanities connected with toil there is another and related idea: there is nothing better for man than to eat and drink and enjoy the fruit of his labor (2:24; 3:13; 3:22; 5:17). This is the only advice that Qoheleth feels he can offer on what is good for man to do. When he gives the advice, he also remarks that the ability to enjoy is a gift of

---

17. The little paragraph on toil in 4:4–6 is a secondary remark on the source of toil and is not part of the main discussion on the results of man's labor.

God (2:24–26; 3:13; 5:18), and at the end of the fourth section he elaborates on that idea. He points out that there are problems even with the advice about enjoyment: God does not give some men the power to enjoy the fruit of their labor (6:1–6); moreover, the appetite of man is never satisfied (6:7–9). And on this note the four sections on toil end. So there is not only a continuity of thought in 1:12–6:9, but there is also a development with regard to the enjoyment idea insofar as the advice is offered four times and then is heavily qualified in the last section.

In 6:6–9 some phrases recall earlier remarks: all go to the same place (cf. 3:20; 2:14–16); man's appetite is not satisfied (4:8; 5:9); what advantage does the wise man have over the fool (2:12–17). Perhaps this is a summing up, and 6:9 marks a major break in the book. The cessation here of "this is vanity and a chase after wind" creates a presumption to that effect, and the final qualification of the enjoyment idea reinforces that presumption. The following lines therefore deserve close scrutiny because they may be the beginning or even the introduction to the next part of the book.

The lines in question are simply 6:10–12, for immediately following them is a collection of proverbs (7:1ff.). In these three verses two ideas are repeated from the first part (what is, is [cf. 1:9, 15; 3:15], and the vanity of many words [cf. 4:17–5:6]), and then a conclusion is drawn from the observations up to this point: who knows what is good for man to do (cf. 2:3; 2:24; 3:12; 3:22; 5:17) and who can tell him what will be after him (cf. 3:22). Is any of this vocabulary taken up again in the material that follows? In 8:7 there is a similar expression: "he does not know what is to be, for who can tell him how it will be"; but this does not seem to have any significance in that it is isolated and does not constitute the beginning or end or the theme of the passage in which it occurs. If we go further, though, we find something which looks quite significant indeed. The words "do not know" and "no knowledge" start occurring with great frequency after 9:1: in 9:1, 5, 10, 12; 10:14, 15; 11:2; and three times in 11:5–6; and this brings us right up to the poem, at the end, on youth and old age (11:7–12:8). The occurrence of "do not know" in 9:5 and its threefold appearance in 11:5–6 mark the ends of sections. If we let the others in between also mark the ends of sections, we get six units (9:1–6; 9:7–10; 9:11–12; 9:13–10:15; 10:16–11:2; 11:3–6). Each one deals with one aspect of the "what comes after" problem, and each says that man does not know (see below).

What about chs. 7–8? The pattern of the verb "not know" in chs. 9–10 calls attention to a similar pattern with the verb "not find/who can find" in chs. 7–8. It occurs in 7:14, 24, 28 (*bis*) and finally three times together in 8:17 at the very end of ch. 8. The first one marks the end of a section as does the triple repetition in 8:17; and if we let the others mark the ends of sections on an analogy with them and with the verb "to know" in chs. 9–10, we get four sections each containing traditional wisdom material and a subsequent comment on it; each one deals with one aspect of the "what is good for man to do" problem, and each says that man cannot find out[18] (see below).

So, to recapitulate, there is the eight-fold repetition in 1:12–6:9 of "vanity and a chase after wind," marking off eight meaningful units which contain eight major observations from Qoheleth's investigation of life, plus digressionary material. A secondary motif runs through the sections on toil (the only thing that he can find that is good for man to do is to enjoy the fruit of his toil), and at the end even this is shown to have limitations. Where this pattern ceases in 6:9 there follows immediately the introduction of two new ideas: man does not know what is good to do nor what comes after him; and another verbal pattern begins. The first idea is developed in four sections in 7:1–8:17. The end of each unit is marked by the verb "find out" and the final section ends with a triple "cannot find out": (8:17) in an *a b a* arrangement (*lōʾ yûkal hāʾādām limṣô*, . . . *wᵉlōʾ yimṣāʾ* . . . *lōʾ yûkal limṣôʾ*). The second idea is developed in six sections in 9:1–11:6. The end of each unit is marked with "do not know" or "no knowledge" and the final section again ends with a triple "you do not know" (11:5–6) and again in an *a b a* arrangement (*ʾênᵉkā yôdēaʿ* . . . *lōʾ tēdaʿ* . . . *ʾênᵉkā yôdēaʿ*.) When this pattern ends we are right at the beginning of the generally recognized unit on youth and old age at the end of the book.

Because of the convergence of indices, it seems almost certain that the patterns uncovered are a deliberate device utilized by the author to provide the main structure of the book. There are three successive patterns embracing exactly all the material between the initial (1:2–11) and concluding poems (11:7–12:8). Where one pattern ends the next begins. The patterns suggest that the book is divided into two main parts (1:12–6:9; 6:10–11:6) and the thought is also thus divided: in the first part Qoheleth is concerned with the vanity of various human endeavors, and in the second part with man's inability to understand the work of God. Each of the two halves indicated has an announcement of its topics at the beginning (1:12–18; 2:3 and 6:10–12) and does indeed pursue those topics. In the second half of the book there is a bipartite construction, and the two parts are paralleled to each other in structuring techniques even down to the triple ending in an *a b a* arrangement. Throughout the book the patterns coincide with meaningful units in the thought (see below). Finally the units match the thought in a repetitive manner and this adds further weight to the argument. If each section indicated by the pattern were on a different topic, the plan would be less certain. But it is a case of verbal repetitions marking out and exactly coinciding with repetitions of ideas. Eight sections are indicated in 1:12–6:9 and each is part of Qoheleth's investigation of the vanity of various features of life, and only there is that investi-

---

18. Save in the first section. Here the effect of the whole section is to say that man cannot find out, but the verb "find," marking the end, is used in the sense of "find fault" with God (see below ad loc).

gation found. In chs. 7–8 four sections are indicated and each is a critique of traditional advice on what is good for man to do; and when the vocabulary repetition ("to find out") stops, so does the idea. In 9:1–11:6 six sections are indicated and each is a repetition of the problem of what comes after; and when the vocabulary repetition ("to know") stops, so does the idea.

Perhaps there are additional indices reinforcing the above, for it may be that Qoheleth used inclusions. There are repetitions in each section which could be so interpreted. What makes one hesitant to affirm their existence is the large amount of vocabulary repetition in the book, and the fact that sometimes the first part of a potential inclusion stands in from the beginning of its section some distance. But in some of the units the repetitions are striking[19] and do invite one to see the repetitions in other sections as inclusions. We shall indicate these possible inclusions below, but they do not constitute the essential argument.

There follow below an outline and a brief paraphrase of each unit of the book to show the train of thought indicated by the structure. The writer is convinced that the patterns discovered should be the basis of future exegesis of the book, and that the material falling in each indicated unit should be interpreted in that context. He is not necessarily convinced that in each case he has captured the correct interpretation, but he wishes to begin that task.

Outline

Title (1:1)
Poem on Toil (1:2–11)

I. Qoheleth's Investigation of Life	(1:12–6:9)	
Double Introduction	(1:12–15)*	*ends with
	(1:16–18)*	"(vanity and) a chase after wind"
Study of pleasure-seeking	(2:1–11)*	
Study of wisdom and folly	(2:12–17)*	
Study of the fruits of toil		
One has to leave them to another	(2:18–26)*	
One cannot hit on the right time to act	(3:1–4:6)**	
The problem of a "second one"	(4:7–16)*	
One can lose all that one accumulates	(4:17–6:9)*	
II. Qoheleth's Conclusions	(6:10–11:6)	

19. E.g., *ʾēn qēṣ lᵉkol*, 4:8 and 16 (the only occurrences of *qēṣ* in the book, save in the editor's epilogue [12:12]); *yôm . . . yôm*, 7:1 and 14; *heḥākām*, 8:1 and 17; *gam ʾahăbâ gam śinʾâ*, 9:1 and 6; *ʿîr*, 9:14 and 10:15; *ʾereṣ*, 10:16–17 and 11:2; *maʿăśēh hāʾĕlōhîm*, 7:3; 8:17; 11:5.

Introduction (6:10–12): man does not know what God has done, for man cannot find out what is good to do and he cannot find out what comes after.

A. Man cannot find out what is good for him
    to do
    Critique of traditional wisdom
        On the day of prosperity and adversity (7:1–14)*
        On justice and wickedness   (7:15–24)*   *ends with "not
                                                          find out/who
                                                          can find out"

        On women and folly   (7:25–29)**
        On the wise man and the king   (8:1–17)***
B. Man does not know what will come after him
    He knows he will die; the dead know   (9:1–6)*
        nothing
    There is no knowledge in Sheol   (9:7–10)*   *ends with
                                                          "do not know/
                                                          no knowledge"

    Man does not know his time   (9:11–12)*
    Man does not know what will be   (9:13–
                                           10:15)**
    He does not know what evil will come   (10:16–
                                           11:2)*
    He does not know what good will come   (11:3–6)***
Poem on Youth and Old Age (11:7–12:8)
Epilogue (12:9–14)

Summary of the Book

1:12–15. Qoheleth begins by stating that he has studied all that is done on earth and he has found that *all is vanity and a chase after wind*. He closes the section with a proverb to the effect that the situation cannot be changed (cf. 3:14–15; 6:10, where the same idea marks the beginning of the second half of the book; 7:13). Possible inclusions (henceforth *Incl.*): *naʿăśâ taḥat/ šennaʿăśû taḥat* in 13 and 14.

1:16–18. Qoheleth has studied wisdom and folly and concludes that the acquisition of wisdom is a *chase after wind*. He closes this second introductory section, as the first, with a proverb and it serves to explain his conclusion. Incl.: *wᵉhôsaptî/yôsîp . . . yôsîp; ḥokmâ; wādāʿat/daʿat; harbēh/bᵉrōb* in 16 and 18. There is a partial chiastic arrangement in the two introductions: (a) "I applied my mind" (13); (b) "I have seen everything" (14); (b) "I have acquired great wisdom . . . my mind has had great experience" (16–17); (a) "I applied my mind" (17). Perhaps it is simply a chiasm; perhaps the "I applied my mind" is an inclusion tying the two introductions together.

2:1–11. Qoheleth studied pleasure-seeking to see what is good for men to do. He undertook great works and did not deprive himself of any pleasure, but he found that *all was vanity and a chase after wind,* for there was no gain. Incl.: *bᵉśimḥâ . . . ûlᵉśimḥâ/śimḥâ . . . śāmēaḥ* in 1–2 and 10; *hebel* in 1 and 11; *maʿăśay* in 4 and 11; *ʿāśâ* in 2–3 and 11.

2:12–17. The author takes up the "wisdom, madness and folly" of 1:17 and presents the results of his study of that aspect of life. He found that, despite the traditional teaching on the superiority of wisdom (2:13–14a), both the wise and the fool suffer the same fate, so what is the value of wisdom (14b–15)? "This also is vanity" (15) is a divider.[20] The idea of one fate is developed (16) and the conclusion stated—"*all is vanity and a chase after wind.*" Incl.: *ḥokmâ . . . heḥākām/heḥākām* in 2–14 and 16; *hakkᵉsîl* in 14 and 16; *ʿāśûhû/šennaʿăśâ* in 12 and 17.

2:18–26. Qoheleth resumes the idea of toil from 2:10–11, and presents the first of four sections on the results of toil. Here he observes that the fruits of one's toil must be left to another, and who knows if he will be a wise man or a fool (18–19). "This also is vanity" in 19 is a divider. In any event the fruits must be given to one who did not work for them (20–21). "This also is vanity" in 21 is a divider. What does a man have from his work but pain and vexation and loss of sleep (22–23). "This also is vanity" (23) is a divider. There is nothing better for a man to do than to find enjoyment in the fruit of his toil, but enjoyment is something God-given and uncertain (an idea to be developed in 6:1–6) and thus it too is *vanity and a chase after wind.* Incl.: *ḥokmâ; daʿat; yittᵉnennú/lātēt* in 21 and 26.[21]

3:1–4:6. Qoheleth presents (perhaps from traditional wisdom) the 14 opposites which have their time (2–8) and immediately applies them to the subject of toil. There is no profit in toil because God has established a time for everything and then has put timelessness in man's heart. Hence man has no sense of the right time to act, and so his toil is fruitless or chancy (9–11). There is nothing better than to find enjoyment in the fruit of one's toil (12–13). We cannot change what God has done (14–15). Incl.: *ʿāśâ . . . ʿāśâ hā ᵓēlōhîm/yaʿaśeh ha ᵓēlōhîm . . . hā ᵓēlōhîm ʿāśâ* in 11 and 14.[22]

---

20. Except in 2:1 "this (also) is vanity/all is vanity/all that comes is vanity" is not only an evaluation, but it also has a structural function as a sort of quarter or half divider within a unit. Cf. 2:15, 19, 21, 23; 3:19; 4:8; 5:9; 6:2; 7:6; 8:10, 14; 11:8.

21. V. 26a is taken in a non-ethical sense (so Barton, Gordis, Ryder, etc.). Qoheleth's judgment that even enjoyment is vanity (26b) is based on the uncertainty of it. This idea will be developed in 6:1–6 and the same judgment repeated in 6:9.—It may be noted that this first section on toil (2:18–26) is strongly tied to the preceding section on wisdom and folly (2:12–17) by the *mots crochets* "hate," "wise," and "fool" in 16–17 and 18–19.

22. If there are inclusions, the 14 opposites stand outside of them in the manner of a text cited for the sake of subsequent comment.—We have put 3:14–15 with the preceding rather than with what follows on an analogy with 2:24; 3:22; and 5:17 where the advice to enjoyment is followed by remarks to the effect that man should accept what God does.

While on the subject of time, Qoheleth adds a further observation (3:16–4:3). There is injustice in the world (16). According to the traditional wisdom, since there is a time and place for everything, then for every work there is a judgment (17).[23] But the author remarks that, not only cannot man predict the times of the opposites in 2–8, he has no grounds for predicting even that there will be a judgment, for man appears to be no different from the beasts in life or in death (18–21). So there is nothing better for man than to enjoy his works, for he has no way of knowing anything of the future to help him determine what else might be good to do (22; the latter is a major thought in the second part of the book, cf. 6:12; 9:1–11:6). In fact, in view of all the evil done on earth, the only ones more fortunate than those who are alive with regard to the knowledge of the future are those not yet born, who have not yet seen the evil done under the sun (4:1–3)! Incl.: *rāʾîtî/ rāʾâ* in 3:16 and 4:3; *hammaʿăśeh* in 3:17 and 4:3.[24]

The author returns to the topic of toil, the idea of oppression in 4:1, perhaps suggesting the envy from which all of man's toil stems (4:4–6). This too is *vanity and a chase after wind;* and by juxtaposing two proverbs, Qoheleth urges not indolence but a handful of quiet, rather than two hands full of toil which is a *chase after wind* (4:4–6). Incl.: *ʿāmāl* in 4 and 6. Perhaps *ʿāmāl* in 3:9 and 4:6 is an overall inclusion for the whole section.

4:7–16. Qoheleth presents his third observation on the results of toil: the problem of the "second." He points out that sometimes a man is alone and has no second one (son or brother) who will benefit from the riches gained by his toil (7–8). "This also is vanity" (8) is a divider. There follows a series of traditional sayings on "two are better than one" (9–12); and this is followed by an obscure example (13–16) which is related to the problem of the second (cf. *haššēnî* in 4:15) and perhaps challenges the "two is better than one" idea: the old and foolish king is perhaps a man who indeed has a "second" after him, but the second turns out to obscure the king's memory.[25] *This also is vanity and a chase after wind.* Incl.: *ʾēn qēṣ lᵉkol* in 8 and 16.

4:17–6:9. This final section on toil begins with a collection of wisdom material on the folly of many words (4:17–5:6). This theme appears again in 6:11 (the introduction to the second part of the book) and toward the end of the second part in 10:12–15; cf. also 12:12. Incl.: *dābār . . . dᵉbārèkā . . . bᵉrōb dᵉbārîm/dᵉbārîm harbēh* in 5:1–2 and 5:6. As Gordis has noted, Qoheleth at times cites "a proverb, part of which is apposite, while the rest of the saying,

---

23. Emending in 3:17 MT *šām* to *mišpāṭ* with CCD. In any event, this is the sense of the sentence.

24. It may be that there are two paragraphs here, 3:16–22 (Incl.: *raʾtî/rāʾîtî . . . lirʾôt* in 16 and 22; *hammaʿăśeh/bᵉmaʿăśā(y)w* in 17 and 22), and 4:1–3 (Incl.: *wāʿerʾeh/rāʾû; naʿăśîm [naʿăśâ] taḥat haššāmeš* in 1 and 3).

25. This interpretation would see *taḥtā(y)w* in 4:15 referring to the king, *lipnêhem* (temporal) in 16 as referring to the king and the heir, and *bô* in 16 as referring to the old king. If *bô* refers to the heir, then perhaps the story is about two men who try to go it alone.

though irrelevant, is quoted for the sake of completeness, a literary practice common to writers in all ages."[26] This practice is evident here as well as in 5:8–12; 7:1–12, 19–21; 8:1–5; 9:13–11:4.

Qoheleth then sets up the ideas that will provide the basis for his final remarks on toil and enjoyment by assembling four pieces of traditional wisdom (5:7–11). Vv. 7–8 are used here as a picture of a hierarchy of greed and of acquisition of goods, and v. 9 states the insatiableness of man's appetite. "This also is vanity" (9) is a divider. The acquisition of goods is often accompanied by the loss of goods (10) and by the loss of enjoyment (11). He then takes up the ideas of acquisition and loss of goods and observes that sometimes a man will accumulate riches and then lose them and have nothing to show for his toil. He repeats for the fourth time that the only good he has been able to discover for man to do is to find enjoyment in the fruit of his toil (5:12–19). Incl.: *bᵉⁱnyan/maᶜǎnēhû*[27] in 13 and 19; *ᵓāmāl* in 14 and 18.

The author points out, however, that there is a serious problem even with this advice (as he has already hinted in 2:24–26 and in his characterizing of enjoyment as a "gift" of God in 3:13 and 5:18). Resuming the loss of enjoyment idea from the beginning of the section, he observes that sometimes God does not give a man power to enjoy the fruit of his toil (6:1–2). "This is vanity" (2) is a divider. The evil of such a situation is developed in 3–6. Incl.: *raᵓîtî/rāᵓâ* in 1 and 6.

Finally Qoheleth takes up from the beginning of the section the idea of the insatiableness of man's appetite (6:7). In this regard what advantage does the wise man have over the fool (8a), especially if the wise man be poor and have little to satisfy any desires (8b). Better is enjoyment of what is at hand than the wandering of desire (a paraphrase of Qoheleth's advice to enjoy the fruits of one's toil), but this too is judged a *vanity and a chase after wind* (9), because a man may not be given the power to enjoy (6:1–6) and because his appetite is insatiable (6:7–9). On this note the first half of the book ends. Incl. for 6:7–9: *nepeš* in 7 and 9; for 4:16–6:9: *rᵉᵓût ᶜēnā(y)w/marᵓēh ᶜēnayim* in 5:10 and 6:9. Some phrases recall earlier remarks: all go to the same place (cf. 2:14–16; 3:20); man's appetite is never satisfied (4:8; 5:9); what advantage has the wise man over the fool (2:12–17).

6:10–12. The introduction to the second half of the book. What God has done is fixed (cf. 1:9; 1:15; 3:15) and man cannot dispute with him; there is vanity in a multiplicity of words (cf. 4:17–5:6). For who knows what is good for man to do, and who can tell him what the future holds in store. Incl.: *nôdāᶜ/yôdēaᶜ* in 10 and 12. There are three interrelated ideas here, but the basic one is that man cannot ascertain what God has done (cf. 3:11), for this idea runs throughout this second half (7:13; 8:17; 11:5). This inability on the part of man is manifested in two ways: in his inability to find out what is good

---

26. Gordis, op. cit., 101. He gives a parallel example from Egyptian literature.
27. Thus LXX, Coptic, Syro-Hexaplar, Vulgate.

to do (developed in four sections in chs. 7–8) and in his inability to know the future (developed in six sections in 9:1–11:6).

7:1–14. Qoheleth assembles a number of proverbs keyed to the word "good," i.e., proverbs which offer advice on what is good for man to do. "This also is vanity" in v. 6 is a divider as usual and separates the proverbs into two groups.[28] The first group extols the advantages of sorrow and adversity, but the effect of the second grouping is to point out the corruptibility of the wise man in the face of adversity. He may become impatient (8), angry (9), complaining (10), and may not possess anything to enjoy, even though wisdom may prolong his life (11–12). The juxtaposition of the two groups speaks for itself, and Qoheleth simply states that what God has done cannot be changed. He offers his usual advice to enjoy the good day; on the evil day one should consider that God has made the evil day as well as the good, so that man *may not find* fault with God.[29] Incl.: *yôm . . . yôm* and *ṭôb . . . ṭôb* in 1 and 14.

7:15–24. Qoheleth cites advice (16–18) on what is good for man to do in view of the problem of retribution, and adds three more sayings (19–22) to the effect that wisdom is good but the righteous man is never totally just (thus explaining 16–18). Perhaps the arrangement of 16–18 is Qoheleth's, perhaps it is prior to him. In any event he has tested it all and found it not helpful. The secret of what God has done is too deep and who can *find it out*? Incl.: *titḥakkam/ʾeḥkāmâ* in 16 and 23.

7:25–29. As Qoheleth tries to add up the sum of things, he investigates the traditional wisdom on the folly of women (26) and that it is good to escape them. But he *did not find* the sum in that material either. In fact he found that men were scarcely better than women with regard to folly. Incl.: *ḥešbôn/ḥiššᵉbōnôt* in 25 and 29.

8:1–17. The author cites the traditional advice that it is good to listen to the wise man and obey the king (1–6a). Yet, he observes, the wise man in fact does not know the essential answers nor does the king deliver from the essen-

28. The connection of "this also is vanity" (6) with the surrounding material has long been a problem. That MT may have suffered damage at this point could be argued from breaks in the text here in 4QKoh (cf. J. Muilenburg, "A Qoheleth Scroll from Qumran," *BASOR* 135 [1954] 26–27). But, as Muilenburg observes, the breaks could simply be erasures and the text need not have diverged in any way from MT. If we take into account the structural function of "this also is vanity" as a divider separating the proverbs into two opposing groups, and if we let it refer to 1–6 and see its explanation in 7–12, MT makes very fine sense as it stands.

29. *ʿal-dibrat šellōʾ yimṣāʾ hāʾādām ʾaḥărā(y)w mᵉʾûmâ*. The translation, "find fault with him," already probable on linguistic grounds (cf. Symmachus; Rashi; Williams; G. R. Driver, "Problems and Solutions," *VT* 4 [1954] 230; Ryder; CCD), is further supported by the fact that the theme of "what comes after" is taken up only in 9:1–11:6 and is absent from the conclusions of the four sections in chs. 7–8. The appearance of the idea in 8:7 is secondary and is not a main point.

tial evils, and man lords it over man to his hurt (6b–9). Incl.: *šilṭôn/šālaṭ* in 4 and 9; *raʿ* in 5 and 9.

Taking up the idea of wickedness from v. 8, Qoheleth presents the problem of retribution once again (10–12a),[30] cites the traditional doctrine (12b–13), but observes that it is not always borne out in fact (10–14). "This also is vanity" (14b) is a divider. He commends enjoyment once again, but confesses three times that man *cannot find out* the work of God (15–17), and this ends the first part of the second half of the book. Incl.: *yôdēaʿ/lādaʿat* in 12 and 17. *Heḥākām* in 1 and 17 is the overall inclusion for the section, and *maʿăśeh hāʾĕlōhîm* in 7:13 and 8:17 is an inclusion tying together the four sections of chs. 7–8.

9:1–6. Qoheleth begins to develop the second idea of the introduction (6:12): man does not know the future (what will be after him). He recalls the traditional teaching that the just man is in the hand of God (1a), but he observes that the just man cannot figure out whether God's sentiments toward him are favorable or unfavorable, and he is always uncertain whether he will meet good or evil in the future. For both the just and the wicked have one fate; in this life the same things happen to each, and afterward they both die (1b–3). But, he observes, citing two proverbs, it is better to be alive than dead (4), for as far as knowledge of the future is concerned man at least knows that he will die; the dead *do not know* anything of what is done on earth after them (5–6). Incl.: *yôdēaʿ* in 1 and 5; *gam ʾahăbâ . . . gam śinʾâ* in 1 and 6.

9:7–10. The author once again commends enjoyment. Man knows that this is his portion in life, for since he is permitted it, God must have approved it. He urges that whatever man does he do it with all his might, for there is *no knowledge* or work or thought or wisdom in Sheol. Incl.: *maʿăśeh* in 7 and 10. But this is all man knows of the future, and in the next four sections Qoheleth cites the wisdom material itself to show that man does not know his time, and does not know what will happen for evil or for good.

9:11–12. The deserving do not receive their due. Rather everyone is subject to a time of misfortune, and a man *does not know* when that time will be. V. 12aβ–b may be a proverb. Incl.: *ʿēt* in 11 and 12b.

9:13–10:15. Man does not know what will come after him. This section consists mainly of previously independent units of wisdom material arranged to create a picture of the uncertainty of the future. At the end of the collection there is also inserted the idea once again of the folly of many words (cf. 4:17–5:6; 6:11). The section is developed in four parts. (a) 9:13–10:1. The future is uncertain because of the vulnerability of wisdom to neglect and folly. Incl.: *ḥokmâ* in 9:13 and 10:1. (b) 10:2–7. Traditional wisdom, which attempts to predict what one will find "on the road" (2–3) and which offers advice on how to keep wise men in high places (4), does not always work out. The im-

---

30. "This also is vanity" (10) divides the observation into two parts as usual.

ages of the "high places" and the "road" are retained and the refutation in 5–7 is given in those terms. Incl.: *hōlēk/hōlᵉkîm* in 3 and 7. (c) 10:8–11. Proverbs arranged in chiastic fashion present six pictures of the unexpected or of the possibility of accident.[31] Incl.: *nāḥāš* and *yiššᵉkennû/yiššōk* in 8 and 11. (d) 10:12–15. Many words are foolish, for *no man knows* what is to be and who can tell him what will be after him. Incl.: *dibrê/dᵉbārîm* in 12 and 14. The overall inclusions for the section are *dābār* in 9:16–17 and 10:12–14; *ʿir* in 9:14 and 10:15.

10:16–11:2. Traditional material is assembled to show that man does not know what evil may happen. There is the possibility of evil even among nobility (16–17) to the detriment of the land (18) and the depletion of state funds (19). Evil can result from even the most careful speech (20). Venture forth, but do not put all the eggs in one basket because you *do not know* what evil may happen (11:1–2). Incl.: *ʾereṣ* in 10:16–17 and 11:2.

11:3–6. What is to happen will happen (3). He who is cautious will never act (4). Venture forth in spite of the uncertain. As you *do not know* how the spirit comes to the child in the womb, so you *do not know* the work of God and you *do not know* what good will happen (5–6). Inc.: *yizrāʿ/zᵉraʿ et-zarʿekā* in 4 and 6. Perhaps the triple *ʾēnᵉkā yôdēaʿ . . . lō tēdaʿ . . . ʾēnᵉkā yôdēaʿ* is an inclusion with *ʾēn yôdēaʿ* in 9:1 and *yādaʿ* in 6:10–12. Once again *maʿăśēh hāʾĕlōhîm* in 11:5 recalls the same phrase in 7:13 and 8:17. It may be that *ṭôbîm*, the last word in 11:6, is intended as an inclusion with *ṭôb* in 6:12 or 7:1.

The Two Poems

There remains to discuss the introductory (1:2–11) and concluding (11:7–12:8) poems which stand outside of the structure described above.

In the introductory piece, "'vanity of vanities,' says Qoheleth, 'vanity of vanities; all is vanity'" (1:2) is an overall inclusion for the book with 12:8 as is generally recognized. The question in 1:3, "What does a man gain by all the toil at which he toils under the sun," provides the context in which 1:4–11 is to be read. There follows a poetic section in 3–8 with a subsequent prose comment in 9–11. The poetry is probably to be divided into two sections: 4–6 on the endless round of events (Incl.: *hôlēk* in 4 and 6 [*bis*]), and 7–8 on the lack of progress in nature and in man's speech, sight, and hearing (Incl.: *mā-lēʾ/timmālēʾ* in 7 and 8). The comment of 9–11 states that there is nothing new, and if something seems to be new, it is because one doesn't remember the previous occurrence. Moreover, the same lack of remembrance will obtain

---

31. 10:10a is obscure. The context (the uncertainty of the future) suggests that it is a picture of iron sharpened beforehand but accidentally blunted, and that we should read *wᵉhûʾ lᵉpānîm* (with CCD). The other problems in the text (the subjects of the verbs, the nature of the *piʿel*, the pointing of *qlql* and its meaning) leave room for a variety of translations.

in the future (Incl.: *hyh* in 9 and 11). Thus there is no profit in toil because nothing is gained, neither progress, novelty, nor remembrance.

The closing poem reinforces Qoheleth's advice on enjoyment. It begins with a prose introduction (11:7–8) which summarizes this final section: enjoy the light, and (as an incentive for enjoyment) remember the darkness that is coming. "All that comes is vanity" (8) is a divider. This advice to enjoy and remember is then developed in a two-part poem: enjoy your youth (11:9–10; Incl.: *bᵉyaldûtèkā/hayyaldût* and *libbᵉkā/millibbekā* in 9 and 10)[32] and remember your grave[33] (12:1–7; Incl.: *bôrᵉkā/habbôr* in 1 and 6; *wᵉšābû/ wᵉyāšûb*[34] . . . *tāšûb*). The second part of the poem is structured by the repetition of "before" (*ᶜad ᵓăšer loᵓ*) in 12:1, 2, 6 and this yields three sections: (a) a general characterizing of old age as the unwelcome time of life (1); (b) old age is the winter of life (2–5); (c) four images of death and the conclusion (6–7). 12:8 provides the overall inclusion for the book with 1:2 and the epilogue is from the hand of the editor.

The two poems, then, single out and express in an arresting way two main thoughts of the book: what profit is there in toil (the point of four of the six sections on vanity in the first half), and the advice about enjoyment (the only good that Qoheleth can find for man to do).

Conclusion

If the above analysis is correct, the book speaks more clearly, but at the same time says much less, than we previously thought. The idea of the impossibility of understanding what God has done (which was always seen as *a* theme) is in reality *the* theme, and it is built on the vanity motif prominent in the first part of the book. The only advice offered is to find enjoyment in life and in the fruit of one's toil while one can (2:24; 3:12–13; 3:22; 5:17–19; 7:14; 8:15; 9:7–9; 11:7–12:8), to venture forth boldly in spite of the uncertain (9:10; 11:1, 4, 6), to fear God (5:6; 11:9), not to work feverishly (4:4–

---

32. Perhaps *hābel* and the end of 11:10 is divider.—The admonition in 11:9 that God will bring one to judgment appears to clash with the previous remarks on judgment in 3:16–21 and 8:10–14. But Qoheleth is a believer and he believes that God is acting; he simply is confessing that he cannot find out what God is doing in his day. And this obtains for God's justice as well. Qoheleth affirms it in principle (11:9), but in the main part of the book he questions it in its manifestations.

33. Reading *bôrᵉkā* with Galling and Scott. MT "remember your creator" has always been felt to be foreign to the context, for according to 11:8 what is to be remembered is the darkness to come. If 12:1 is the opening line of the second part of the poem as seems indicated by the repetitions "enjoy" (11:8 and 9) and "remember" (11:8 and 12:1), and if 12:1 is meant to state the theme of the second part as 11:9a does for the first part, then the difficulty becomes acute. If the author is using inclusions, *bôr* in 1 would go nicely with *bôr* in 9, and this may explain the choice of the word.

34. MT *wᵉyāšōb*.

6), not to put all the eggs in one basket (11:2), and not to waste words trying to puzzle things out (1:18; 4:17–5:6; 6:10–11; 10:12–15). The "be not too just, be not too wicked" advice in 7:16ff., frequently seen as a major thought of Qoheleth, is not Qoheleth's message at all, but is something he judges not helpful. Similarly, the various collections of proverbs are not "Qoheleth's favorites" offered by way of advice as previously treated, but they are either cited to be criticized or they are arranged and juxtaposed to produce various negative effects.

In 12:9 the editor remarks that Qoheleth taught the people knowledge and he weighed, scrutinized, and arranged many proverbs. If this analysis is correct, Qoheleth was an extremely skillful arranger of proverbs, and there is a greater depth of meaning to the editor's remark than we had hitherto suspected.

4

QOHELETH'S WORLD
AND LIFE VIEW

H. Carl Shank

Within the scope of Old Testament ethical problems falls the viewpoint of Qoheleth, or the Preacher, of Ecclesiastes. A superficial reading of the book reveals a man who definitely has a negative viewpoint of life in its many facets. If indeed the book is a unity, composed by one wise man, then the theme of pessimism or cynicism becomes a suggested option. But the ethical questions arising from such an understanding of the book become crucial. Can a thoroughly pessimistic view of life have any place in the canonical books of Scripture? What exactly is the goal of Qoheleth's ethics? Further, what does the *God* of Qoheleth really have to do with his life and standards of conduct? Again, does not the recurring theme of "there is nothing better for a man than that he should eat and drink and make his soul enjoy good in his labor" (cf. 2:24; 3:12, 13, etc.) denote a sort of Epicurean sentiment?

Qoheleth's Ethical Perspective: Critical Views

Of course the modern critics of the Bible have seized upon the pessimism-cynicism suggestion with a vengeance. Morris Jastrow has suggested that the

From *Westminster Theological Journal* 37 (1974): 57–73. Reprinted by permission.

book teaches an ethical cynicism, where, in the face of no real goal to life, good humor is still to be maintained.[1] A popular view, held until recently, noted the phrase "Vanity of vanities" and attempted to draw certain parallelisms in thought and perspective between Qoheleth's notion of "vanity" and Heraclitus's view that "all is flux."[2] However, most critical scholars today reject this argument as unconvincing. The recognized modern critical writer, G. Von Rad, has related the book to a supposed stage in Israel's religious evolution at which "belief in Yahweh's action in history grew weak" and Ecclesiastes "fell back on the cyclical way of thinking common to the East."[3] D. Kidner comments that Von Rad's argument rests on "precarious assumptions." Along with the questionable premise that the thinking of the Ancient Near East was "cyclical," the dating of the book still remains too much of an open question to make definite conclusions concerning the strength of belief "in Yahweh's action in history."[4]

R. B. Y. Scott in the Anchor Bible series, suggests the following concerning Qoheleth's ethic:

> His ethic has no relationship to divine commandments, for there are none. It arises rather from the necessity of caution and moderation before the inexplicable, on the acceptance of what is fated and cannot be changed, and finally on grasping firmly the only satisfaction open to man—the enjoyment of being alive. The author is a rationalist, an agnostic, a skeptic, a pessimist and a fatalist (the terms are not used pejoratively!).[5]

Scott adds that Qoheleth teaches "philosophical nihilism" and has no real "religious" point of view. In response to such a characterization of Qoheleth's ethics, we note that Scott, along with Von Rad, assumes the non-Christian ethical construct of a God, hidden behind an "impenetrable veil," and One who can offer no clear revelation to Qoheleth. Qoheleth's "God" is the Great Unknown of neo-orthodox theology.[6] Qoheleth's wisdom lay in "recognizing the limitations of human knowledge and power,"[7] affirms

---

1. *Cf.* Morris Jastrow, *A Gentle Cynic* (Philadelphia: J. B. Lippincott, 1919).

2. *Cf.* Carl Knopf, "The Optimism of Ecclesiastes," *Journal of Biblical Literature*, XLIX (1930), 195–99.

3. G. Von Rad, *Old Testament Theology* (New York: Harper and Row, 1962), p. 454.

4. Derek Kidner, "Wisdom Literature of the Old Testament," *New Perspectives on the Old Testament,* ed. J. Barton Payne (Waco: Word Books, 1970), p. 125.

5. R. B. Y. Scott, *Qoheleth,* in the Anchor Bible (New York: Doubleday, 1965), pp. 191–92.

6. This is substantially true of the view expressed in G. A. Buttrick, et al. (eds.), *The Interpreter's Bible,* Vol. V (New York: Abingdon, 1956), p. 22: "He (Qoheleth) does not doubt the existence and sovereignty of God, but his God is absentee, lost in the distance, not only apparently careless of mankind but at variance with it."

7. Scott, p. 206.

Scott. Consequently, man cannot have an absolute good in the universe; he must remain satisfied with the *relative* good found in "relishing being alive."[8] It does seem that Scott relies upon some kind of Kantian noumenal-phenomenal distinction at this point. At the very least, his scheme is based upon a faith-knowledge dialectic where Qoheleth's faith (if he possesses any) has nothing to do with his intellectual comprehension and explanation of the world about him.

Is indeed the goal of Qoheleth's ethics some deterministic yet strangely "hidden" and silent Elohim-God, who barely resembles Israel's covenant Yahweh? Is Qoheleth's situation that of an ethical dilemma arising from hopeless pessimism? Must we finally agree with the non-Christian ethical view that since it is hopeless and foolish to look for perfection in this world and since, after all, God and man on Qoheleth's model are subject to certain limitations it is best to seek to improve conditions to some extent, at least? Must we conclude that man should enjoy himself (2:24; etc.) and work with all his might (9:10), whatever God may say?

Qoheleth's Ethical Perspective: Conservative Views

In response to critical views, evangelicals have attempted in various ways to justify Qoheleth's seemingly negative attitude about life. For the most part, they have recognized the distinctively recurring phrases in Ecclesiastes.[9] However, it seems to me that they have not really dealt honestly with them.

Leupold analyzes the phrases "under the sun," "vanity of vanities; all is vanity," and suggests that Qoheleth *deliberately* concerns himself only with the things of this world. Revelation and the world to come are, for the sake of argument, temporarily ruled out. It is by this "as if" technique that Leupold explains Qoheleth's seemingly negative outlook on the world.[10] *Actually*, however, Qoheleth really does "fear God and keep his commandments."

Even Hengstenberg, though he has some valid penetrating remarks on the message of Ecclesiastes, points out that the theme, or themes, are difficult to delineate. In fact the whole book, including these recurring themes, is "unintelligible except on the historical presupposition that the people of God was in a very miserable condition at the time of its composition."[11] The Persians held dominion over the people of God. They were in a state of deepest misery and had consequently fallen prey to vanity. The radiant glory of Solomon's day was no more

---

8. Ibid., p. 196.

9. There are six of these recurring phrases in the book of Ecclesiastes; the phrases and Scriptural references are listed in this section.

10. This is especially apparent in H. C. Leupold, *Exposition of Ecclesiastes* (Columbus: Wartburg Press, 1952), pp. 92–93.

11. E. W. Hengstenberg, *Commentary on Ecclesiastes* (Philadelphia: Smith, English, and Co., 1860), p. 45.

(1:12–18), and this was a time of persecution.[12] The date of composition was either contemporaneous with or after the time of Malachi. Thus, Qoheleth, in demonstrating the utter vanity of this life, would enable the people to appreciate fully the "fear of God" and "what a precious treasure man has in God."[13] Yet, even if one accepts a late, post-exilic dating and non-Solomonic authorship, both of which are unsettled in scholars' minds, what about the seemingly "obvious" tone of resignation demonstrated over and over again in these phrases? Even on the historical construct of Hengstenberg and others they may still seem to portray Qoheleth as a man of "questionable" or "confused" ethics.

The frankness of the introductory note to the Scofield Bible concerning the recurring phrases and the entire book plays havoc with conservative "glossing over" or "dressing up of " the thought of Qoheleth.

> This is the Book of man "under the sun," reasoning about life; it is the best man can do, with the knowledge that there is a Holy God, and that He will bring everything into judgment. . . . Inspiration sets down accurately what passes, but the conclusions and reasonings are, after all, man's.[14]

The specter of pessimism once more appears on the horizon of Qoheleth's thought.

Although these conservative writers have different emphases and methods of interpretation, they will all agree on one crucial ethical area, namely the situational perspective of Qoheleth. Qoheleth is a man who, though he does fear God and stresses the keeping of His commandments (12:13), looks at the world about him from the standpoint of reason that has very little relationship with his "blind faith" in the Creator. A distinct dichotomy between faith and reason can be clearly seen in Leupold, Delitzsch, and Scofield when they deal with the recurring phrases. Even Hengstenberg does not totally escape this faith-reason dialectic. He mentions that Qoheleth's pervasive use of the name *Elohim* shows that "the problem before the writer is considered from the point of view of Natural Theology with the aid of experience and of reason as purified by the Spirit of God."[15] Finally, Sierd Woudstra, who criticizes Leupold for his nature-grace dichotomy in interpreting Qoheleth's thought, falls into speaking of two concurrent lines of thought prevalent in Qoheleth: "Koheleth is on the one hand dealing with life as he observed it, while on the other hand he knew and was convinced by faith that things were different."[16]

---

12. Ibid., pp. 2–16.

13. Ibid., p. 16.

14. Quoted in J. Stafford Wright, "The Interpretation of Ecclesiastes," *The Evangelical Quarterly* (1946), pp. 20–21.

15. Hengstenberg, p. 26.

16. Sierd Woudstra, "Koheleth's Reflection Upon Life," (unpublished Th.M. Thesis, Westminster Theological Seminary, 1959), p. 38. Notice Woudstra's evaluation of Leupold on p. 106.

However, Woudstra here raises an important issue in the interpretation of the ethical perspective of Qoheleth. If there does exist a distinction here, that distinction is *not* between faith and reason but between faith and *sight*, i.e. between "faith". (that comes from special revelation) and that revelation presently available to any natural man as he perceives the creation about him. Of course, such a distinction can be seen in the New Testament record (cf. Rom. 1:18–32; Acts 14:15–17; Acts 17:22–31). But, *in what sense* and *to what degree* is such a "distinction" relevant to Qoheleth?

To begin with, Qoheleth was not merely a theologian working from the construct of "natural theology" who then attempted to understand God's creation without the interpretative key of special revelation. As we shall demonstrate later, he looked upon life and the world from the perspective of an Old Testament believer who had understood the reality of the curse of God placed upon life "under the sun" in Gen. 3. Hence, Qoheleth's wisdom and knowledge of this world was not merely that of a propositional and sense-experience sort. He approached the world and the life-situation by presupposing a Creator God who had indeed revealed Himself in creation, in the fall and in the subsequent history of redemption. He stood in a culture which knew Yahweh and the world about them in terms of direct revelation given through the Law and the Prophets. Consequently, his knowledge of anything must presuppose his knowledge of God, which sprang from a proper attitude of the fear of God. Thus, Qoheleth's "faith" and "sight" were not something wholly distinct from and independent of each other (cf. below, Phrase 4).

But also, they do not *oppose* one another in the book of Ecclesiastes. The historical-redemptive *antecedents* of Qoheleth's sight-perspective find their point of reference in the fall and curse of Gen. 3. Intimations to such a reference-point are found in an exposition of some of his recurring phrases and their contexts (cf. below, Phrase 4). Moreover, the twin-idea of all men being "of dust" (3:20; 12:7) and "turning or returning to dust again" (3:20)/"to the earth as it was" (12:7) when they die, no doubt has its primary reference in Gen. 3:19: "In the sweat of thy face shalt thou eat bread till thou return unto the ground; for out of it wast thou taken; for dust thou art and unto dust shalt thou return."[17] Further, the *consequences* of Qoheleth's sight-perspec-

---

17. Comparing the Hebrew of Gen. 3:19 with Eccles. 3:20 and 12:7 we notice some interesting syntactic parallels:

שׁב אל-העפר (Eccles. 3:20)
אל-עפר תשׁוב (Gen. 3:19)
וישׁב העפר אל-הארץ (Eccles. 12:7)
שׁובך אל-האדמה (Gen. 3:19)

Hengstenberg maintains that the foundation of Eccles. 3:20 is found in Gen. 3:19 (op. cit., p. 118) while *allusion* is made to Gen. 3:19 in Eccles. 12:7 (cf. p. 253).

tive merely drive him to acknowledge that wisdom resides in fearing God and keeping His commandments (12:13). Consequently, any claim that Qoheleth's ethic falls into the imperfect ethical thought of the Old Testament and that we must therefore expect some sort of faith-reason, or rather faith-sight, *dichotomy* cannot be maintained.

Yet, in another sense, since Qoheleth does refer back to the fall and the resultant curse, he like Paul in Acts 14 (cf. Acts 17 and also Rom. 1) makes a case that is largely restricted to that revelation made available by the Creator God to all natural men who live in the light of the fall. Qoheleth gives the natural man an astoundingly lucid description of what he can behold in this world and his life which should drive him to seek God and His self-revelation in Jesus Christ. To demonstrate this we notice two points.

First of all, to the Lycaonian Gentiles Paul and Barnabas in Acts 14:15ff. restrict their case to that revelation available to these people in the Creator God (vs. 15) providentially giving them "rains and fruitful seasons filling your hearts with food and gladness" (vs. 17). F. F. Bruce suggests that the imagery here is drawn from several Old Testament texts, one of which is Eccles. 9:7 (cf. below, Phrase 5).[18] This "gladness" was a gift of God to these Gentiles by which they should have discerned His providential rule over them.[19] It was therefore foolish and vain for them to attempt to perform that worship before Paul and Barnabas which, by the light of even natural revelation alone, belonged only to the Creator.

Then, also, the theme of foolishness for unregenerate men not recognizing the "power and divinity" of the God of the creation in which they live and move is brought out clearly in Rom. 1:18ff.[20] These unrighteous acts of the

---

18. *Cf.* F. F. Bruce, *Commentary on the Book of Acts* (Grand Rapids: Eerdmans, 1954). The term for gladness (εὐφροσύνη) is used in the LXX of Eccles. 9:7 and translates שׂמחה. Other possible references to Old Testament imagery for vs. 17 are Ps. 4:7 and Isa. 25:6. At the very least, the Apostles may be alluding to the passage in Eccles. 9:7.

19. "This εὐφροσύνη can also be gratefully understood as the gift of God by which even the heathen may discern his providential rule, Acts 14:17." (R. Bultmann, article on εὐφρνίυω/εὐφροσύνη. Vol. II, *TWNT,* ed. G. Kittel (Grand Rapids: Eerdmans, 1964), p. 774.

20. M. D. Hooker maintains that Paul in Rom. 1:18–32 had the figure of Adam in mind: "In these verses he deliberately described man's predicament in terms of the biblical narrative of Adam's fall. Not only does the language of this section echo that of Gen. 1:20–6 but the sequence of events is reminiscent of the story of Adam in Gen. 1–3." (M. D. Hooker, "A Further Note on Romans 1," *NT Studies* 13 (Jan., 1967), p. 181; cf. also her "Adam in Romans 1," *NT Studies* 6 (1959–1960), pp. 297–306).

C. K. Barrett develops this thesis in *From First Adam to Last* (London, 1962, pp. 17–19) and claims that the moral wickedness described in Rom. 1 is the *direct* result of the Fall.

Finally, Robert Haldane in his *Exposition of the Epistle to the Romans* (Banner, 1960) notes that the wrath of God "was revealed when the sentence of death was first pronounced, the earth cursed and man driven out of the earthly paradise . . ." (p. 55).

We might therefore be able to draw a redemptive-historical link between the Fall/Curse, Qoheleth and Paul in Rom. 1 and hence in Acts 14 and 17.

Gentiles in the light of God's natural revelation proceeded *not* from a mere deficiency in mental capacity but from oral obtuseness, or foolishness (v. 22).[21] Again, F. F. Bruce points out that the term used by Paul for "fool" probably refers back to the "fool" of the Old Testament Wisdom Literature.[22] Here we have a tie-in with Qoheleth's exposition in Ecclesiastes. As natural men observe the creation about them there are only two possible options for a philosophy of life. One is to claim the "wisdom" of this world and thus become fools in the sight of God. The other is to recognize the stark reality of the picture Qoheleth paints for him and to heed the command, "Fear God and keep His commandments" (cf. below, Phrase 6). True wisdom resides in this alone.

Before we consider the recurring phrases, it is necessary to make some preliminary remarks on the method of interpretation of Qoheleth's ethic in these phrases. To begin with, we should attempt to understand the book in the apparent way Qoheleth has composed it. He has done so by using certain phrases which occur over and over again throughout the twelve chapters. I think that J. Stafford Wright has a valid hermeneutical principle in mind when he suggests that examination of these recurring phrases reveals, at the very least, Qoheleth's thought in the immediate context of the book.[23]

Secondly, Qoheleth's directive in 12:13 and the remark in vs. 14 skillfully summarizes and concludes his whole ethical stance. Qoheleth's ethical integrity is grounded in the practice of the fear of God along with the keeping of His commandments, and however we analyze the rest of the book we must not contravene Qoheleth's own ethical conclusion.

Third, we must remember that Ecclesiastes appears in the broader context of the Wisdom Literature of the Old Testament. That literature, though similar in some formal characteristics with other Ancient Near East Wisdom Literature, cannot be identified with it in its ethical perspective. Qoheleth's wisdom has its foundation clearly laid in the fear of the Lord.

Finally, we must understand Qoheleth's ethical perspective in the general context of the rest of the Old Testament and in the light of the One who embodied this wisdom in the New Testament, even Jesus Christ. We affirm that Qoheleth does not disagree with other Old Testament thought. Rather, he writes in the context of the doctrines of the Fall and man's sin. He does not dispute their revelatory character and relevance to his situation; he assumes

21. *Cf.* F. F. Bruce, *Epistle to the Romans,* Tyndale Series (Grand Rapids: Eerdmans, 1963). Calvin says that impiety here should be joined to unrighteousness (*Commentary on the Epistle of Paul the Apostle to the Romans,* p. 68).

22. *Cf.* F. F. Bruce, *The Epistle to the Romans.* He also notes that parallels exist between later Israelite Wisdom Literature (cf. Wisdom 12–14). Hooker (op. cit.) makes a similar point in her exposition of this section.

23. Wright, op. cit., p. 22 has a rather uncritical way of suggesting this hermeneutical principle. Nevertheless, I feel he has a valid principle in mind.

their validity for his life and world view. Also, he looks forward in hope to the New Testament in his doctrine of the fear of the Lord and the coming judgment of the secret thoughts of man.

Qoheleth's Ethical Perspective in Light of the Recurring Phrases

Phrase 1: "All is vanity" or "This is vanity" (1:2, 14; 2:1, 11, 17, 26, 15, 19, 21, 23; 3:19; 4:4, 8, 7, 16; 5:7 (6), 10 (9); 6:2, 4, 9, 11, 12; 7:6, 15; 8:10, 14; 9:9; 11:8, 10; 12:8 repetition of 1:2)

This phrase is the most dominant and pervasive of all the recurring phrases in Ecclesiastes. Hengstenberg disagrees with those who would attempt to make this phrase the *one* theme of the book since it does not sufficiently explicate some of the other material in the book. Yet its dominance in Qoheleth's thought renders it a key to the interpretation of life "under the sun."

Woudstra states the main exegetical question concerning this class of phrases well:

> Is Koheleth only saying that man's accomplishments under the sun are transitory in character, are devoid of any permanence, or is he saying that human existence and everything that goes with it is futile and meaningless?[24]

The latter, Leupold holds, gives the term *hebel* (הבל) a pessimistic connotation not warranted by the facts.[25] He claims that the term refers to "that which is fleeting and transitory and also suggests the partial futility of human effort."[26] Woudstra, on the other hand, opts for the latter description of *hebel* and denies that this implies a pessimism that the critics would like to see here.

A thorough study of the word in the contexts mentioned above reveals that the term takes on different connotations in different contexts. Theophile Meek says that "in this short book, *hebel* would seem to be used in at least five different senses: 'futile' (most frequent, e.g., 1:2), 'empty' (e.g., 6:12), 'sorry' (e.g., 6:4), 'senseless' (e.g., 8:14), and 'transient' (e.g., 11:10)."[27] He therefore proposes that the term takes on different meanings in different contexts. With respect to other Old Testament literature, *hebel* can refer to that which is "unsubstantial, evanescent" as far as a basis for religious trust is concerned (cf. Jer. 1:15; 51:18; 16:19). In Ps. 39:4ff., man is in a "turmoil over vanity" (v. 6), over the labor to attain breaths of wind. His "precious things" cannot endure because they partake of the nature of "vanity."

24. Woudstra, p. 38.
25. Leupold, p. 41.
26. Ibid.
27. Theophile J. Meek, "Transplanting the Hebrew Bible," *Journal of Biblical Literature*, 79 (1960), p. 331.

The power of Meek's suggestion in the immediate context of Ecclesiastes lies in the fact that it seems to give the term the flexibility of connotation that Qoheleth evidently employs in these recurring phrases.[28] Different "aspects" of the idea of vanity are employed by Qoheleth to vividly illustrate the reality of the curse of God placed upon the work of man after the Fall (cf. Gen. 3:17–19). Therefore, an attempt to find a "static" meaning to *hebel* in Ecclesiastes, as Woudstra and others do, fails to take note of the richness of the concept as used by Qoheleth.

Those aspects which are available to every man, and from which none can entirely escape, are a life and labor that are wearisome (cf. Job 7:3), filled often with sorrow and pain (cf. Job 3:10; Ps. 25:18; 73:16)[29] and will only end up in physical death, at the very least. Also, Qoheleth tells us that this created order partakes of the character of "vanity" (cf. 7:15; 9:9). Yet, man's effort in this context is given to him as a gift of God (3:13, 14; 6:2). Therefore, natural man cannot claim that his efforts are "meaningless" or that the *situation* in which he finds himself forces him to sin, since God made labor a good gift. It is the fear of God alone and the keeping of His commandments which can give men the ability to enjoy this gift of labor. Yet, Qoheleth's faith does not change the character of a created order which now partakes of the character of vanity (cf. Rom. 8 and below). Consequently, excruciating moral problems do exist for Qoheleth because the ground after the curse brought on by the fall becomes an occasion for temptation.

Phrase 2: "under the sun" (1:3, 9, 14; 2:11, 17, 18, 19, 20, 22; 3:26; 4:1, 3, 7, 15; 5:13, 18; 6:1, 5, 12; 8:9, 15, 17; 9:3, 6, 9, 11, 13; 10:5)

This second phrase forms the immediate context of a world which has the constitution and course of "vanity." It has reference to the place where the toil of man occurs and is tantamount to על־הארץ (cf. 8:14, 16; 11:2). Notice that this phrase is unique to Qoheleth.

Phrase 3: "striving after wind" (1:14, 17; 2:11, 17, 26; 4:4, 6, 16; 6:9)

With the exception of 4:6 this expression is always joined to the phrase containing the word "vanity." A man may determine or make up his mind to accomplish something eternally significant in a creation subjected to vanity, yet no matter how hard he tries Qoheleth tells him it will be a fruitless endeavor (cf. 1:14 and use of רשות). A man in his toil "under the sun" grasps after the wind and attains precious little for all his labor.

---

28. Note also the variability of connotations in the use of the term עלם in Ecclesiastes: 1:4; 3:11, 14; 9:6; 12:5.

29. Even as early as Gen. 4:2 in the history of redemption Eve was overcome by the discovery of the vanity of this earthly life. This is expressed in the naming of "Abel": הבליהי־הבל רעה.

Phrase 4:

(a) *"I perceived"* (1:17; 2:14; 3:22)
(b) *"I said in my heart"* (2:1, 15; 3:17, 18; 9:1)
(c) *"I gave my heart to consider"* & *variations* (1:13, 17; 2:3; 7:25; 8:9, 16; 9:1)

Most interpreters have more or less considered this class of phrases as indicative of a thoroughgoing research activity, primarily involving mental conception of various empirical facts. Leupold maintains that these phrases merely indicate an experiment of Qoheleth in rational thinking, thinking that, for the time-being, is unaided by enlightened reason and revelation from God.[30] As noted above, Hengstenberg would disagree with Leupold's conjecture and claim that this class of phrases demonstrates Qoheleth's *enlightened* reason operating in the sphere of natural theology. But again, revelation has very little to do with Qoheleth's perception of this world of vanity.

However, we must maintain, contrary to the majority of critical and conservative commentators, that Qoheleth's perception as indicated in this class of phrases refers to a knowledge which is a "reflex-action" of his fear of God and which penetrates to the essence of the *meaning* of what this world of vanity is all about. Surely, Qoheleth does perceive the vanity "under the sun" which does not *exclude* the intellectual element of knowledge of these things. Yet that perception also *includes* a deep, spiritual insight into the effects of the curse of God upon life and labor "under the sun."

Two very common Hebrew words (ראה and ידע) are used to denote the sight-action involved here. Commenting on 1:17, Delitzsch notes that "... *death* is knowledge penetrating into the depth of the essence of things, by which wisdom is acquired and in which wisdom establishes itself."[31] However, he distinguishes between this "type" of knowing and the "intellectual" experience recorded in verse 16—"my heart hath seen (ראה) wisdom and knowledge in fullness." "The seeing here ascribed to the heart is meant of intellectual observation and apprehension . . ."[32] As to ידע, Qoheleth uses it to refer to a spiritual perception (cf., for example, 3:12, 14; 8:5; 9:12; 10:14; 11:2, 5). In 7:25f. notice that spiritual conception arising from *revelation,* not from experimental data, intellectually

30. Leupold, p. 55.
31. Franz Delitzsch, *Commentary on the Song of Songs and Ecclesiastes* (Grand Rapids: Eerdmans, 1970 reprint), p. 230.
32. Delitzsch reasons thus: ". . . for all perception, whether it be mediated by the organs of sense or not (as prophetic observing and contemplating), comprehends all, from mental discernment down to suffering, which veils itself in unconsciousness, and the Scripture designates it as seeing" (Ibid.) Much of this comment seems to proceed from his particular view of psychology, which tends to break up the psycho-physical unity of man into artificial compartments.

found and studied, accounts for the acknowledgment of the truth in v. 29: "God made man upright." Indeed, a man's own reasoning ability functions in the context of vanity too (cf. 8:16, 17)!

But, furthermore, the distinction which Delitzsch (and others) makes between the ראה-seeing and the ידע-seeing cannot be sustained either on general Christian-theistic anthropological grounds or on specific exegetical grounds in Ecclesiastes.

As to the latter consideration, we recognize the close tie between ראה and ידע in 6:3–6. In verses 3 and 4 Qoheleth states that even an "untimely birth" comes and goes in the context of vanity, just as a man who lives many years (vs. 3) lives in the context of vanity. On that consideration there is no difference. However, what is better about this "untimely birth" than the long-lived man without a burial and without "his soul being filled with good" is that at least this child "hath not seen the sun nor known it" (שמש לא־ראה ולא־ידע). A purely "intellectual perception" of life under the sun and a deeper, spiritual perception are brought so close together grammatically that they are interdependent.

Secondly, in this class of phrases we have Qoheleth using the term לב (καρδία in LXX), "I said in my *heart*, etc." While Leupold relates all of these sayings to the realm of empirical experiences, Qoheleth does not do so. Rather, Qoheleth employs the bond that exists between religion and ethics which is found in the Wisdom Literature's concept of "heart." Yes, it is true that the will, aims, principles, thoughts, and intellect of man are found in the heart (cf. Prov. 18:15; Job 8:10; Jer. 23:20; 11:20). Yet, also, the "heart" describes the whole person (Ps. 22:26; Prov. 23:15f., etc.) and in it dwells the "fear of God" (cf. Jer. 32:40). How can Qoheleth, out of an ethic dominated by the fear of God, look on the world solely from an intellectual, empirical sense that is somehow to be *distinctly differentiated* from "heart" consideration of the world? Surely, Qoheleth perceives this world of vanity from the "unity and totality of the inner life represented and expressed in the variety of intellectual and spiritual gifts."[33]

Phrase 5: *"There is nothing better for a man than that he should eat and drink and make his soul enjoy good in his labor"* (2:24; 3:12, 13, 22; 5:18, 19; 8:15; 9:7, 9)

It has been claimed by the critics that Qoheleth here expressed his "questionable ethic" by approving of some form of Epicureanism. However, the six occurrences of this phrase support nothing of the sort. In His gracious wisdom God has given Qoheleth the insight to a proper understanding of how man is to labor in light of the curse. True, it is hard work, and the ground

---

33. Notice the article on καρδία by Baumgarten and Behm in *TWNT,* Vol. III, ed. G. Kittel (Grand Rapids: Eerdmans, 1965), pp. 609–10.

does not easily give its riches to man. Yet man's attitude in all his labor should be to rejoice in it (8:15) and work with all his might. This is what belongs to man in the context of vanity (3:22).[34] In the midst of life's confusion mankind receives a call from God to rejoice. In this redemptive-historical "time of ignorance" when God patiently "suffered all the nations to walk in their own ways" (cf. Acts 14, 17) Qoheleth counsels all men as to their labor before their Creator.

Therefore the readers are not led into some Epicurean work-ethic or "to the desperate attempt . . . to snatch what they can while there is still time."[35] This toil cannot endure for eternity since it takes place "under the sun." Hence, the *wise* reader will see that that which abides is the eternal work of God (3:11, 14, 15) and that all men must place their fear in Him alone (3:14; cf. 2:22–26) and not in their vanishing works done under the sun. In this very practical situation there is truly "nothing better" for a man to do than to rejoice in what God has providentially given him (cf. 1 Sam. 27:1).

Phrase 6: Instances employing some variation of "fear God" (3:14; 5:7; 7:18; 8:12, 13; 12:13)

If we ask ourselves why it is that Qoheleth possessed an unusually keen perception (cf. Phrase 4) of the actual condition of man and his world (cf. Phrases 1–3) and yet understood his role in that context of vanity (Phrase 5), we must reply that Qoheleth practiced the fear of God. In that fear he found wisdom and knowledge and hence could understand the Fall and its effects "under the sun" (Prov. 1:29; 2:5; 1:7; 9:10).

With respect to ethics, Qoheleth found the fear of the Lord the foundation of his faith and practice in a world in which human wisdom is limited. His keenness of insight and exceeding fruitfulness of thought was ensured by his fear of God. That fear also ensured the integration of the theoretical and the practical in Qoheleth's perception of this world subjected to vanity. Indeed, we have noted this in the examination of the fourth class of recurring phrases. Therefore Qoheleth's God was not some "hidden" Great Unknown who did not have very much to do with his ethical point of view. Rather, Qoheleth found that all of our knowing and applying of personal ethics must be related to humble faith in the Creator God.

Since he knew that worship takes place in the presence of the living God, Qoheleth could stress the fear of Him against the foolish multitude of form-ritualism that was then prevalent within the Temple (5:1–7). Further, since he knew that all our labor partook of the character of "vanity," he had to affirm that, instead of attempting either to frustrate God's pur-

---

34. חלק man's due or his portion.
35. F. N. Jasper, "Ecclesiastes: A Note for Our Time," *Interpretation* 21 (1967), p. 265.

poses or to add to them, we should rather submit ourselves to them, in reverence to our God (3:13ff.).

Finally, Qoheleth joined the "keeping of God's commandments" to the general imperative "Fear God" (12:13) to indicate to men that their ethical standard must be the revealed Word of God. Of course, Qoheleth knew that men will attempt to hide their works from the searching eye of God, yet he nails his hearers to this truth of "fearing God" by pointing to the truth of the coming judgment of God (12:14). Certainly, many evil things are done in this context of vanity which are hid to men's eyes, yet God will reveal them all at a future judgment day to take place in the coming Messianic Age (cf. Mal. 3:5).

How do we relate the ethical situation and conclusions of Qoheleth to that of the believer today? New Testament evidence in Rom. 8:18–22 tells us plainly that a state of "vanity"[36] *now* exists and that it had a beginning and will have an end. Before its beginning recorded in the curse of Gen. 3 stands a God and a κτίσις without vanity, and at its end stands the hope of a "new heavens and a new earth" no longer under that curse. The coming of the Messiah and the subsequent Age of the Spirit have brought freedom from that curse and from the effects of vanity only in principle; the full realization of that liberation awaits the Second Advent. Indeed, the Messiah came into this world of vanity and took upon Himself the labor (ʾamal) of a cursed world. We read in Isaiah 53:11 that the Suffering Servant "shall see the fruits of the *travail* (ʾamal) of his soul *and be satisfied*." Therefore, in contradiction to Qoheleth who stood in an age of the history of redemption among wise and foolish men, both of whom could never overcome the inevitable fact of death, Christ came and conquered death for the believer. The New Testament believer lives in the present light of Christ who has come and who has delivered us from the bondage of sin and death.

However, until he comes again, we live in the stark reality of the suffering which characterizes a world under the curse (Rom. 8:18). How then shall we view life and labor today? We may regard Qoheleth's thoughts on life and labor as developed from his recurring phrases as a normative pattern of experience to be applied by way of *analogy*[37] to our situation today. Qoheleth's analysis functions as a vivid reminder for the natural man of the reality of the

---

36. Notice Paul's use of the term ματαιότης for "vanity," which is the same term used in the LXX rendering of Ecclesiastes for this word.

37. The principle of analogy is a hermeneutical principle used in the interpretation of the Old Testament in light of the New. It refers to the embodiment of a certain principle of redemptive truth which can *constantly recur* in the history of redemption. Although it may probably be more fully developed in the New Testament, there is no inherent demand in analogy for fulfillment in an anti-type.

curse. For the believer Qoheleth's ethic remains meaningful since it finds the present situation rooted in the past declaration of the curse of God upon the creation "under the sun" and moving toward the future renewal of the cosmic order in the hopeful certainty of God's just Judgment of the innermost thoughts of men at the Second Advent (12:14).[38]

---

38. Since the judgment spoken of in 12:14 cannot take place now before men since the hidden things are not able to be seen by men, Qoheleth refers to a future judgment. Further, the primary objective reference of מִשְׁפָּט (κρίσει) is to the Day of Judgment recorded in the New Testament (cf. Rom. 2:16; 1 Cor. 4:5; 1 Tim. 5:24, 25).

QOHELETH

ENIGMATIC PESSIMIST OR GODLY SAGE?

Ardel B. Caneday

The enigmatic character and polarized structure of the book of Qoheleth is not a defective quality but rather a deliberate literary device of Hebrew thought patterns designed to reflect the paradoxical and anomalous nature of this present world. The difficulty of interpreting this book is proportionally related to one's own readiness to adopt Qoheleth's presupposition—that everything about this world is marred by the tyranny of the curse which the Lord God placed upon all creation. If one fails to recognize that this is a foundational presupposition from which Ecclesiastes operates, then one will fail to comprehend the message of the book, and bewilderment will continue.

Introduction

T he book of Qoheleth,[1] commonly known as Ecclesiastes, is perhaps the most enigmatic of all the sacred writings. It is this quality

From *Grace Theological Journal* 7 (1986): 21–56. Reprinted by permission.

1. Though the meaning of קֹהֶלֶת continues to be much debated, the sense accepted here is connected with the Hebrew verb for assembling (קָהַל), and its form suggests some kind of office-bearer (the feminine ending). Qoheleth was one who assembled a congregation for the purpose of addressing it, thus the Preacher. See H. C. Leupold, *Exposition of Ecclesiastes* (Grand Rapids: Baker, 1966) 7.

which has been a source of sharp criticism. Virtually every aspect of the book has come under the censure of critics—its professed authorship,[2] its scope and design, its unity and coherence, its theological orthodoxy, and its claim to a place among the inspired writings.

A superficial reading of Qoheleth may lead one to believe he is a man with a decidedly negative view of life in its many facets. This negative quality has been disproportionately magnified by liberal critics and conservatives alike. Understandably, then, Qoheleth has become the delight of critics and the embarrassment of conservatives. Embarrassment has led to greater perplexity about the book, and perplexity has brought negligent disuse of this valuable book.

Certainly the viewpoint of Qoheleth upon the world and life must be included in any discussion of OT ethical problems. If the book is indeed a unity, the composition of a single wise man, what is its theme? Is it pessimistic? Can a completely pessimistic view of life be admitted a place in the canon of Holy Scripture? Does not the recurring theme of "a man can do nothing better than to eat and drink and find satisfaction in his work" (cf. 2:24; 3:12, 13; etc.) suggest an Epicurean influence? Perhaps Stoicism, too, has influenced Qoheleth, for he claims, "All is vanity" (1:2; etc.). What exactly is Qoheleth's view of the world and of life? What was the source of his ethics? Is Qoheleth the record of a man's search for meaning gone awry, ending in cynicism? Or, is it the book of a godly wiseman who gives orthodox counsel for directing one's path through the labyrinth of life?

Qoheleth in the Hands of Liberal Critics

Modern critics have seized upon the alleged disunity of Qoheleth and upon the presumed contradictions. This alleged antithetical character has led critics to disavow the single authorship of Qoheleth, to discredit the theological expressions, to disclaim its ethics and view of the world and of life, and to displace the book from its authority and position as one of the writings of Holy Scripture.

Earlier critics, such as Tyler, postulated a late date (ca. 200 B.C.)[3] for the book in order to accommodate the alleged influence of Greek philosophical

---

2. The Solomonic authorship has been widely rejected by scholars, both critical and conservative. Some noted conservatives opt for a post-exilic dating of the book. See, e.g., E. W. Hengstenberg, *Commentary on the Book of Ecclesiastes* (reprint; Minneapolis: James and Klock, 1977) 1–15 and E. J. Young, *An Introduction to the Old Testament* (Grand Rapids: Eerdmans, 1952) 339–41. Young suggests that the author, being post-exilic, placed his words into the mouth of Solomon, employing a conventional literary device of his time (p. 340). However, in favor of Solomonic authorship see G. L. Archer, "The Linguistic Evidence for the Date of 'Ecclesiastes,'" *JETS* 12 (1969) 167–81.

3. Thomas Tyler, *Ecclesiastes* (London: D. Nutt, 1899) 30–32.

schools. Tyler sought to explain the discordance within Qoheleth in terms of conflicting influences from Epicureanism and Stoicism.[4] To Tyler the recognition of discontinuity and discordance within Qoheleth is an assumed fact without need of proof. Hence, it is of little consequence for Tyler to claim Greek philosophical influence upon a late Hebrew writer, subject to the erosion of the ancient Jewish faith.[5]

Tyler disallows any attempt to demonstrate a genuine continuity in Qoheleth which would show that it has no real discordant or antithetical character and especially no "obvious contradictions, as for example, that between the Stoic and Epicurean. . . ."[6]

> One might fancy that the author of Ecclesiastes intended that the contrarities of this book should in some sort reflect and image forth the chequered web of man's earthly condition, hopes alternating with fears, joys succeeded by sorrows, life contrasting with death. It must not be supposed, however, that we can find an adequate explanation in the hypothesis that the author of Ecclesiastes arranged his materials in a varied and artistic manner.[7]

The denial of an overall literary plan for Qoheleth and a dislike for its ethical expression, which motivated Tyler's criticism,[8] also motivates other negative criticisms. Recent critics do not identify Qoheleth's philosophy as being derived from or influenced by Greek schools.[9] Yet, Qoheleth's literary method is still looked upon as a "most serious defect."[10] Assuming the accuracy of this assessment, Jastrow seeks to recover the true and original words of a purely secular Qoheleth by stripping away additions and corrections of later pious redactors who sought to reclaim the book.[11] In this manner he essays to isolate the interpretation of pious commentators and the maxims which were added to counterbalance the objectionable character of the book.[12]

Other critics represent the alleged discontinuities of Qoheleth in varying manners. Siegfried divided the book among nine sources.[13] Yet, none of the

---

4. Tyler (ibid., 54) states, "Our book possesses a remarkable antithetical character, its contrasts not unfrequently assuming the form of decided and obvious contradiction. This antithetical character is especially marked in those two great thoughts of the philosophical part of the book—the Stoic, ALL IS VANITY; and the Epicurean, EAT, DRINK, AND ENJOY."

5. Ibid., 33.

6. Ibid., 54.

7. Ibid.

8. See Ibid., 63–64 where Tyler concludes that קֹהֶלֶת must be the personification of *Philosophy,* a designation in which the speculations of several philosophers are embodied.

9. See, e.g., R. B. Y. Scott, *Qoheleth* (AB; New York: Doubleday, 1965), p. 197.

10. Morris Jastrow, *A Gentle Cynic* (Philadelphia: Lippincott, 1919) 124.

11. Ibid., 197–242.

12. Ibid., 245ff.

13. See the citation by George Barton, *Ecclesiastes* (ICC; Edinburgh: T. & T. Clark, 1971) 28.

scholars who attempt to reconstruct the words of Qoheleth by isolating redactors' statements demonstrate why the book should have attracted such an
effort on the part of pious interpolators and sages to legitimatize it. It could
have been easily suppressed or dismissed. Gordis properly points out,

> But that the book was subjected to thoroughgoing elaboration in order to
> make it fit into the Biblical Canon is an assumption for which no real analogy
> exists, indeed is contradicted by the history of the Apocrypha and the Pseud-
> epigrapha after their composition.[14]

Recent critics recognize a basic unity in Qoheleth, abandoning the assumption of widespread interpolation. Yet, Qoheleth continues to be viewed
negatively in its ethics and world and life view. Scott sees both heterodoxy balanced by "unimpeachable orthodoxy."[15] Yet, it is the divergence from the orthodox which is emphasized. Scott states, "It denies some of the things on
which the other writers lay the greatest stress—notably that God has revealed
himself and his will to man, through his chosen nation."[16] He adds further
that,

> In place of a religion of faith and hope and obedience, this writer expresses a
> mood of disillusionment and proffers a philosophy of resignation. His ethic
> has no relationship to divine commandments, for there are none. It arises rath-
> er from the necessity of caution and moderation before the inexplicable, on
> the acceptance of what is fated and cannot be changed, and finally on grasping
> firmly the only satisfaction open to man—the enjoyment of being alive. The
> author is a rationalist, an agnostic, a skeptic, a pessimist, and a fatalist (the
> terms are not used pejoratively!).[17]

Even for Scott it was necessary for an orthodox interpreter to affix the two
closing verses (12:13, 14) in order "to safeguard the faith of the uncritical
reader,"[18] and to assure Qoheleth a place in the canon.

The critics, with unified voice, decry Qoheleth's ethics and his world and
life view as being opposed to that of the remainder of the OT. He is perceived
as a maverick among the sages who propounded incompatible propositions.

Qoheleth as Vindicated by Conservatives

In response to liberal critical views, several conservative scholars have attempted to vindicate the apparently negative view of life in Qoheleth and have

14. Robert Gordis, *Koheleth* (New York: Schocken, 1968) 71–72.
15. Scott, *Qoheleth,* 191.
16. Ibid.
17. Ibid., 191–92.
18. Ibid., 194.

affirmed its rightful place in the canon of Holy Scripture. Among evangelicals there is a general acknowledgment that Qoheleth is the composition of one individual.[19] However, many evangelicals agree with liberal critical opinions concerning Qoheleth's world and life view.

The Jewish conservative scholar Gordis assumes a negative character about Qoheleth's world and life view and seeks to alleviate some of the tension of his polarized expressions. He resolves the alleged dilemma of antithetical expressions in Qoheleth by accounting for many of the "apparently pious sentiments" as quotations cited for the purpose of discussion.[20] For example, Gordis claims that יוֹדֵעַ (8:12) is used by Qoheleth to introduce "a quotation of conventional cast which he does not accept."[21] But the verb claimed to be introductory appears in the middle of the portion it is claimed to mark off as a quotation.

Leupold, in laying out introductory principles for the interpretation of Qoheleth, states that the recurring phrase, "under the sun," indicates that Qoheleth deliberately restricted his observations and explanations of human events to a human perspective. By this Leupold means that Qoheleth, in his observations and reflections upon life, assumed a position of complete neglect of revelation and the world to come. He spoke from the perspective that God had not revealed Himself, and, furthermore, that God is inaccessible.[22] In actuality, though, Qoheleth was a "true man of God who is offering invaluable counsel."[23] For Leupold, Qoheleth was a rationalistic apologist who sought to lead his readers to true happiness by showing how miserable life is "under the sun," that is to say "apart from God." He attempted to direct men toward God by seeking to convince them rationalistically of their despair apart from God.

The *New Scofield Reference Bible* extends Leupold's approach.

> Ecclesiastes is the book of man "under the sun" reasoning about life. The philosophy it sets forth, which makes no claim to revelation but which inspiration records for our instruction, represents the world-view of the wisest man, who knew that there is a holy God and that He will bring everything into judgment.[24]

19. This is true even of those who reject Solomonic authorship. Some have maintained that Solomon was the original author, but that at a later time, before the exile, the book was edited and enriched (see Young, *Introduction to OT,* 340–41).

20. Gordis, *Koheleth,* 174.

21. Ibid., 283; cf. 287.

22. Leupold, *Ecclesiastes,* 28; cf. 42–43.

23. Ibid., 30.

24. C. I. Scofield, ed., *New Scofield Reference Bible* (New York: Oxford University, 1967) 696. This interpretive approach virtually abandons Qoheleth to the grasp of liberal critics, for one wonders how such an espousal of worldly wisdom could possibly hold any valid claim to canonicity. This approach agrees that Qoheleth hopelessly contradicts himself, but such contradiction is accounted for by a not-so-lucid device of separating *revelation* from *inspiration.* See, e.g., the note on 9:10 concerning Qoheleth's characterization of the dead: "This statement is no more a divine revelation concerning the state of the dead than any other conclusion of 'the Preacher'

Both Leupold and the *New Scofield Reference Bible* have misunderstood Qoheleth's use of his phrase "under the sun." He did not employ it to restrict his perspective to common ground with natural man. He was no mere philosopher who, working from a system of "natural theology," sought to understand God's creation without the interpretive revelation of the Creator. The phrase "under the sun" is not a restriction upon the *manner* of Qoheleth's reflections, but it circumscribes the *sphere* of those things which he observed in contrast to that sphere in which God's reign knows no opposition. The expression, "under the sun," therefore, speaks of the earth upon which man dwells as does Qoheleth's phrase, "all that is done under heaven" (cf. 1:13, 14; etc.).

An older commentator, Moses Stuart, energetically tried to vindicate Qoheleth from charges of impiety. However, he too accepts the charge that Qoheleth's book contains blatant contradictions and several impious conclusions. Nevertheless, Stuart acquits the author by suggesting that those objectionable portions must be understood in the same way as the "objectors" who appear in the apostle Paul's letters.[25] Stuart characterizes the book as a replaying of the struggle through which Qoheleth's mind had passed when he set himself on the course of philosophical inquiry. Along this course it does not matter that doubts and improper conclusions "had passed through the author's mind, for they had greatly perplexed and disturbed him. The passing through his mind does not stamp them with the authority of opinions settled, deliberate, and final."[26]

(1:1). No one would quote 9:2 as a divine revelation. The reasonings of man apart from revelation are set down by inspiration just as the words of Satan (Gen. 3:4; Job 2:4–5; etc.) are recorded. But that life and consciousness continue between death and resurrection is directly affirmed in Scripture . . . " (p. 702). Such an approach vitiates the whole character of Qoheleth's book. If one isolates 9:10 from the context of Qoheleth's burden, one may argue that Qoheleth did not believe in the conscious existence of the dead. But to assert such a conclusion goes far beyond Qoheleth's intention. Qoheleth does not concern himself with the state of man after death. He addresses the matter of death from the vantage point of things done "under the sun," i.e., the realm of the living (see 9:3, 6, 9). His purpose is to celebrate life, for as long as man has breath he has influence and activity in all "the things done under the sun" (9:6). But once a man dies, he no longer has anything to do with the activities of man "under the sun" (9:10). It is the same perspective the King Hezekiah held in his prayer to the Lord who spared his life. "For the grave [sheol] cannot praise you, death cannot sing your praise; those who go down to the pit cannot hope for your faithfulness. The living, the living—they praise you, as I am doing today; fathers tell their children about your faithfulness" (Isa. 38:18–19). In the same way Qoheleth only seeks to urge men to the full enjoyment of life *now*, "for it is now that God favors what you do" (9:7), for "anyone who is among the living has hope" (9:4).

25. Moses Stuart, *A Commentary on Ecclesiastes*, ed. and rev. by D. C. Robbins (Boston: Dreper and Halladay, 1880) 36–39.

26. Ibid., 39. He states further, "It only shows what embarrassments the writer had to remove, what perplexities to contend with. The question is not, whether this or that occupied his mind, which he has recorded in his writing, but whether this or that was *adopted* by him, and made up a part of his settled and ultimate opinion" (pp. 39–40).

Hengstenberg also succumbs to the claim that Qoheleth wrote several contradictions and antithetical assertions in expressing his ethics and world and life view. However, Hengstenberg seeks to vindicate Qoheleth from the charge of self-contradiction by means of a different approach. For him an understanding of the historical milieu out of which the book of Qoheleth arose is absolutely necessary. He states, "This book is unintelligible except on the historical presupposition that the people of God was [sic] in a very miserable condition at the time of its composition."[27] He claims that the book was composed in post-exilic days (contemporary with or slightly later than Malachi)[28] when the Persians held dominion over God's people. They were in a most miserable condition, slaves in their own land. Heathens ruled over them. Degradation, injustice, and misery ruled everywhere. The glorious splendor of Solomon's days had long passed and the Jews were now in a time of persecution.[29]

With this understanding of the times of Qoheleth, Hengstenberg finds it easy to take the various apparently contradictory or impious expressions and place them into the mouths of tyrannized impious Jews. Qoheleth only quotes them as reflecting the popular sentiment of the times. So, Hengstenberg says, "Vanity of vanities was the universal cry: alas! on what evil days have we fallen! They said to one another, 'How is it that the former days were better than these?' Ecclesiastes vii.10."[30]

Hengstenberg's method of interpretation is observed in his remarks upon Eccles. 9:5–7. Of Qoheleth's words, "the dead know nothing" (9:5), he says,

> Such is the language of natural reason, to those whose eye all seems dark and gloomy that lies beyond the present scene, because it fails in this world to discern the traces of divine retribution. The Spirit says on the contrary: "the spirit returns to God who gave it."[31]

Hengstenberg then explains in his comments on 9:7 that Qoheleth had spoken in vv. 1–6 "as the representative of the then prevailing spirit of the people," but in v. 7 he takes up the cause of God "to oppose the popular views and feelings."[32]

Hengstenberg, along with many evangelicals, has followed many liberal scholars in dating the book late based upon internal evidence. The external evidence for Solomonic authorship has been almost universally rejected by

27. Hengstenberg, *Ecclesiastes,* 45.
28. Ibid., 10–11.
29. Ibid., 2–16.
30. Ibid., 45.
31. Ibid., 212.
32. Ibid., 213.

scholars.[33] Along with an appeal to its language,[34] scholars cite the condition of Qoheleth's times as an argument against Solomonic or early authorship.[35] As widely accepted as this argument may be, it seems to be begging the question. If, indeed, Qoheleth must be understood as post-exilic in order to interpret it and to make its meaning intelligible, then what continuing value does it have for God's people? Certainly, it can be argued that it is useful for men in hard times and when under affliction; but Qoheleth's perspective is not so restricted. He touches upon virtually every conceivable condition of life and his verdict upon it all is the same, whether prosperous or poor, wise or foolish, industrious or slothful, whether times are good or bad (cf. 7:13, 14). Qoheleth was not provincial in his world view; he set out to explore "all that is done under heaven" (1:13). He states with sincerity and not exaggeration, "then I saw all that God has done. No one can comprehend what goes on under the sun" (8:12).

The nature of the book itself argues against Hengstenberg and others who would find internal historical evidence to place it during the post-exilic Persian domain over Palestine. The book defies such attempts. The book presents a world and life view which is in accord with the rest of Scripture. It does not occupy itself with local phenomena such as Hengstenberg claims. Quite to the contrary, it depicts life which is *universally* true throughout all of earth's history since the fall of man in the garden. The book deals with things which are common among men everywhere without a necessary connection to a particular historical milieu. An element common to many conservative scholars is their assessment of Qoheleth's ethics and world and life view. For them, Qoheleth was a man who, though he feared God, looked upon the world around him from the vantage point of a "reason" that had little to do with his faith in the Creator. They see a dichotomy between faith and reason.[36] This view hinders the grasping of Qoheleth's true world and life view.

One final trend among some conservative scholars must be addressed. This is the trend to differentiate between "appearance" and "reality." One says of Qoheleth's world and life view, "There is much that superficially viewed, has the appearance of disordered confusion. But that this is the real state of the case is here emphatically denied."[37] Again concerning the theme of the book, it is asserted

33. See, e.g., the arguments of Christian D. Ginsburg, *Coheleth* (London: Longmans, Green, Longmans, and Roberts, 1861) 245ff.

34. See Archer, "Linguistic Evidence for the Date of 'Ecclesiastes,'" 167–81 for a technical defense of Solomonic authorship.

35. See Ginsburg, *Coheleth,* p. 249; Stuart, *Ecclesiastes,* pp. 38–39.

36. Cf. H. Carl Shank, "Qoheleth's World and Life View As Seen in His Recurring Phrases," *WTJ* 37 (1974) 61. Hengstenberg (*Ecclesiastes,* 26) states, "The problem before the writer is considered from the point of view of Natural Theology with the aid of experience, and of reason as purified by the Spirit of God."

37. See the article attributed to Greene, "The Scope and Plan of the Book of Ecclesiastes," *Biblical Repertory and Princeton Review* 29 (1857) 422.

The problem really discussed is the *seeming* inequalities of divine providence. These are reconciled with the justice of God, as they are in the book of Job reconciled with his mercy and goodness.[38]

These comments fall into a dichotomous pattern because they refer to Qoheleth's observations of the world as things he only judged to be "apparent." Sierd Woudstra clearly expressed this perspective: "Koheleth is on the one hand dealing with life as he observed it, while on the other hand he knew and was convinced by faith that things were different."[39]
Shank astutely observes,

> Woudstra here raises an important issue in the interpretation of Qoheleth. If there does exist a distinction here, that distinction is *not* between faith and reason, but between faith and *sight*, i.e. between "faith" (that comes from special revelation) and that revelation presently available to any natural man as he perceives the creation about him. . . . But, *in what sense* and *to what degree* is such a "distinction" relevant to Qoheleth?[40]

Qoheleth did not look upon the world from the perspective of a *tabula rasa*. Nor was his observation of creation and "all that God has done" (8:17) conducted upon the foundation of "natural theology." His reflections upon this world and life are not the aimless ramblings and superficial remarks of one given to "sense-experience theology." Rather, Qoheleth's whole approach was governed by foundational presuppositions: his firm beliefs that God had revealed Himself through the biblical themes of creation, the fall of man, and the ensuing history of redemption; and that God had cursed man and the earth so pervasively that nothing was left untouched by evil.

Qoheleth lived among a people who knew the Lord God and his relationship to the world through the special revelation of the *Torah*. Therefore, his knowledge of the world and of life was regulated by his antecedent knowledge of God, the one whom he feared. This being true, Qoheleth's "faith" and "sight" were not two entirely distinct and independent modes of observation.

"Faith" and "sight" do not oppose one another in Qoheleth. His "sight"[41] (his perception of this world and life) *is* his "faith" put into operation to consider "all that God has done under the sun" from the orientation of his firm belief in the fall and the curse of man as recorded in Genesis 3.

38. Ibid., 423–34. Cf. Walter Kaiser, Jr., *Ecclesiastes* (Chicago: Moody, 1979) 17.
39. Sierd Woudstra, "Koheleth's Reflection upon Life" (unpublished Th.M. thesis; Westminster Theological Seminary, 1959) 58. He criticized Leupold for his nature/grace dichotomy (p. 106). But see Woudstra's attempt to Christianize Qoheleth (pp. 91ff., esp. pp. 99–101).
40. Shank, "Qoheleth's World and Life View," 61.
41. Cf. ibid., 68–70, where Shank astutely discusses Qoheleth's phraseology, "I perceived."

He looked upon the world and all of life from the vantage point of a genuine OT believer who well understood not only the reality of the curse of God placed upon life "under the sun," but also its pervasive effect upon everything "under heaven." It is just such a world and life that Qoheleth depicts in vivid terms.

Qoheleth Revisited

Thus far it has been the burden of this chapter to suggest that it is the assumed antithetical character and presumed contradictions which have hindered correct interpretation of Qoheleth. Many commentators suggest that more than one mind was operative in the composition of the book. Even some evangelicals portray Qoheleth as a combination of at least two divergent philosophies or perspectives: natural reason devoid of special revelation and orthodox affirmations of faith (though they be few). It is the thesis of this chapter that Qoheleth's enigmatic character cannot be resolved by following either of these two conventional lines of interpretation. The enigmatic character and polarized structure of the book is not a defective quality reflecting opposing and contradictory philosophies. On the contrary, the book's antithetical character is a deliberate literary device set in Hebrew thought patterns designed to reflect the paradoxical and anomalous nature of the world which Qoheleth observed. The difficulty of interpreting this book and of understanding its message is proportionally related to one's own readiness to acknowledge the true nature of this world—a world in bondage to the tyranny of the curse placed by God upon all creation (cf. Rom. 8:20ff.). If one fails to recognize this foundational presupposition of Qoheleth, then he will fail to comprehend the message of the book.

Qoheleth's Arrangement

Many scholars have contended that Qoheleth has no cohesive plan or design. Long ago Delitzsch stated:

> A gradual development, a progressive demonstration, is wanting, and so far the grouping together of parts is not fully carried out; the connection of the thoughts is more frequently determined by that which is external and accidental and not unfrequently an incongruous element is introduced into the connected course of kindred matters. . . . All attempts to show, in the whole, not only oneness of spirit, but also a genetic progress, an all-embracing plan, and an organic connection, have hitherto failed, and must fail.[42]

42. Franz Delitzsch, *Commentary on the Song of Songs and Ecclesiastes*, trans. M. G. Easton (reprint in *Biblical Commentary on the Old Testament*, by C. F. Keil and Franz Delitzsch; Grand Rapids: Eerdmans, 1950) 188.

Hengstenberg follows suit:

> A connected and orderly argument, an elaborate arrangement of parts, is as little to be looked for here as in the special portion of the Book of Proverbs which begins with chapter X., or as in the alphabetical Psalms.[43]

Surely such assertions are extreme, for even a cursory reading of Qoheleth should convince anyone that its character is quite different from the book of Proverbs.[44] With the book of Proverbs one can select at random a single verse or two and observe a complete unity of thought in them that may not have any real connection with what precedes or follows. Yet this does not hinder interpretation of its meaning. However, Qoheleth is not at all so characterized. "It is useless to take a text and ask 'What does that mean?' unless we have in our minds some scheme for the whole book into which that text must fit."[45] The book of Proverbs may be read at several sittings, disconnected and randomly without disrupting one's understanding of its isolated parts. However, Qoheleth is like the book of Job; it must be read with great attentiveness given to its design and scope, for apart from the context of the complete book, any isolated portion will be wrongly interpreted. It is precisely because this principle has not been observed that so many contradictory interpretations have been spawned. When detached from the overall design of the book, any one of Qoheleth's refrains or expressions may be given extremely negative interpretations. So it is that his recurring phrase, "Meaningless! Meaningless! Utterly meaningless! Everything is meaningless" has been dealt with as the exasperated outburst of a cynical pessimist. Qoheleth's repeated, "A man can do nothing better than to eat and drink and find satisfaction in his work" has been segregated from his theme and corrupted to become the slogan of the indulgent Epicurean sensualist, "Let us eat, drink, and be merry, for tomorrow we die!"[46] "So I hated life, because the work that is done under the sun was grievous to me" (2:17) is ascribed to a slothful pessimist. Examples of "decontextualized" misinterpretations of Qoheleth could be multiplied many

43. Hengstenberg, *Ecclesiastes,* 15. He continues to say, "Such matters of plan and connection have been thrust into the book by interpreters who were incapable of passing out of their own circle of ideas, as by degrees became evident from the fact that no one of these arrangements gained anything like general recognition, but that on the contrary each remained the sole property of its originator and of his slavish followers." Concerning the theme of the book, he writes, "It is quite misleading to represent the work as occupied with a single narrow theme. . . . A superficial glance at its contents will amply show that they are of far too rich and varied a nature to be comprehended under one single theme" (p. 16).

44. See Stuart, *Ecclesiastes,* 28ff.

45. Cf. J. Stafford Wright, "The Interpretation of Ecclesiastes," in *Classical Evangelical Essays on Old Testament Interpretation,* ed. by Walter Kaiser, Jr. (Grand Rapids: Baker, 1973) 136.

46. See F. C. Thompson, ed., *The New Chain-Reference Bible,* 4th ed. (Indianapolis: B. B. Kirkbridge, 1964) 199 in the section "A Complete System of Biblical Studies."

times. But these serve to illustrate how his words in various portions have been isolated from one another so that when they are retrieved and placed back together, one is left only with a mutilated Qoheleth. With such a method, no two pieces fit together. Is it any wonder that critics and conservatives alike hear so many strange and contradictory voices in Qoheleth?

However, the solution to determining Qoheleth's arrangement and design is not to go to the other extreme. One states,

> There is clear and consistent plan in the book of Ecclesiastes . . . one in fact of the most strictly logical and methodical kind. Not only is the argument well conducted, conclusive and complete, but its various points are so admirably disposed, its divisions so regular, and its different parts so conformed in structure as to give evidence that the whole was carefully considered and well digested before it was put together.[47]

One must keep in mind that these are the words of one who wrote at a time prior to the present resurgence of interest in Hebrew studies, which has brought with it a heightened sensitivity to the many peculiarities of the language and its literature. Recent studies of Qoheleth have shown a much greater appreciation for the qualities of Hebrew literature and its thought patterns which find their matrix in the Near Eastern and not the Western mind.[48]

Nevertheless, the structure of Qoheleth remains elusive. Once its scheme is traced out, it must still be acknowledged that the progression of its argument is not readily detectable. In many respects the book defies the Western mind that looks for clear breaks in thought around which it may be outlined. Like 1 John, its contours are fluid. Its boundaries are obscure. It is characterized by reiteration and recurring phrases. It is cyclical as it traverses a course around its subject. As the apostle John treated the life which is in union with Christ, he chose a spiral course for considering the manifold character of fellowship in the life of Christ.[49] The subject is of such magnitude that a glance at it from one perspective will not suffice. So it is with Qoheleth. His subject, too, is immense. A single gaze upon the world and upon life from a remote vantage point could never do justice to its multiform character.

Although Qoheleth's arrangement is difficult to determine, certain structural devices do come to light. Setting aside the book's title (1:1), epigram (1:2; 12:8), and the epilogue (12:9–14), one finds that Qoheleth begins and ends with a poem. The first poem is on the endless round of events in which man forever comes up short in his laborious toil (1:3–11). The book ends with another

---

47. [Greene], "The Scope and Plan of Ecclesiastes," 427.

48. See J. A. Loader, *Polar Structures in the Book of Qohelet* (Berlin: Walter de Gruyter, 1979).

49. Cf. Donald Burdick, *The Epistle of John* (Chicago: Moody, 1970) 14–15; Robert Law, *The Tests of Life* (reprint; Grand Rapids: Baker, 1968) 1–24.

poem in which Qoheleth calls upon men to enjoy life while they yet have breath, for if death does not cut one off in mid-life, old age will deteriorate one's satisfaction with life and still death will finally wrench the spirit from the body (11:7–12:7). It is these two poems which set the tone and direction of Qoheleth's reflections upon life. Focusing upon the inscrutability of divine providence, Qoheleth guides his readers to acknowledge the meaninglessness of events under the sun. He directs the reader's focus away from an attempt to understand providence and toward enjoyment of life as the gift from God. "Enjoyment of life," not a search for meaning, should be man's guiding principle.[50]

There is much to commend Addison Wright's view of the structure of Qoheleth which he suggests in his provocative study.[51] He tries to demonstrate that there is a break between 6:9 and 6:10. The first half of the book (1:12–6:9) is characterized by the verbal pattern "all is vanity and a chase after wind." The cessation of this phrase at 6:9 signals a major break in the book.[52] The lines following this (6:10–12) form a transition to a different verbal pattern which is carried out throughout the remainder of the book. These verses introduce two themes which are developed in what follows: (1) what is good for man during his lifetime? and (2) who can tell man what will come after him?[53] Wright points out that chapters 7 and 8 are structured around the first of these themes. It is developed in four sections with each marked by the verb מָצָא.[54] The second motif expressed in 6:12 is developed in 9:1–11:6. The end of each unit is marked with the verb יָדַע or the noun דַּעַת.[55] Though one may not agree with all the details of Wright's analysis, there are grammatical indicators which suggest his general divisions.

The structural development of the book can be summarized as follows. The title (1:1) and the poem (1:3–11) set the tone and direction of Qoheleth's reflections by focusing upon the fruitlessness of man's toil in contrast to the incessant endurance of the earth. The first major section (1:12–6:9) shows that man's toil is vanity and "a chase after wind." The second half of the book (after the transition of 6:10–11) develops two themes: "what is good for man" (7:1–8:17) and "man does not know what will come after him" (9:1–11:6). The poem on youth and old age (11:7–12:8) and the epilogue (12:9–14) conclude Qoheleth's considerations.[56] However, this struc-

50. Robert Johnston, "'Confessions of a Workaholic:' A Reappraisal of Qoheleth," *CBQ* 38 (1976) 12–18. See also his study in *The Christian at Play* (Grand Rapids: Eerdmans, 1983) 95–102.

51. Addison G. Wright, "The Riddle of the Sphinx: The Structure of the Book of Qoheleth," *CBQ* 30 (1968) 313–34.

52. Ibid., 322–23.

53. Ibid., 322.

54. Ibid., 323.

55. Ibid., 324.

56. Ibid., 325.

tural pattern does not deny that there is an overlapping of themes between sections. For example, the inability of man to comprehend life's meaning and his failure to see what will happen after he is gone first appears in 3:11 and 3:22. Though 1:12–6:9 can be characterized as Qoheleth's investigation of life and 7:1–11:6 (after the transition of 6:10–11) as his conclusions, there is an intermingling of both in each portion. It is this fact that prohibits any rigid outline of the book.

Qoheleth Interpreted: The Prologue

Qoheleth knew the great expanse of the subject he was about to undertake, so he prepared his plan of investigation accordingly. He says, "I devoted myself to study and to explore by wisdom *all that is done under heaven*" (1:13, italics added). His inquiry into the meaning of life and his examination of the character of this world were not restricted to provincial peculiarities, nor was his reflection narrowly conceived. He deliberately opened up his observation to the *whole* world and to events common among men universally. This he did in accordance with wisdom,[57] a wisdom guided by preestablished beliefs which show themselves throughout his discourse.

Qoheleth bursts upon his reader with his concise and vigorous exclamations: "'Meaningless! Meaningless!' says the Preacher, 'Utterly meaningless! Everything is meaningless'" (1:2). The intensity of the expression could hardly be exceeded. With such brilliance the book commences.

Now when the preacher gives prominence to words of such strength and to an expression so captivating, one would suppose that there would be little need to look further for the theme which the book seeks to develop and to prove. However, it has not so impressed some scholars. Hengstenberg claims,

> It is quite misleading to represent the work as occupied with a single narrow theme. . . . A superficial glance at its contents will amply show that they are of far too rich and varied a nature to be comprehended under one such single theme.[58]

But Qoheleth puts his arresting expression concerning meaninglessness in the position that a book of this nature would normally place its theme. Furthermore, the phrase, "everything is meaningless" (with its variations),[59] is the most dominant and pervasive of all Qoheleth's recurring phrases in the book.

---

57. Cf. Stuart's discussion of "wisdom" (*Ecclesiastes,* 50ff.) where he points out that, for Qoheleth, the contrast between wisdom and folly is not equivalent to the Proverbs' use where wisdom is piety and folly is wickedness. In Qoheleth, wisdom bears the sense of sagacity and folly, the lack of it.

58. Hengstenberg, *Ecclesiastes,* 16.

59. Cf. 1:2, 14; 2:1, 11, 15, 17, 19, 21, 23, 26; 3:19; 4:4, 7, 8, 16; 5:7, 10; 6:2, 4, 9, 11, 12; 7:6, 15; 8:10, 14; 9:9; 11:8, 10; 12:8.

Also, as the book opens, so it closes with an exclamation of meaninglessness (see 12:8). Therefore, it seems advisable to adopt 1:2 as the theme which Qoheleth seeks to prove throughout the entirety of the book.

Phrases with the word הבל appear no less than 30 times. Of this class of phrases, Woudstra well states the main exegetical question, "Is Koheleth only saying that man's accomplishments under the sun are transitory in character, are devoid of any permanence, or is he saying that human existence and everything that goes with it is futile and meaningless?"[60] This latter sense of הבל is rejected by Leupold as "a pessimistic meaning . . . that is not warranted by facts"[61] in Qoheleth. He avows that the word can only refer in Qoheleth to "that which is fleeting and transitory, and also suggests the *partial* futility of human efforts."[62] On the other hand, Woudstra defends the latter sense of הבל and denies that it implies pessimism.[63]

One should not be too hasty to translate הבל with a single word as do most translations.[64] The word הבל, meaning "vapor" or "breath," is employed figuratively of anything that is "evanescent, unsubstantial, worthless, vanity."[65] The particular sense of the word must be derived from its usage in any particular context. It is employed as a designation for false gods (Deut. 32:21; 1 Kings 16:13, 26; 2 Kings 17:15; Jer. 2:5; 8:19; 10:8, 15; Jon. 2:9; Ps. 31:6). The term הבל also represents the exasperated sentiments of individuals.[66] Job complains about the brevity and uncertainty of his life; it is an exasperation to him (Job 7:16).[67] The use of הבל in Ps. 39:5, 6 is similar to its use in Qoheleth:

> You have made my days a mere handbreadth, the span of my years is nothing before you. Each man's life is but a breath. Man is a mere phantom as he goes to and fro; He bustles about, but only in vain; he heaps up wealth, not knowing who will get it.[68]

The majority of the uses of הבל in the OT appear in Qoheleth, yet even here the word is more flexible than most translations would suggest. There are four general categories into which Qoheleth's use of הבל can be placed. First, there are passages in which the word expresses "meaninglessness" in the most general sense. Among these, 1:2 and 12:8 are the most prominent, for

---

60. Woudstra, "Koheleth's Reflection upon Life," 38.
61. Leupold, *Ecclesiastes*, 41.
62. Ibid. Italics added.
63. Woudstra, "Koheleth's Reflection upon Life," 38.
64. KJV, "vanity"; NASB, "vanity"; NIV, "meaninglessness."
65. BDB, 210–11.
66. For example, Isa. 49:4. The servant Israel says, "I have labored in vain [רִיק], I have spent my strength for nothing [תֹהוּ] and vanity [הֶבֶל]."
67. Cf. Job 7:16 with Eccles. 2:17.
68. NIV, Eccles. 5:16–17.

they summarize the whole book in compressed form. Other passages in this category are 2:1, 26; 4:16; 5:7, 10; 6:4; 7:6; 9:9. Second, the author employs הבל to express his vexations arising from the laboriousness of his work and his inability to control the disposition of his possessions when he departs from the earth (2:11, 17, 19, 21, 23; 4:4, 7, 8; 6:2). Third, the expression is used of Qoheleth's frustration over the delay of retribution. Retribution, adequate, appropriate, and final does not take place in the present world. The connection between wickedness and condemnation, righteousness and deliverance is not direct and obvious but shrouded and often turned upside down (2:15; 6:9; 7:15; 8:10, 14). Finally, הבל is employed by Qoheleth to vent his deepest vexation with this present world—his lament over the brevity of life and the severity of death (3:19; 6:12; 11:8, 10; cf. 12:8 following the graphic portrayal of death). The quality of life is "empty" and "vacuous" and its quantity is entirely "transitory" and "fleeting."[69] How appropriate, then, is הבל with its many nuances to express the nature of this world and life in it!

Shank sums up well Qoheleth's employment of הבל:

> Different "aspects" of the idea of vanity are employed by Qoheleth to vividly illustrate the reality of the curse of God placed upon the work of man after the Fall (cf. Gen. 3:17–19). Therefore, an attempt to find a "static" meaning to *hebel* in Ecclesiastes . . . fails to take note of the richness of the concept as used by Qoheleth.[70]

Indeed, Qoheleth does announce his theme in 1:2. It is not narrowly conceived nor is it too singular. The theme of evanescence, unsubstantiality, meaninglessness, vanity is carefully carried through the whole book as a weaver threads his theme color throughout his fabric. It is sufficiently broad in its formulation, for it accurately summarizes the full contents of Qoheleth (if one does not restrict the word הבל to a rigid or static meaning).

What the Preacher states with pithy conciseness in 1:2, he restates in further summary form before he begins the body of his work. This he does in 1:3–11 in the form of a *compendium*. The opening poem serves as an abstract which compresses the essence of the book into a brief introduction.

The Preacher first asks, "What does man gain from all his labor at which he toils under the sun?" (1:3). Qoheleth clearly indicates by his question the inquiry that led to his announced verdict of evanescence and meaninglessness (1:2). The query expresses in typical Hebrew concreteness the quest for the *meaning* and *purpose* of life in this present world. This often escapes the occidental mind which posits the question in more abstract terms. Qoheleth's fondness for the book of Genesis[71] throughout his work influenced how he

---

69. Cf. Victor Hamilton, "hebel" in *Theological Wordbook of the Old Testament*, vol. 1, ed. by R. Laird Harris, Gleason L. Archer, Bruce K. Waltke (Chicago: Moody, 1980) 204–5.

70. Shank, "Qoheleth's World and Life View," 66.

71. See Charles C. Forman, "Koheleth's Use of Genesis," *JSS* 5 (1960) 256–63.

framed his question. As scholars have observed, wisdom literature in the OT is "within the framework of a theology of creation."[72] Thus, one can understand why Qoheleth structured his inquiry based upon man's divinely appointed occupation within creation (cf. Gen. 2:5, 15) rather than ask abstractly, "What is the meaning of life?" His interest is not economical but truly philosophical; it does not concern pecuniary profits but life's purpose and meaning.

Qoheleth states his conclusion (1:2); then he asks the question to which his conclusion is the answer (1:3). He then turns to prove his conclusion about this world and man's part in it by means of the poem in 1:4–11. This introductory poem serves as a compendium in which the message of the book is summarized. Qoheleth seeks to establish his conclusion of 1:2 by rehearsing the inflexible cyclical nature of the world and its enduring character in contrast to transitory and evanescent man. He declares, "Generations come and generations go, but the earth remains forever" (1:4). The earth, methodically plodding along in its routine course, does not skip a beat of its rhythm to celebrate a man's birth nor to mourn his death.

This rhythmic uniformity of seasons and events forms the context within which man dwells. It provides stability so that much of his life becomes routine; there are not shocking surprises every day. Man can depend upon the recurrence of the daily appearance of the sun. As it sets in the westerly sky in the evening, so it shall rise in the east the next morning (1:5). Man has come to recognize the course of the wind which brings warmth or cold. It, too, is cyclical. Daily the winds change their direction bringing a variety of weather conditions (1:6). Man does not need to fear that the seas will swallow up the land, for though the rivers and streams all flow into the ocean, the sea does not overrun its boundaries. The waters dissipate and return as rain upon the land to keep the rivers flowing to the sea (1:7).

Times and seasons are a blessing to man, for God promised a regularity and uniformity upon which man could depend. "As long as the earth endures, seedtime and harvest, cold and heat, summer and winter, day and night will never cease" (Gen. 8:22). However, this blessing which gives man some measure of predictability about life becomes wearisome to him. Uniformity and repetition breeds monotony in this cursed world. Regularity has an eroding effect; it wears man down. So it is that Qoheleth declares, "All things are wearisome, more than one can say. The eye never has enough of seeing, or the ear its fill of hearing" (1:8).

Man comes to expect the recurrence of events. Even in man's brief existence upon the earth, he comes to learn that even those few things that may occur only once in his lifetime are not new (1:9). The joy of discovery is

---

72. Walter Zimmerli, "The Place and Limit of the Wisdom in the Framework of the Old Testament Theology," *SJT* 17 (1964) 148.

dampened by earth's stubborn uniformity. As one excitedly exclaims, "Look! This is something new," the excitement quickly fades with the realization that, "It was here before our time" (1:10).

Uniformity; regularity; methodical, orderly recurrence; cyclical, rhythmic routine; these are all descriptive of the world which Qoheleth observed. But there is an intruder which interrupts man's part in the profound cycle of events. It is the culprit which transforms the beauty of uniformity into a monotonous machine which mercilessly carries the sons of Adam through the corridors of time into oblivion (1:11). It is the curse which has put a blight upon everything. Nothing has escaped its clutching grasp. Surely, God's providential directing of the affairs of this world is carried out with uniform precision and beauty, yet the curse hides the full character of the one who governs the universe.

Such is the broad, sweeping picture that Qoheleth portrays in his compendium (1:3–11). The stage, with its backdrop and props, obstinately endures as earth's systems methodically press on with no apparent direction, for everything about it repeats itself. Much to the grief of the actors, they themselves have no such permanence. "Generations come and generations go, but the earth remains forever" (1:4). To add insult to injury, even the product of their work falters with them (1:3), so they become forgotten men (1:11). Such is the scene which stirs Qoheleth with vexation to announce with startling boldness, "'Meaningless! Meaningless!' says the Preacher, 'Utterly meaningless! Everything is meaningless'" (1:2).

It is Qoheleth's prologue which sets the theme, the tone and the movement of the whole book with its incessant repetition. The book takes on the shape of the world as it imitates the cadence of creation by the use of its many recurring phrases and themes. Not only has Qoheleth captured with words the pointlessness of man's life of labor in a world which outlasts him, uninterrupted by man's coming and going, but he also leads his reader to *sense* the incessant rhythm of the world by his own calculated refrains. It is precisely this recurrent character of Qoheleth with its polarized structure which should aid the reader to a proper interpretation of the book. Rather, it has become the chief point of criticism and dispute.

Qoheleth Interpreted: The Recurring Themes

As Qoheleth develops his world and life view it is imperative to observe his pattern. He sets before the reader motifs and themes, all calculated to support his verdict announced in 1:2. Qoheleth's argument will be considered under four headings: 1) polarity of themes, 2) theology of creation, 3) elusiveness of meaning, and 4) celebration of life.

Polarity of Themes

The antithetical character of Qoheleth is not to be resolved by positing contradictory thought patterns within Qoheleth himself, nor by appealing to the voices of presumed editors, redactors, and glossators as the liberal critics do. Rather the polarity of structure and expression found in the book reproduces the *character of this world.* As the world which Qoheleth observed is characterized by its ceaseless recurrent cycles and paradoxes of birth and death, war and peace, and the like (cf. 3:1–8), giving it an enigmatic quality, so Qoheleth reproduces its pattern in literary form, repeatedly turning back upon himself to reiterate and restate themes and observations upon various subjects which support his verdict.[73] This he does by casting his work into a polarized structural form as illustrated by 3:1–9.[74] Just as there is no place "under the sun" to find a tranquil resting place devoid of life's vexations where the movement of this world ceases to erode the strength and vitality of man, so Qoheleth's composition does not permit its readers to settle their minds with contentment upon a particular portion of his book. There is always tension as various observations and reflections upon life are juxtaposed in polarity. He hates life (2:17), yet he commends its enjoyment (2:24ff.). Death (7:1ff.) and life (9:4ff.) hold prominency in Qoheleth's polarized expressions. On the one hand he can say, "The day of death is better than the day of birth" (7:1) and on the other "a live dog is better off than a dead lion" (9:4). Illustrative of this polarized character of Qoheleth, 7:16, 17 stand out: "Do not be overrighteous neither be overwise—why destroy yourself? Do not be overwicked, and do not be a fool—why die before your time?" It is these paradoxical observations and expressions which characterize the book and cause such great difficulty for so many exegetes. The tension cast by Qoheleth's observations and reflections is unrelenting.

Qoheleth involves the *whole* reader in an incessant movement of thought as he carefully weaves his various strands of thread into a multiform fabric, fully reflecting this world and life in it. His literary image reflects the harsh realities of this present world as he places side by side contradictory elements to portray the twisted, disjointed and disfigured form of this world (see 1:15; 7:13). Man as observer is not exempted from the tension. His emotional and mental involvement in the contradictions of this world create a complexity of thought, motives and desires. Qoheleth was a man torn by the presence of evil and vexed by the ravages of injustice, oppression and death. He compels his reader to confront this diverse nature of this paradoxical world in which evil has supplanted the good. In this world wickedness drives out justice (3:16). Oppression replaces charity (4:1ff.). Everything is marked by twisting and incompleteness (1:15). In the place of sweet labor (which was man's original allotment), the sweat of the brow embitters one's work with the brine of wearisome and laborious toil which is fruitless (cf. Gen. 3:17–19; with Eccles. 2:11, 17f., etc.).

73. See Shank, "Qoheleth's World and Life View," 57–73 for an excellent study of Qoheleth's recurring phrases.

74. Cf. Loader, *Polar Structures in the Book of Qohelet,* 29ff.

The world which Qoheleth observed is cursed; it is disjointed; it is upside down. Death and decay dominate. The appointment of every man has become the grave. As a man is born, so he must die (3:1). He comes into a world naked and leaves stripped of all the profits from his labors (5:15–17). He leaves his wealth to be squandered by one who has not worked for it (2:17–21), or it falls into the hands of a stranger by some misfortune (6:1–2). But the greatest evil of all is the fact that death is no respecter of persons (9:3). It comes upon men so haphazardly, often leaving the wicked to live long in their wickedness (7:15).

In this paradoxical world no man knows what shall befall him—whether love or hate (9:1), good or evil (7:14), prosperity or destruction (11:6). An adequate and appropriate retribution is absent from this present world. The connection between wickedness and condemnation, righteousness and reward is hidden and apparently non-existent (cf. 2:15; 6:9; 7:15; 8:10, 14). It is upon this subject that Qoheleth's polarized expressions have caused his readers to become most disconcerted and unsettled. For on the one hand he complains that wickedness has driven out justice in the place where one would expect to find equity (3:16). Yet, he quickly offsets the present scene with an expression of confidence that "God will bring to judgment both the righteous and the wicked, for there will be a time for every activity, a time for every deed" (3:17). Qoheleth vents his grief that sentences for crimes are not quickly executed (8:11). Yet, he again expresses confidence that the final day will bring justice where it is now absent (8:12–13). But immediately Qoheleth turns the reader back to view the paradox that vexes him most: "There is something else meaningless that occurs on earth: righteous men who get what the wicked deserve, and wicked men who get what the righteous deserve. This too, I say is meaningless" (8:14).

Herein lies the chief source of Qoheleth's dilemma; divine providence in this present world disproportionately distributes deserts—the wicked prosper and the righteous flounder (cf. Job 21:4–33; Ps. 73:4–12; Jer. 12:1–4). The almighty God who rules this world hides himself behind a frowning providence. It seldom appears that the benevolent God who created the universe has control of his own creation. It rarely seems that a rational and moral being gives motion to the world. Even the beauty of uniformity plagues man's thoughts about God. Uniformity becomes monotony in the present cursed world, for it is precisely upon the basis of the world's disjointed regularity that men scoff at God and his promises (see Mal. 2:17; 3:14–15; 2 Pet. 3:3–7). The present world order becomes the occasion for wicked men to jeer God and for righteous men to vex their souls that divine justice is so long delayed. It is precisely this character of the world which gives rise for the need of patient endurance on the part of the righteous as they await the fulfillment of God's promises of justice and deliverance (cf. 1 Pet. 3:8–13, 15).

Theology of Creation

The Preacher's occasion and purpose for writing his book is found in his opening question: "What does man gain from all his labor at which he toils under the sun?" (1:3). He asks this question repeatedly (2:22; 3:9). This may seem to be a rather narrowly conceived question for setting the theme of Qoheleth which is broad in its discussions and investigations. It has been stated earlier that Qoheleth's interests were not merely to investigate the measure of profits gained from labor, but the inquiry expresses tangibly man's quest to know the meaning and purpose of life. The entire book of Qoheleth is a reflection upon life in this world in order to search out its meaning. The theme question found in 1:3 is conceived in terms of man's original divine mandate to work in paradise and to subdue the earth by ruling over it as king (Gen. 2:5, 15; 1:28). The creation motif holds a significant place in the formulation of Qoheleth's thoughts. He acknowledges, as does the Genesis account, that man was made from the dust of the ground and will return to it (Eccles. 12:7; 3:20; cf. Gen. 2:7; 3:19); that man was designed to live in companionship (Eccles. 4:9–12; 9:9; cf. Gen. 1:27; 2:21–25); that man is bent toward sin (Eccles. 7:29; 8:11; 9:3; cf. Gen. 3:1–13); that human knowledge is derived and has God-given limitations (Eccles. 8:7; 10:14; cf. Gen. 2:17); and that God is sovereign over all (Eccles. 3:10–13; cf. Gen. 1:28–30; 3:5).

Johnston observes, "Perhaps most importantly, Ecclesiastes and Genesis exhibit substantial agreement as to the central focus of the creation motif—that life is to be celebrated as a 'good' creation of God."[75] But the problem that exists for Qoheleth is the intrusion of sin and God's curse upon all creation and, in particular, upon man. When God created man, his design was that man till the soil as an extension of God's hand to carry on the work which God had made (Gen. 2:4–7). Man's purpose, then, was to work upon the earth, an earth which yielded readily to the hands of Adam to produce only those things which "were pleasing to the eye and good for food" (cf. Gen. 2:9). But the curse of God came upon man and his environment because of Adam's rebellion. It changed the scene drastically so that no longer would man's work be pleasurable. Instead it is characterized by laboriousness and pain and yields a meagerly disproportionate return for the energy expended (Gen. 3:17–19). Thorns and thistles grow where once beautiful and luscious produce sprang forth. Man was made to eke out a living under adverse conditions. His whole life became involved with this effort. Thus, the real question of the meaning of life is the query Qoheleth asks: "What does man gain from all his labor at which he toils under the sun?" What does man have left when all his painful and wearisome toil is complete? What goal is there for a life which is so consumed with such endless and exhausting drudgery? If there is meaning to life, where is it concealed?

---

75. Johnston, "'Confessions of a Workaholic,'" p. 22.

It is Qoheleth's orientation to the Scriptural account of creation which forms his presuppositional basis for a world and life view. He recognized a great disparity between his world and that which came directly from the creative hand of God; the curse had intruded to disrupt the harmony of creation. The evil that Qoheleth observed "under the sun" was not inherent in nor of the essence of creation, but was externally imposed. The curse of Gen. 3:17ff. becomes in Qoheleth's language *disjointedness and discontinuity* or kinks and gaps which are irrevocable (1:15) because they have been imposed by God (7:13). By the curse God subjected creation to the frustration of bondage and decay (cf. Rom. 8:19–21), creating the enigma which bewilders men. The world has been turned upside down, so that it bears little resemblance to the pristine paradise that it once was. For Qoheleth, then, the world was neither what it once was nor what it will be. Therefore he designed his book, not to "wrest some form of order from chaos"[76] or to *master* life, but to bring men to acknowledge that this world and life in it is marked by aimlessness, enigma, and tyranny. Qoheleth upholds the creational design to celebrate life as a divine gift which is to be enjoyed as good, something to be cherished reverently and something in which man delights continually.[77] This, perhaps, is the greatest enigma in Qoheleth—his bold assertion of the meaninglessness of life "under the sun" and his resolute affirmation that life is to be celebrated joyfully. The fact that he unequivocally maintained both is not proof that Qoheleth was a double-minded man—secular and religious. He was not a pessimist who saw nothing better than to indulge the flesh. He was a godly sage who could affirm both the aimlessness of life "under the sun" and the enjoyment of life precisely because he believed in the God who cursed his creation on account of man's rebellion, but who was in the process, throughout earth's history, of redeeming man and creation, liberating them from the bondage to decay to which they had been subjected (cf. Rom. 8:19–21). *Because* Qoheleth was a man of faith, he held this perspective, for it was through his faith in the God who revealed himself that Qoheleth knew what the world once was and what it will be again. It was because of this orientation that so many enigmatic and antithetical considerations and observations are held in proper tension within his mind and within his book.

Elusiveness of Meaning

The identification of 1:3 as the theme question, the question of life's meaning, is confirmed by the book itself. In 3:9–11 Qoheleth reveals the breadth of the question. It was no mere *economic* question about one's wealth, but it was a *philosophical* inquiry about life's meaning and purpose. After a poetically

76. G. von Rad, *Old Testament Theology,* vol. 1, trans. D. M. G. Stalker (New York: Harper and Row, 1962) 420.
77. Cf. Johnston, "'Confessions of a Workaholic,'" 22–23.

structured recitation of the divine appointment of affairs which touch every man in this cursed world (3:1–8), Qoheleth breaks forth with his thematic question, "What does the worker gain from his toil?" (3:9). The relentless tide of events described by Qoheleth is reminiscent of the cosmological cycle earlier recited (1:4–11). It is precisely to such unalterable and rhythmic recurrence of events "under the sun" that the Preacher affixes his question of meaning (1:3 before the poem in 1:4–11; 3:9 after the poem in 3:1–8). Man is part of the cyclical flux of time and circumstance "under the sun." He both inflicts adversity and suffering upon others and is victimized by the incessant recurrence of events. Man struggles for life and meaning in an environment that taunts him with its paradoxes: birth and death, weeping and laughter, love and hate, war and peace, and the like. Such a relentless and inflexible cycle of events extends beyond the grasp of man's control and understanding. Qoheleth never suggests that a man should resign himself *passively* and put forth no "effort to avert the times and the circumstances."[78] Yet, his purpose is not to aid his reader to *search* for order so as to master life.[79] Von Rad is misguiding when he offers the following wisdom literature's intention: "There was surely only one goal, to wrest from the chaos of events some kind of order in which man was not continually at the mercy of the incalculable."[80]

Though Qoheleth surely is not a passive victim of the cruelties of the endless rounds of this life, neither does his focus become the task of mastering life, straining to "wrest some form of order from chaos."[81] Rather, his entire concentration is on how one directs his life through the labyrinth of this meaningless life; it is guidance and counsel to his readers to enjoy life in spite of the inscrutable and enigmatic world in which they live.

On the one hand, precisely where one might expect pessimistic resignation from Qoheleth, the notion is resisted. On the other hand, he does not counsel his readers to search for order in an attempt to manipulate life. It is his burden to show from his consideration of life's limits and enigmas the futility of man's attempt to understand the whole of life and thus to master it. He counsels his readers to replace false and illusory hopes of understanding providence (thereby manipulating life) with a well-established, joyful confidence that creation is God's gift.[82]

One may be puzzled about the connection between the question of 3:9 and the statement of 3:10. However, if one remembers that the inquiry of 3:9 is not economic but the basic question of life's meaning, the connec-

---

78. See the improper conclusion of Louis Goldberg, *Ecclesiastes* (Grand Rapids: Zondervan, 1983) 64.

79. Cf. Johnston, "'Confessions of a Workaholic,'" 26–27.

80. G. von Rad, *Wisdom in Israel*, trans. J. D. Martin (New York: Abingdon, 1972) 316.

81. von Rad, *Old Testament Theology*, vol. 1, 421.

82. Johnston, "'Confessions of a Workaholic,'" 26.

tion is clear. If every event in this cursed world has its appointed time (depending not upon human influence but upon the determination and providence of God), "what does the worker gain from his toil" (3:9)? What purpose and meaning does life hold? In response to his inquiry, Qoheleth says, "I have seen the burden God has laid on men" (3:10).[83] What is this burden (הָעִנְיָן)? Hengstenberg refers it back to the moil and toil of v. 9, "to which men subject themselves in that they desire, and yet are unable to effect anything, because everything comes to pass as it has been fixed and predetermined by God."[84] However, the inquiry of v. 9 is not so restricted but is a philosophic question relative to the basic meaning and purpose of life. It does not merely have in view moil and toil. Rather, it encompasses the whole of life's activity in a cursed world where labor and life is subjected to drudgingly irksome and fruitless efforts. Thus, the *burden* spoken of in v. 10 is not to be identified as simply the moil and toil in which men are occupied.

The quest in v. 9 is linked with v. 11 through v. 10. The burden (הָעִנְיָן) is comprised of this: "He has made everything beautiful in its time. He has also set eternity in the hearts of men; yet they cannot fathom what God has done from beginning to end" (3:11). To express the fact that God has made everything *beautiful* in its time, Qoheleth uses יָפֶה as a synonym for טוֹב. Yet, the beauty can hardly be that goodness which the Lord God observed in the work of his hands at the beginning (cf. Gen. 1:31, etc.), for creation's subjugation to bondage and decay had not yet come. But after the fall, God's creation was pervasively marred by the curse as is seen in the paradoxes of human affairs listed by Qoheleth (3:1–8). The beauty of which the Preacher speaks consists in this, that what occurs among men comes to pass at its appointed time as a constituent portion of the whole of God's work among men.[85]

Not only has God ordered the affairs of all creation beautifully, he also has put אֶת־הָעֹלָם in the hearts of men (בְּלִבָּם). The suffix in בְּלִבָּם refers to the הָאָדָם in v. 10. How is הָעֹלָם to be understood? Some older commentators attempted to translate the word in the sense of the Arabic ʾlam as "knowledge" or "understanding."[86] With this interpretation, מִבְּלִי אֲשֶׁר is translated "without which," so that the sense of the text is: "He has also set *knowledge* in the hearts of men, *without which* they cannot fathom what God has done from beginning to end."[87]

---

83. See Kaiser, *Ecclesiastes*, 53–54 concerning the singular לִבְנֵי הָאָדָם.
84. Hengstenberg, *Ecclesiastes*, 104.
85. Cf. Delitzsch, *Ecclesiastes*, 259.
86. Cf. Stuart, *Ecclesiastes*, 174–75. But see Delitzsch's response to this, *Ecclesiastes*, 260.
87. Stuart's strained conclusions on 3:11 are inconsistent with his comments on 8:17. See Stuart, *Ecclesiastes*, 173–74 and 308.

This exegetical course is rejected by most commentators.[88] Apparently Luther took אֶת־הָעֹלָם to mean "the world," "the desire after the knowledge of the world," or "worldly mindedness."[89] However, it seems best to follow the lead of Delitzsch and others who take הָעֹלָם as "eternity."[90]

The "eternity" which God has put into the hearts of men is a certain inquisitiveness and yearning after purpose. It is a compulsive drive, a deep-seated desire to appreciate order and beauty, arising because man is made in the image of God. It is an impulse to press beyond the limits which the present world circumscribes about man in order to escape the bondage which holds him in the incessant cycle of the seasons and in order to console his anxious mind with meaning and purpose.[91] It is man's desperate attempt to make sense out of what seems senseless and meaningless. Yet, הָעֹלָם must not be restricted to this, but also must include a residual knowledge of God's eternal power and divine nature which God has placed in every man (cf. Rom. 1:19),[92] for it is this knowledge which gives man his sense that there is purpose and meaning (though it entirely eludes him).

This compulsive desire to appreciate the beauty, symmetry and order of creation shows itself differently at various levels. Aesthetically man seeks to appreciate creation's beauty as he imitates his creator by fashioning beauty with his own hands. Philosophically man pursues knowledge of the universe to know its character, composition and meaning. Theologically man seeks to discern creation's purpose and destiny. Since man has this craving for meaning, a deep-seated inquisitiveness and capacity to learn how everything in this world fits together, he seeks to integrate his experience into a meaningful whole. He yearns to connect the various pieces of his experience to see each portion in the context of the whole of his life. He desperately desires to have a meaningful understanding of the world and of life to give him direction and mastery. He is like Qoheleth who sought to add "one thing to another to discover the scheme of things" (7:27).

Herein then is the task or burden which God has laid upon the sons of Adam: the search for meaning in a disjointed and topsy-turvy world. It is not a burden because man is a creature who has only limited and derived knowledge. It is a heavy and frustrating burden because man's quest for meaning is now performed in a cursed world wherein inexplicable paradox dominates—there is birth and death, hate as well as love, and more war than peace fills the earth. It is this kind of world, uniform yet twisted and marked by gaps, which Qoheleth explored and declared to be meaningless.

88. See Delitzsch, *Ecclesiastes,* 260.
89. Attributed to Luther by Delitzsch, *Ecclesiastes,* 260.
90. Ibid., 261.
91. Ibid.
92. Otto Zöckler, *Ecclesiastes,* trans. William Wells, in vol. 5, *Commentary on the Holy Scripture,* ed. by J. P. Lange (Grand Rapids: Zondervan, 1960) 67.

In spite of the fact that God has "made everything beautiful in its time" (an orderly arrangement even of chaos), and despite the certainty that "He also has set eternity in the hearts of men," Qoheleth declares, "yet they cannot fathom what God has done from beginning to end" (3:11c). This incapacity of man is emphasized repeatedly by Qoheleth to establish the meaninglessness which he announced at the beginning as his theme. The inability to discover God's purposes and design from events and experiences is an essential thread which Qoheleth weaves into the fabric of his work. The elusiveness of meaning becomes the dominant motif in 6:12–11:6. Man is reminded that he "cannot discover anything about his future" (7:14; cf. 3:22) because God has made both good and evil to befall men quite haphazardly. Is proof needed for the inscrutable ways of God? Qoheleth declares, "In this meaningless life of mine I have seen both of these: a righteous man perishing in his righteousness, and a wicked man living long in his wickedness" (7:15). The tyrannies and the benevolences in this world, both caused by God, come upon men with disparity and inequity, for "righteous men get what the wicked deserve and the wicked get what the righteous deserve" (8:14). God has not revealed to men the secrets of the purposes which move his actions (cf. Deut. 29:29).

Man's limitation and fractional knowledge, as he seeks to "add one thing to another to discover the scheme of things" (cf: 7:27), is emphasized in 8:7–8a: "Since no man knows the future, who can tell him what is to come? No man has power over the wind to contain it; so no one has power over the day of his death." The disproportionate allotment of God's providence ruins men's illusory hopes of mastering life and discovering the divine meaning and purpose for life's experiences and events. "There is something else meaningless that occurs on earth: righteous men get what the wicked deserve and wicked men get what the righteous deserve" (8:14). Who would challenge Qoheleth? He is right! The incongruities and paradoxes that baffled Qoheleth bewilder every man. It is this disharmony and absurdity that compelled Qoheleth to impart to his readers a realistic perspective:[93]

> When I applied my mind to know wisdom and to observe man's labor on earth—his eyes not seeing sleep day or night—then I saw all that God has done. No one can comprehend what goes on under the sun. Despite all his efforts to search it out, man cannot discover its meaning. Even if a wise man claims he knows, he cannot really comprehend it [8:16–17].

Celebration of Life

It is precisely in the contexts where Qoheleth magnifies and emphasizes man's bewilderment that so many scholars have failed to understand Qoheleth. His candid and realistic confessions followed by counsel have brought severe criticism. On the one hand, he is accused of pessimism for his acknowl-

---

93. Cf. 9:1–3, 11–12.

edgment of the elusiveness of meaning and, on the other hand, he is said to be orthodox because of his counsel to sane living (see 12:13–14). At some places his counsel is viewed as grossly defective. Delitzsch asserts, "If Koheleth had known of a future life . . . he would have reached a better ultimatum."[94] Delitzsch is referring to 3:12–14:

> I know that there is nothing better for men than to be happy and do good while they live. That every man may eat and drink, and find satisfaction in all his toil—this is the gift of God. I know that everything God does will endure forever; nothing can be added to it and nothing taken from it. God does it, so men will revere him.

Now wherein lies the shortcoming of Qoheleth's counsel? He urges men to do good (טוֹב) and to be glad (לִשְׂמוֹחַ). The enjoyment to be derived from life is coordinate with obedience to divine commandments.[95] This is how men are to conduct themselves as long as they are living (בְּחַיָּיו). Furthermore, that which a man may eat or drink or find satisfying in his toil is confessed as "the gift of God." Above all, Qoheleth acknowledges that what God does, though it may be perplexing to man, he does "so men will fear him" (3:14). How could Qoheleth be more orthodox? Is not this the counsel of one who considers the eternal, the future existence of man? If Qoheleth did not believe in the resurrection, why would he counsel men to behave obediently, fearing God? What is there to fear, if it is not God's judgment of *resurrected* men?

Qoheleth's world and life view was not fashioned according to a natural theology restricted to the affairs of men "under the sun." If that were the case, he would have counseled his readers to revelry, for he saw in this world that it is the wicked who live long (7:15; 8:14). He does not envy the way of the ungodly as Asaph began to do, nearly to his own destruction (cf. Ps. 73:3–17). If Qoheleth had no belief in final retribution—the demise of the wicked and the rewarding of the righteous—his counsel would have been, "Let us eat and drink, for tomorrow we die" (see 1 Cor. 15:32), the very philosophy of which he is often accused. Qoheleth does not yield to pessimism and despair nor to an ascetic withdrawal, nor to an anesthetic desensitized denial of evil. Instead, from the recognition that what the righteous and wicked receive is inverse to their deserts (8:14), he moves directly to his holy counsel: "So I commend the enjoyment of life, because nothing is better for man under the sun than to eat and drink and be glad. Then joy will accompany him in his work all the days of the life God has given him under the sun" (8:15).

---

94. Delitzsch, *Ecclesiastes*, 262. In contrast to the negative interpretation by Delitzsch, see R. N. Whybray, "Qoheleth, Preacher of Joy," *JSOT* 23 (1982) 87–98.

95. See Delitzsch, *Ecclesiastes*, 262 concerning a discussion of Qoheleth's use of טוֹב in 3:12.

Qoheleth's perspective upon the incongruities of this life is the same as Job's who said of the wicked: "Their prosperity is not in their own hands, so I stand aloof from the counsel of the wicked" (Job 21:16). Qoheleth says,

> Although a wicked man commits a hundred crimes and still lives a long time, I know that it will go better with God-fearing men, who are reverent before God. Yet because the wicked do not fear God, it will not go well with them, and their days will not lengthen like a shadow [8:12–13].[96]

Qoheleth formed his world and life view with divine creation and divine retribution in mind. This creator-retributor perspective gives Qoheleth equilibrium and stability to dwell in a world subjected to the curse of God. The creation motif serves as the source of Qoheleth's counsel to celebrate life with joy, for it is a *good* creation of God. The eschatological judgment motif is behind his caution to behave obediently in view of the divine retribution which will reward the righteous and condemn the wicked. This counsel is gracefully harmonized by Qoheleth in his admonition to the young man:

> Be happy young man, while you are young, and let your heart give you joy in the days of your youth. Follow the ways of your heart and whatever your eyes see, but know that for all these things God will bring you to judgment. So then, banish anxiety from your heart and cast off the troubles of your body, for youth and vigor are meaningless [11:9–10].

The joy and freedom of following one's desires is not to be dampened by knowledge of coming judgment but only controlled. This is not counsel to indulgent and indecent conduct but to freedom and joyful celebration of God's good gift of life, tempered by the knowledge that the God who created life also holds men accountable to revere him. The free pursuit of the heart's desires and whatever the eyes see is to be done within the moral boundaries of God's commandments (see 12:13). Qoheleth's counsel encourages one to celebrate life, unshackled from a search for the meaning of life.

Qoheleth Interpreted: The Epilogue

Upon concluding his graphic poem on aging and death, Qoheleth closes the body of his book with the theme with which he began: "'Meaningless! Meaningless!' says the Preacher. 'Everything is meaningless!'" (12:8; cf. 1:2). But the verdict is not the final word that Qoheleth has for his readers. Instead, he leaves them with a closing word of counsel on how to behave in a world that is aimless and meaningless as the result of the Creator's curse upon it.

---

96. See Michael Eaton, *Ecclesiastes* (Tyndale Old Testament Commentaries; Leicester: Inter-Varsity, 1983) 41–42. His comments are appropriate against those who presume an interpolated contradiction in these verses.

That counsel is not in the least out of character with the theme of the book. He concludes, "Now all has been heard; here is the conclusion of the matter: Fear God and keep his commandments, for this is the whole duty of man. For God will bring every deed into judgment, including every hidden thing whether it is good or evil" (12:13–14).

Qoheleth, throughout his book, had repeatedly raised the motif of eschatological judgment to motivate obedient behavior despite the fact that rotters advance in prosperity and live long in this world while the righteous flounder in their struggles and succumb early to the curse of death (cf. 3:16, 17; 5:4–7; 8:11–14; 11:9). The final judgment serves as a chief orientation to which Qoheleth directs his readers to steer them through the labyrinths of this meaningless life. The fear of God who shall judge men is to temper and regulate man's ethical actions and decisions throughout his sojourning here. And so it is appropriate that Qoheleth sums up the duty of man: "Fear God and keep his commandments" (12:13; cf. 3:14; 5:7; 7:18; and 8:12–13 three times).

Fearing God is motivated by the fact that "God will bring every deed into judgment." These two great themes, fearing God and an appointed time for divine judgment, serve as integral elements in the development of Qoheleth's world and life view. They were not mere addendas to a series of unconnected discursive sayings and affirmations. Rather, the conclusion serves as the knot which secures the ethical threads carefully woven into the fabric of the work. Qoheleth asserts this to be the case, for he says, "Now all has been heard; here is the conclusion of the matter" (12:13a).

Consistent with his counsel throughout the book, Qoheleth does not permit his reader to despair even though "everything is meaningless." He counsels men to fear God and to obey him because there is a time for judgment when they will give account of their conduct and secrets, whether they be good or evil. These last words can hardly be taken in a crippling manner. Qoheleth did not design his words concerning the all-searching eye of God (v. 14) to *inhibit* human enjoyment and behavior nor to cast his readers into *introspective* questioning of motives. Rather, knowledge of divine judgment should *regulate* one's conduct with a *prospective* gaze of expectation toward the day when justice shall eradicate all iniquity, when divine mercy shall purge out all oppression, when the righteous shall flourish as the wicked are cut off (cf. 3:16–17; 8:12–14).

Qoheleth's World and Life View Summarized

As Qoheleth made his thorough investigation (1:13) of all that is done under heaven, he was governed by basic presuppositional beliefs which are expressed throughout his work. These presuppositions largely arise out of his knowledge of God's revelation of himself in Genesis 1–11. Foundational to his philosophical pursuit of meaning is his firm recognition that the world with all its systems, and man in particular as actor, operate under the curse of God. This he expresses in terms of things *twisted* and things *lacking* (1:15). The presence of evil is not to be attributed to the essence of creation but as a foreign element imposed upon it, for "Who can straighten what he [God] has made crooked?" (7:13). Furthermore, God did not capriciously impose this curse, but "God made mankind upright, but men have gone in search of many schemes" (7:29). Thus, it is the curse which accounts for the inequity, the tyranny, the oppression, the disparity of providence, and especially for the presence of death and its haphazard encroachment without respect to men's characters (cf. 9:1–3).

This basic presuppositional belief that the world is not what it was *originally* nor what it will be *finally* governs Qoheleth's ethical world and life view. This is due to the fact that the transformation of the world is not accomplished by some evolutionary process inherent within creation itself, but by the God who created the universe and also subjected it to its present frustration under the curse and who will finally liberate it (cf. Rom. 8:19–21).

For Qoheleth, then, there is a second and much more ultimate presupposition which regulates all his observations of this evil world and his wise counsel on how to live in it. The entire book rests solidly upon the assumption that the Lord God of Israel is the Creator and Governor of all things. He is the *Creator* who set all things into motion (12:1; 11:5). He is the *Sovereign* who governs all that he has created. He does not merely permit or allow the present suffering and evil in the world. Qoheleth acknowledges that it is God who *causes* both the good and the bad to befall men irrespective of their characters (7:14–15). It is God who gives a man wealth and yet may not give him the enjoyment of it, an evil which is vexing to men (6:1–2). Though it is God who gives both the good and the evil, he is not to be charged with doing evil; he is only to be feared precisely because of all that he does among men (3:14).

God is also perceived by Qoheleth as *Incomprehensible Wisdom,* for the creator/creature distinction, aggravated by the curse, hides God behind a frowning providence which hinders man from discovering life's meaning in this cursed world (3:11; 7:13–14; 8:16–17; 11:3–6). Man's knowledge of what God does as he observes the world is fractional and frustrated by the perplexing paradoxes. It is precisely this fact, namely, that almighty God has hidden his full character behind a disparate providence, that necessitates his special revelation.[97]

---

97. Shank ("Qoheleth's World and Life View," 68) astutely states, "We must maintain contrary to the majority of critical and conservative commentators, that Qoheleth's perception . . . refers to a knowledge which is a 'reflex-action' of his fear of God and which penetrates to the essence of the *meaning* of what this world of vanity is all about. . . . That perception also *includes* a deep, spiritual insight into the affects of the curse of God upon life and labor 'under the sun.'"

The antithetical quality of Qoheleth must be understood within this frame-work. The proposal of liberal critics that the oscillations of thought and ex-pression are to be attributed either to a dialogue between two or more speak-ers or the result of glossators and redactors must be rejected.[98] Furthermore, the proposed solution of many conservative scholars also must be laid aside. The suggestion that Qoheleth's book is indicative of a man who wavers be-tween secular and religious perspectives, oscillating to and fro, filled with doubts and perplexities, yet finally arising above them, has no true correspon-dence to the nature of Qoheleth. Even the attempt to resolve the paradoxical nature of the book by suggesting that the evils and inequities, of which the Preacher complains, are only an "apparent anomaly"[99] must be disallowed.

The paradoxical expressions and antithetical observations of God's disparate providence do not find their explanation from some internal struggle in Qoheleth between faith and reason. Nor are they resolved by postulating that they are the result of a dichotomy between sacred and secular perspectives. Rather, Qoheleth reflects the *real* world in its present state which is in conflict with the way it once was and the way it will be again. It is the curse, causing the twisting and incom-pleteness (1:15) of all things, that accounts for the dilemma which confronts man. Qoheleth hides no evil nor does he seek to deny it as merely apparent. He con-fronts the reality of evil and seeks to bring his readers to do the same. Yet, on the other hand, Qoheleth maintains an unwavering belief in the God who created and who will judge all men. For after all is said and done, it is God who has ar-ranged the world as it is so that men will fear him (3:14).

Qoheleth does not shrink from acknowledging that it is God who has made both the good times and the bad (7:14). Yet, he never resorts to a fatalism which encourages either pious passivity or Epicurean indulgence. He takes the pathway of wisdom. The fact that God has inscrutably arranged this world under the per-plexity and frustration of the curse, caused Qoheleth to declare, "Therefore, a man cannot discover anything about his future" (7:14b). Man is not to busy him-self with the inscrutable. He is not to become occupied with trying to determine which course it is that is divinely chosen for him.

Qoheleth makes it clear that it is futile to seek to determine from the course of providential events whether or not divine approval rests upon one's amoral decisions, however great or small they may be. Searching divine providence to determine one's course of action is not piety, but folly which leads to inac-tivity and failure. For "whoever watches the wind will not plant; whoever looks at the clouds will not reap" (11:4). The mystery of providence is un-fathomable and inscrutable (11:5). "No one can comprehend what goes on

98. Cf. Eaton, *Ecclesiastes,* 37–39.

99. See [Greene], "The Scope and Plan of Ecclesiastes," 424. This view is too much domi-nated by presuming that the final retribution cuts its line *now* with vividness. See also ibid., 424–25. Cf. Kaiser, *Ecclesiastes,* 17.

under the sun. Despite all his efforts to search it out, man cannot discover its meaning. Even if a wise man claims he knows, he cannot really comprehend it" (8:17). Trying to discern providence will drive one mad, for it presumes that God's providence bears a direct and invariable correspondence to the events among men. Such misguided efforts cause men to turn upon God in bitterness or berate themselves when evil days befall them, thinking that suffering is always caused by particular sins.

Qoheleth counsels against "providence reading," for those who follow such a course fail to succeed at anything (11:4). Instead, since no man can know which endeavors will prove fruitful, the proper approach to life is to give oneself to the responsibilities at hand *with freedom* and *diligence,* and to await the course of events to determine one's success (11:6). All the days a man is given ought to be enjoyed (11:8), for "it is now that God favors what you do" (9:7b). Life is a divine gift to be enjoyed to its maximum as long as there is breath in the nostrils, for "even a live dog is better off than a dead lion" (9:4). Life is an endowment to be presently celebrated in the presence of the Creator (12:1). The enjoyment of life is to be the dominant motif of one's existence upon this earth, not the mercenary fixation of a miserly workman who hoards his earnings to satisfy his soul when he retires from his labors. The days of trouble come too quickly and unpredictably upon men eroding their pleasure and enjoyment (12:1–2). This perspective upon life is not sensual; it is realistic. It is governed by the fact that this world is cursed, and the ultimate curse is death (9:1, 3). Death is not something to be desired as a release from the prison of the body (as in Neoplatonism), for it wrenches man away from the environment in which he was designed to dwell (cf. Ps. 115:16–17). Death is no friend but an enemy which violently tears a man apart, severing the spirit from the body (12:7). This is the perspective that the whole Bible takes upon death (cf. Isa. 38:10–20; 2 Cor. 5:1–5).

For Qoheleth, then, two opposing realities serve to motivate his expressions in 9:5–10: (1) the curse of death comes to every man, and (2) the gift of life is man's to be enjoyed to its fullest "all the days of this meaningless life that God has given you under the sun" (9:9). His whole description of the dead in 9:5–6 is defined carefully—"never again will they have a part in anything that happens under the sun" (9:6b). His interest is not to describe theologically the *state* of the dead (as Jehovah's witnesses might contend), but he portrays the dead in relation to this world; they have nothing more to do with it. It is for this reason that Qoheleth so often reiterates his celebration of life:

> Go, eat your food with gladness, and drink your wine with a joyful heart, for it is now that God favors what you do. Always be clothed in white, and always anoint your head with oil. Enjoy life with your wife, whom you love, all the days of this meaningless life that God has given you under the sun—all your

meaningless days. For this is your lot in life and in your toilsome labor under the sun. Whatever your hand finds to do, do it with all your might, for in the grave, where you are going, there is neither working nor planting nor knowledge nor wisdom [9:7–10].

Conclusion

Qoheleth was no *enigmatic pessimist*. He was not a man who recorded the battle of tormenting and conflicting thoughts that raged inside his own mind as he oscillated between orthodox piety and indulgent secularism. Qoheleth was a *godly sage*. He was a righteous man regulated by his knowledge of and devout fear of the God of Israel. It is precisely because he was a God-fearing man that Qoheleth was capable of giving expression to such paradoxical and anomalous matters without denying the presence of evil in this world or without destroying his belief in God. Qoheleth records a godly man's reflections upon a cursed world subjected by God to vanity and frustration. It is the character of such a world which accounts for the polarized expressions and paradoxical and anomalous matters without denying the presence of evil in this world or without destroying his belief in God. Qoheleth records a godly man's reflections upon a cursed world subjected by God to vanity and frustration. It is the character of such a world which accounts for the polarized expressions and paradoxical observations in his book. It is precisely what one scholar dogmatically denied: "That the author of Ecclesiastes intended that the contrarities of his book should . . . reflect and image forth the chequered web of man's earthly condition, hopes alternating with fears, joys succeeded by sorrows, life contrasting with death."[100]

What Paul asserts in a few words in Rom. 8:19–21, Qoheleth investigates at length. Where Paul spoke generally, the Preacher descended to uncover the particulars. Though Paul had the privilege of knowing that Christ will restore all things and even now, in principle, has begun to do so (cf. 1 Cor. 15:54–57), both he and Qoheleth share one biblical assessment of the character of this world and of life in it since the fall. It is cursed! It is disjointed! It is upside down! It is in bondage to decay! It is meaningless! It needs to be liberated!

What Qoheleth saw obscurely in the coming day of final retribution, the apostle Paul makes clear: "creation itself will be liberated from its bondage to decay and brought into the glorious freedom of the children of God" (Rom. 8:21). It is for the final redemption of God's people that creation awaits, for then will it be set free from what is now twisted and lacking (Eccles. 1:15).

---

100. Tyler, *Ecclesiastes*, 54.

6

THE SCOPE AND PLAN
OF THE BOOK
OF ECCLESIASTES

In order to gain the proper understanding of any treatise, it is necessary to gain clear and correct ideas of its scope and plan. There is no book of the Old Testament to which this remark applies with greater force than Ecclesiastes, and none in which the neglect of it has been and must be attended with more serious injury to its exposition. Its proverbial dress creates a special need of taking comprehensive views of the writer's main design, and not being diverted from this by cleaving too anxiously to the tenor of each individual expression. The ill success of too many attempted expositions has shown, that if the clue thus furnished to all its intricacies and windings be not discovered or be lost sight of, the book becomes a labyrinth, within whose mazes the improvident adventurer is hopelessly entangled; and each verse becomes to him a new passage leading to fresh perplexity, however honestly and assiduously he may labor upon its interpretation. The general truths inculcated by proverbs of course admit either of being taken in their widest extent, or of receiving an indefinite number of particular applications. Which of these expresses the precise intent of the writer, in each individual case, can

Reprinted from *The Biblical Repertory and Princeton Review* 29 (July 1857): 419–40.

never be learned from the inspection of single sentences by themselves, but only from a discovery of the place which it holds in the discussion of his theme. And an erroneous view of this theme or of the method of its discussion, will necessarily involve attaching meanings to passages very different from those which they were intended to bear.

Another difficulty connected with that just spoken of, and of a like nature, arises from the absence of particles in every case to indicate the connection or the relation of dependence which the various sentences or paragraphs sustain to each other. This is partly due to the venerable simplicity of the Hebrew language, in which such particles do not abound, and with which it agrees better to suggest relations by the juxtaposition of related ideas, than formally and precisely to state them. It is also partly due to the proverbial style already referred to, which characteristically delights to state truths in the general and the absolute, leaving their limitations and specific relations to be gathered from the connection in which they are adduced.

The inattentive and superficial reader might infer from the peculiarities now stated, and which would be among the first to attract his attention, that this book was composed of loose and detached sentences, without orderly consecution or intimate coherence. This mistaken view was in fact taken by Grotius, who supposed that Ecclesiastes contained no proper discussion of any one theme, but a miscellaneous collection of the varying opinions of different sages upon topics connected with human happiness. He thus explained those contradictions or diversities of judgment which he imagined to be found in the book; and likewise escaped the necessity of regarding any sentiment as authoritative or inspired which he was disinclined to accept. It is but a slight modification of this opinion of Grotius to regard the book as a record of the various opinions maintained in a learned assembly or society presided over by Solomon.

Another view, which rises above this conception of a chaos of discordant materials, and yet assumes the existence of conflicting sentiments in the book, endeavors to reconcile these into a common unity by the hypothesis of a dialogue between two voices, one that of an earnest but rash inquirer, the other his sage and experienced teacher, who endeavors to curb the hasty impatience and inconsiderate views of the former, and to inculcate upon him the lessons of sobriety and heavenly wisdom. But the harmony of the sentiments here maintained can be vindicated without the necessity of this theory, which finds no support from any intimations in the text itself. The same may be said of the opinion which supposes instead of different speakers, different states of mind in the same speaker; who begins the discussion in a tumult of doubt between conflicting views, and speaks now under the influence of one, now of another, as they respectively obtrude themselves upon him, until at the close of the whole he ultimately reaches clear and settled convictions.

Among those who admit a single theme consistently discussed, there is still a divergence as to what that theme is, arising principally from an undue predominance being given to some one part of the book or class of passages in it, instead of each being held in its just subordination and relations. Some have paid too exclusive attention to what is said of the vanity of earthly pursuits. So Jerome, and after him the commentators of the middle ages, generally made of it an argument for the renunciation of the world and a life of monasticism. So in modern times Umbreit thought it to be a treatise on the chief good, which the author tinged with skepticism and gloom endeavors to show is unattainable. Others, looking solely at such passages as declare that it is good for a man to eat and to drink and to enjoy life, have charged the author with Epicurean sentiments, as though worldly pleasure were in his esteem the highest form of good, and what men should chiefly strive after. This view, and that first stated are directly antagonistic and mutually destructive. The author cannot teach both that earthly pleasure is vanity and that it is the chief good. The book will be involved in endless complication and self-contradiction upon either of these views. The only way to harmonize it is to suffer one class of statements to modify and assist in explaining the other. To him whose heart is inordinately set on earthly things, and who fancies that by accumulating whatever affords gratification, he can fill and satisfy his soul, every thing will prove vanity as regards this impracticable end which he is seeking; for his desires invariably outrun his acquisitions, his feverish toil is incompatible with serene enjoyment; their continued possession in the future is uncertain and their loss at death inevitable. Still, he who knows how to use the world, who contentedly and thankfully receives the good things which God gives him, and without immoderate desires partakes of them rationally and in obedience to the will of God, will find in them much real satisfaction. This life has a positive value, which should not be overlooked; and it is a lesson of no small consequence, how it may be rendered most peaceful and happy. The enjoyment of life, which this book commends, is as far as possible from a wild and senseless revelry, which it denominates insane and profitless, 2:1, 2; it is an enjoyment which is connected with doing good, 3:12, and is indulged with a constant recollection of the judgment of God, 9:9. Piety holds the key to the chamber of happiness. There is no entrance but by her aid. He who would really extract from the world such enjoyment as it is capable of affording, can only do so by obedience to her injunctions. Otherwise, be a man's possessions what they may, they will end in vanity and emptiness. This is the aspect under which the happiness of men in the present life is here presented, and if this is Epicurean, the whole Bible is so too.

Others have given too exclusive prominence to such passages as 1:4–11, 3:1–15, 3:13, 14, 9:11, in which the fixed and permanent order of things in the universe is insisted upon, and the regulation of everything is referred to the will of God; and they have hence drawn the conclusion that the book contains fatalistic sentiments, teaching the doctrine of an undeviating, inexorable fate, which leaves no room for human freedom, and allows no man to obtain profit from his labor. This fate it is vain to think of resisting; man must just submit and get whatever good his present circumstances put within his reach. But this is as much as the preceding a distortion of what is here taught. It is indeed asserted that man is not the uncontrolled arbiter of his own fortune; not, however, because he is a creature of fate, but because he is a subject of the wise and righteous government of God. The doctrine is not that of fate, but of Providence: and this, too, is intimately connected with the theme here discussed. As we look upon the world, everything seems to be moving at random, or to be directed by man's free will. Men act as they please, and the allotments distributed to each bear no manifest relation to their respective characters. There is much that, superficially viewed, has the appearance of disordered confusion. But that this is the real state of the case is here emphatically denied. The assertion is made and the proof given, that instead of confusion the most perfect and beautiful order prevails. Whether men see his hand or not, God is guiding and directing all; and everything is, as respects his consummate plan, just as it should be. He has dissociated sin and happiness; and no man can alter that arrangement so as to bring together what have been thus divinely separated. He who seeks for happiness in ways of worldliness and sin, seeks for what, by the very constitution of the universe, cannot be.

Too great prominence has again been sometimes given to such passages as 3:17, 5:8, 11:9, 12:7, 14, and on the basis of these the future state and the coming judgment have been made the grand lesson here inculcated, as though it were the intention of the writer to turn the thoughts of his readers from the seeming inequalities of this world to the world to come, where all shall be rectified or explained. The error in this view is simply that of limiting the discussion within too narrow a range. The future judgment is explicitly asserted, and is one of the elements in the proper presentation of the subject. But this is not the sole view that is here taken, nor the sole answer which is returned to the perplexing problem of human life. It is most unaccountable how some writers have been able so utterly to misconceive the teachings of this book as to deny to its author any confident persuasion of the immortality of the soul, or anything more than a hesitating admission of its possibility. In basing this opinion upon 3:19–21 and 9:4–6, they not only interpret these passages incorrectly, even altering the text for this purpose, as will be seen hereafter, but bring them into irreconcilable conflict with such passages as those referred to above; a difficulty from which Knobel endeavours to escape by a German critic's ready weapon, the denial of the genuineness of 12:9–14.

Attention has sometimes been directed to too great an extent to the seemingly miscellaneous character of the proverbs, in such passages as 4:5, 6, 9–13, 6:1–7, 7:1–9, 21, 22, 10:1–11:6, and the conclusion has hence been drawn that the design of the book is to give rules for the conduct of life, and to teach wisdom in general. This goes to the extreme of extending the theme too widely, as the preceding to that of unduly restricting it. Its aim becomes thus too vague and indefinite, and the main drift of the discussion is lost sight of. The writer does not spread his thoughts over the whole range of human action or the proprieties of life; but he has one definite subject before him, to which a proper treatment of the book will show that all his remarks are directed, and that with a closeness of argument and a clearness of presentation worthy of the wise king of Israel.

The problem really discussed is the seeming inequalities of divine providence. These are here reconciled with the justice of God, as they are in the book of Job reconciled with his mercy and goodness. In other words, while Job had especially to do with the sufferings of the pious, Ecclesiastes contemplates the same subject chiefly from the side of the prosperity of the wicked. The difficulty to be explained is thus stated by the writer, 7:15, "There is a just man that perisheth in his righteousness, and there is a wicked man that prolongeth his life in his wickedness." And 7:14, "There is a vanity which is done upon the earth; that there be just men unto whom it happeneth according to the work of the wicked; again, there be wicked men to whom it happeneth according to the work of the righteous." This apparent anomaly is shown not to be inconsistent with the righteousness of God's government. The position taken and established is, 8:12, 13, "Though a sinner do evil an hundred times and his days be prolonged, yet surely I know that it shall be well with them that fear God, which fear before him; but it shall not be well with the wicked, neither shall he prolong his days, which are as a shadow; because he feareth not before God." The solution which is furnished is twofold:—1. A proper estimate of men's fortunes and of their characters will show these inequalities to be much fewer than they appear to be. 2. There is a righteous government to rectify whatever inequalities may temporarily exist.

It is most interesting to observe the harmony of the grand lessons inculcated by Job and by Ecclesiastes. No two books could well be more unlike in their style and method of discussion. The problem upon which they are engaged is one of the most perplexing of human life. They approach it, too, from quarters the most diverse. And yet the principles which underlie their solutions are identical. The book of Job reconciles the sufferings of the pious by saying, (*a*) Their afflictions though a seeming evil are a real good. (*b*) The perfections of God are an ample security for the rectitude and goodness of his dispensations. Ecclesiastes says of the prosperity of the wicked, (*a*) It yields no real good, but vanity and vexation of spirit. (*b*) The justice of God secures that all is, and shall be, right under his holy government.

That the main design of this book has been correctly stated, shall be shown hereafter in detail. Before proceeding to this, however, it may be readily established in a general way by the testimony of the author himself. This is in the first place given in a formal manner at the close of the book, 12:13, 14, "Let us hear the conclusion of the whole matter: Fear God and keep his commandments; for this is the whole duty of man," i.e., the whole of his duty and destiny, his entire welfare, all that concerns him is centered here and depends on this single thing. "For God shall bring every work into judgment with every secret thing, whether it be good, or whether it be evil." In other words, man's true welfare is only to be secured by fearing God and obeying his will; for in spite of any present appearances to the contrary, every good deed, open or secret, shall be divinely rewarded, and every evil deed divinely punished. This is given by the author as the final result of the experience, observations, and reasonings recorded in his book. And this is precisely what has been already represented to be its aim.

A second mode in which the writer declares himself as to this point, is by certain forms of statement which recur again and again from the beginning to the close. We cannot be mistaken in deducing from these the topic which is ever in his thoughts, and to whose illustration his whole argument is directed. There are two series of these statements; one of which contains the negative, and the other the positive view of his subject. Their combination will give a just conception of his idea. The first consists of those in which it is repeatedly declared of all those accumulations and sources of gratification which men so eagerly covet, and after which they so increasingly toil, that they are vanity and pursuit of wind (Eng. ver., vexation of spirit). They are no real good, but constantly disappoint their possessors of the satisfaction which they had hoped by this means to obtain. The second series consists of those, in which it is declared that there is nothing better for a man than to eat and to drink, and to enjoy the fruit of his labor; and this is the gift of God to them that please him. That this is not an Epicurean sentiment, has been already seen. The eating and drinking which Solomon commends, is not the gratification of sensual appetite. To eat and to drink, by a common figure in all languages, denotes to partake of what may be either pleasurable or painful. Comp. Ps. 24:8, 36:8; Heb. 6:4, 5; Job 21:20; Matt. 20:23. Here the connection determines it to refer to what is pleasurable. In 2:24, 3:18, 5:18, "to eat and to drink" is explained by the parallel phrase, "to enjoy good," and in 3:22, "to rejoice," stands as its equivalent. In 2:25, "Who can eat more than I?" certainly does not mean who is a greater glutton, but who has more sources of gratification at his command? And in 5:19, 6:2, to eat riches, wealth, and honor, can only mean to enjoy them. The meaning of this class of passages then is, that enjoyment, pleasure, happiness is a greater good than all these vain acquisitions which are attended with so little satisfaction. And enjoyment is God's gift to them that are pleasing in his sight. We thus reach once more the theme before propounded. Outward prosperity may be in possession of the wicked; but this is empty and unsubstantial. It does not necessarily confer happiness. This is only for the good.

The scope of this book being thus settled, we proceed to consider its plan. It is of course conceivable that the writer might discuss his theme without any orderly arrangement or methodical disposition of parts. He might merely give expression to his reflections upon it as they spontaneously occurred to him or were suggested by accidental association, without aiming to govern himself by any strict logical sequence. Some have maintained that this is the case with the book of Ecclesiastes. It is so with another book of Solomon's, the Proverbs. It is to some extent the case with other books of the Old Testament as well as with admired productions of uninspired genius. And it would cast no reflection upon the ability or excellence of this book to admit the same thing here.

Others have been of the opinion that the writer had a general plan in his mind, which he followed in the main, yet not so strictly but that he has indulged upon occasion in considerable digressions. Others have thought that there was a plan originally, but it has been obscured by negligent transcription and derangement of the text; and attempts have been made by transpositions and re-arrangement to restore it to its supposed original form and thus bring to light its proper plan; but the results have been as unsatisfactory as the procedure was unauthorized and the premises groundless. We must take the text as we find it, which there is no reason to believe has been corrupted. The deficiency of arrangement which has been alleged, does not exist; and the alterations which have been proposed are not improvements. There is a clear and consistent plan in the book of Ecclesiastes, which needs no changes nor mutilations in order to its discovery; one in fact of the most strictly logical and methodical kind. Not only is the argument well conducted, conclusive and complete, but its various points are so admirably disposed, its divisions so regular, and its different parts to confirmed in structure, as to give evidence that the whole was carefully considered and well digested before it was put together. This differs perhaps from the prevalent opinion, but we are convinced that they who complain of a want of method, *hærent in cortice*.

It would be tedious and confusing to enumerate in all their details the various divisions proposed by different commentators. Very many of them, however diverse in their minor subdivisions, will be found to rest ultimately upon the same essential scheme, the division of the book into two parts or grand leading sections. These are sometimes made unequal by assigning four chapters to the first and eight to the second; at other times equal, so that each contains six chapters. The principle assumed as the basis of the division is in either case the same, that the first contains the theoretical and the second the practical portions of the subject; the first establishes the vanity of earthly things, and the second the duties and obligations which this involves, and how man should demean himself in this vain world. There is so far a foundation for these schemes, that the tone of the book does become more hortatory and practical as it approaches its close; but the line of separation between its doctrine and exhortation is not so sharply defined as to render such a division between them practicable, as is shown in fact by the divided sentiment of those who undertake it. Hitzig's division into three parts of four chapters each, appears to be a lame attempt to mediate between the views already recited.

The most satisfactory division is, in our judgment, that into four parts, which was proposed by Vaihinger in the "Studien und Kritiken," for 1848, and has since been adopted by Keil and others. It is a modification of that of Ewald (whom Heligstedt follows) which is itself an improvement upon that of Köster, all of whom assume the same number of sections. His scheme is the following, viz.

    I.   1:2–2:26.
    II. 3:1–5:20.
    III. 6:1–8:15.
    IV. 8:16–12:14.

It has a sanction of an external kind, inasmuch as it seems to be indicated by the writer himself, winding up each part by a formal statement of the conclusion of his argument, which in the first three is given in almost identical terms. This is the more worthy of note, as Solomon has indicated the divisions of his Song in a precisely similar way by the recurrence of a refrain. Its full justification depends upon its being shown that it is coincident with the actual course of the discussion, and that every part, without forcing or the assumption of arbitrary senses, fits into the scheme thus presented. Vaihinger was prevented from exhibiting this in a satisfactory manner by his predilection for strophes of equal length, into which he fancied the whole to be in the most precise manner subdivided. This encumbered his view and rendered it too artificial; while his too zealous pursuit of a merely mechanical regularity led him to lose sight of the proper divisions of the thought and of that regular structure which actually does exist. Each section contains, in addition to a brief conclusion, three subdivisions, not counted off into precisely the same number of verses, but with entire freedom as to length, and arising out of the nature of the subject discussed. Of the four principal sections the first and second are preliminary, the third contains the main body of the argument, and the fourth is supplementary.

The first and second sections are intended to pave the way for the discussions proper, by presenting facts and reasonings, upon which the considerations alleged for the settlement of the question at issue are then based. The first section, chaps. 1 and 2, contains a preliminary argument from Solomon's own experience, designed to show that happiness is not in man's own power; that all his striving and toiling, though it may surround him with every source of gratification his heart can desire, is powerless to give that gratification itself. After announcing 1:1, the author, he proceeds to state his theme, 1:2, 3, the vanity of men's toil and acquisitions; they cannot yield the happiness so confidently expected from them. To the illustration of this theme he now proceeds. He first, 1:4–11, lays down the postulate essential to the validity of any general deductions from an individual experience of the uniformity of sequences in the world, where the same phenomena are constantly repeating themselves. The earth, with its established laws, abides through every shifting generation. The sun, the wind, the rivers in their constant motions, maintain their uniformity. The same is true, v. 8, of every thing; one would never have done telling, seeing, hearing the numberless examples of like purport. The thing that hath been, it is that which shall be. There is nothing new. Things will happen in all time to come just as they have done in the past; though there is too little disposition to remember and profit by the lessons of experience.

Having thus established the universality and permanence of uniform sequences in the world, he proceeds to state his own experience with its results. The same results must, from the principle just laid down, follow in every like case; whence he is warranted in drawing from these premises the universal conclusion at which he is aiming. His experience is given first in general, 1:12–18, and then with more detail, 2:1–11. The general account of it is rendered more emphatic by its repetition in precisely the same form, vv. 12–15, vv. 16–18. He describes first his favorable situation for trying a satisfactory experiment, v. 12, v. 16, he was a king, and superior to all former dwellers in Jerusalem; the experiment itself, vv. 13, 14a, v. 17a, he tested everything, whether wise or foolish; the result, vv. 14b, 15, vv. 17b, 18, it was all empty and unsatisfactory. There was in everything he attempted something crooked that could not be made straight, or deficient that could not be rendered complete. There was always something to render the unalloyed happiness that he sought, unattainable; and that something could not be got rid of, for it arose from a vice inherent in earthly things. He then goes on, 2:1–11, to specify more particularly some of the methods in which he sought happiness but failed to find it; merriment, conviviality, splendid buildings, fine grounds, retinues, wealth, music. In fine, he surrounded himself with everything his heart desired; and yet surveying it all while still in the secure possession of it, he found it emptiness and vanity. It did not yield him happiness.

In addition to the unsatisfactory nature of these things in themselves, the brevity of their possession, and the uncertainty of what shall become of that which has been accumulated with so much pains and toil, are alleged, 2:12–23, as fresh reasons for disappointment and vexation. Solomon had tried his experiment under circumstances as favorable as any man could have, v. 12, and yet he found that whatever might be the intrinsic superiority of wisdom over folly, it could not preserve from death, which would consign him to oblivion, vv. 13–17, and hand over all his acquisitions, so painfully accumulated, to no one knows whom, vv. 18–23. And yet, for such a good as this, so unsatisfactory, so fleeting, and so precarious, men will toil and make themselves miserable all their days.

The conclusion from this experience of his own is drawn, vv. 24–26. Translated as it is in the common version, ver. 24 yields a good sense, and is conformed to 3:12, 13, 22, 5:18, 8:15. The meaning would be, that enjoyment or happiness is a better thing than all these unsatisfying accumulations which have been described, and which men toil so to obtain. The precise form of the conclusion in the original Hebrew is, however, slightly different. The word rendered "better," is not properly in the comparative degree. It should be read, "Good is not in man (*i.e.* within his power or control) that he should eat and drink, and that he should make his soul enjoy good in his labour." Man has not the ability in himself to extract enjoyment from his acquisitions. The ability to enjoy, which is quite distinct from the possession of things to be enjoyed, is the gift of God. Solomon's experience is conclusive upon this point; for no man could go beyond what he did. As enjoyment is the gift of God, he assigns it only to the good; but to the wicked he gives the empty and vexatious toil of accumulating what shall afterwards be converted to the uses of the good.

This point thus proved from Solomon's personal experience is in the second section, chaps. 3–5, proved again from current facts of observation. He here passes from what he had himself done and felt to what he had seen. The structure of the argument is precisely the same as before. There is first a postulate essential to its validity, 3:1–15, then the facts observed, 3:16–4:16, then reasonings upon them, 5:1–17, and finally the conclusion, 5:18–20. The uniform sequences of the first postulate are in the second, to meet the exigencies of this new argument, traced to their source in the all-embracing and admirable plan of God. He has a scheme in which every event, and all the multifarious actions of men, with the time of their occurrence, are definitely arranged. This scheme is, v. 11, a beautiful one, though from their prevailing worldliness men do not comprehend it. (So the English version. It is probable, however, that this verse ought to be translated, "He hath set eternity in their heart, because no man can find out the work that God maketh from the beginning to the end"; i.e., He gives men an idea of the vastness and eternity of his plan from their very incapacity to comprehend the whole of it.) Human welfare consisting, v. 12, in happiness and goodness, is, v. 13, constituted the gift of God by this, v. 14, permanent and unalterable plan, whose aim is to lead to piety, and which, v. 15, embraces within itself that uniformity of sequence before insisted on.

He next proceeds to allege various facts, of constant occurrence in the world, upon which his argument is to be constructed. The first is 3:16, unrighteousness in halls of justice. It is so grievous an anomaly, that tribunals which are looked to for the rectifying of abuses existing elsewhere, should themselves originate injustice from which there appears to be no appeal; and this seems to be so serious an exception to his grand doctrine, that justice rules in the world and happiness attends right-doing, that he pauses to give its explanation before adducing the other facts which he has to allege. His postulate ensures, v. 17, that this seeming inequality shall be rectified by God's future judgment, though meanwhile its existence is temporarily permitted, vv. 18–21, to prove men and to exhibit to them their frailty; for, however they may tyrannize over each other, death shall level them with the brutes. And yet how few consider their immoral nature, in which their real eminency lies? The conclusion previously drawn is valid, therefore, even in this case, v. 22, happiness which requires no crime in order to its attainment, is better than the gains of the unjust judge, which he can no longer enjoy (ראה ב) after death.

We are certainly not disposed to yield to those who would alter the text of 3:21, so as to change its assertion of man's immortality into an expression of doubt, "Who knoweth whether the spirit of man goeth upward, etc.," for the mere sake of making the writer contradict himself, and express a sentiment unworthy of his inspiration.

The remaining facts alleged are, 4:1–3, oppressions so grievous as to make life a burden; vv. 4–6, the envy attendant upon success, which is an argument not for idleness but for moderation; vv. 7–12, the selfish toil of the solitary, unmindful of the advantages to be derived from society; vv. 13–16, the temporary nature of the most brilliant rewards of wisdom, illustrated by the case of one who raised himself by wise conduct from poverty to a throne and yet who, after all, formed one in the endless procession of mankind unremembered and unpraised.

In proceeding to reason upon the facts now stated, he first, 5:1–7, utters a caution against being seduced to irreligion, to a neglect of religious duty, or to inconsiderate language reflecting upon God's providence by such contemplations. In regard to the case of oppression, which was the first that had been alleged, he appeals, v. 8, to the fact that there is always a tribunal higher than those by whom it is perpetrated, to which appeal may be made, and ultimately, as the highest of all, there is the tribunal of God. Ver. 9 continues the same thought, and should be rendered, "Moreover a profit to the land in all is a king served by the field" (i.e., land. Comp., field of Zoan, Ps. 70:12, 43). Good government by a supreme officer, to whom respect and obedience are yielded, is a great blessing to a country. It is a source of the rectification of abuses such as those described. These wrongs, which are acknowledged to exist, find redress therefore in a superior government, human or divine.

In respect to the other cases alleged, considerations are adduced, vv. 10–17, freshly confirming the truth to which they point, of the unsatisfying nature of human toil and accumulations. The first is, v. 10, to the insatiable character of human desire, which always outruns acquisition, however great that may be. The second, v. 11, that wealth is consumed by others more than by its owners. The third, v. 12, that it occasions disquiet of mind. The fourth, vv. 13–16, that its possession is uncertain and brief. Its owner may lose it by "evil travail," by some unfortunate enterprise. He will certainly be stripped of the whole at death, and leave the world as naked as he entered it. And yet for so empty a good as this he will, v. 17, spend all his days in painful and distressing toil.

The conclusion is, vv. 18–20, that not riches but enjoyment is the thing to be desired. The capacity to enjoy is independent of, and additional to worldly accumulations, and is the gift of God. He to whom God gives it shall not distress himself with frequent recollections of past sorrows, or anxious solicitude for the future. The condition of this gift has been stated before, 2:26, and is not here repeated. Men may be striving after it all their days and never attain it, if they do not seek it in that way in which, according to his uniform plan, he chooses to bestow it. Happiness and goodness are by him linked together. And only they who possess the latter can gain the former.

Having settled this preliminary point, both by his own experience and observation, he is now prepared in the third section, 6:1–8:15, to grapple with the main question. He has shown, but without stating as yet to what he means to apply it, that enjoyment is preferable to worldly accumulations, that it does not necessarily result from them, but is the gift of God, and its bestowment is regulated by his grand and beautiful plan. The next step, and this constitutes the central portion of the whole book, is to apply this to the explanation of the inequalities of divine providence. Three considerations are adduced as furnishing the solution of this perplexing problem, so that we have, as in the preceding sections, three divisions and a conclusion. The inequalities in question may be explained,

1. 6:1–7:15, by a just estimate of men's outward fortunes.
2. 7:16–29, by a just estimate of their characters.
3. 8:1–14, by a reference to government, human and divine, which will sooner or later distribute evenhanded justice.

In relation to the fortunes of men it is shown, chap. 6, that prosperity may not be a good. For a man may have wealth and honor and everything he wishes, and yet never have any enjoyment of them. The same is true of other forms of outward good, numerous children and long life, which even putting the case in the most extravagant and exaggerated form, may yield no pleasure. Human desires are insatiable. The advantages of the wise over the fool is that he knows that the sight of the eyes is better than the wandering of the desire; he contents himself with what he has in actual possession, instead of allowing his desires to prove unsatisfied after unattained good. This incapacity of worldly things to yield enjoyment is, v. 10, a permanent and unalterable fact, because it rests upon the ordinance of God. As man is mere man, he cannot contend with nor set aside that connection between earthly things and dissatisfaction which the Almighty has established. Hence, vv. 11, 12, if external prosperity in so many cases only increases what is empty and unsatisfying, what real good or intrinsic advantage is there in it? In point of fact, no man knows in his ignorance of the future whether outward prosperity will be an actual good to him or not.

Having thus presented one side of the subject, that prosperity is not always nor necessarily a good, he goes on, 7:1–14, to state the converse, that adversity or affliction is not necessarily an evil, but may be, and often is, a greater good than prosperity itself. This is expressed by bringing together a number of proverbs, showing, vv. 1–4, that scenes of sadness, and, vv. 5, 6, what may occasion present pain, may prove more salutary in their effect than festivity and mirth. Ver. 7, "Oppression maketh a wise man mad"; the opportunity or the habit of oppressing others will turn the head of the best of men. Such elevation so abused will be no advantage, but the most serious spiritual injury. "And a gift," i.e., one received as a bribe by a person exercising judicial functions, "destroyeth the heart," blinds or corrupts the understanding. It is better, vv. 8, 9, to wait the issue of God's dispensations than impatiently to fret and find fault with them, or, v. 10, to contrast the real or imaginary discomforts of the present with the pleasures of the past, as though a condition less agreeable were therefore worse. This is not a wise view of the case, for, vv. 11, (marg.) 12, there is something better than outward good, and which may be furthered by affliction. Besides, vv. 13, 14, affliction is the appointment of God, which man cannot alter; and it and prosperity are distributed in the manner that they are "to the end that man should find nothing after him," that he may not anticipate the future, but may be kept in a state of constant dependence and trust in God for whatever lies beyond the present; which would not be so much the case if there were some evident rules for the distribution of good and evil. Whence it is, v. 15, that men often seem in the divine allotments to be treated irrespective of their characters, the just man perishing in his righteousness, and the wicked prolonging his life in his wickedness.

This, then, is the first consideration adduced for the settlement of this difficult enigma. The perishing of the one may not be in reality the evil that it is supposed to be, nor the prolongation of the life of the other the good that it is imagined. So that while their fortunes, viewed externally, appear to be in contrast with their characters, if we but penetrate beneath the surface the opposition will disappear.

The second consideration is drawn, 7:16–29, from the character of men. Those whom we suppose to be suffering unjustly, may not be so good as we think they are. Conformity to the preceding might lead us to expect a converse to this argument also, but it does not admit of one. When bad men prosper, it is not because they are inwardly better than they outwardly appear. There is, v. 16, an excess of seeming righteousness, or of what passes for it in the estimate of its possessor and of others, which will as surely and as justly be visited with destruction as, v. 17, the opposite extreme of wickedness. That the caution, not to be "righteous overmuch," cannot mean that there is danger of possessing too much real piety is apparent not only from the absurdity of such a sentiment in itself, its opposition to other passages in this book where piety is inculcated without any such limit, and the incongruity of such an utterance from an inspired writer; but also, from v. 18, where the fear of God is declared to be an effectual preservative against this extreme, as well as its opposite. What precise form of religious excess Solomon had in his mind, it may not be easy to determine, as he does not more precisely define it. It may have been purposely left indefinite, with the view of covering all such pseudo-religious manifestations, as Pharisaical ostentation, sanctimoniousness and self-righteous conceit, censoriousness of others, multiplied acts of uncommanded will-worship, etc. Wisdom will, v. 19, be a surer protection against all such errors and excesses than ten valiant captains with their armies would be to a city.

Besides the fact already stated, that much which passes under the guise of piety is not really such, but is as punishable as grosser acts of sin; it is added, vv. 20–22, that none are faultless in deed and word, as every man's heart must assure him with regard to himself; and, vv. 23–29, notwithstanding the original uprightness of man's nature, the truly virtuous and good are as one in a thousand. Whether the abandoned woman, v. 26, is spoken of with the view of instancing a particular sin of great enormity, or whether she is, as some suppose, the personification of folly or sin in general, ensnaring men by its meretricious charms, the sense of the entire passage is not affected.

A right application of the considerations already urged will doubtless remove a large proportion of the apparent inequalities of providence. Those which still remain are provided for by the third consideration, 8:1–14, of the existence of a righteous government. After bestowing, v. 1, a passing commendation on the wisdom which can solve such perplexing enigmas as this, and can dissipate the gloom which they occasion, he proceeds, vv. 2–5, to refer to the righteous awards of human government. The obligation of obedience to its authority is attended with a divine sanction. Persistence in evil provokes its penalties, good conduct escapes them. The doctrine is precisely that of Rom. 13:1–5. It is not that human governments are never unjust and oppressive; the contrary is admitted and provided for, v. 9. But the administration of justice is the design for which they are ordained of God and instituted amongst men; this is the professed end of those who conduct them; and in spite of every perversion this is to a considerable degree really accomplished.

From human government, considered as rectifying disorders, he passes in the last clause of v. 5 to God's supreme control, employing language similar to that used, 3:1, of the same subject, only adding to his previous announcement that God has a time for everything in his admirable plan, the fact which is of equal consequence here, that he has "judgment" likewise. Everything is harmoniously disposed precisely at the right time, and all is equitably administered upon principles of justice. The meaning of v. 6 is obscured by an improper rendering of its particles. Instead of "because . . . therefore," it should read "for . . . for." God's harmonious and equitable administration is not productive of misery to men. But the greatest of human misery, man's utter ignorance of the future, his inability to resist the assaults of death or to escape from peril by his wickedness, are so many proofs that the sovereign control of all things is vested not in his hands, but in those of God, whose sway must be well-ordered and just. Rulers inflicting injury upon their subjects, v. 9; the wicked honored (with burial), v. 10; the righteous maltreated (lit. they who have done right must go from the holy place and be forgotten in the city) and such delays of justice, v. 11, as encourage men in their transgression, do not prevent but that, vv. 12, 13, the most exact justice shall be meted out to all. This shall be the case notwithstanding the apparent contrariety of the fact, v. 14, that the fate of the wicked sometimes seems to befall the just, and *vice versa*. The enigma is now solved, as far at least as a solution is practicable. The considerations adduced embrace all that can be offered in its explanation. The section is accordingly brought to a close, v. 15, by the standing formula which these reasonings have served freshly to confirm, that enjoyment is the best thing which earth affords. That serene enjoyment which is the portion only of the good, is to be preferred above all those accumulations which the wicked may possess, and which men are tempted to do wickedly in order to obtain.

The fourth section, 8:16–12:14, is, as has been before said, supplementary to the preceding. It does not re-open the argument, which is not finished, but is occupied with the removal of discouragements and the enforcing of practical lessons. We have, as in former cases, three divisions and a conclusion. The remaining mystery of this subject need be no obstacle to human joy, 8:16–9:9, nor to the most strenuous activity, 9:10–11:6, while in both their joy and their activity men should be mindful of death and judgment, 11:7–12:8. The conclusion follows, 12:9–14.

After all that can be said toward their explanation, there are yet, 8:17, insolvable mysteries in divine providence. No one can tell, 9:1, by God's treatment of particular individuals, whether they are objects of his love or hatred, v. 2, the good and the bad appear to fare alike, vv. 3–6, the existence of sin and death involve the most perplexing mysteries. But this, vv. 7–9, should prevent no one from enjoying life with a constant sense of the divine favor.

Nor is it any obstacle to the most energetic action, v. 10, but the reverse. When it is said that "there is no work, nor device, nor knowledge, nor wisdom in the grave whither thou goest," it is manifest that this is no denial of a future state of intelligent activity, any more than, vv. 5, 6, where the meaning is more fully explained by saying that the dead "have no more a portion for ever in anything that is done under the sun," i.e., in this world. Men should labor with their might. It is true, vv. 11, 12, that the results attained do not always correspond with what might be expected from the means employed. And yet on the whole and as a general rule, 9:13–10:20, wisdom is advantageous and folly is ruinous. And, 11:1–6, this general certainty, even though no positive assurance of a successful result can be attained in each individual case, is a sufficient warrant and incitement to vigorous exertion.

The advantages of wise action are first illustrated, 9:13–16, by the case of a city delivered by a poor wise man from the siege of a powerful king. The same thought is then exhibited in a series of apothegms to the close of chap. 10. This passage, it will be perceived, is directed to precisely the same point with the entire book of Proverbs. And it is observable to what an extent the style of the two books is here identical, possessing the same terse brevity and the same lack of connection between the individual sentences, while all conspire to teach the same general truth. The attempt to force a more intimate connection upon this passage than the writer designed or than its nature will allow, has resulted in the strangest misinterpretations. Thus because rulers are referred to, vv. 4–7, and again, vv. 16, 17, and v. 20, it has been quite common for interpreters to insist upon explaining all the intermediate verses in reference to the same subject. So vv. 8–10 are made to teach the evils resulting from premature or ill-concerted attempts to throw off the yoke of bad government; and v. 18, the injury arising to the edifice of the state from negligent rulers, whose revels and avarice are supposed to be described, v. 19. Upon the wretched government, under which it is thus (with the help of 8:2–5, perverted to precisely its opposite sense, and v. 17 being pronounced spurious, as inconsistent with the context) made out that the author must have lived, is based the conclusion that this could not have been written by Solomon. Our answer to which is, that the argumentation has about as much connection with the text as Geier's notion that the times spoken of, 3:2–8, are the seven periods of the church militant.

The propriety and even necessity of acting upon a general presumption, without demanding particular certainties, is variously illustrated, 11:1–6. Even where there seems so little antecedent likelihood of return as in casting bread upon the waters, it should be done in the hope of finding it after many days. The possibility of some time needing their assistance, is a reason for making friends everywhere by benevolent action. When the clouds are full, they empty themselves upon the earth, it may be sometimes uselessly on the rock or on barren land, yet on the whole the benefit is immense. So a tree may fall this way or that, on one man's land or another's, but it will be likely in any case to do somebody good. If a man were to insist on certainties, or even on having always the most favorable conditions prior to his acting, he would never do anything. "He that observeth the wind, shall not sow; and he that regardeth the clouds shall not reap." As, therefore, we neither understand God's natural, nor his providential operations, the only proper course is to be diligent in right action; some of it will succeed, even if all does not.

After placing death and the coming judgment before its readers as a solemn fact which should never be lost sight of amid their pleasures, and which should influence all their conduct, the book is brought to a formal close. The conclusion of the entire discussion is stated to be: Fear God and keep his commandments; for this is the whole welfare of man; for God shall bring every work into judgment, with every secret thing, whether it be good or whether it be evil.

"CONFESSIONS OF A WORKAHOLIC"

A REAPPRAISAL OF QOHELETH

Robert K. Johnston

This chapter seeks to reopen the question of the hermeneutical posture taken with regard to Qoheleth (Ecclesiastes). It goes beyond the question of Qoheleth's intent (his specific reason for writing), by inquiring into his intentionality (his underlying consciousness, i.e., the implied author's tone or stance toward his world). The discussion moves along the following lines: (1) structural, (2) philological, (3) thematic, (4) comparative, and (5) textual. In each of these categories, there is no attempt at exhaustive analysis. Rather, a theological interpretation is offered in the hope of challenging those critics who would reduce Qoheleth too quickly to a cynical or pessimistic posture.

In order that this objective be accomplished, the affirmative side of Qoheleth's thought is purposely emphasized. In the process, undue weight is given to Qoheleth's advice to enjoy created life as a gift from God. In reality, this advice serves in the text as a brief counterpoint to the main argument—Qoheleth's discussion of man's inability to discover the key to life's meaning. This latter theme is Qoheleth's intent. That is, it is the occasion and

From *Catholic Biblical Quarterly* 38 (1976): 14–28. Reprinted by permission.

purpose for the writing of this text. But interspersed within the discussion are hints of Qoheleth's intentionality—his mind-set or underlying consciousness.[1] It is this that surfaces within his admonition to enjoy life as a gift from God, the Creator. Qoheleth is skeptical in his intent, but affirmative in his intentionality.

The direction of this interpretive essay suggests that Qoheleth's stance toward life has been clouded by commentators unable to break out of their alien (to Qoheleth) work-dominated mind-sets. Qoheleth need not be considered[2] as standing in resignation on the periphery of the wisdom tradition. Rather he can be understood as indirectly, but fondly, calling the tradition back to a central focus—the enjoyment of life itself. The *"art* of steering" (Prov. 1:5), not the *"task* of mastering life"; God's *gift* of life, not man's *effort* at control; the aesthetic over the ethical—this Qoheleth affirms.

How to Understand Qoheleth?

Gerhad von Rad, in his book *Wisdom in Israel,* makes the comment in passing that Qoheleth's concern in discussing God's determination of the "times" (*ʿēt*) "is, in the last resort, not a theoretical one, or a theological one, but an explicitly pastoral one."[3] Scholars have, in interpreting Ecclesiastes, rightly pointed out the problematics of translating *qōhelet* as "preacher." Without challenging the linguistic side of the argument, I propose that if Qoheleth's advice in his work as a whole is examined from within its own hermeneutical presuppositions, then the reader will find the epithet "preacher," in the sense of "pastor," to be an appropriate one, at least theologically, if not linguistically. It is my thesis that we have done Qoheleth an injustice both by viewing his work as the extremity of Israelite wisdom's theological speculation and by interpreting its spirit to be one of overarching resignation and despair. Qoheleth is not merely giving his reader the pessimistic results of his attempt to wrest meaning from life. Rather, his book is constructed as a "guide to *life.*"[4]

---

1. I am grateful to Brian W. Kovaks for the use of the terms "intent" and "intentionality" (borrowing from Husserl) in regards to wisdom literature. (Kovaks, "Structure of Intentionality in Wisdom: Foundations of Ethics and Value in the Aphoristic Literature," paper presented to SBL, Southeastern Sectional Meeting, March, 1974.)

2. Cf. James Crenshaw, "The Eternal Gospel (Eccl. 3:11)," *Essays in Old Testament Ethics* (eds. J. Crenshaw, J. Willis; J. Philip Hyatt Festschrift; New York: KTAV, 1974) 29–30, 46, 48, who argues that Qoheleth's mood was one of "tragic pessimism." "Historical existence is for him a living *in tormentis.*" Crenshaw believes that Qoheleth "swims alone against the powerful stream of the whole 'wisdom establishment.'" "Unable to draw strength and courage from a vital relationship with God, who seems not to have been a 'You' to him, Qoheleth can only say: 'whether it is love or hate man does not know' (9:1). Here stands secular man. . . ."

3. G. von Rad, *Wisdom in Israel* (tr. J. D. Martin; New York: Abingdon, 1972) 227–28.

4. D. B. Macdonald, *The Hebrew Philosophical Genius: A Vindication* (Princeton: Princeton U. Press, 1936) 211.

Qoheleth is not turning his back on the whole wisdom undertaking, as von Rad[5] posits. He is calling it to return to the central focus of wisdom itself and its chief referent—life. As Roland Murphy has pointed out, "The kerygma of wisdom can be summed up in one word: life."[6] Commentators have had trouble, however, applying this insight to Ecclesiastes.[7] For there, the Biblical text begins bleakly, "Vanity of vanities; all is vanity" (1:2), and moves on to exclaim, "Therefore, I hated life ..." (2:17). Although there is throughout the book a constant counterpoint given—that man is to enjoy life (2:24–26; 3:12–13; 3:22; 5:17–19; 7:14; 8:15; 9:7–9; 11:9–12:1), biblical scholars have most often subordinated this theme, choosing instead to view the vanity motif (or some variant of it) as the focus of Ecclesiastes. Parenthetically, it is usually noted that Qoheleth does observe that God *may* give man some *small* pleasure along the way to *ease* his existence.[8] Qoheleth's advice to enjoy one's food and drink is, therefore, interpreted by these commentators as being bitter-sweet, possibly even ironic.

For example, in his seminal article on wisdom literature, Zimmerli describes Qoheleth as one "who feels this freedom of God as a painful limitation of his own impulse to go out into the world by wisdom and to master the world."[9] It is life inhibiting. Again, von Rad in his excellent book *Wisdom in Israel* defines Qoheleth's "three basic insights round which his thoughts continually circle" as the following:

1. A thorough, rational examination of life is unable to find any satisfactory meaning; everything is "vanity." 2. God determines every event. 3. Man is unable to discern these decrees, the "works of God" in the world.[10]

5. von Rad, *Wisdom in Israel*, 265.

6. Roland Murphy, "The Kerygma of the Book of Proverbs," *Int* 20 (1966) 9; cf. Walter Brueggemann, *In Man We Trust: The Neglected Side of Biblical Faith* (Richmond: John Knox, 1972) 14; Norbert Lohfink, *The Christian Meaning of the Old Testament* (tr. R. A. Wilson; Milwaukee: Bruce, 1968) 140: "Man's purpose must be that those years be truly filled with 'life' .... This is the automatic assumption of the ancient Israelite wisdom, based on experience, whenever it mentions death."

7. An exception is D. B. Macdonald, *Hebrew Philosophical Genius*, 138, though Macdonald's understanding of Qoheleth's view of God largely vitiates his findings. Norbert Lohfink, in *Christian Meaning of the Old Testament*, 152, recognizes in Qoheleth's thought a "love for life, one based upon God." Cf. also Edwin Good, *Irony in the Old Testament* (Philadelphia: Westminster, 1965) 173, 190.

8. Cf. Roland Murphy, "Ecclesiastes," JBC, I, 535; R. B. Y. Scott, *Proverbs: Ecclesiastes* (AB, 17; Garden City, N.Y.: Doubleday, 1965) 191, 221: "Thus, in place of a religion of faith and hope and obedience, this writer expresses a mood of disillusionment and proffers a philosophy of resignation." According to Qoheleth, man can "enjoy such passing happiness as God may grant him."

9. Walther Zimmerli, "The Place and Limit of Wisdom in the Framework of the Old Testament Theology," *SJT* 17 (1964) 157.

10. von Rad, *Wisdom in Israel*, 227–28.

What is conspicuously ignored in this listing is anything of the acceptance and enjoyment of life as a gift from God—something central to the wider wisdom tradition. Von Rad's conclusion is in basic agreement with that of R. B. Y. Scott, Roland Murphy, Walther Zimmerli, James Crenshaw, and Robert Gordis (in his earlier writings): "Koheleth has come to terms with his situation, even if it is with a resignation that can leave no reader unmoved."[11]

Although Gordis in his earlier writings adopted such a position concerning Qoheleth's alleged resignation, he has become dissatisfied with such a negative appraisal.[12] In *Koheleth—the Man and His World*, he discards his earlier focus upon Qoheleth's "resignation" and understands the "basic theme of the book" to be "*simhâ,* the enjoyment of life."[13] Edwin Good concurs with Gordis, quoting him when he says:

> For Koheleth, joy is God's categorical imperative for man, not in any anemic or spiritualized sense, but rather as a full-blooded and tangible experience, expressing itself in the play of the body and the activity of the mind, the contemplation of nature and the pleasures of love.[14]

And Norbert Lohfink expresses a similar viewpoint in his chapter "Man Face to Face with Death." Although Qoheleth's hatred of life has arisen from the stark fact of death, according to Lohfink, this is an intermediate stage. Qoheleth's final attitude, and the posture from which he writes, is his recognition of life's joys. We should accept "the gift of happiness in the present moment from the hand of God."[15]

The Analysis

Gordis, Good, and Lohfink are minority voices among scholars of Qoheleth. There is, I believe, ultimately a hermeneutical bias that has caused their position to be ignored. However, before discussing this possibility, it is necessary to look at the text itself in order to reacquaint ourselves with certain data from it that is often passed over.

11. Ibid. 223. Cf. Scott, *Proverbs: Ecclesiastes,* 191; Zimmerli, "Place and Limit of Wisdom," 157; Murphy, "Ecclesiastes," 535; Crenshaw, "The Eternal Gospel," 28; Robert Gordis, *The Wisdom of Ecclesiastes* (New York: Behrman House, 1945) 23.

12. It is interesting to note that in reworking his article on "Koheleth the Man" for his book *Koheleth—the Man and His World* (3d ed.; New York: Schocken, 1968), Gordis deleted several paragraphs from his previous discussion which had appeared in *The Wisdom of Ecclesiastes* (1945), including the following: ". . . his attitude stemmed not from a full-hearted acceptance of the world, as preached by religion, but from a sense of frustration and resignation by his philosophy" (Gordis, *The Wisdom of Ecclesiastes,* 23).

13. Gordis, *Koheleth,* 131.

14. Ibid., 119, quoted in Good, *Irony in the Old Testament,* 192.

15. Lohfink, *Christian Meaning of the Old Testament,* 154–55.

Structural Remarks

Addison Wright has with some justification labeled the problem of the book of Ecclesiastes' structure, "The Riddle of the Sphinx."[16] It is, thus, with a certain tentativeness that one looks at the overall unity of the book to learn from it concerning Qoheleth's intention and intentionality. In doing so, however, one finds that several interesting structural devices do in fact come to light. Ignoring the book's title (1:1), epigrams (1:2; 12:8), and epilogue (12:9–14), one discovers that Qoheleth begins with a poem concerning the "profit"-lessness of man's toil (1:3–11) and ends with another poem calling man to enjoy life while he can (11:9–12:7). From a focus upon the vanity of toil, Qoheleth turns to sing a paean of praise to life as it was meant to be lived, though he hastens to add that we all grow old and die. These two poems set the tone and direction of Qoheleth's investigation and reflection. From a focus on the pointlessness of a work orientation—on the profitlessness of man's toil when it is absolutized and, thus, misused—Qoheleth turns to argue for the importance of enjoying life from God as a gift while we can. "Enjoyment," not "work," is to be our controlling metaphor of life.

Secondly, regarding structure, Qoheleth's advice in his writing is sometimes held to fall into two sections. If the first extends from 1:2 through 6:9, and the second, from 6:10 through 11:16, as Addison Wright suggests, then Ecclesiastes 6:7–9 can be understood as a summary paragraph of the first part of Qoheleth's presentation. The form of this section is consistent with other sequences of ideas within the first half of Qoheleth (see below, ["Selected Texts"] for a discussion of 2:18–26; 3:1–15; 3:16–4:3; 4:4–16; 5:9–6:6). Each begins with a negative judgment concerning life's toil and meaning, which is then contrasted with advice to live life authentically and/or joyfully, which, in turn, is hastily qualified lest this affirmative advice be misinterpreted and changed into the *key* to life's mystery.

Thus in 6:7–8, Qoheleth begins with his negative conclusion: there is no advantage, no self-profit, either in toil or in wisdom. He then counters with the positive assertion in 6:9, "Better is the sight of the eyes than the wandering of desire." This, in turn, is qualified by the concluding, oft repeated phrase, "This also is vanity and a striving after wind" (RSV). By making this melancholic qualification, Qoheleth is not taking back his preferred advice, but hedging it against any false apotheosis. It is best to look at *(mar'ēh)* the

---

16. Addison Wright, "The Riddle of the Sphinx: The Structure of the Book of Qoheleth." *CBQ* 30 (1968) 313–34. Cf. James Crenshaw, who also speaks of the mystery of the book's structure: "The attempts at structural analysis on the basis of logical coherence and stylistic characteristics have failed to create a consensus, due chiefly to their subjective nature. Perhaps this failure bears witness to the aphoristic quality of the book, and suggests that the author may not have arranged his 'collection of sentences' in any logical fashion, but permitted random observations to intrude at will" (Crenshaw, "The Eternal Gospel," 26–27).

world honestly and openly; in doing so, however, one must not think he has mastered life's mystery.

According to Wright, in the second half of Ecclesiastes, the basic thrust of the argument revolves around the fact that we cannot "ascertain what God has done."[17] After a brief introduction (6:10–12) Qoheleth groups his ideas loosely into two sections. In the first (chs. 7–8), man is said to be unable to find out (*māsāʾ*) what is good to do. In the second (9:1–11:6), man is said to be unable to know (*yādaʿ*) the future. Turning to chapters seven and eight, we note that Qoheleth concludes this phase of his discussion as follows: "Therefore I commend enjoyment, because there is nothing good for man under the sun but to eat and to drink and to rejoice; for this will accompany him in his toil during the limited days of his life which God gives him under the sun" (8:15). Man is to enjoy life while he can, even given the stark reality that God's work on earth remains undiscoverable (8:16, 17).

In an analogous way, Qoheleth concludes his assessment that life's future remains unknowable (9:1–11:8; I believe Wright is mistaken in grouping 11:7–8 with the concluding poem) by offering the positive advice: "Light is sweet, and it is pleasing to the eyes to see the sun" (11:7). We are, he says, to enjoy the years we live (11:8), though he quickly adds that our days of darkness will come. Again the same pattern of a qualified optimism is present. Man can enjoy his life in the present, though he should be mindful of its transitoriness.

Philological Concerns

Turning to philological considerations, we observe that most of the internal unity of the book is provided by Qoheleth's repeated use of certain words and phrases, e.g., "vanity," "under the sun," "gift," "I knew." In the context of this chapter, three of Qoheleth's favorite expressions have particular relevance.

(1) *rāʾâ:* The verb *rāʾâ* is used by Qoheleth forty-seven times, having the general meaning of "to see." Although the nuance of *rāʾâ* varies, it is particularly interesting in our context to note Qoheleth's usage of *rāʾâ* in the sense of "to look into or at." Here, *rāʾâ* means to center one's interest, or thoughts, outside one's self, focusing them instead upon the object viewed. Depending on what is focused upon, such "intentionality" can be done with apprehension (11:4), with interest (3:22), or with joy (2:1). Three different times Qoheleth joins vectorially the word *rāʾâ* to the words *ṭôb* (good) and *āmāl* (labor) (2:24; 3:13; 5:17; cf. 2:1; 5:18; 6:9). Rather than continuing to manipulate his surroundings, rather than continuing to vainly work at mastering life, man, Qoheleth suggests, should instead *rāʾâ* (indwell, look into, enjoy, look at) the good in all of his labor. The same words *rāʾâ beṭôb* are used by Qoheleth in parallel with *ʾănasskâ beśimḥâ* (pleasure) in 2:1. To

17. Wright, "Riddle of the Sphinx," 330.

"see," in this sense of the word, is not to manipulate but to commune with and to enjoy the world. It is to let the *object* of one's vision become a *subject* as well.[18]

(2) *ʿml:* The root *ʿml* occurs in Ecclesiastes thirty-four times (*ʿāmāl*, n., twenty-one times; *ʿāmēl*, adj., five times; *ʿāmal*, v., eight times). Qoheleth associates two words with *ʿml* (work): *ḥēleq* (share, portion, lot. 2:10, 21; 3:22; 5:17, 18; 9:9) and *yitrôn* (profit, advantage: 1:3; 2:11; 3:9; 5:15). In his work (*ʿāmāl*) at mastering life, Qoheleth was seeking to gain some advantage over (*yitrôn*), some profit—some leverage in which he might approach his world as its master. Repeatedly Qoheleth makes his point that such toil is of no advantage (*yitrôn*). With this profit-motive, Qoheleth contrasts his advice to enjoy one's portion (*ḥēleq*) in this life (3:22; 5:17; 9:9). The same word (*ḥēleq*) is used elsewhere in Scripture in speaking of each soldier's "fair-share" of the booty (Gen. 14:24), and again, in speaking of that rightful "portion" of land that was to be allocated to the tribe of Simeon (Jos. 19:9).[19] In Ecclesiastes, one's work (*ʿāmāl*) is viewed both as one's portion (*ḥēleq*) and as one's attempted profit (*yitrôn*). Whether *ʿāmāl* is viewed as creative or destructive, enjoyable or dreary, depends upon which of these rubrics it is placed under.

(3) *śmḥ:* The root *śmḥ* occurs seventeen times in Ecclesiastes. Qoheleth's advice to man is that he accept his lot with joy (*śimḥâ*, "gladness," "mirth," "pleasure"; cf. 2:26; 5:19; 8:15; 9:7), and that he enjoy (*śamaḥ*, "rejoice in," "be glad"; cf. 3:12, 22; 5:18; 8:15; 11:8, 9) the days of his life that are granted him by God. In the OT *śāmaḥ* can denote either the communal jubilation of the festival or cult gathering (e.g., Ps. 45:16), or the individual's mood of joy in his heart (e.g., Prov. 14:13). It is interesting to observe that the Septuagint translated this word into the Greek as *euphrosynē*, and as such, it is used by the NT writers to speak of natural or common joy (e.g., the joy of a festive meal; cf. Luke 12:19), in contrast with one's joy in Christ (*charā*).[20] Thus Paul states in Acts 14:16, 17: "God let all the nations follow their own ways; and yet he did not leave himself without testimony, bestowing blessings, giving rains from heaven and fruitful seasons, filling your hearts with food and gladness (*euphrosynēs*)." It

---

18. This understanding of *rāʾâ* is in marked contrast to the NAB translation of *rāʾâ* in Eccles. 2:24: "To provide (*rāʾâ*) himself with good things by his labor." Cf. R. Murphy, *The Book of Ecclesiastes and the Canticle of Canticles* (*Pamphlet Bible Series* 38, New York: Paulist Press, 1962) 29.

19. Crenshaw misinterprets the import of *ḥēleq* when he writes: "One of the reasons for the scepticism is Qoheleth's recognition that *hakkol* [everything] is denied him. Only a *ḥēleq* is granted him, and even this is a direct *gift* of God." Crenshaw believes the root *ntn* (to give) is indicative of Qoheleth's pessimism, for it suggests that salvation is no longer automatic. Rather than suggest the portion of divine blessing, Crenshaw believes *ḥēleq* has been "neutralized" in Qoheleth and made to suggest God's distance and unknowableness (Crenshaw, "The Eternal Gospel," 28–34).

20. Rudolf Bultmann, "*euphrainō*," *TWNT,* II, 773.

is to this gift of God, the blessings of life given by the Creator to his creatures, that Qoheleth also appeals. We are to "rejoice" in our youth (Eccles. 11:9).

Thematic Analysis

Norbert Lohfink rightly understands Qoheleth's theme to be three-pronged: (1) death as the limit imposed upon human existence; (2) the hatred of life and the disillusionment that results from this realization; and (3) the reality of the present moment as a gift from God to be enjoyed.[21] Lohfink is correct in understanding the basic contours of the book, though somewhat limited by his preoccupation with death.

Reformulating Lohfink's thematic insights, I would understand Qoheleth to be concerned, first of all, with the limits of man's toil. These go beyond the fact that man's common lot, his destiny, is death (cf. 9:2, 3; 2:15; 3:19; 5:12–16; 6:6; 7:2; 8:8; 12:1–7). Other limits include the realization that man lives out his life amidst an indiscernible moral order (cf. 7:15; 8:14); that wisdom is transitory at best and life uncertain (cf. 4:13–16; 9:13–16); and that wisdom is fragile and easily defeated in the presence of riches and folly (cf. 9:16–10:1). Given all this, the arrogance of man's effort to control his fate is laughable.

Man's attempt to work at mastering life is misdirected, according to Qoheleth, not only because life's experiences belie the attempt, but also because it constitutes an effort to transgress upon divine independence. God is sovereign and inscrutable (cf. 3:11; 6:10–11; 7:13, 14, 23, 24; 8:17). Thus, we can neither find out what we are to do (cf. 6:12a; 7:29; 8:16, 17), nor know what will come after us (cf. 6:12b; 9:11–15; 10:14; 11:4–6).[22] Given life's experiences and God's inscrutability, all of man's activities have the mere weight of one's breath (*hebel*); they are like a chasing after wind (*rᵉ'ût rûaḥ*, 1:14).

Having noted (1) a range of limits imposed on man's experience, and (2) the resultant folly of man's attempt to master his life, Qoheleth (3) reasserts the sage advice that man's lot (*ḥēleq*) is to enjoy (*rā'â* or *śāmaḥ*) the life that God gives (*nātan*) him. Man's active participation and engagement in the world is not to be manipulative or assertive, but rather a "seeing" (*rā'â*: 2:24; 3:13; 5:17; cf. 9:9), or a rejoicing (*śāmaḥ*: 5:18; cf. 3:22, 8:15) in the good in all his labor, an affirming as "good" (*ṭôb*) of his eating and drinking (2:24–26; 5:17; 8:15; 9:7), a rejoicing in all one's present activities (3:22), and an affirmation that life was meant to be lived joyfully in community (9:9; 4:9–12). Qoheleth preaches that there must be an acceptance of life as given by God with both its joys and sorrows (7:14), and he argues for an active participation and engagement with life, despite its uncertainties (11:1–6).

---

21. Lohfink, *Christian Meaning of the Old Testament*, 140–55.

22. I am indebted to Wright ("Riddle of the Sphinx," 323) for pointing out the interesting repetitions of the word *māṣā'* (to find out) in Eccles. 7:1–8:17, and of the word *yāda'* (to know) in Eccles. 9:1–11:6.

Comparative Analysis

Walther Zimmerli, in his article, "The Place and Limit of Wisdom in the Framework of Old Testament Theology" (1964), understands the place of wisdom to be "within the framework of a theology of creation."[23] This is particularly true of Ecclesiastes which echoes much of Genesis 1–11.[24] Thus, Qoheleth recognizes, as does the Genesis creation accounts, that man is made from the dust and will return to it (Eccles. 12:7; 3:20; cf. Gen. 2:7; 3:19); that man was meant to live in companionship (Eccles. 4:9–12; 9:9; cf. Gen. 1:27; 2:21–25); that man is inclined to sin (Eccles. 7:29; 8:11; 9:3; cf. Gen. 3:1–13); that human knowledge has certain God-given limits (Eccles. 8:7; 10:14; cf. Gen. 2:17); that life is tiring toil (Eccles. 9:4–6; 11:8; cf. Gen. 3:19, 24; Gen. 4); and that God is sovereign (Eccles. 3:10–13; cf. Gen. 1:28–30; 3:5).

Moreover, Qoheleth is in agreement with the writer in Genesis who viewed the order and regularity of nature as a sign of God's graciousness and blessing (Gen. 8:21ff.). Thus, Qoheleth writes: "He has made everything beautiful in its time . . . I know that there is nothing better but that a man rejoice and do good in his life" (3:11–12).[25] Perhaps most importantly, Ecclesiastes and Genesis exhibit substantial agreement as to the central point of the creation motif—that life is to be celebrated as a "good" creation of God. Seven times in the opening chapter of Genesis, God looks at his creation and calls it "good" (*ṭôb*). Similarly, Qoheleth views life and concludes: "There is nothing better [lit., *ṭôb*, "good"] for a man, than that he should eat and drink, and that he should make his soul enjoy good (*ṭôb*) in his labor. This also, I saw was from the hand of God" (2:24).

Creation theology provides a strong contextual suggestion concerning Qoheleth's intention. If Ecclesiastes is part of the wisdom tradition, and wisdom finds its place in creation theology—moreover, if Qoheleth shows within his work a direct acquaintance with and dependence on the book of Genesis—

23. Zimmerli, "Place and Limit of Wisdom," 148.

24. Cf. Charles Forman, "Koheleth's Use of Genesis," *JSS* 5 (1960) 256–63; H. W. Hertzberg, *Der Prediger* (KAT, 17; Stuttgart: Mohn, 1963) 230: "Es ist kein Zweifel: das Buch Qoh ist geschrieben mit Gen. 1–4 vor den Augen seines Verfassers; die Lebensanschauung Qoh's ist an der Schöpfungsgeschichte gebildet."

25. In the quotation, an important phrase has been omitted. Qoheleth states that although God has made everything beautiful in its time, God has also "put the timeless into their hearts, without man discovering from beginning to end the work God has done." The word *hā'ôlām* ("timeless") has eluded precise definition, but the import of the passage does not seem to be the questioning of creation's order, but rather of man's ability to discover its secret and mystery. The key which would unlock the universe's secret remains with God. However, although the future-oriented secret of life eludes our grasp, we can still enjoy, in the present, life's beauty as it unfolds. Qoheleth does not deny the goodness of created life. (For a discussion of these verses, see also ["Selected Texts"]).

then it is not in the least surprising that Qoheleth seeks to affirm life as something to be celebrated and enjoyed as good, as something to be beheld reverently and interacted with joyously.

Scholars who have failed to see the connection between Qoheleth's advice to enjoy life and the affirmations of the Genesis creation accounts have sought to locate parallels in other directions. Both Gordis and Murphy believe that Qoheleth, in returning to the theme of enjoying the pleasures that God gives in this life, is "echoing the kind of advice" found in *Gilgamesh*.[26] In that tale, Siduri, the barmaid, tells Gilgamesh:

> Gilgamesh, whither rovest thou?
> The life thou pursuest thou shalt not find.
> When the Gods created mankind,
> Death for mankind they set aside,
> Life in their own hands retaining.
> Thou, Gilgamesh, let full thy belly.
> Make thou merry by day and by night.
> Of each day make thou a feast or rejoicing,
> Day and night dance thou and play!
> Let thy garments be sparking fresh,
> Thy head be washed; bathe thou in water.
> Pay heed to the little one that holds on to thy hand,
> Let thy spouse delight in thy bosom!
> For this is the task of mankind![27]

The similarities are indeed striking, but several differences cannot be glossed over. First, though ultimate meaning in life is illusive for Qoheleth as for Gilgamesh, Qoheleth believes we should still work and even "enjoy" our toil. He does not believe that man should only play, as Siduri does, and even warns against such an approach to life explicitly (Eccles. 2:1–11).

A second difference in these two works is apparent in Eccles. 9:7ff., where Qoheleth's advice most closely parallels that of Siduri. Tellingly, Qoheleth gives his justification for his advice, and it is far from the spirit of the Gilgamesh epic. He states, "Go to it, then, eat your food and enjoy it, and drink your wine with a cheerful heart, for *already* God has accepted what you have done" (NEB, italics mine). There is no resignation, nor is there an apotheosizing of play.[28] We are to enter life joyfully for God has ordained it.

---

26. Murphy, "Ecclesiastes," 492; Gordis, *Koheleth*, 54.
27. *ANET* 90a.
28. For a contrasting position, see R. B. Y. Scott, *Proverbs: Ecclesiastes*, 246.

Selected Texts

In discussing the structure of Ecclesiastes, I suggested that its poetic frame provides some indication of the alternatives which Qoheleth attempts to juxtapose—the "profit"-lessness of man's toil over against a recognition that life should be lived in joy. Qoheleth takes up these possible approaches to life time and again in his discussion. Because of the need to counter a false direction within the wisdom tradition, Qoheleth emphasizes the misuse of toil that results from a "work orientation" toward life, rather than dwelling on the joy inherent in life itself. Nevertheless, within the limitations imposed by his primary intent for his writing, Qoheleth presents the alternatives—"work" or "enjoyment" as one's controlling stance, or metaphor, toward life (i.e., one's intentionality).

This he does by making use of a dialectical, or alternating, pattern for his argument (I referred to this in discussing 6:7–9 earlier in this chapter. This pattern is also found in the movement from the opening to the concluding poems, and in the general shape of 7:1–8:17 and 9:1–11:8 discussed above). At least six times, including 6:7–9 (cf. 2:18–26; 3:16–4:3; 4:4–16; 5:9–12:6), Qoheleth presents his case using an approach which follows this structural framework: first, a lengthy presentation of some critical or negative observation concerning life which calls man's toil and effort into question; secondly, a brief statement of an alternate "playful" approach to life through which, man might better view his activity in the world; thirdly, the insertion (varying in length) of a hastily drawn qualification in order to protect against any interpretation of Qoheleth's positive advice which would turn it into another absolute which transgresses upon life's limitations and God's freedom.

It is the third-prong of this framework which has often been viewed differently by wisdom scholars. Those, for example, who have understood Qoheleth's posture to be that of a cynic have seen the role of these negative rejoinders in the text to be that of undermining and vitiating the previously proffered advice to find joy in life. Instead, Qoheleth should be understood (at least in the six instances noted above), as not having taken back or undercut his positive advice by this third aspect of his argument, but rather of having framed its positive import within its proper and needful limits. We have already seen the shape of this dialectic in operation in the poetic framework which Qoheleth provides for his discussion. Qoheleth in the opening poem portrays the vanity of man's toil. Then in the concluding poem he turns to suggest that man should rejoice in his youth, although he immediately adds that we all will grow old and die. By naming this melancholic qualification at the end of his poem in praise of life, Qoheleth is not taking back his advice. Rather, he is qualifying it against any false apotheosizing of joy by setting it within its God-given boundaries. Qoheleth does not want to fall back into the trap he has criticized as being vain—that of "mastering" life through one's self-effort (in this case, through one's joy). Man is to center his interest on the joy of the present, states Qoheleth, for any future-oriented "workful" approach toward discovering some ultimate meaning is vitiated by death.

Let us briefly observe how Qoheleth's use of negative qualifiers in the text to serve as "rightful limits" on these joyful admonitions rather than as "attempted retractions" applies to the remaining passages cited above:

Eccles. 2:18–26: In light of the fact that man must often indiscriminately leave the fruit of his toil to another, work has no ultimate value, suggests Qoheleth (2:18–23). Instead man is to eat and drink and *enjoy* his labor (2:24a). However, lest one believe that he now has the key to life's meaning, Qoheleth quickly reminds his readers that such enjoyment is dependent upon the hand of God. Man's pleasure depends on God's good pleasure, and the divine action cannot be neatly categorized or programmed by man (2:24b–26). Such an attempt would be a "striving after wind" (2:26).

Eccles. 3:1–15: Differences in interpretation of this passage would center upon 3:11b and 3:14, 15. Qoheleth believes that although God has made everything beautiful in its time, man cannot find out the key to life's meaning. Though beautiful, life remains mysterious and unmanipulatable (3:1–11). It is best, therefore, to enjoy God's present gifts to man as they unfold in life. These include both one's leisure and one's work (3:12–13). Such enjoyment however, Qoheleth hastens to add, rests in God the giver and not upon man's ability to control his world (3:14, 15). Qoheleth's positive advice in this passage is that man rest actively in the present which is given to him by God.

Eccles. 3:16–4:3: Qoheleth, here, recognizes the fate of both the righteous and the wicked to be the same—that which all men share even with the beasts: death (3:16–21). Given such an awareness, man should enjoy his lot in life now (3:22a), for the future is a mystery (3:22b) and injustice and oppression predominate (4:1–3). Although one's posture of joy toward life is transient, and although it does not reflect any ultimate meaning or insight, Qoheleth believes such happiness is authentic, nonetheless, as an approach to the present, even granted its moral problematics.

Eccles. 4:4–16: In these verses, Qoheleth continues his discussion on the vanity of toil by centering on the selfishness of man the "worker." All toil and all skill in work come out of a sense of rivalry or greed, states Qoheleth (4:4–8). Life, however, is meant to be lived in community (4:9–12). All such egocentric labor is, thus, pointless. Moreover, it will be rejected by those following after him (4:13–16). The alternatives are presented—the vanity of working at life alone, over against a recognition that life's toil and rest must be shared in community.

Eccles. 5:9–6:6: Qoheleth describes the vanity of seeking life's meaning in the possession of riches—riches both cause anxiety and are transitory (5:9–

16). What is good in life (while it lasts) is to enjoy life's riches which come from God, i.e., man's work and his leisure (5:17). It is important to remember, however, that even the power to be able to enjoy life is a gift from God. Man cannot hope to find enjoyment apart from such divine empowerment. Furthermore, without the empowering and thus the joy, life's good things are of no account to man (5:18–6:6).

In each of the above sections, I have purposely chosen to emphasize the affirmative side of Qoheleth's thought, in order that his underlying intentionality might surface. Set within Qoheleth's discussion of man's inability to discover the key to life's meaning are his admonitions to enjoy life as a gift from God, the Creator. As was stated at the outset, Qoheleth is skeptical in his intent, but affirmative in his intentionality. This distinction has too often been overlooked, and thus the text misunderstood. Qoheleth does not want to undermine his advice to enjoy life. He only wants to place it within the larger context of man's mistaken attempts to master life, given the mystery of life itself.

Conclusions

Qoheleth's intent in his writing is to pass judgment upon man's misguided endeavors at mastering life by pointing out its limits and mysteries. He would prefer that man replace such false and illusory hopes with a confidence based in the joy of creation as God's gift. The above analysis, while by no means exhaustive, is perhaps suggestive of the kinds of support possible for this interpretation. In conclusion, let me suggest a possible reason (one lying beyond the text itself) for the fact that this interpretation has largely been ignored by some wisdom scholars.

Walter Brueggemann, in his article, "Scripture and an Ecumenical Life-Style" (1970), discusses the five-fold nature of Biblical wisdom. His fourth point is that the biblical sages recognized "that life had been called good (Gen. 1:31), that it is for our enjoyment, celebration, appreciation."[29] However, in reworking this article for his opening chapter in *In Man We Trust* (1972), Brueggemann changed this spoke of wisdom's wheel to read, "Man is meant for an orderly role in an orderly cosmos. His rightful destiny is to discern that order and find his responsible share in it."[30] Brueggemann, in changing his wording from "celebrating" to "finding his responsible share" has shifted the focus ever so slightly from man as "player"—one who enjoys and celebrates life—to man as "worker," and in doing so has subtly misread the wisdom tradition. Rather than wisdom being understood as the "*art* of steering,"[31] it is viewed as man's *search* for order, his attempt to *master* life.

---

29. *Int* 24 (1970) 14.
30. Brueggemann, *In Man We Trust*, 23.
31. von Rad, *Old Testament Theology* (tr. D. M. G. Stalker; New York: Harper and Row, 1962) I, 421.

Brueggemann unfortunately has redirected his focus away from the celebrative aspect of the wisdom tradition. He has moved from the aesthetic, into the ethical mode of thinking.[32]

Brueggemann is following von Rad on this point, who is guilty of the same ambiguity and subtle misdirection. In summarizing wisdom's intention, for example, von Rad says, "There was surely only one goal, to wrest from the chaos of events some kind of order in which man was not continually at the mercy of the incalculable."[33] Several pages later, however, von Rad states: "The teachers here are working out only one perception with great keenness: Constitutive for man's humanity is the faculty of hearing. If he is not constantly listening to the order established by God, then he is lost."[34] Does the wise man "listen" or does he "wrestle"?

Von Rad states,

> The expression of what was known was something which one could freely enjoy. The teachers were aware of primeval wisdom's sporting with man (Prov. 8:31) and, in their own way, participated in that sport. The expression of what was true required poetic form; for Israel too, it was an aesthetic phenomenon.[35]

In the first volume of his *Old Testament Theology,* von Rad again rightly describes wisdom's posture:

> The purpose which these maxims are intended to serve could be called, rather than teaching, an art for living or at least a certain technique for life. The wise men who came later very picturesquely described wisdom as an art of steering (תחבלות, LXX κυβέρνησις, Prov. 1:5), the art of piloting oneself through the confusion of life.[36]

Von Rad saw wisdom's aesthetic dimension, aptly capturing its essence in his phrase "the *art* of steering." Unfortunately, he seems to have been unable in his reflection on wisdom to remain focused outside of "salvation-history" (work-dominated) categories. Thus he more often characterized wisdom as man's attempt at the "*task* of mastering life"—his straining to "wrest some form of order from chaos."[37]

There is a subtle but profound difference in viewing wisdom as the "*art* of steering" as opposed to "the *task* of mastering life." It is to Brueggemann's and von Rad's credit that they were able, however inconsistently, to break out of an alien work-dominated mind-set and to view wisdom from within its own

32. Cf. von Rad, *Wisdom in Israel,* 316.
33. Ibid., 308; cf. von Rad, *Old Testament Theology,* I, 420.
34. von Rad, *Wisdom in Israel,* 316.
35. Ibid.
36. von Rad, *Old Testament Theology,* I, 421.
37. Ibid., 418, 420.

hermeneutical presuppositions, i.e., as the aesthetic phenomenon that it is. Nevertheless, we must point out their inconsistency, and by doing so suggest something of the difficulty involved in remaining inside the mind-set of the wisdom writers.

Returning to Ecclesiastes, it becomes apparent that if the goal of OT wisdom is seen to be that of mastering life, of wresting from its chaos some order, then Qoheleth must be viewed as carrying out a frontal assault upon the tradition as a whole, and his advice to enjoy the "small" gifts (both work and play) that come man's way from God, as resigned or ironic conclusions that carry little consolation. If, however, the goal of Biblical wisdom is understood aesthetically as the "art of steering," and its theological focus is seen as resting squarely in creation, then Ecclesiastes' advice to enjoy life's work and play as given by God must be re-evaluated in this light. Rather than turning his back on the whole wisdom undertaking, as von Rad suggests, Qoheleth might better be understood as restating the central focus of the wisdom tradition itself.[38] For Qoheleth, life in all of its dimensions is a question of common grace, not of hard work.

The title of Wayne Oates' amusing book, *Confessions of a Workaholic*, might well serve as the subtitle for Ecclesiastes as well.[39] Man's efforts at self-justification are misplaced: the mystery of the world's order, the shared fate of its citizens, and the lack of discernible progress all militate for Qoheleth against an obsessive work-orientation. Instead Qoheleth calls his readers to approach life receptively, enjoying its gifts from God as they unfold.

38. von Rad, *Old Testament Theology*, I, 455: "So the Preacher's book is better understood as a skeptical marginal note on the tradition of the wise men, although of course it is a very bitter one."

39. Wayne Oates, *Confessions of a Workaholic* (New York: World, 1971).

THE THEOLOGY
AND PURPOSE
OF ECCLESIASTES

Duane A. Garrett

Ecclesiastes has been subjected to a bewildering array of interpretations.[1] Conservative Christians have generally assumed that the purpose of Ecclesiastes is to show the futility of the world over against eternity;[2] that is, the book is evangelistic. This was the view of the Reformers and Puritans (Whitaker, Pemble, Cocceius, Matthew Poole, Matthew Henry), and John Wesley. In like manner, Ralph Wardlaw used Ecclesiastes to point to the cross.[3] Today, however, the interpretation of this book is anything but unified.

1. One recent interpretation of Ecclesiastes is exceedingly strange. Zimmermann *(Inner World of Qohelet,* 1–97) argues that Qoheleth was a highly neurotic, impotent bureaucrat with homosexual tendencies. His reading is, to say the least, arbitrary.

2. For a brief survey of interpretations from G. Thaumaturgus to Luther, see R. E. Murphy, "Qohelet Interpreted: The Bearing of the Past on the Present," *VT* 32 (1982): 331–37, which has been expanded in his commentary *(Ecclesiastes,* xlviii–lvi). For a survey of early interpretation in the LXX, the Syr, and Jerome, see S. Holm-Nielsen, "On the Interpretation of Qoheleth in Early Christianity," *VT* 24 (1974): 168–87.

3. R. Wardlaw, *Exposition of Ecclesiastes* (1868; reprint, Minneapolis: Klock & Klock, 1982).

A Pessimistic Skeptic?

In recent years scholars have emphasized the pessimism and apparent skepticism of the book. Scott describes the message of Ecclesiastes under the following points: (1) The endless motion that we see brings about no real change and no real profit. (2) Everything that happens seems to be predetermined, but no one can comprehend what will happen to him. Hence life is an enigma and a waiting on fate. (3) The theory that retribution always overtakes wickedness is contradicted by experience. (4) Death is the universal negation of all values. In the same way, misfortune can overcome every kind of virtue.[4] Crenshaw, too, argues that the Teacher rejects the ways of the traditional sages as futile; that he regards God as distant, inscrutable, and capricious; and that, since death cancels every gain in life, one should at least enjoy a woman, wine, and food while health allows.[5]

Delitzsch also adopted a negative view of Ecclesiastes. He urged that Ecclesiastes on the whole shows that the Old Testament was inadequate and incomplete. The book is in many ways dark and pessimistic and points out the need for a New Testament. Delitzsch explained that the fear of death evident in the book is a result of its outlook being pre-Christ and asserted that its notion of the fear of God is not balanced by understanding of the love of God.[6] He implied that Ecclesiastes is the low point of the Bible: "In the Book of Koheleth the Old Covenant digs for itself its own grave."[7]

Although all of the points made by the above scholars could be supported with ample citations from the text, they do not tell the full story and in fact misconstrue its message. The Teacher's faith in the justice of God and the goodness of his commands runs far deeper than these analyses imply (e.g., 8:12–13; 11:9).[8] Even where the Teacher does not know and cannot explain, his response is a response of faith (e.g., 3:16–17 . . .). His recommendations that the reader enjoy life, moreover, arise not from a skeptic's despair but from a profound understanding of human mortality.

Finally, Ecclesiastes is not the inferior piece of theology that Delitzsch asserts it to be. It should not be looked upon as dark and inferior just because it is pre-Christ and therefore does not reflect the fullness of the revelation of God. The entire Old Testament would suffer from such an evaluation.

4. Scott, *Proverbs and Ecclesiastes*, 202–3.
5. Crenshaw, *Ecclesiastes*, 23–28.
6. Delitzsch, *Ecclesiastes*, 182–84.
7. Ibid., 182.
8. Cf. Whybray, *Ecclesiastes*, 27.

The Preacher of Joy?

R. N. Whybray contends that seven pessimistic sections within Ecclesiastes each have, usually toward the end, an exhortation to rejoice. His division of the text is described in the following chart:

Text	Problem Described	Exhortation to Rejoice
1:12–2:26	*Pleasure does not satisfy*	*2:24–26*
3:1–15	*Ignorance of the future*	*3:12*
3:16–22	*Injustice*	*3:22*
5:9–19	*Wealth does not satisfy*	*5:17*
8:10–15	*Injustice*	*8:15*
9:1–10	*God inscrutable; death certain*	*9:7–9*
11:7–12:7	*Old age and death*	*11:9–10; 12:1*

Thus the text would seem to be saying that the best thing one can do is to rejoice in the face of life's unresolved problems. For Whybray, therefore, the Teacher is not the teacher of dour pessimism but the preacher of joy.[9] To this Fox replies that true joy (i.e., "intense happiness") is not so much an option for the Teacher as mere pleasure and that even pleasure is not wholeheartedly endorsed.[10] Indeed, it seems excessive to call the Teacher a "preacher of joy"; his distress is too great for that. Also the term implies that the goal of Ecclesiastes is to drive the reader toward joy, and this emphasis obscures the theological dimension of the book.[11] Its aim is to drive the reader to God. Whybray has, however, provided a good counterbalance to those who emphasize the negative in Ecclesiastes.

9. R. N. Whybray, "Qoheleth, Preacher of Joy," *JSOT* 23 (1982): 87–98. The above chart does not appear within Whybray's article. It is my summation of his argument. Whybray also argues that texts that look very pessimistic (e.g., 4:2–3) need to be read in context. However, compare his more recent commentary (*Ecclesiastes*, NCB [Grand Rapids: Eerdmans, 1989], 17–31).

10. Fox, *Qohelet*, 70; cf. p. 62.

11. Whybray himself appears to shy away from calling the Teacher a "preacher of joy" in his later (1989) commentary on Ecclesiastes. He instead speaks of him as a realist and also gives a good deal of attention to the Teacher's theological emphasis (*Ecclesiastes*, 24–28). At the same time, Whybray's general approach is unchanged. For example, on 3:12 he comments that "Qoheleth's intention here is to lay emphasis on man's possibility of happiness" (*Ecclesiastes*, 74).

A Thinker Caught in the Tensions of Life?

Loader attempts to demonstrate that the Teacher everywhere draws together opposing realities in life (wisdom and folly, power and powerlessness, talk and silence, etc.). These "polar opposites" bring about tensions that the book openly acknowledges but does not always resolve. Or, to put it more precisely, the only resolution is that life is devoid of security or meaning. Following this method, Loader argues that every passage in the book except the prologue and 7:8–10 has the polar pattern.

Thus, for example, in the tension between wisdom and folly, wisdom is found to be relatively superior. But in the tension between wisdom and the realities of life, wisdom is found to be worthless since life often contradicts the teachings of wisdom, and the wise share the fate of fools anyway.[12] Loader describes the tensions in a simple diagram.[13]

Thought:	Generally accepted wisdom
Counterthought:	Folly
Tension:	*Relative* priority of wisdom

and

Thought:	Generally accepted wisdom
Counterthought:	Life's happenstances
Tension:	Worthlessness of wisdom

Loader's analysis here is illuminating.[14] Even so, his approach has a number of problems, not the least of which is that his presentation is often quite confusing.[15] It is significant that he begins his analysis with 3:1–9, which does contain a list of polar opposites,[16] and then goes on to find polar opposites everywhere. In short, 3:1–9 has been made programmatic for the entire book. He often forces the notion of polar opposites on passages where it does not belong.

12. Loader, *Polar Structures*, 35–66.
13. J.A. Loader, *Ecclesiastes: A Practical Commentary*, trans. J. Vriend, TI (Grand Rapids: Eerdmans, 1986), 33. I have here cited the simpler form of the diagram as it appears in his commentary rather than the more technical form fround in the monograph.
14. But cf. Fox, *Qohelet*, 32–33.
15. Ibid., 115, n. 38.
16. Even here, however, the text does not establish the kind of polar tension Loader claims to see, that humanity is trapped between forces of life and death and is in a state of insecurity (*Polar Structures*, 29–33). Rather it teaches the reader what it means to be mortal and urges acceptance of the fact of mortality.

For example, he examines 11:1–6 under the heading "risk and assurance" and argues that the tension of the passage is that there is no security in life.[17] While it is true that these concepts play a part in this text, it is artificial to claim that Ecclesiastes is concerned with maintaining a polar opposition here. Instead, it is simply telling the reader how to obtain a measure of financial security by minimizing risk. . . . Loader's analysis is questionable in other areas as well; he wrongly concludes, for example, that the Teacher rejects the notion of retribution altogether.[18]

Ecclesiastes contains a great deal of tension, and many ambiguities are left unresolved; however, to say that the book is preoccupied with the idea of polar opposites or even uses the concept as a primary method of analysis is a considerable exaggeration. At the same time, Loader has forced us to reckon with the tension of unresolved contradiction in Ecclesiastes. Life, in short, has many unanswered questions.

An Apologetic Work?

Eaton attempts to interpret Ecclesiastes as essentially an apologetic work. He observes that much of the book does not take God into account and is characterized by gloom and pessimism. He argues that when God is introduced, however, the "under-the-sun" terminology drops out and the Teacher speaks of the joy of man (2:25; 3:12; 5:18, 20; 11:7–9) and the generosity of God (2:26; 3:13; 5:19).[19] Like earlier Protestant scholars, he asserts the book to be evangelistic and apologetic: "What, then, is the purpose of Ecclesiastes? It is an essay in apologetics. It defends the life of faith in a generous God by pointing to the grimness of the alternative."[20]

On the other hand, if Ecclesiastes is an apologetic work, it is surely unlike any other defense of the faith we know. It raises more questions than it answers. It is also doubtful whether we can legitimately separate two viewpoints within Ecclesiastes—the one being the worldly, under-the-sun perspective and the other being the true, evangelistic heart of the Teacher. As noted earlier, those who read Ecclesiastes as pessimism and skepticism do not do so without substantial support from the text. Also, one would not expect in an apology such a frank *carpe diem* ("seize the day," a statement of the brevity of life) as in 11:10. While Eaton has correctly observed

17. Ibid., 66–69. Loader is able to maintain his polar opposite only by some peculiar exegesis of vv. 1–2. His analysis makes the Teacher in effect a champion of antiwisdom in which prudence and imprudence in the final analysis are equals.

18. Ibid., 96–105. Loader's conclusion is strange since he also contends that the tension posed by the problem of retribution is maintained. But if the doctrine is simply rejected, in what sense does a tension exist?

19. Eaton, *Ecclesiastes*, 45.

20. Ibid., 44.

that the Teacher believes both in God and in his goodness and generosity, we cannot say that Ecclesiastes is evangelizing *in the conventional sense*. The Teacher's words are unlike those of the prophets and apostles. Nevertheless, he does drive the reader to God (see below).

The Original Existentialist?

Scholars have long noted the similarities—at times superficial and at times profound—between Ecclesiastes and existentialist philosophy.[21] M. Fox has recently exploited these similarities to the full. Drawing heavily upon *The Myth of Sisyphus* by A. Camus, he paints a picture of the Teacher as a man wrestling with the absurdity of the world.

He argues that the Teacher's main concern is the *"the rationality of existence*. This rationality [the Teacher] denies, calling everything *hebel*" although rationality itself remains an "irreducible value."[22] Fox further contends that the Teacher does not so much challenge wisdom as bemoan the fact that wisdom is not rewarded. Fox concludes that the Teacher, having faced the absurdity of life, "affirms the grasping of *inner experience*, emotional and intellectual, as the one domain of human freedom."[23]

Although acutely aware of the negative side of wisdom, the Teacher is himself committed to it. He has a "compulsion for knowledge." He is a Sisyphus whose triumph comes at the moment when he has pushed the rock of inquiry up to the very peak, to the point of lucidity, even though the knowledge gained by that struggle may be painful and the rock inevitably rolls back down the hill before full illumination is attained.[24]

Fox is correct that the rationality of existence is for the Teacher a more fundamental problem than mere matters of material wealth and pleasure. Nevertheless, these too are a part of his quest to understand what makes life worth living. He does not deal in abstractions. Similarly, the Teacher's challenge to the intellectual quest is far more fundamental than grief over the wise not being adequately compensated. More significantly, he doubts whether it is possible for the wise to find the answers to their questions at all (7:23–24).

Fox has correctly observed that other sages were also aware of the limitations of wisdom,[25] and he is also correct in noting that the Teacher does not attack traditional wisdom but rather grieves over the "inevitability of ignorance."[26] Nevertheless, the Teacher looks upon the intellectual quest—what

---

21. Cf. Gordis, *Koheleth*, 112–21.
22. Fox, *Qohelet*, 10. It is here possible to give only a brief summary of Fox's conclusions (far too brief to do his work justice).
23. Ibid., 11. Cf. p. 77, "By exploiting our limited possibilities we become most fully human."
24. Ibid., 117–20.
25. For example, Agur (Prov. 30:3–4); Fox, *Qohelet*, 109.
26. Ibid., 111–12.

Fox calls the "wisdom imperative"—as a road with no destination. He will not play the part of the scholar who walks the road simply for the sake of being on the journey. If there is no goal, if "truth" can never be attained, what is the point? He will not (and here is Fox's fundamental error) play the part of Sisyphus and forever be pushing the rock up the hill just to see it roll down again. He abandons the intellectual quest not because of a collapse of nerve but out of conviction that it was a manifest failure. It has been for him what the quest for righteousness had been for Saul of Tarsus. In Ecclesiastes he turns away resolutely from the search for truth through reason although rejecting neither the validity of reason itself nor the moral insight of traditional wisdom.

His solution to the dilemma of absurdity is thus not what Fox perceives it to be. He does not celebrate emotional and intellectual experiences as the givers of human value. To be sure, he does counsel that his readers enjoy the fleeting pleasures of life and assures them that these pleasures can be appreciated as long as their transitory nature and limited value are understood.

Nevertheless, the Teacher's arguments drive the readers not to the self but *to God* as the only giver of permanent worth—not simply to doctrines about God or to the teachings of the wise but to the very person of God. Thus he does not deny but rather emphasizes that much about God is beyond our ability to know. Even if, however, he does as Paul in Athens and preaches the unknown God, it is nevertheless *God* he preaches and not *humanity.* The Teacher anticipates the existentialists in perceiving the absurdities they see, but his response is quite different.

Reflection for the Wise

If Ecclesiastes is to be understood as having an evangelistic purpose, it can only be interpreted as such within its genre and context. The work is written for the educated elite in the ancient Near Eastern setting. It is addressed, in short, to the "wise."

Childs rightly notes that "Koheleth's (the Teacher's) sayings do not have an independent status but function as a critical corrective (to conventional wisdom), much as the book of James serves in the New Testament as an essential corrective to misunderstanding the Pauline letters."[27] The book is unintelligible if it is not assumed that it is primarily addressed to an aristocratic audience. The implied readers were people who were likely to have access to the king and to the circles of power. They were people for whom the pursuit of wealth was a real possibility and not just a fantasy and who had the leisure time for intellectual pursuits.

27. Childs, *Introduction to the Old Testament,* 588.

Some of his audience were adherents of traditional, conventional wisdom. He warns these readers of the limits of wisdom. Many were wealthy bureaucrats or were at least comfortable in their situations. For these the Teacher is trying to strip away the illusion of having achieved permanence and value in life. Still others knew the Babylonian and Egyptian skeptical philosophy and already were familiar with pessimistic literature. To these he asserts that although life is often arbitrary, despair and cynicism are not appropriate responses. The wise reader will enjoy the good things life offers and yet maintain reverence for God.

Ecclesiastes could be accurately described as a report on the failed quest for eternal life. In this it stands well in the tradition of ancient Near Eastern literature, especially the *Epic of Gilgamesh*. "Eternal life" is not merely perpetual existence. It includes this, but it is especially the sense that one's life and work are fundamentally meaningful rather than of no lasting value. A writer seeks "immortality" through the masterpiece of literature, an athlete wishes to be "immortalized in the record books," and an actor desires to live forever through fame (all of which the Teacher would pronounce futile).[28] The search for value also includes the hedonist's attempt to make life worth living through pleasure, the politician's effort to control life through power, and the intellectual's attempt to master life through knowledge. Ecclesiastes therefore examines not only the specific question of life after death but also the vain attempts to gain genuine personal worth through wealth and pleasure, through accomplishments and power, and through knowledge.

The Teacher tells his readers how to live in the world as it really is instead of living in a world of false hope. In short, *Ecclesiastes urges its readers to recognize that they are mortal*. They must abandon all illusions of self-importance, face death and life squarely, and accept with fear and trembling their dependence on God.

Recognition of personal mortality leads necessarily to three conclusions. First, all pretense of pride in oneself must be abandoned. For the ruling elite this means a humble acceptance of the limitations on both their political power and on their ability to achieve intellectual comprehension of life.[29]

Second, life should be enjoyed for what it is—a gift of God. The book counsels that while avoiding the temptation to consider pleasure to the point of being the goal of life, one should not miss the fleeting joys life affords. This too is an act of humility, for it is an admission that one's work is not as one

---

28. See 9:1; 12:12.

29. Loader, *Ecclesiastes*, 15: "For all those who have been disillusioned by the discovery that the all-embracing systems on which they relied were not in fact reliable, how thrilling and astonishing it is to discover that in Scripture itself a similarly disillusioned and desperate voice may be heard." He notes that Ecclesiastes "cries out" for "a deliverance from the misery of meaninglessness."

might wish and that it has no eternal validity. It is also, ironically, an antidote to the madness of the quest for wealth. Although money is ostensibly sought for the pleasure it can provide, personal happiness and the enjoyment of life's pleasures are often the price paid for wealth.

Third, and most important for us and for the book, one must revere God. To refuse to do so is to deny one's dependency on God.

Reflections on Creation and the Fall

One other aspect of the theology of Ecclesiastes that deserves mention is its theological and literary dependence on the early chapters of Genesis. In these chapters humanity is subjected to a life of toil and condemned to death. The presentation of God in Ecclesiastes as absent and hidden arises directly from Gen. 3 (where humanity loses access to God). The frequent refrain that all is "meaningless" may be a play on the name of Abel, the murdered son of Adam.[30] More to the point, the Teacher ponders what has become of *ʾādām* ("humanity, Adam") as a result of sin. Ecclesiastes can also be called a collection of reflections on creation and the fall, or even reflections on the continuing significance of creation and the fall. The reasons for this are not difficult to imagine. Genesis tells the story of how humans—originally in a state of life, paradise, and innocence—fell into guilt, toil, and mortality. Ecclesiastes tells how persons now made weak and mortal should live.

---

30. In Hebrew both are written הבל. C. C. Forman, "Koheleth's Use of Genesis," *JSS* 5 (1960): 256–63.

9

INTRODUCTION TO ECCLESIASTES

J. Stafford Wright

Background

Ecclesiastes is one of the most puzzling books of the Bible. Its apparently unorthodox statements and extreme pessimism caused its inclusion in the canon of Scripture to be questioned.[1] However, because historically it has been thought to have been the work of Solomon . . . , its place in the canon of Scripture was generally secure. . . .

The correct interpretation of the Book of Ecclesiastes will harmonize with the rest of the OT even though, as always, we need to consider the fuller revelation of the NT. Rather than treating texts and verses in isolation from the total argument of the book, this commentary shows how the book may be taken as a whole in a way that is worthy of its inclusion in Scripture.

Unity

It is always wise to accept the unity of any book unless it is absolutely clear that more than one hand has been at work in its writing. Early in the present

Taken from the book, *The Expositor's Bible Commentary,* vol. 5 edited by Frank E. Gaebelein. Copyright © by the Zondervan Corporation. Used by permission of Zondervan Publishing House.

1. See R. Beckwith, *The Old Testament Canon in the New Testament Church* (Grand Rapids: Eerdmans, 1985), pp. 297–304.

century, numerous literary scholars were busily engaged in trying to determine the sources of many books, whether they were the work of one or more writers and redactors. This activity included the works of Homer and Shakespeare as well as books of the Bible.

Two factors led some Bible scholars to surmise that Ecclesiastes had more than one writer: (1) the literary forms, especially the groups of proverbs, and, more significantly, (2) the apparent blend of unorthodox and orthodox statements. Thus the author(s) seemed to regard man as caught in blind destiny, with his only sensible course being to make the most of life and enjoy himself (ch. 3). Yet periodically what could be an orthodox corrective appears (e.g., 2:26), and the book is rounded off with a wholly orthodox summary.

Among the multiple authorship theories, the simplest postulates three writers (so McNeile and Barton). The original writer (*Qoheleth,* "the Preacher") was a rebel against piety and held a pessimistic view of life in relation to God. His thoughts were toned down—or even contradicted—by an orthodox redactor who emended the text. He belonged to the *Ḥasîdîm* ("holy ones," "saints"), who were forerunners of the Pharisees. Another writer of the regular Wisdom school, a *ḥāḵām* ("wise man"), incorporated a series of traditional proverbs. This is the simplest division of the book, but others claim to have discovered more writers at work.[2]

On the other hand, many commentators (e.g., Delitzsch) always have maintained the unity of the book—with the possible exception of the closing comments. Recent commentators have paid more attention to psychological understanding than to purely literary features.

Gordis, for example, believes that the alleged differences do not need the explanation of different authors: "Reared in the bosom of Jewish tradition and seeking to express in Hebrew a unique philosophic world-view possessing strong overtones of skepticism, Koheleth falls back upon the only abstract vocabulary he knows, that of traditional religion, which he uses in his own special manner" (p. 74).

Gerhard von Rad writes:

> There is, to be precise, an inner unity which can find expression otherwise than through a linear development of thought or through a logical progression in the thought process, namely through the unity of style and topic and theme, a unity which can make a work of literature into a whole and which can in fact give it the rank of a self-contained work of art. This is all the more so in the domain of ancient Near Eastern literature which, in any case, must be measured by different standards. A specific, unifying function is fulfilled by a small number of leading concepts to which Koheleth returns again and again, concepts such as "vanity," "striving after wind," "toil," "lot" etc. Nor can the modern reader escape the quite dispassionate—in contrast to Job—restrained

---

2. E.g., D. C. Siegfried (*Prediger und Hoheslied,* 1898) has nine.

solemnity and weight of his diction. Thus the book is more than a secondarily edited collection. No other collection of proverbs, not even that of Sirach, presents such clearly defined intellectual characteristics.[3]

Currently, the growing consensus favors viewing the book as having an identifiable literary integrity. Crenshaw observes that "both forms and content give the impression of a sustained argument" and that the content "proclaims a coherent message, a single point, which it declares again and again with complete abandon" (p. 35). For those who support the literary integrity of the book, there are four possible approaches: (1) some view the book as primarily the work of a single author that has been augmented by editorial glosses along the way; (2) others view the author as presenting the claims of tradition wisdom only to refute them from his wealth of experience; (3) still others believe that the apparent differences of perspective in the book can be accounted for by an author who records his changing viewpoints over the years; and (4), finally, a fourth group suggests that the book represents a dialogue between the author and a philosophical antagonist.

Though it is common for the literary integrity of the book to be defended in scholarly circles, one should not confuse this with single authorship. Whybray concludes that "the wise commentator will assume that the material comes in its entirety from the hands of Qoheleth alone . . . and will attempt to understand it as such before resorting to theories of interpolations" (p. 19). Fox, however, has raised the interesting question of whether Qoheleth is presented as the author of the book at all. He contends that the author is quoting Qoheleth as a form of instruction to his son (12:12) ("Frame Narrative," pp. 83–106):

> The frame-narrator presents himself not as the creator of Qoheleth's teachings, but as their transmitter. He keeps himself well in the background, but he does not disappear. Insofar as the frame-narrator presents himself as having selected certain of Qoheleth's teachings to transmit, he is indeed analogous to an editor . . . [but] the frame-narrator is composing the sayings, not merely gathering them. (Fox, *Qoheleth and His Contradictions*, pp. 311–12).

In this sense perhaps the author's presenting the sayings of Qoheleth is much like the Gospel writers who gathered, composed, and presented the words of Jesus. As Fox observes, however, there are numerous examples of this type of frame-narrative in the wisdom literature of the ancient Near East (ibid., pp. 312–13).

Certainly whether one considers the author to be Qoheleth or not, the cohesiveness of the book is now well established and widely accepted. While the issue of editorial activity remains somewhat open, Fox sensibly observes that "even if we could identify certain glosses, we could not credibly associate them with specific types of thought" (e.g., allocating some verses to a *ḥāsîd* and others to a *ḥākām*) (ibid., p. 163). [JHW][4]

---

3. *Wisdom in Israel* (Nashville: Abingdon, 1972), p. 227.

4. The editors wish to express their appreciation for the helpful contributions made by John H. Walton (associate professor of Old Testament at Moody Bible Institute), the major ones of which are identified by [JHW] (passim). See also his *Ancient Israelite Literature in Its Cultural Context* (Grand Rapids: Zondervan, 1989), esp. pp. 187–89.

This commentary assumes a single writer, Qoheleth, except possibly for the closing verses (see introduction to comments on 12:9–12). It recognizes that the author looks at life from several angles, deliberately at times raising the arguments that would occur to his readers. Nevertheless, he is always firm in his conclusions. A central argument emerges throughout the book. . . .

Authorship

Traditionally, the authorship of the book has been ascribed to Solomon. This is implied in the opening verse, where the author, Qoheleth, is described as the "son of David, king in Jerusalem." Again at 1:12 he states, "I, the Teacher [Qoheleth], was king over Israel in Jerusalem." Yet commentators of all schools till recently emphasized that the Hebrew belongs to a time considerably later than that of Solomon. . . . Here, however, we first want to see how far the contents of the book tally with Solomon's authorship.

The tradition of David as singer and psalmist is borne out by an early reference at Amos 6:5 and is taken seriously in the light of the lament for Saul and Jonathan (2 Sam. 1:17–27). We ought to take Solomon's reputation for wisdom equally seriously and see his court as the center that drew wise men from all quarters to discuss problems of living in a difficult world (1 Kings 4:34).

Solomon was on the highroad of trade and culture. He had important contacts with Egypt, including an Egyptian wife, and Egypt had a wealth of wisdom literature. This literature includes poems that reason about the problems of life.[5] Other known writings of a similar type come from Babylon.[6] Presumably, Solomon too listened, collected, and added to the literature by facing the realities of life and showing the way through for the God-fearing person.

So we begin by treating Solomonic authorship seriously. Since many modern commentators, however, completely reject such authorship, their reasons for doing so must be considered. Apart from the linguistic objections, it is suggested that certain passages cannot have come from Solomon's pen: e.g., sorrow for the oppression of the weak (4:1) and for corruption in government (5:8–9), the proper attitude to the king from the subject's point of view (8:2–5; 10:20), and unworthy rulers who do not properly distinguish good subjects from bad (9:1–2). If Solomon felt so strongly about these wrongs, surely he would have put them right.

---

5. E.g., A Dispute Over Suicide (also referred to as The Dispute Between a Man and His Soul, *ANET*, pp. 405–7) and A Song of the Harper (*ANET*, p. 467).

6. E.g., The Epic of Gilgamesh (*ANET*, pp. 72–99) and A Pessimistic Dialogue Between Master and Servant (*ANET*, pp. 437–38).

The style of writing suggests that it was the subject who had suffered rather than the king. This is far from conclusive. A king or president may be aware of mismanagement by local authorities, however much he may want to rectify it. Solomon had a number of local officers (1 Kings 4:7–19); and, as always happens, complaints from his subjects would come to his notice from time to time. Unfortunately, he sagged in his moral actions as he grew older, both in the concessions he made to his pagan wives (1 Kings 11:4–6) and in his treatment of his subjects (cf. 1 Kings 12:14). Some men know what is wrong and make a profession of repentance but never clinch a decision by putting things right. With local rulers of considerable influence, Solomon probably found himself in the position of his father, David, who excused a murder with words: "These sons of Zeruiah are too strong for me" (2 Sam. 3:39). On the positive side, according to a fair translation of 5:8–9, the rule of a king is contrasted favorably with the rule of power-hungry governors and their servants.

Some scholars support a late date for Ecclesiastes by a possible reference at 2:8 and 5:8 to the Persian provincial system. . . . Solomon, however, could use the word translated "province" (cf. 1 Kings 20:14–15, 17) of the areas he had divided his kingdom into (1 Kings 4:7). Doubtless, the twelve officers directly responsible to him arranged with local suppliers, who in turn fixed things with juniors, somewhat like the system of tax gathering in Roman times.

Others see a reference at 7:19 to the committees of Ten who governed the cities of Palestine in Greek times. All the verse says, however, is that "Wisdom makes one wise man more powerful than ten rulers in a city," *ten* being an obvious round number, as we might say "a dozen" (cf. Lev. 26:26; Num. 14:22; Job 19:3; Isa. 5:10; et al.).

There are, in fact, no passages in the book that rule out the possibility of Solomonic authorship. Commentators who look for a later date cannot agree on criteria for dating in any of the rather general references to contemporary situations and events. Although this commentary holds that Solomon was Qoheleth, the author, it would not be fair to force this view on the reader. Certainly it is not out of the realm of possibility that a later author is presenting the words and teachings of Qoheleth (= Solomon). (For the non-Solomonic authorship view, see E. J. Young, *An Introduction to the Old Testament* [Grand Rapids: Eerdmans, 1960].)

On the other hand, granting that Solomonic authorship cannot be ruled out, one must fairly ask how strong is the case that Solomon should be equated with Qoheleth? Certainly his identification as the "son of David, king in Jerusalem" (1:1) strengthens the identification. However, it must be realized that any king of Judah could be identified as a "son of David." Though the claim in 1:16 of being wiser than all who ruled Jerusalem before him initially appears practically moot in the mouth of Solomon (who was preceded only by his father, David), the possibility that he is including non-Israelite kings over Jerusalem and the unlikelihood of a successor to Solomon plausibly making such a claim would favor identification of Solomon as Qoheleth. It must still be asked, though, why the name of Solomon was avoided. If Solomon was Qoheleth, why not just say so? If there is some attempt to conceal Solomon's identity, it certainly was not totally successful—nor was it very heartily attempted. Perhaps the title was a well-known one for Solomon and no other identification was necessary. [JHW]

Given all the uncertainty and difference of opinion regarding authorship, this commentary will treat Qoheleth anonymously. Thus, except when there are intentional references to Solomon, [this chapter uses] the title that stands at the head of 1:1. Older versions have familiarized readers with the translation "Preacher," but the note on 1:1 explains a preference for "Teacher" in this commentary.

Date

Although, as it has already been suggested, the contents of the book do not demand a date later than Solomon, its language has been treated by most modern commentators as conclusive of a later period. All quote the dictum of Delitzsch: "If the Book of Koheleth were of Old Solomonic origin, then there is no history of the Hebrew language" (p. 190). While this categorical statement may need some correction in the light of more recent discoveries, it obviously must be taken seriously.

The question is not one of the inclusion of a few Aramaic words, which by themselves are now recognized as unreliable criteria for dating. Aramaic had succeeded Hebrew as the spoken language of Israel by the time of Christ. Although it uses the same script and is closely related to Hebrew in vocabulary and constructions, it is not a derivative of Hebrew. Aramaic is used at Genesis 31:47; Ezra 4:8–6:18; 7:12–26; Jeremiah 10:11; and Daniel 2:4–7:28. It had become a trade language as early as the time of Isaiah (2 Kings 18:26).

It has been held that Ecclesiastes contains so much Aramaic influence that it cannot be dated before the Persian period (SOTI, p. 464). The problem is not so much that the author introduced Aramaic words and constructions but rather that to the expert ear he expressed himself often in a sort of Hebraized Aramaic. Gordis sums the book up as "written in Hebrew, by a writer who, like all his contemporaries, knew Aramaic and probably used it freely in daily life" (p. 61). One might compare him to a preacher who quotes the KJV but modernizes it as he goes along—viz., changing, e.g., "saith" to "says," "him that cometh" to "him who comes," "they did all eat" to "all of them ate," etc.

Some commentators have gone further than this, supposing the book to be a translation from an Aramaic original.[7] If this had been the case, one would have expected that all the Aramaisms would have been smoothed out. Moreover, a writer who wished to pass off his work as Solomonic would certainly have composed his original in Hebrew, not Aramaic.

It also has been argued that the book uses Hebrew words that are transitional between classical and Mishnaic Hebrew (Crenshaw, p. 31). The Mishnah is the collection of Jewish oral laws and traditions that were reduced to writing during the second century B.C. Although this contention is often accepted as a mark of a late date, it has been questioned by D. S. Margoliouth (JE, 5:33).[8]

The relationship to Mishnaic Hebrew has been called into question in a recent monograph by Fredericks, who argues that the language is a preexilic northern dialect. He suggests that features of this dialect were later incorporated in Mishnaic Hebrew, thus the similarity with Qoheleth. [JHW]

In yet another approach, an article by M. J. Dahood called attention to linguistic and other resemblances between Ecclesiastes and Phoenician literary forms and suggested that the book was written by a Jew or Jews living in Phoenicia soon after the Fall of Jerusalem in 587 B.C.[9]

Although this was attacked by Gordis (e.g., in an appendix to his commentary), it has been taken up by G. L. Archer in "The Linguistic Evidence for the Date of Ecclesiastes." He concludes:

1. There is no known Hebrew writing with which Ecclesiastes as a whole can be matched linguistically.

2. Comparative evidence shows that the original Hebrew text of Ecclesiastes was singularly lacking in vowel letters (*matres lectionis*). These were inserted more frequently in later Hebrew to assist pronunciation but are not found in Phoenician inscriptions.

3. Certain inflections, pronouns, and participles are characteristic of Phoenician.

4. Certain words and phrases resemble Phoenician usage—e.g., "under the sun" (used twenty-seven times in Ecclesiastes) is found elsewhere only in two Phoenician inscriptions. The series "seven . . . eight" (11:2) is typical of Phoenician usage.

Archer holds that Solomon himself wrote the book, adopting the standard linguistic presentation expected for a work of this kind. He compares the development of choral poetry among the Greeks; since the Dorian Greeks were

---

7. F. Zimmermann, *JQR* 36 (1945); H. L. Ginsberg.

8. Hebraists will find a list of Aramaisms and Mishnaic words in Barton, pp. 52–53.

9. *Biblica* 33 (1952). The validity, however, of Dahood's conclusions that Qoheleth's use of vowel letters suggests Phoenician connections has been seriously undermined by Anton Schoors, "The Use of Vowel Letters in Qoheleth," *Ugarit Forschungen* 20 (1988): 277–86.

the most famous original writers of this kind of poetry, it became a tradition for all subsequent choral poetry to be composed in this dialect. Since at present, however, we have no Phoenician parallels to the wisdom type found in Ecclesiastes, we must treat this part of Archer's theory as a hypothesis that could be clinched by further discoveries.

Archer does not suggest a further possibility—viz., that Solomon used a scribe with a Phoenician background, just as he used the Phoenician, Hiram of Tyre, in constructing the temple (1 Kings 7:13–14). A similar suggestion is often held to account for variations of style and language in Paul's epistles. The thoughts would then be Solomon's, which he gave to his scribes, but the form of the Hebrew would be colored by the scribe's Phoenician background.

Dahood and Archer have presented a strong case, but they are still very much a minority. We, therefore, must consider how far the standard view of lateness of language necessarily rules out Solomon as the original author. All that the language shows on this view is that the book in its present form was written later than Solomon's day. This need not be the date of its composition, any more than the language of the Mishnah indicates that all its material was first composed in the second century B.C.

As well as priest and prophet, there were wise men (Jer. 18:18). Their task and joy would have been to treasure and discuss specialized sayings and discussions of what we call the wisdom type (cf. 12:9–12). Some of their conclusions would be written, others oral. From what we know of the gathering of the rabbis to debate the application of the laws to specific situations, we can similarly imagine gatherings of wise men to study and thrash out the problems of life.

As the living language inevitably changed, the language of a popular treatise like Ecclesiastes would keep step in the discussion groups, until eventually the book was seen more and more to have a place in the inspired canon and its form then fixed in writing.

Folk songs offer a modern analogy. Collectors of old songs in America and Britain are fully aware of changes in diction and expression down the ages, and it would be difficult to date a modern presentation of any folk song on linguistic grounds, which is what some try to do with Ecclesiastes.

If we then follow the tradition of the Bible that Solomon was the hero of the wise, his bequests would represent for the circles of the wise what Moses and the Law were for the rabbis.

Those who believe that one cannot make out a fair case for Solomonic authorship may well follow E. J. Young, a firm believer in the full inspiration of the Bible. Young holds that a later writer put his own thoughts into Solomon's mouth and indicates this by adopting a strange title for himself, without ever saying "I, Solomon." One might go a step further than Young and hold that Solomon was traditionally known to have said, "Meaningless!

Meaningless! . . . Utterly meaningless! Everything is meaningless." These may be the only words that come directly from the "son of David, king in Jerusalem" (1:1–2). The new Teacher takes up where Solomon left off, uses the words as a text, and puts himself in Solomon's place so as to discover how he came to reach his conclusion about life.

It is, therefore, entirely plausible that the words of Solomon (Qoheleth), preserved by wise men over several centuries, were eventually recorded by a new Teacher (the author of the book?) in his own dialect or in the Hebrew of his time period. Whether this scenario or another is true, given our state of knowledge, it is best to conclude with Eaton:

> Our conclusion must be that the language of Ecclesiastes does not at present provide an adequate resource for dating. It is possible that a particular style was adopted for pessimism literature. The possibility that a northern dialect of Hebrew was used must be left open. Equally it is possible that its dialect is Phoenicianizing. Certainly no other document possesses precisely the same characteristics, and no reliable date can be given this way. (p. 19) [JHW]

Place of Origin

One naturally assumes Palestine as the place of origin for the Book of Ecclesiastes, and most scholars accept this. Based on references to the weather (1:5–7) and anatomy (11:5; 12:1–7), some have suggested Alexandria as the book's place of origin (e.g., Plumptre, E. Sellin); but the references are too general to be specifically Egyptian. Also, one would expect a resident of Alexandria to show some Greek influence in his style, since the Alexandrian Jews were Greek speaking and were responsible for the translation of the LXX. Arguments for Greek influence, however, are not strong. . . .

Certainly the author gives the impression of writing from Jerusalem (1:1, 16). In default of any other compulsive evidence, we may accept Jerusalem as the place of origin for the Book of Ecclesiastes.

Destination

Ecclesiastes was clearly written as a discussion guide for people prepared to think out their response to God's unseen hand in life and history. Although it contains practical advice, it would appeal to a different public than Proverbs. One may rather link it to Job. The Wisdom writings have a twofold scope. First, they set out the rules of life for an individual who wishes to be a member of a prosperous society and who looks for the right way to build up a God-fearing conscience. These rules form the Book of Proverbs.

Society, however, is not ideal; mankind has a fundamental twist, and there will always be cases where a person finds things happening to him that he cannot reconcile with the promises of Proverbs. He may suffer when he expects the temporal blessings of God, and others who deserve punishment may prosper. This second scope of Wisdom writings is taken up by Job and Ecclesiastes, each in its own way. Job shows the nature of testing and something of Satan's challenge, but Ecclesiastes explores these things more widely. . . .

Occasion

If the Book of Ecclesiastes was written by Solomon, the occasion of its writing was in his last years. In 2:1–11 he describes a lifetime of accumulating wealth, and in chapters 11–12 he writes as one beginning to experience the onset of old age. He writes for young men who might learn from his experiences (11:9; 12:1; cf. Prov. 1:8 et al.).

Purpose

The theme of the book appears in the prologue: "Meaningless! Meaningless! . . . Everything is meaningless." The general conclusion comes in the epilogue, which speaks of fearing God and keeping his commandments because we must one day give account to him. The meaning and purpose of the book must be discovered within this framework. Life in the world is subject to frustration; but man can still accept his circumstances, even enjoy them, and find strength to live life as it comes.

Where does one start to build a way of life that transcends the meaninglessness of the world? Can purpose for life be found in nature, money, self-indulgence, property, position, intelligence, philosophy, and religious observances? Obviously, some of these pursuits are better than others, but all encounter some crowning frustration that invalidates them as solutions to the problem of living. The world does not contain the key to itself. It can be found only in God. Roughly speaking, this is the theme of chapters 1–6.

If God exists and is concerned for man's response to him, why has he made life so frustrating? The answer is that God originally made man perfect, but man fell and thus brought frustration into the human race (7:29).

How much does this frustration prevent us from recognizing God's plan in every circumstance? God does not show anyone what only he can know (3:11; 7:14). Indeed, the attempt to discover this brought about the Fall (Gen. 3:5). But God has implanted in man the sense of an eternal existence (3:11), and in this man rises above the rest of the animal world. Since there is a total plan, there must be some way that man can fit into it; but how can he do so if he does not know what the plan is?

The book tells man to begin where he is, with the assumption that God has his purpose for today. To fulfill this purpose man must use his God-given sense as well as his own experience of himself and that of others. God has a proper time for each thing to be done (3:1–8), and recognizing this allows man to accept life as it comes (3:11a), even though he knows he has fitted no more than one piece in the great puzzle.

Thus we are directed from speculation (e.g., 8:16–17) to observation. It is right to meditate on the total work of God, but we are to glorify God in the common things of life; i.e., we are to make the fullest use of the present moment. There may be times of stress and strain and special calling; but the norm is to eat, drink, and live our daily life as those who gladly rejoice in God's good gifts and intend to use them to his glory. This is the theme of the refrains (2:24–26; 3:12–13, 22; 5:18–19; 8:15; 9:7–9).

In all this there is nothing unworthy. In fact, it tallies with the NT teaching that we are to eat and drink and do all our actions to the glory of God (1 Cor. 10:31; Col. 3:17), since he has generously given us everything for our enjoyment (1 Tim. 6:17).

Several comments must be made, however:

1. The book offers insight to thoughtful readers who want to know how to develop a God-centered worldview. Its advice is compatible with the Sermon on the Mount, in which Christ said that we are to accept food, drink, and clothing as the gifts of God and are to seek God's kingdom and righteousness (Matt. 6:25–33). In the same sermon he referred to those who would be called to undergo suffering precisely because they sought to fulfill God's righteous commands (Matt. 5:10–12). Ecclesiastes also faces the fact of the suffering of the righteous but sees it in relation to the frustration in the world rather than as part of the witness to God's righteousness (e.g., 5:8). It teaches that we need not do something out of the ordinary in order to do God's will. Similarly, Paul advised the zealous convert to remain in the sphere in which God called him (1 Cor. 7:17) though later he may be called to some special service.

2. Interestingly, the book makes no suggestion of living a life of self-sacrifice, so as to spur the reader on to a life of philanthropy or self-deprivation. Qoheleth would most likely identify self-sacrifice as meaningless if it is motivated by any degree of self-satisfaction. We need to remember that the author is not trying to describe the life of faith or what our faith responsibilities are. Rather, he is contrasting a self-centered life style with a God-centered one. It is needless for the person of faith to be glum about life's anomalies or adversities. The Teacher's approach is through philosophy, not through an assumed source of revelation (much like C. S. Lewis's *Mere Christianity*). He does not discuss moral obligation to the law of God, though that is no reason to think that he was ignorant of the law [JHW]. Ecclesiastes expresses this faith as "I see" (2:24) and "I know" (3:14; 8:12). One may compare this with Paul's words in Romans 8 where, after speaking about how the whole creation is subject to frustration (v. 20), he declares, "We know that in all things God works for the good of those who love him, who have been called according to his purpose" (v. 28).

3. The book is not against serious thinking; it is itself a deep and thoughtful work. But it demands a recognition of the limitations of human philosophy (e.g., 3:11; 8:16–17).

4. The refrains do not mean "Do what you will." Man is accountable to God, not simply to himself; he has a duty to work and moral responsibilities to society. The book contains warnings against self-indulgence that exploits others for personal advantage (e.g., 8:8–9).

Christians may ask how the stress on using and enjoying life tallies with the NT command "Do not love the world" (1 John 2:15). The answer is that the Teacher (Ecclesiastes) would have agreed fully with John's next statement that "everything in the world—the cravings of sinful man, the lust of his eyes and the boasting of what he has and does—comes not from the Father but from the world. The world and its desires pass away" (vv. 16–17). One could hardly find a better statement than this of the whole theme of Ecclesiastes (e.g., 2:1–11; 5:10). Life in the world has significance only when man remembers his Creator (12:1).

There always have been two kinds of teaching about the way to holiness. One is by withdrawal as far as possible from the natural in order to promote the spiritual. The other is to use and transform the natural into the expression of the spiritual. While each kind of teaching has its place, some people need one emphasis rather than the other. Ecclesiastes definitely teaches the second.

Literary Form

While the Book of Ecclesiastes is unanimously included in the larger literary category of wisdom literature, the specific literary genre of the book is somewhat uncertain. It has been likened to the so-called pessimism literature known from the ancient Near East (see footnotes 5 and 6). But these are not works of the same genre; they merely include observations about the meaninglessness of life and some advice concerning the enjoyment of life that show some similarity to the content of Ecclesiastes. So, for instance, a section from the Egyptian "A Song of the Harper" commends enjoyment of life:

> Hence rejoice in your heart!
> Forgetfulness profits you,
> Follow your heart as long as you live!
> Put myrrh on your head,
> Dress in fine linen,
> Anoint yourself with oils fit for a god.
> Heap up your joys,
> Let not your heart sink:
> Follow your heart and your happiness,
> Do your things on earth as your heart commands.

> (Translation from M. Lichtheim, *Ancient Egyptian Literature* [Berkeley: University of California Press, 1976], 1:196–97)

Likewise, from the "Epic of Gilgamesh":

> Gilgamesh, whither rovest thou?
> The life thou pursuest thou shalt not find.
> When the gods created mankind,
> Death for mankind they set aside,
> Life in their own hands retaining.
> Thou, Gilgamesh, let full be thy belly,
> Make thou merry by day and by night.
> Of each day make thou a feast of rejoicing,
> Day and night dance thou and play!
> Let thy garments be sparkling fresh,
> Thy head be washed; bathe thou in water.
> Pay heed to the little one that holds on to thy hand,
> Let thy spouse delight in thy bosom!
> For this is the task of [mankind]!
>
> (*ANET*, p. 90; cf. Eccles. 9:7–9)

Beyond this similarity in content, Fox also identifies some similarities in form between Ecclesiastes and some of the wisdom literature of Egypt, including Kagemeni, Ptahhotep, Neferti, Onchsheshonqy, as well as in the Sumerian Instructions of Shuruppak, the Aramaic Words of Ahiqar, and even in the biblical Book of Deuteronomy (*Qoheleth and His Contradictions,* pp. 312–15). Though most of these are works from the wisdom genre, the use of frame-narrative is not limited to a particular genre.

Tremper Longman suggests that once the frame is removed, the Book of Ecclesiastes can be seen to follow the same format as an Akkadian genre that he identifies as fictional royal autobiography (*Fictional Akkadian Autobiography: A Generic and Comparative Study* [Winona Lake: Eisenbrauns, 1990]), the closest comparison being found in the Akkadian Cuthean Legend of Naram-Sin. Just as the pessimism of Ecclesiastes served to identify it with a particular branch of wisdom literature, so Longman suggests that the style of an author addressing himself identifies Ecclesiastes with fictional royal autobiography. Furthermore, Longman suggests that the genre identification is sound enough to determine that royal fiction is also a characteristic of Ecclesiastes. By this he means that the writer is not really Solomon. The material is presented as the wisdom of Solomon (= Qoheleth) and stylistically framed in the first person.

Beyond the question of genre are a number of recognizable literary forms used in the Book of Ecclesiastes. Among the more prominent are aphorism (short truth statements; cf. 7:1–8; 10:1–3, 8–15), admonition (advice using imperative or jussive forms; e.g., 5:1–4), and didactic narrative (short story with a moral; e.g., 4:13–16; 5:13–17; 9:13–16) (for discussion of these, see Whybray, pp. 20–21).

A combination of all these features suggests that the author of Ecclesiastes was truly cosmopolitan in the breadth of his literary exposure. Deft and sophisticated use of several ancient Near Eastern genres and numerous wisdom motifs and forms make him a fine example of Israel's literary elite. [JHW]

Theological Values

Ecclesiastes does not pretend to preach the Gospel. Rather, it encourages the reader to a God-centered worldview rather than falling victim to frustrations and unanswered questions. None of its contents has to be rejected in the light of the NT. Although the NT revelation is vastly greater than that in Ecclesiastes, the two are not devoid of similarities (e.g., James 4:13–17). Like the people of God in Solomon's time, believers today are subject to the unexpected changes and chances common to mankind. Yet they know that God works through every vicissitude of life. Respecting the future, which for Solomon was shrouded in a shadow land, Christians have the glorious hope of being in the presence of Christ himself (2 Cor. 5:6; Phil. 1:23).

The writer of Ecclesiastes was no humanist. He named God some forty times, and six times he spoke of the fear of God (3:14; 5:7; 7:18; 8:12–13; 12:13). He used the general name Elohim and not Yahweh, the covenant name of God. This may be because he was writing about God in relation to the whole of mankind. Another possibility may be that as the OT period drew to its close, there was a growing reluctance to use the sacred covenant name in daily speech. Hence, when Ecclesiastes reached its final form—even if Solomon had been the author and had used the covenant name—reverence would have required the use of Elohim.

So far as man's state before God is concerned, the book contrasts two classes of humanity. One comprises the God-fearing (3:14; 5:7; 7:18; 8:12–13; 12:13), righteous (3:17; 7:15–16, 20; 8:14; 9:2), good (9:2), and wise (frequently mentioned, e.g., 10:2). The other comprises the sinners (2:26; 7:26; 8:11; 9:2, 18) and the wicked (3:17; 7:15; 8:10, 12–14; 9:2); both terms describe deliberate villains. There is also frequent mention of fools (e.g., 5:4), a term that does not mean a jester or merely unwise person, but one who is godless and wicked (cf. Pss. 14:1; 53:1). It is especially descriptive of those who act wrongly because they do not make any effort to discover the will of God. At the same time the book recognizes that there is no such thing as sinless perfection (7:20).

Strangely, there is no reference to repentance and forgiveness. There are, however, two references to sacrifices (5:1; 9:2), the second of which is linked to moral evil and uncleanness. Lest we downgrade Ecclesiastes because of its silence about repentance and forgiveness, we should take into account that a book on godly morals need not necessarily deal with these things. Rather, it assumes that the reader knows about repentance and forgiveness.

Canonicity

The Book of Ecclesiastes forms one of the five Megilloth (rolls or scrolls), and it was read by the postbiblical Jewish community on the Feast of Booths (Tabernacles). One cannot say how early the various festival readings were fixed. However, the discovery of fragments of the book at Qumran shows that it had status in the middle of the second century B.C. Later, the schools of Hillel and Shammai argued over whether it "defiled the hands." The phrase means the opposite to what it appears to the English reader and indicates that the book was so fully inspired of God that elaborate ritual washing was needed by the reader who handled it. Hillel favored its inclusion in the canon; Shammai opposed this. Shammai's opposition seems to us to be on trial grounds, mostly resting on superficial contradictions; e.g., joy is commended at 8:15 but spoken of critically at 2:2 and 7:3.[10]

The book apparently was in the canon at the time of Christ, since the Jewish Council of Jamnia in A.D. 90 did not meet to put books into the canon but to discuss whether a few disputed books, already regarded as canonical, should remain in it. Undoubtedly, the association of Ecclesiastes with Solomon aided its retention, whereas Ecclesiasticus (cf. "The Apocrypha and Pseudepigrapha," EBC, 1:161–75) was not under consideration, because it was written by Ben Sira after God's direct inspiration was believed to have ceased.

Jamnia, however, did not close the debate. When Jerome made his Latin translation of the Bible in the fourth century, he noted that many Jews were still not happy about some theology in the book.

If we look for confirmation of Ecclesiastes by quotation in the NT, there is little doubt that Paul referred to it in Romans 8:20, where he spoke about the complete futility of the world system. Other parallels with the NT, though not quotations, are noted in the commentary.

Text

The Hebrew text of the Book of Ecclesiastes is in good condition. There are only a few places where one needs to give serious attention to the possibility of error by a copyist. The LXX is a rather formal Greek translation of the Hebrew and was possibly made in the first half of the second century B.C. There is also a Syriac translation, likewise quite formal. Its date, while uncertain, is later than the LXX.

The recent finds of fragments of the Hebrew text at Qumran show only very slight variants, chiefly in spelling. Therefore, we may accept the conclusion of Gordis that "fundamentally we read Koheleth today in the form in which it left its author's hands" (p. 128).

---

10. Beckwith, *Old Testament Canon*, pp. 297–304.

10

THE WORLD VIEW
OF KOHELETH

Robert Gordis

I

The reconstruction of the precise stages in Koheleth's spiritual odyssey that we have proposed is confessedly an act of the imagination, rooted though it be in the facts before us. On the other hand, the conclusions at which he ultimately arrived are clear, for he set them forth in the book he left behind him. Personal experience or reflection, most probably both, had robbed him of the traditional Jewish faith in the triumph of justice in this world, preached by the Prophets, or in the redress of the balance in the hereafter, as affirmed by the forerunners of Pharisaic Judaism, who were his contemporaries. Moreover—and this was a deprivation he felt even more keenly—he had lost the assurance that man could fathom the meaning of life.

The modern reader might expect that Koheleth would be led by his views to deny the existence of God, but that was impossible to an ancient mind, and especially to a Jew. Even the Epicureans, who denied the gods' intervention in human affairs as a fundamental element of their outlook, did not deny their being. In the ancient world, atheism, the denial of God, referred to the view that the gods did not intervene in human affairs. Koheleth, a son of Israel,

From Robert Gordis, *Koheleth—The Man and His World: A Study of Ecclesiastes*, 3d ed. (New York: Schocken, 1968), 122–32. Reprinted by permission.

175

reared on the words of the Torah, the Prophets and the Sages, could not doubt the reality of God for an instant. For him, the existence of the world was tantamount to the existence of God.

It was on the question of God's relation to men that Koheleth parted company with the conventional teachers of his time. For all the barrage of platitudes of the Wisdom teachers, there was not a shred of proof that God wished to reveal the true Hokmah, the secret of life, to men. Similarly, there was tragic evidence to contradict the confident assertion of the moralists:

> Say to the upright that it shall be well with him, for he shall eat the fruit of his doings. Woe to the wicked! It shall be ill with him, for the reward of his hands shall be given him. (Isa. 3:10, 11)

The Psalmist had sung:

> I have been young, and now am old, yet I have never seen an upright man forsaken, and his offspring begging bread. (Ps. 37:25)

His words might be a prayer or a pious hope; they were scarcely the result of empirical observation!

With justice in human affairs an illusion, and truth unattainable, Koheleth is left with very little upon which to build. All that is certain is that man has an innate desire for happiness. Since God has created man, He has also created this impulse. It thus becomes clear that God's fundamental purpose for mankind is the furthering of man's pleasure.

We may put it another way: Koheleth's metaphysics postulates the existence of God, coupled with His creative power and limitless sovereignty. But beyond these attributes, Koheleth refuses to affirm anything about his God, except that He has revealed His will to His creatures by implanting in man an ineradicable desire for happiness. Koheleth's morality accordingly recognizes the pursuit of happiness as the goal. His religion is the combination of his theology and his ethics.

In substance, this is Koheleth's world-view, but setting it forth in systematic abstract categories gives it a lifelessness and a dogmatic cast that are completely alien to Koheleth's personality. For it robs the book of its most attractive qualities, the informality and tentativeness with which the author sets forth his ideas, his amused doubts even with regard to skepticism, his insights into human nature with all its weaknesses and pretenses, and his basic sympathy for men in their lifelong quest for happiness, elusive and fleeting at best. Above all, there is the haunting sadness of one who in earlier years had known and shared larger hopes for man upon earth.

The contradictions that troubled earlier readers are, in part, normal variations in temper and mood and, in part, the consequence of his clear-sighted recognition that no one, not even he, has a monopoly on truth. These contrasting passages are not among the least of Koheleth's charms.

Thus the basic theme of the book is its insistence upon the enjoyment of life, of all the good things in the world. There is the love of woman—and the singular is noteworthy—

> Enjoy life with the woman whom you love
> Through all the vain days of your life,
> Which God has given you under the sun,

but the counterpoint of melancholy is never absent:

> Throughout your brief days,
> For that is your life's reward
> For your toil under the sun. (9:9)

With a moving sense of the transitoriness of life, he calls for the vigorous and full-blooded enjoyment of all it affords, food and drink, oil and fine clothes, beautiful homes and music:

> Whatever you are able to do, do with all your might, for there is neither action nor thought nor knowledge nor wisdom in the grave toward which you are moving. (9:10)

In practice, Koheleth advocates a moderate course, not very different from the attitude of the Rabbis of the Talmud:

> שלשה דברים מרחיבין דעתו של אדם בית נאה אשה נאה וכלים נאים
> Three things bring a sense of ease and contentment to a man: a beautiful home, an attractive wife, and fine clothes. (Ber. 57b)

What set his standpoint apart from theirs was that his attitude stemmed not from a full-hearted acceptance of the world, as preached by religion, but from a sense of frustration and resignation, induced by his philosophy.

For Koheleth, nothing really counts if truth and righteousness cannot be attained. Yet man lives and God rules, and God's manifest will is man's happiness, not that it matters overmuch, but this at least is certain.

II

In Koheleth, form and substance are so closely interwoven that any restatement becomes a distortion. His view of life is best gathered from his own words, or at least from a summary of the book as he wrote it.

The work opens and closes with his fundamental judgment, "Vanity of vanities, all is vanity" (1:2; 12:8). In the opening section, Koheleth declares that the natural world about us presents a changeless cycle without novelty or progress. The four elements of the universe, the earth, the sun, the wind and the sea, repeat their monotonous courses interminably. Against this background, man's petty strivings are folly (I, 1:2–11).

Koheleth then takes on the role of King Solomon, and tells how he had experimented with wisdom and wealth, goals for which men are wont to struggle and squander their lives. Truth he found unattainable, and wisdom a source of misery. As for physical pleasure, it may offer a temporary satisfaction, but it is not an absolute or enduring good. Nonetheless, it is God who has endowed man with the desire for happiness; to enjoy life is therefore the only commandment of which man can be certain; to fail to obey it is to be a sinner before God (II, 1:12 to 2:26).

Not only are the processes of nature beyond man's power to contravene, but even human actions are preordained. All human activity is useless, above all the search for truth. Only joy remains for man as the gift of God (III, 3:1–15).

Bitterly, Koheleth condemns the world in which the powerful are unjust and the weak victimized. Nor can one be certain of a just retribution in the hereafter, as some would believe. Only joy is a sensible goal in life (IV, 3:16 to 4:3).

A favorite doctrine of the preceptors of youth is the value of diligence and hard work. Analysis reveals, however, that the reasons usually advanced for these virtues are worthless. The creative skill in which men glory is largely a disguise for their desire to compete with and outstrip their fellows (4:4). Some men claim to toil for the sake of their families, the advantages of which, Koheleth finds, are much overrated, being largely physical (4:9ff.). As for the desire for fame, "the last infirmity of noble minds," that is the greatest illusion of all, for all men are quickly forgotten (4:13–16). The conclusion is inescapable—hard work is folly and only ease is sensible (V, 4:4–16).

A few brief comments now follow on the basic institutions of society. Religion is part of the accepted order, and a sensible man should do his duty to the temple. He should visit the sanctuary at proper intervals, offer his brief prayers, and pay his vows by which the ritual is maintained. Koheleth scorns the religious ecstatic, but even more, the man who evades his obligation (VI, 4:17 to 5:6). He then turns to the political scene and finds that corruption is inherent in the very nature of government, with its endless hierarchy of officials. In a difficult verse, he seems to pay tribute to agriculture as the basic pursuit of society (VII, 5:7–8).

He now turns to a basic drive in the lives of men. Few vices are more widespread than the lust for wealth, and few bring less genuine satisfaction. Diligence and thrift are hardly more than expressions of greed. Men struggle and toil to amass riches, finding only that the dependents and parasites about them augment their responsibilities, but bring no increased pleasure in life. Greed often drives men into ill-starred ventures that wipe out overnight the patient accumulation of a lifetime. Even if a man does not lose all his fortune, some one else will inherit it all, after he goes down into silence. Whoever his heir, be it his child or kinsman, fundamentally he is a stranger to him (6:2). Hence it is better to seize joy before it is too late forever (VIII, 5:9 to 6:9).

Man remains incapable of changing the predetermined character of events or even of penetrating the mystery of existence—that is the fundamental tragedy (IX, 6:10–12).

There now follows a collection of proverbs dealing with the good life, linked together by the opening word *tōbh,* "good." These traditional apothegms are made to serve Koheleth's outlook. Man must not expect too much from life in order to avoid disappointment. Since life is unchanging, it is as foolish to weave elaborate hopes for the unborn future as to glorify the dead past. Good and evil are both to be accepted as part of the pattern ordained by God (X, 7:1–14). Man should avoid extremes, whether of saintliness or of wickedness, and strive after "the golden mean." In a world where nothing is predictable to man, hewing close to the center is the safest course (XI, 7:15–25).

Koheleth has little confidence in the character of men. Upon women, however, he pours out the vials of his bitterness and wrath—testimony that he had loved them and lost (XII, 7:26–29).

With regard to the political status quo, Koheleth urges submission to the king, not merely because of the oath of allegiance that he exacts from his subjects, but because of the royal power. The unpredictability of events and the perils of life in a mysterious universe are reflected and heightened in a royal court, where the ruler's caprice and the intrigues of the courtiers make survival, let alone advancement, a difficult and risky art (XIII, 8:1–9).

Noting how successful evil-doers are often eulogized as public benefactors in their last rites, Koheleth turns to the problem of reward and punishment. He does not altogether deny the principle of retribution. However, the long delays that occur before God metes out punishment to the sinner and the numerous cases where there is no discernible difference between the lot of the righteous and that of the evil-doer, act as a stimulus for men to do wrong. Hence, the quest for justice is futile—only joy remains (XIV, 8:10 to 9:3). This latter theme is then expanded in an eloquent call to man to enjoy life with all the zest at his command, before unknown perils crush him and death ends all sensation and activity (XV, 9:4–12).

Though Koheleth cannot overcome his natural bias for the wise man as against the fool, he knows how slight is the respect that wisdom commands and how easily all its achievements can be negated by stupidity (XVI, 9:13 to 10:1).

Another proverb collection, miscellaneous in character, now follows. Koheleth urges the same practical virtues as the conventional Wisdom teachers, but generally on more realistic grounds that are in harmony with his basic viewpoints—man's inability to know the future and his duty to enjoy life while he can (XVII, 10:2 to 11:6).

In the closing sentences, Koheleth rises to eloquent heights. Joy is God's great commandment for man. The time for joy is youth, the period of vigor and zest. Koheleth, from the vantage point of his own experience, calls upon the youth to "remember his Creator" before the shadows begin to lengthen and presage the end. With the unforgettable "Allegory of Old Age," Koheleth sounds the note of man's inevitable dissolution and death. Vanity of vanities, all is vanity (XVIII, 11:7 to 12:8).

The Epilogue, consisting of the six concluding verses of the book (12:9–14), are an addition by an editor, who knew Koheleth as a Wisdom teacher and a collector and composer of Hokmah literature. Fascinated by the book, the editor is fearful lest the reader be led away from the eternal verities and he calls upon him, having heard everything, to fear God and keep His commandments.

III

From this summary it is clear that Koheleth does not present a systematic philosophy in the grand manner of Aristotle, Spinoza, Hegel or Kant, but that is less of a defect than may appear. For nothing is as certain as the fact that the elaborate systems of philosophies upon which they spend their life's energies ultimately pass away, and only scattered insights, minor details in their patterns of thought, become abiding elements in man's approach to reality. Only the flashes of illumination endure to light up men's path in a dark and mysterious world.

Basic to Koheleth, as we have seen, is the skeptical outlook, which, rooted in his temperament, was nurtured also by his position among the well-to-do classes of society. Essentially, a skeptic is one who refuses to be convinced without proof; concerning the shape of things to come, where such evidence cannot be forthcoming, he remains without faith. The skeptic finds it possible to be suspended in a state of perpetual doubt with regard to the future, because as a rule he finds his lot in the present not unbearable. Being generally a beneficiary and not a victim of the status quo, he feels no powerful urge to achieve or even to envisage a better world. That drive tends to arise among the submerged groups in society, who find existence intolerable without the hope of a change. Koheleth, on the other hand, rejects the older prophetic faith which expressed itself in such concepts as the End-Time and the Messianic Age. At the same time, he is unable to accept the newer Pharisaic doctrine of life after death or the Apocalyptic faith in the imminent end of the world through a Divine cataclysm. He is, of course, at the farthest remove possible from the mystic, the social reformer or the revolutionary.

Undoubtedly, Koheleth's failure to respond actively to social injustice and political tyranny constitutes a crucial defect, so that our age cannot find in him the motive power toward the building of a better world that is so abundant in the Hebrew prophets. In the face of the towering evils of our own day coupled with the breath-taking vision of a more abundant life for all men, now for the first time within realization, Amos and Isaiah are incomparably more inspiring guides than the disillusioned sage of Jerusalem.

Yet for all Koheleth's remoteness from the fever and the fret of the world and his apparent lack of concern with social problems, his view of life does furnish a basis, at least, for men's age-old struggle against any order in which "man has power over his neighbor to do him harm." For Koheleth, joy is God's categorical imperative for man, not in any anemic or spiritualized sense, but rather as a full-blooded and tangible experience, expressing itself in the play of the body and the activity of the mind, the contemplation of nature and the pleasures of love. Since he insists that the pursuit of happiness with which man has been endowed by his Creator is an inescapable sacred duty, it follows that it must be an inalienable right.

To be sure, Koheleth never drew the implications of these premises, in facing the social, economic, and political ills of his day. His conservatism was, as has been noted, an amalgam of intellectual, temperamental and social factors. But had he been confronted by the logic of his position, we may well believe that he would have been too honest to deny the conclusion that a system of society which denies inalienable rights to men is not God-ordained, and that men have the duty as well as the right to change it. He lacked the Prophets' faith that right would triumph, but at least he shared their conviction that it should. His passionate outcry against life because of human oppression (4:1ff.) should guard us against imagining that he was complacent in the face of oppression. If, as a rule, he deprecated where he would have condemned, he never committed the blasphemy of regarding the status quo as the acme of perfection. He was no apologist for folly enthroned in high places and did not hesitate to call evil by its right name.

Koheleth's principal value, however, lies not in this implication for the social scene, but in his explicit concern with the individual. The temperamental difference between Koheleth and the Prophets must not blind us to the guidance he offers men in meeting those ills that must be transcended because they cannot be transformed. It is true that nowhere does Koheleth preach the virtue of courage in so many words. For him courage is not a conscious ideal, nor even an idea—it is far more, an inborn, pervasive quality. Every line in his book is instinct with the spirit of clear-eyed, brave and joyous acceptance of life, for all its inevitable limitations.

And these limitations *are* inevitable, however unwilling a youthful and activistic generation may be to confess it. However successful men may become in molding the pattern of the world nearer heart's desire, they will still encounter pain and frustration in life, in meeting which they will require dignity and courage and the saving grace of good humor. The mounting doubts, fears and tensions of our own day, carried to unconscionable lengths though they may be, have served at least to remind us of this truth.

This need for resignation is independent of any given set of political, social and economic conditions. It inheres in the character of the universe and the nature of man. For he is a creature whose reach is always greater than his grasp, with a boundless imagination weaving hopes and desires far beyond the capacity of his brief, earth-bound existence to fulfill. As Koheleth observes, "All a man's toil is for his wants, but his desires are never satisfied." In teaching men to taste life's joys without self-deception and to face its sorrows without despair, Koheleth performs an everlastingly significant function.

The several factors that played their part in gaining admission for the book of Koheleth to the canon of Scripture have been discussed. . . . Undoubtedly the tradition of Solomonic authorship and Koheleth's unique style, particularly his unconventional use of a religious vocabulary and his citation of proverbs for his own special purposes, proved decisive factors.

Yet with it all, there was much in the book that was a stumbling-block to the devout. That it was never dislodged may be due in part to the naïveté and lack of historical perspective of many of its readers. But, basically, its preservation is a tribute both to the fascination of the book and to the catholic taste of the creators of the Biblical canon, who saw in every honest seeker after truth a servant of the one source of truth.

Moreover, ancient and medieval readers were not so naïve as their modern successors are wont to believe. That the basic theme of the book was *simḥah,* the enjoyment of life, was clearly recognized by Jewish religious authorities who thus explained the custom of reading *Koheleth* in the synagogue on the Feast of the Tabernacles, the Season of Rejoicing. But whatever the motives that led to the preservation of the book, we cannot be too grateful.

Koheleth would have been shocked, even amused, to learn that his notebook was canonized as part of Holy Scripture. But the obscure instinct of his people was building more truly than it knew when it stamped his work as sacred. Two millennia after Koheleth's day, a pietistic movement arose in Eastern European Jewry at the farthest possible remove from the temper of the ancient sage of Jerusalem. Yet a classic tale of the Hasidic tradition reveals a remarkable affinity with Koheleth. One day, Rabbi Bunam of Pshysha found his beloved disciple Enoch in tears. The Rabbi asked him, "Why are you weeping?" and Enoch answered, "Am I not a creature of this world, and am I not made with eyes and heart and all limbs, and yet I do not know for what purpose I was created and what good I am in the world." "Fool!" said Rabbi Bunam. "I also go around thus." Thus Koheleth, too, went about, seeking the purpose of life and lamenting his ignorance. His book is the record of his wandering and his sorrow, and of the peace he finally attained.

In the deepest sense, Koheleth is a religious book, because it seeks to grapple with reality. The Psalmist had sung:

A broken and contrite heart,
O God, Thou wilt not despise. (Ps. 51:19)

This cry of a sensitive spirit wounded by man's cruelty and ignorance, this distilled essence of an honest and courageous mind, striving to penetrate the secret of the universe, yet unwilling to soar on the wings of faith beyond the limits of the knowable, remains one of man's noblest offerings on the altar of truth.

11

THE IDENTIFICATION
AND USE
OF QUOTATIONS
IN ECCLESIASTES

R. N. Whybray

O ne of the most important aspects of the study of the wisdom of Qoheleth is the problem of its relationship to the earlier wisdom of the Old Testament, particularly as represented in the gnomic or proverbial literature collected in Proverbs 10–29.[1] The problem may be expressed in the following way: did Qoheleth regard himself as an exponent of "wisdom" in the same sense as the authors of the book of Proverbs? Was it his purpose to oppose the teaching of his predecessors in its entirety, or merely to modify certain aspects of it? Do the occasional apparently contradictory statements in the book show him to have been himself subject to doubts or contradic-

From *Vetus Testamentum Supplements* 32 (1981): 435–51. Reprinted by permission.

1. See especially K. Galling, *Die Krise der Aufklärung in Israel* (Mainz, 1952); H. Gese, "Die Krisis der Weisheit bei Koheleth," *Les sagesses du proche-orient ancien* (Paris, 1963), pp. 139–51 = *Vom Sinai zum Zion* (Munich, 1974), pp. 168–79; H. H. Schmid, *Wesen und Geschichte der Weisheit* (Berlin, 1966), pp. 186ff.; M. Hengel, *Judentum und Hellenismus* (Tübingen, 1969), pp. 210ff. = E. tr. *Judaism and Hellenism* (London, 1974) 1, pp. 115ff.; G. von Rad, *Weisheit in Israel* (Neukirchen, 1970), pp. 292ff. = E. tr. *Wisdom in Israel* (London, 1972), pp. 226ff.

tions, or was he rather quoting older sayings only to refute them? Or are we to follow some of the older critics and regard certain verses as having been added to the original text by interpolators?[2]

Some progress towards the solution of these problems may perhaps be obtained by looking again at the question of the supposed quotations of earlier wisdom sayings in the book of Qoheleth and at the way in which they fit into their contexts. However, the *identification* of such quotations constitutes a problem. Some sayings in the book certainly stand out from their contexts as sayings which are self-contained: they make good sense on their own. But are they in fact quotations from earlier literature, or were they composed in traditional fashion by Qoheleth himself? Can one distinguish between two kinds of such sayings: quotations, and original compositions by the author of the book?

In this essay it is not possible to attempt any major contributions to the solution of the many unsolved problems of the book. What I wish to undertake is some discussion of these putative quotations. It is to Robert Gordis that we owe most of our insights into the use of quotations in the Old Testament books and particularly in Qoheleth. One question, however, he left open as probably insoluble: in his book *Koheleth—The Man and His World: A Study of Ecclesiastes*[3] he wrote: "Whether Koheleth is quoting proverbs already extant, or composing them himself, is difficult to determine." If in fact there is no way of identifying Qoheleth's quotations, any attempt to draw conclusions about the way in which he used them is obviously doomed from the start. What are the possibilities? The kind of sayings which we are discussing might be quotations from some earlier written or oral collection, or quotations by Qoheleth of sayings composed earlier by himself, or passages in which he dropped the discursive style which he mainly employed in his book, and reverted to that of the more conventional wisdom writer. If they are actual quotations of sayings composed by someone other than himself, they may be from an earlier age—contemporary, for example, with the sayings in Prov. 10–29, many of which must probably be dated in the period of the monarchy—or they may be sayings composed by Qoheleth's own contemporaries. In view of all these possibilities it is indeed probable that the question of authorship— that is, Qoheleth's or another's—will not be capable of solution in all cases. Nevertheless it may be possible to point to some sayings where Qoheleth's

2. As maintained especially by C. Siegfried, *Prediger Salomonis und Hobeslied* (Göttingen, 1898[2]), and E. Podechard, *L'Ecclésiaste* (Paris, 1912).

3. (New York, 1955), p. 100 (repr. 1978). His articles "Quotations in Wisdom Literature," *JQR*, N.S. 30 (1939/40), pp. 123–47 = J. L. Crenshaw (ed.), *Studies in Ancient Israelite Wisdom* (New York, 1976), pp. 220–44, and "Quotations in Biblical, Oriental and Rabbinic Literature," *HUCA* 22 (1949), pp. 157–219 = *Poets, Prophets and Sages* (Bloomington and London, 1971), pp. 104–59, should also be consulted.

authorship is highly improbable: where we are, in other words, almost certainly dealing with quotations by him of sayings composed by others. If this can be done even in a few cases it will be possible to consider the reason for his employment of them and the use to which he put them.

In order to bring my remarks within the compass of this essay I propose here to confine myself to *one* type of saying: the single poetical verse or distich. I shall also confine my comparative material mainly to Prov. 10–29, chapters which contain the oldest extant collections of such sayings in the Old Testament, and it will be to these chapters that I refer when I use the term "Proverbs."[4] My purpose is to attempt to identify those sayings which because of their similarity to those in Proverbs and for other reasons appear to be quotations from earlier wisdom literature. These are the only ones which offer to the investigator some measure of objective control. It is not my intention to deny the existence of other quotations in Qoheleth, that is, from a period close to that of Qoheleth himself; but I know of no certain method by which such cases can be distinguished from Qoheleth's own writing.

What are the criteria which, when applied to such sayings, offer a high probability that they are quotations of earlier traditional wisdom sayings? Taking Proverbs as the norm, there are, it seems to me, four such criteria. Such sayings must be

1. sayings which are self-contained: that is, which when considered independently of their contexts express complete thoughts;
2. sayings which in *form* correspond closely to sayings in Proverbs;
3. sayings whose *themes* are characteristic of Proverbs, and at the same time in partial or total disagreement or tension either with their immediate contexts or with Qoheleth's characteristic ideas expressed elsewhere in the book;
4. sayings whose *language* is free from late features such as those of the language of Qoheleth, and is either that of classical Hebrew or more particularly of early wisdom literature.

It is of course possible that Qoheleth himself composed sayings identical in all respects with those in the book of Proverbs. We should then be dealing with examples of *pastiche* of an obsolete style. But in view of the fact that—as we shall see—Qoheleth's normal practice when he composed short wisdom sayings was to compose them in his own contemporary style, this would seem to be improbable.

In Qoheleth there are, according to my investigations, at least forty sayings to which the first two of these criteria apply: that is, which are self-contained,

4. Specifically to Prov. 10:1–22:16, 25–29.

and whose form is paralleled in Proverbs;[5] but most of these fail to conform to one or other, or both, of the last two criteria: in other words, either their language (vocabulary or grammar) is late, and indeed frequently identical with that of Qoheleth himself, or their theme differs from any of the themes occurring in Proverbs—and again is frequently identical with one of Qoheleth's own characteristic themes.

If we leave aside a number of doubtful cases there are then two groups of potentially independent single-distich sayings in the book. Of these, a study of those which resemble Qoheleth in style or theme would be rewarding, but would require a separate investigation. I intend in what follows to confine myself to the other group: those sayings which are *in every respect* indistinguishable in character from those in Proverbs. Of these there are—at least—eight clear examples: 2:14a, 4:5, 4:6 (omitting the final words, "and a striving after wind"), 7:5, 7:6a (i.e. omitting "This also in *hebel*"), 9:17, 10:2, 10:12.

Before a detailed investigation of these eight sayings is undertaken, one characteristic of them as a group should be mentioned which may be significant but which will not be pursued here. Although these eight sayings *individually* are indistinguishable from those in Proverbs, there is one respect in which *as a group* they have affinities with Qoheleth rather than with Proverbs: as in the rest of the book of Qoheleth, only *one* word for "fool" is used in them. All these eight passages except 6:6 refer to the fool or fools, and in each case the word *kᵉsīl* is used. This differs from the usage of Proverbs, which has five words for "fool," of which four (*pᵉtī, kᵉsīl, ᵉwīl, lēṣ*) are used frequently either by themselves or in contrast to *ḥākām*, "wise."

Quotations of Older Wisdom Sayings in Qoheleth

Each of the eight sayings referred to above will now be examined in respect of the three criteria of form, theme and language. That they all conform to the fourth criterion of being self-contained sayings will be self-evident.

1. 2:14a The wise man has eyes in his head,
   but the fool walks on in darkness.

a) *Form*. This is an antithetical saying in which, as in many similar sayings in Proverbs, the subject of each clause is placed first. The structure (nominal clause followed by participial clause) is paralleled in Proverbs, e.g. in 12:15:

---

5. Further study is needed of these. At least the following (some of which may require emendation to restore them to their original form) ought to be considered as possible quotations: 1:4, 8b, 15, 18 (omitting *kī*), 2:14a, 4:4, 6 (omitting *ūrᵉᶜūt rūaḥ*), 9, 11 (omitting *gam*), 13 abᵅ (to *ūkᵉsīl*), 17aᵝ (i.e. *qārōb . . . zābaḥ*, with some emendation), 5:2 (omitting *kī*), 9a (to *tᵉbūʾāh*, adapted), 6:7, 9a, 7:1, 2a (to *mišteh*), 3, 4, 5, 6a, 7 (omitting *kī*), 8, 9, 8:1b, 4 (omitting *baᵃšer*), 8aᵅᵝ (to *hammāwet* and omitting *likᵉlōʾ ʾet-hārūaḥ*), 8a–b (omitting *wᵉ*), 9:4b (omitting *kī*), 17, 18, 10:2, 8, 9, 11, 12, 19, 11:1, 4.

The way of a fool is right in his own eyes,
but a wise man listens to advice.

b) *Theme.* The theme of the conduct respectively of the wise man and the fool and its consequences (here implied rather than explicitly stated) occurs frequently in Proverbs and is there often expressed through the metaphor of walking: words like walk, way, stumble, path etc. are characteristic.[6] The phrase "to walk in the paths of darkness" itself occurs in Prov. 2:13, though in connection with unrighteousness rather than folly. That this saying is a quotation in its present context is shown by the fact that it is immediately followed by a comment which is characteristic of Qoheleth and challenges it: "And yet I perceived that one and the same fate will befall both."[7]

c) *Language.* All the words used in the saying occur in classical Hebrew. There is no trace of late words or usage. Everything points to the saying being a quotation.

2. 4:5   The fool folds his hands
and consumes his own flesh.

a) *Form.* This saying has synthetic parallelism consisting of two participial clauses, a form which is found also in Prov. 20:8:

A king sitting on the throne of judgment
winnows all evil with his eyes.

The second half is short, but not more so than, for example, Prov. 19:17.

b) *Theme.* The theme that laziness leads to ruin is very frequent in Proverbs.[8] The present context, however, speaks of the frustration caused by toil, a theme which is characteristic of Qoheleth.

c) *Language.* Each word occurs frequently in classical Hebrew or in Proverbs. The expression "fold the hands" (*ḥābaq yādayim*) occurs elsewhere only in Prov. 6:10 and 24:33, where as here it is an image of laziness. The expression "consume (literally, 'eat') one's own flesh," whose meaning is uncertain,[9] occurs

---

6. E.g. Prov. 10:17, 12:15, 13:20, 14:8, 12, 15:10, 19, 24, 16:25, 19:2, 3, 21:16, 22:5, 28:26.

7. *ʾet-kullām* means "both" here and in 7:18. So Gordis, *Koheleth,* p. 222; K. Galling, *Prediger* (Tübingen, 1969[2]), p. 90; A. Lauha, *Kohelet* (Neukirchen, 1978), p. 41; and cf. R. N. Whybray, "Qoheleth the Immoralist? (Qoh 7:16–17)," in J. G. Gammie et al. (ed.), *Israelite Wisdom . . . in Honor of Samuel Terrien* (New York, 1978), pp. 200f.

8. E.g. Prov. 10:4, 5, 12:11, 24, 27, 13:4, 15:19, 18:9, 19:15, 24, 20:4, 13, 28:19.

9. The view of several commentators that it refers to starvation consequent upon the fool's failure to provide food for himself may well be right. Cf. L. Koehler-W. Baumgartner, *Lexicon in Veteris Testamenti Libros* (Leiden, 1953), p. 43: "verzehrt (innerlich) sich." Even G. R. Driver, "Problems and Solutions," *VT* 4 (1954), p. 228, had no solution to offer: "Whatever this expression may connote. . . ." Mic. 3:3 and Ps. 27:2, cited by some commentaries in this connection,

only here and in Isa. 44:26: its absence from Proverbs is thus not significant. This saying appears to be a clear example of a quotation from earlier wisdom.

> 3. 4:6   Better is a handful with quiet
>   than two fistfuls with trouble.[10]

a) *Form*. The omission of the final words *ūrᵉᶜūt rūaḥ*, "and striving after wind," a phrase characteristic of and peculiar to Qohelet,[11] improves both metre and parallelism and leaves a so-called *ṭōb*-saying characteristic of Proverbs.[12]

b) *Theme*. Beyond the attainment of a sufficiency, wealth is not worth the toil involved in acquiring it. This is certainly a theme of Qoheleth's and is in fact elaborated in the verses which immediately follow; but similar sayings occur in Proverbs:

i. Prov. 14:30 points out the importance of tranquillity:

A tranquil mind gives life to the flesh,
but envy makes the bones rot.

ii. Prov. 17:1 also praises the virtue of tranquillity in terms similar to the saying under consideration:

Better is a dry morsel with quiet
than a house full of feasting with strife.

iii. Other sayings in Proverbs (15:16, 17, 16:8, 19, 28:6) also prefer a modest income with righteousness to wealth accompanied by trouble.

The final words of the verse, however, are clearly Qoheleth's own comment on an older saying: "and striving after wind."

c) *Language*. All the words used are those of classical Hebrew. *mᵉlōʾ kap*, "handful," occurs also in 1 Kings 17:12. *ḥopnayim*, "two fists," occurs once in Proverbs (30:4) and in five other Old Testament passages but not elsewhere in Qoheleth. The whole phrase *mᵉlōʾ ḥopnayim*, "two fistfuls," occurs in Exod. 9:8 and Lev. 16:12. *naḥat*, "quiet, tranquillity," occurs three times

---

are irrelevant because they refer to the eating of the flesh of others, not to eating one's own flesh. The idiom is probably a quite different one. Isa. 49:26, where Israel's oppressors are to be made to eat their own flesh and drink their own blood, is also almost certainly of an entirely different order.

10. There is no need to follow Galling (*Prediger*, p. 98) and others in emending *naḥat* and *ᶜāmāl* by adding the copula. The two nouns are adverbial accusatives (so Gordis, *Koheleth*, p. 241; H. W. Hertzberg, *Der Prediger* (Gütersloh, 1963), p. 102).

11. 1:14, 2:11, 17, 26, 4:4, 6, 6:9. The word *rᵉᶜūt* does not occur elsewhere in the Old Testament.

12. I.e., sayings characterized by the construction *ṭōb . . . min-*, "Better (is) . . . than . . . ". There are sixteen examples of this type of saying in Prov. 10:1–22:16 and 25–29, viz. 12:9, 15:16, 17, 16:8, 19, 32; 17:1, 19:1, 22, 21:9, 19, 25:24, 27:5, 10, 28:6.

iin Qoheleth but also in Prov. 29:9, twice in Job and once in Isaiah. Only *ʿāmāl* might suggest that Qoheleth is the author, since this word occurs in the book twenty-two times. But it is by no means peculiar to him, and in the sense in which it is used here ("misery, trouble") it occurs in Prov. 31:7 in addition to the many occurrences in the Old Testament in the sense of "wickedness." The saying is thus in every way indistinguishable from the sayings in Proverbs, and although it is not impossible that Qoheleth is the author, the addition of the final words suggests that it is a quotation.

4. 7:5   It is better to listen to a wise man's rebuke
            than (is) a man listening to the song of fools.

a) *Form.* The *ṭôb*-saying is of course characteristic of Proverbs. The slight anomaly in which an infinitive ("to listen") is paralleled by a noun ("a man") is also attested in Proverbs, e.g. Prov. 21:9:

It is better to live in a corner of a roof
than (is) a contentious woman and a brawling household.[13]

b) *Theme.* The themes of the value of listening to the wise and of the contrast between the speech of the wise man and of the fool are both characteristic of Proverbs. Elsewhere in the book of Qoheleth—for example in the story of the wise man whose advice was not sought (9:14–15)—Qoheleth questions the assumption that the wise man's advice is likely to prevail.

c) *Language.* All the words used here are normal Hebrew vocabulary and have no particular affinities with the language of Qoheleth. *gᵉʿārāh*, "rebuke," occurs nowhere else in Qoheleth but three times in Proverbs and several times elsewhere in the Old Testament. In Prov. 27:10 it is used in a very similar saying:

A rebuke goes deeper into a man of understanding
than a hundred blows into a fool.

There is a similar saying in Prov. 13:1. The fact that this saying (7:5) has been joined to the next by *kī*, "for" although the one was clearly not originally the continuation of the other supports the view that it is a quotation by Qoheleth of an earlier saying.

5. 7:6a   (omitting the first word *kī* and also omitting 6b,
            "This also is *hebel*"):

Like the crackling of thorns under a pot,
so is the laughter of the fool.

13. So NEB. On the difficult phrase *bēt ḥāber* see the commentaries.

a) *Form.* The comparison of two things expressed as nouns or nominal expressions is very frequent in Proverbs, and the wordplay here (*sīr*, "thorn"; *sīr*, "pot") is reminiscent of pairs such as *zādōn, qālōn* (Prov. 11:2). The second half of the saying is rather short, but we may compare Prov. 10:26.

b) *Theme.* The emptiness of fools is revealed in their laughter. Prov. 29:9 has a similar reference to the laughter of fools, and their speech is compared to a thorn in Prov. 26:9. References to their empty babbling are frequent, e.g. Prov. 10:14, 14:3, 7, 15:2, 14, 18:6, 7. This theme is itself not opposed to the ideas of Qoheleth, but the context shows that the saying is a quotation. In spite of the word *kī*, "for," at the beginning it is clearly not the continuation of verse 5, since there is a change of reference: verse 5 is about the song of fools but verse 6 about their laughter. The two verses are both quotations and were originally independent one of the other. The addition of the final words "This also is vanity" (*hebel*), a characteristic comment of Qoheleth's and not part of the metrical line, suggests that here too he is quoting an older saying.

c) *Language.* The language has no particular affinities with that of Qoheleth, *sīr*, "pot," is frequent in the Old Testament, but does not occur in Proverbs and occurs only here in Qoheleth. *sīr*, "thorn," though rare, is as old as Hos. 2:8 and Amos 4:2. *śāḥaq*, "laugh," a word which occurs frequently in the Old Testament, is found three times in Proverbs but only here in Qoheleth.

6. 9:17 Wise men's words (spoken) in calm are worth hearing rather than a ruler's shouting among fools.

a) *Form.* If the above rendering is correct[14] this is a comparison-saying of the same kind as Prov. 17:10:

A rebuke goes deeper into a man of understanding
than a hundred blows into a fool.

b) *Theme.* The superiority of the wise man with his calm speech is a theme which occurs very frequently in Proverbs. The noun *naḥat*, "calm, quiet," is used in a very similar context in Prov. 29:9:

If a wise man quarrels with a fool
he meets with rage and scorn and there is no quiet.

But the immediately preceding story of the poor man whose advice was not heeded (verses 14–16), which expresses Qoheleth's own view, is clearly different from the tenor of this saying, which again suggests that it is a quotation.

14. The commentaries differ about the syntactical relationship of *nišmāʿîm* to its context (see Gordis, *Koheleth*, pp. 190, 312; Galling, *Prediger*, p. 115; Hertzberg, *Prediger*, p. 183). Galling translates: "Worte der Weisen in Ruhe gehört, sind mehr als . . . ". I have followed Lauha's translation (*Kohelet*, pp. 175, 178).

c) *Language. naḥat* has already been discussed under 4:6. *mōšēl,* "ruler," frequent in the Old Testament, occurs five times in Proverbs and only twice in Qoheleth (7:19, 10:5) where the word *šallīṭ* is also used for "ruler." There are thus no affinities with the language of Qoheleth.

7. 10:2 The wise man's understanding inclines him to the right,
          and the fool's to the left.

a) *Form.* This saying in antithetical parallelism consisting of two nominal clauses may be compared with several in Proverbs including Prov. 10:16:

The wage of the righteous leads to life,
the gain of the wicked to sin.

b) *Theme.* The theme of the contrast between the respective fates of the wise man and the fool is characteristic of Proverbs. But the optimism of this older saying is negated by the pessimistic comment of Qoheleth in the previous verse: "A little folly outweighs wisdom and honor."[15]

c) *Language.* This is normal classical Hebrew. There are no affinities with the language of Qoheleth.

8. 10:12 The speech of a wise man brings him favour,
          but the lips of a fool destroy him.

a) *Form.* This pattern of nominal clause followed by verbal clause in antithetic parallelism is also found in Proverbs, e.g. Prov. 10:7:

The memory of the righteous is a source of blessing,
but the name of the wicked will rot.

b) *Theme.* The themes of the importance of wise speech and of the consequences of wise and foolish talk are characteristic of Proverbs. As in the cases of 7:5, 9:17 and 10:2 the optimism of this saying is in contrast with Qoheleth's views on the improbability of the wise man's words being heeded.

c) *Language.* Again, there are no affinities with the language of Qoheleth. *ḥēn,* "favor," frequent in the Old Testament, occurs also frequently in Proverbs, sometimes in sayings very similar to the present one:

13:15   Good sense wins favor,
         but the way of the treacherous leads to their destruction.[16]

28:23   He who rebukes a man will win favor[17]
         rather than he who flatters with his tongue.

---

15. Or "an abundance of wisdom" (Gordis, *Koheleth,* pp. 190, 315).

16. Reading *ʾēdām* for *ʾētān* with some commentaries and the NEB. See L. H. Brockington, *The Hebrew Text of the Old Testament. The Readings Adopted by the Translators of the New English Bible* (Oxford and Cambridge, 1973), p. 161. Cf. LXX.

17. Omitting the difficult *ʾaḥᵃray,* "after me," which may however be a corruption. One MS has *ʾaḥᵃrāw,* which is accepted by the NEB (see Brockington, p. 167) and translated by "in the end."

But it occurs in only one other passage in Qoheleth (9:11). *bāla'* (Piel), "swallow up, destroy," occurs frequently in the Old Testament, but this is the only example in the wisdom books of its use in the sense of bringing ruin on a person.

Qoheleth's Use of His Quotations

The eight sayings discussed above are, then, all examples of sayings whose themes are characteristic of the teaching of Prov. 10–29. Since their form and language are also those of an earlier period we may conclude that they are older sayings (not necessarily the only ones, but the only really clear examples) which Qoheleth incorporated into his book as quotations. Why did he do this? What use did he make of them? A consideration of these questions may shed light on Qoheleth's relationship to earlier wisdom: that is, on the extent to which he agreed with it and the extent to which he parted from it.

It will be seen as the study proceeds that he used these sayings in two ways. Some of them he quoted with full approval, either making no comment of his own or confirming and elaborating the statements which they make. Others he used in the course of a more complex kind of argument in which he distinguished between absolute and relative truths. It will be observed that in no case did he quote one of these sayings simply in order to contradict or refute it completely.

Sayings to Which Qoheleth Gave Unqualified Approval

10:3 is a saying by Qoheleth himself in which he expresses approval of the older saying 10:2. Having quoted the older saying

> The wise man's understanding inclines him to the right,
> and the fool's to the left,

he added, in prose, his own comment: "Even on a journey, when the fool is traveling he lacks sense, and says about everyone else, 'He is a fool'" (or perhaps, "He tells everyone else that he himself is a fool"). The late form *k'šehassākāl* (Qere *k'šessākāl*) and the use of the word *sākāl*, "fool" (five times in Qoheleth and only twice elsewhere in the Old Testament—Jer. 4:22; 5:21) suggest that this is a comment made by Qoheleth himself.

10:13 similarly is a comment by Qoheleth, though it purports to be the continuation of the older saying in 10:12. The older saying is as follows:

> The speech of a wise man brings him favor,
> but the lips of a fool destroy him.

Qoheleth's comment is:

> The beginning of his speech is folly,
> and the end of his speech wicked madness.

The use of the words *siklūt*, "folly" and *hōlēlūt*, "madness," both of which are peculiar to and characteristic of Qoheleth, shows that this is not the second half of an original double proverb but an addition made by Qoheleth himself. Verse 14 is a further elaboration of the theme by Qoheleth in prose, again—like verse 13—restricting the scope of the discourse to the fool alone.

In 7:5 and 7:6, as has already been pointed out, Qoheleth has joined together two older sayings, the first about the speech of the wise man and the fool and the second about the empty laughter of the fool. He has also added his own comment, "This also is *hebel*," which clearly refers to and approves of these sayings in their contempt for fools.

In all these cases, then, Qoheleth quoted older sayings and gave them his full approval. Why did he do this, and what exactly did he find to approve of in the older wisdom? The usual modern—and, I think, correct—interpretation of these older sayings in which the wise man is contrasted with the fool is that it is possible for a man to achieve success and happiness by imitating the former and avoiding the behavior of the latter.[18] But is this what Koheleth understood by these sayings? Did he agree with their essentially optimistic teaching?

If we look more closely at his comments it will be clear that this is not the case. In all the instances which we have just considered there is a significant fact to be noticed: whereas the older or the first saying presents two modes of conduct for comparison, those of the wise man and of the fool, Qoheleth's comment refers only to one of these: the foolish one. Thus 10:2 contrasts the "understanding" (*lēb*) of the wise man and that of the fool, but verse 3 speaks only of the fool as he walks along calling others fools. Again, 10:12 contrasts the speech of the wise man and the fool, but verse 13 only develops the thought about the fool's speech, and verse 14 likewise. Finally the two older sayings in 7:5 and 6 have been selected and arranged so that whereas verse 5 contrasts the wise man's rebuke with the song of fools, verse 6 speaks only of fools and their laughter. The comment "This also is *hebel*" made by Qoheleth at the end betrays his purpose in all this: it is the vanity of life as exemplified by the behavior of the *fool* which he wishes to emphasize.

Qoheleth valued these older sayings, then, not because they teach, by contrasting two modes of conduct, that one can be happy if one wishes by choosing wise conduct rather than foolish, but because they offer evidence congenial to his own view, that the world is at least as full of fools as it is of wise men. "*This*," he says, "is vanity." In other words, Qoheleth has completely reinterpreted the wise-foolish contrast of the older sayings, seeing in them a meaning

---

18. In some sayings in Proverbs this is clearly implied, e.g., Prov. 13:14:
   The teaching of the wise man is a fountain of life,
   that one may avoid (*lāsūr min-*) the snares of death.

quite different from that which we are accustomed to see in them. For him they express not an optimistic teaching but a pessimistic one: the presence of folly in the world is—to use his own imagery—the fly in the ointment (10:1) which makes ineffective the wisdom existing in the world, which if only it existed without the counterweight of folly would make it a good world.

Thus in the cases which we have considered, Qoheleth only "approved" the older wisdom because he interpreted it in a sense which fitted his own view of the world; and the way in which he has commented on it shows that he believed that although wisdom and folly co-exist in the world, folly predominates. As he himself said in 10:1, "A little folly outweighs wisdom." It is for this reason that he has placed a saying—whether of his own composition or not—which mentions only folly immediately after each saying which mentions wisdom and folly together. In this way he succeeds in each case in concluding his reflection with all the emphasis placed on the tragic, or at least frustrating, existence of folly.

Sayings to Which Qoheleth Gave Relative Approval

The conclusion reached in the foregoing section is confirmed by the use which Qoheleth made of the other older sayings which we have identified. The passages in which these occur belong to the type which Galling called the "gebrochene Sentenz," in which Qoheleth cites a traditional truth and accepts it as far as it goes while also pointing to other facts of life which seriously weaken its effectiveness and so lead to a pessimistic rather than an optimistic conclusion.[19]

2:12–17 is a passage devoted to a discussion of wisdom and folly in which the quotation from older wisdom, verse 14a, plays a supporting role in an otherwise self-contained argument of this type. It is preceded by verse 13, a verse whose authorship is indicated by the use of the words *yitrōn*, "advantage, profit" and *siklūt*, "folly," both of which are peculiar to and characteristic of Qoheleth: "And I saw that wisdom is more profitable than folly as light is more profitable than darkness." This statement of a traditional truth receives its fatal qualification, again in the words of Qoheleth himself, in verse 15: "But I said to myself, the fate of the fool will befall me also: why have I been so very wise?"

In verses 16 and 17 this pessimistic thought is pursued further. The older saying, verse 14a, is inserted after verse 13 to support the original optimistic proposition:

The wise man has eyes in his head,
but the fool walks on in darkness;

---

19. K. Galling, "Kohelet-Studien," *ZAW* 50 (1932), pp. 277–92; "Stand und Aufgabe der Kohelet-Forschung," *ThR*, N.F. 6 (1934), p. 369; *Die Krise der Aufklärung in Israel*, pp. 14ff. More detailed analysis of this type of pericope is to be found in F. Ellermeier, *Qohelet* I/1 (Herzberg, 1967).

and to this Qoheleth, before going on to his further remarks in verses 15–17, has made a direct comment in the same vein: "But I also reflected that one and the same fate will befall both."

There is, then, no question of Qoheleth's quoting an earlier saying simply to refute it. He himself has already expressed his approval of its truth in verse 13. The teaching of the older wisdom, then, is true; but it cannot in the long run overcome the vanity or meaninglessness of life.

The older saying 9:17 is set in a similar context. Throughout the section 9:13–18 the ability of the wise man to achieve what force cannot achieve is accepted, but so also is another fact of life which can entirely negate its value: the wise man's advice is rarely heeded. Verses 14–15, which tell the story of the poor wise man who could have saved the city but whom no-one remembered at the crucial time,[20] already demonstrate both of these truths. Verses 16–18 then make the point again, indeed twice over. Verse 16a, which is probably a quotation of a popular adage, makes an absolute statement about the superiority of wisdom: "Wisdom is better than force." Verse 16b, whose use of the word *miskēn*, "poor," peculiar to Qoheleth, clearly indicates its authorship, states the second truth in a direct comment on the preceding story: "But the poor man's wisdom was despised and his words were not heeded." Verse 17, the older saying, picks up from verse 16b the word *nišmāʿîm*, "heard, heeded," and repeats the first truth:

> Wise men's words (spoken) in calm are worth hearing (*nišmāʿîm*) rather than a ruler's shouting among fools.[21]

This is then qualified in verse 18 in a poetical saying of Qoheleth's own composition (shown by the use of *harbēh*, "much," peculiar to Qoheleth among the wisdom books and used fifteen times by him):

> Wisdom is better than weapons of war,
> but a single incompetent (*ḥōṭēʾ*)[22] can destroy much good

(i.e. its good effect). The older saying (verse 17) is, then, quoted to confirm the truth that wisdom is better than force, a truth which Qoheleth himself accepts, though in conjunction with the other, depressing, fact of life.

---

20. So most modern commentaries. The alternative interpretation, according to which the poor man did save the city but was subsequently forgotten, is less probable in the context.
21. See note 14 above.
22. Cf. Prov. 19:2. Gordis, *Koheleth*, p. 310, translates by "fool."

Finally, in 4:5 and 6 Qoheleth uses two older sayings to express a similar two-part argument, this time on the value of hard work and its corresponding drawbacks. 4:5,

> The fool folds his hands
> and consumes his own flesh,

expresses the thought that work is indispensable to life, while 4:6,

> Better is a handful with quiet
> than two fistfuls with trouble

makes the point that, while the former statement is true, overwork in order to make a fortune is not worth the candle. Qoheleth's final words "and striving after wind" stress the truth of the second saying.

Concluding Observations

It is now possible to give some tentative answers to the questions posed at the beginning of this article.

1. His use of wisdom sayings from an earlier period shows that Qoheleth regarded himself as a wisdom writer in the Israelite tradition. Whenever possible he made use in the course of his arguments of the insights of the wisdom of the past.

2. His purpose in quoting these sayings was not to demonstrate their falsity. He quoted them because he accepted their truth.

3. His approval of them, however, was of a distinctive and characteristic kind. He saw in the contrast which they make between wisdom and folly not the optimistic doctrine that man is free by choosing wisdom to seek and obtain success and happiness but rather the pessimistic one that folly generally prevails over wisdom, so that life is meaningless.

A further observation may be made about Qoheleth's *selection* of older sayings. Although the examples discussed above may not be the only quotations which he makes from the wisdom of an earlier period—there are a number of other sayings which may belong to this category, though the evidence for this seems to me to be less conclusive[23]—nevertheless the sayings in the book which do not by their theme or language betray a late origin are very few. For the most part Qoheleth seems to have been unable to find sayings which he could use to express or support his radical teaching, and so he mainly went his own way, guided simply by his personal observation of the world.

23. Especially 6:7, 7:7, 7:8, 11:1, 11:4.

It may also be noted that all the sayings which he quotes from earlier wisdom are "secular": that is, they deal with themes such as wisdom and folly, work and idleness, the quiet life and the troubled life, success and failure, not with righteousness and wickedness or with piety and impiety. They represent only one side of the teaching of older wisdom represented by Prov. 10–29.

Unresolved Questions

Finally some questions which remain unsolved may be noted.

1. Study is needed of the fairly numerous sayings in Qoheleth mentioned earlier which have the form of sayings in Proverbs, but whose language shows them to be contemporary with Qoheleth. Some of these express views which are characteristic of Qoheleth himself; others are reminiscent of Proverbs in theme as well as in form. If we are to discover whether these are quotations or the work of Qoheleth himself, some examination of their function in their present contexts will be necessary.

2. A further question concerns the possibility that some of the sayings expressed in late language may be older sayings whose language has been "modernized." As has already been pointed out, even in those sayings which are clearly quotations from earlier wisdom the only word used for "fool" is *kᵉsîl,* a limitation of vocabulary which corresponds to Qoheleth's own usage but not to that of Proverbs. It is possible that in some of these sayings Qoheleth himself substituted *kᵉsîl* for some other word, although it should be noted that Ben Sirach, writing somewhat later, shows no such limitation of vocabulary. But this question requires further thought.

Part 2

SPECIFIC THEMES
AND PASSAGES
IN THE BOOK
OF ECCLESIASTES

12

QOHELETH,
PREACHER
OF JOY

R. N. Whybray

Qoheleth is generally regarded as having taken a very sombre view
of life. The seven passages where he recommends the whole-
hearted pursuit of enjoyment, therefore, constitute a problem.[1] The purpose
of this article is to re-examine these seven texts and their contexts in an attempt to understand their place in his thought. They are: 2:24a; 3:12; 3:22a;
5:17; 8:15a; 9:7–9a; 11:7–12:1a.

From the *Journal for the Study of the Old Testament* 23 (1982): 87–98. Reproduced by permission of Sheffield Academic Press.

1. Many early translators and commentators, both Jewish and Christian, recognized the
problem and sought to avoid it by spiritualizing, allegorizing or paraphrasing these passages (see
C. D. Ginsburg, *Coheleth,* London, 1861 (reprinted in *The Song of Songs and Coheleth,* New York,
1970), 27–243 for a detailed history of interpretation up to that date). C. Siegfried in *Prediger
und Hoheslied* (Nowack's *Handkommentar* II/3), 1898 attempted a solution by means of his
theory of multiple authorship: the passages are additions by a Sadducee influenced by Epicurae-
anism to an original work expressing an un-Hebraic view of life. Theories of multiple authorship,
together with somewhat analogous theories of the presence of numerous glosses or of the book
as a sustained dialogue between two persons with different viewpoints, have now been abandoned, and the question is now recognized as being one of the consistency or inconsistency of

It may first be noted that these texts are arranged in such a way as to state their theme with steadily increasing emphasis and solemnity. First comes the plain statement:

> There is no better thing for man to do than[2] to eat and drink and find enjoyment in his toil. 2:24a

To the next two statements an asseverative phrase is prefixed:

> So I realized (*wᵉyāda ᶜtî*) *that* there is no better thing for them[3] to do than to be happy and enjoy themselves as long as they live. 3:12

> So I understood (*wᵉrā*ʾîtî)[4] *that* there is no better thing than that a man should be happy in his work. 3:22a

The fourth has a more solemn introduction:

> *Take note of what I have discovered* (*hinnēh ᵃšer-rā*ʾîtî): it is good and right[5] to eat and drink and find enjoyment in one's toil. 5:17

Qoheleth's own thought. The majority of modern scholars try to find some consistency in it and to interpret Qoheleth's advocacy of the pursuit of happiness as in some way the consequence of his sombre view of the world. They vary greatly, however, in their estimates of the spirit in which he gives this advice. These estimates range from the view of (e.g.) M. Hengel, *Judaism and Hellenism*, London, 1974, 126 that "only the possibility of '*carpe diem*' . . . can give meaning, albeit very limited, to life," through G. A. Barton's estimate of Qoheleth's attitude as "manly and healthy, if not inspiring" (*Ecclesiastes* (ICC), 1908, 49) to the view that Qoheleth preserved a lively faith in God's goodness in spite of everything. Few writers, however, have taken the view that the sense of joy expressed in these passages is in fact the keynote of the book. Among them are R. Gordis, *Koheleth—The Man and His World*, New York, 1955 (even more clearly in the third edition, New York, 1968, 131); M. A. Klopfenstein, "die Skepsis von Qoheleth," *Theologische Zeitschrift* 28 (1972), 97–109; and R. K. Johnston, "'Confessions of a Workaholic': A Reappraisal of Qoheleth," *CBQ* 38 (1976), 14–28. Cf. also S. Holm-Nielsen, "The Book of Ecclesiastes and the Interpretation of It in Jewish and Christian Theology," *ASTI* 10 (1975–6), 50f.; E. M. Good, *Irony in the Old Testament*, London, 1965, 168–95.

2. MT *ʾēn-ṭôb bā*ʾādām *šeyyōkal* is, literally, "It is not good for man that he should eat. . . . " But in view of the similar phrases in 3:22 and elsewhere in the book it appears necessary, with almost all modern commentators, to assume the haplography of *memm* before *šeyyōʾkal*, giving "*than* that he should eat." J. A. Loader, *Polar Structures in the Book of Qohelet* (BZAW 152), Berlin, 1979, 38, 41 and N. Lohfink, *Kohelet* (Die neue Echter Bibel), Würzburg, 1980, defend MT and translate accordingly: but it is improbable that Qoheleth would have used almost identical expressions here and in 3:22 with different meanings. This consideration also tells against the suggestion that the sentence should be taken as interrogative. Emendation of *bā*ʾādām to *lā*ʾādām is however unnecessary in view of a similar use of *bᵉ* in 3:12.

3. *bām* (for the use of *bᵉ* see 2:24) refers to *hā*ʾādām in verse 11, understood collectively: see G.-K. § 145m. Emendation to *bā*ʾādām (R. Kroeber, *Der Prediger* (Schriften und Quellen der Alten Welt, 13), Berlin, 1963: K. Galling (HAT 18²), 1969; W. Zimmerli, *Prediger* (ATD 16/1³), 1980 is not necessary. Gordis's view that *bām* is a dittograph is consequently gratuitous.

4. The context shows that *rā*ʾāh is here used to introduce a conclusion drawn from the preceding observations.

5. So several commentators including Gordis (who takes *ṭôb* ᵃšer *yāpeh* as "an idiom heightening the effect, like 'good and proper.'"). Possibly *ṭôb* should be taken with the preceding phrase (so Kroeber; H. W. Hertzberg, *Der Prediger* (KAT 17/4), 1963; A. Lauha, *Kohelet* (BKAT), 1978): "Take notice of what I have discovered to be good: it is right to eat. . . . " The general sense is not affected.

The fifth is expressed in even more decided terms:

> *So I praise joy:* for there is no better thing for man to do under the sun than to eat and drink. 8:15a

In the sixth Qoheleth has changed to the imperative mood. He now positively urges his young pupil to follow his advice:

> Go, eat your bread with joy . . . , drink your wine with a cheerful heart . . . Always be dressed in white . . . Do not fail to anoint your head with oil . . . Enjoy life with the woman you love. 9:7a, 8, 9a

In the seventh and last the advice is given, again in the imperative, in the form of a personal address to the young man:

> Be happy, young man, in the time of your youth, and let your heart be cheerful[6] while your youth lasts . . . ; follow the promptings of your heart . . . Banish worry . . . ; cast off trouble . . . Remember your Creator[7] . . . 11:9a, 10a; 12:1a

These seven texts are clearly more than mere marginal comments or asides. They punctuate the whole book, forming a kind of *Leitmotiv;* they increase steadily in emphasis as the book proceeds; and the last, the most elaborate of them all, directly addressed to the reader, introduces and dominates the concluding section of the book in which Qoheleth presents his final thoughts on how life should be lived and why. It would be arbitrary to deny that they play a significant part in the exposition of Qoheleth's thought. In order to discover what part they play we must examine their contexts.

The immediate contexts (2:24–26; 3:10–15; 3:22b; 5:17–19; 8:14–15; 9:7–10; 11:7–12:1) give reasons for the advice which Qoheleth offers. The point which occurs most frequently is that of God's gift: the opportunity to enjoy life is given by God himself. The words "give" and "gift," with God as giver, occur with great frequency in these passages. Three other reasons are also adduced: the necessity of accepting one's lot, which is unchangeable (2:26; 3:14; 3:22b; 5:18; 9:9); the brevity of life (5:17b; 9:9b; 11:9; 12:1b): and man's ignorance of the future (3:11; 3:22b; 8:14). These apparently depressing considerations are turned by Qoheleth into positive incentives to enjoy all the more what God gives in the present. How this can be so becomes clearer when we turn our attention to the more remote

---

6. Literally, "may your heart make you cheerful." But no emendation is necessary.
7. The form *bōr'e(y)kā* (the same as that of the *plural* noun with suffix) is strange. Various explanations have been given of it (see especially Hertzberg, Gordis, Lauha). The Versions understood it as meaning "your Creator," and there is insufficient reason to emend it or to translate it otherwise.

contexts. As will be seen, each of these seven passages is closely related to a particular theme and to a particular section of the book.[8]

1. 2:24–26 is the concluding paragraph of the section 1:12–2:26. Here "Solomon," after seeking satisfaction in life by the acquisition first of pleasure and then of wisdom, looks back on his efforts and expresses his disillusionment: he "hates life" (2:17); he hates his fruitless toil (2:18). Even the immense efforts which he made to enjoy himself (2:1a) have given him no lasting satisfaction (2:1b–2, 10–11). Then in 2:22–23 we are told why: it is precisely because he tried so hard and relied on his own efforts that in the end all he has achieved is worry and strain:

> What good does a man derive from all the toil and effort with which he toils under the sun? For his whole life is one long round of anxiety, and his business brings nothing but worry. Even at night his mind is not at rest.

Qoheleth's answer to this problem is then given in verse 24: man should "eat and drink and *find enjoyment* in his toil"; but this is possible only when it comes "from the hand of God." *God* may *give* joy and pleasure; man can never achieve it for himself, however hard he may try.

2. 5:9–19, on wealth, makes a similar point. Wealth does not satisfy (verse 9); it does not last; and it may be lost more quickly than it has been gained (verses 12–13); moreover a man cannot take it with him when he dies. Like Solomon, all he gets is worry:

> What profit can he show after toiling to earn the wind, with all his life spent in the dark, with much worry, sickness and irritation? 15b–16

Again comes the answer that it is best "to eat and drink, and find enjoyment in one's toil" (verse 17), because this is God's gift. In another part of his book (4:6) Qoheleth summed up the lesson of both these sections with a quotation from an older saying:

> Better is a handful with quiet
>   than two fistfuls with toil[9]

—to which he added a further comment of his own: "and chasing after the wind."

---

8. No comprehensive theory is here put forward or assumed regarding the structure—if any—of the book as a whole, nor are the seven passages discussed below to be regarded as implying any such theory. The purpose of the discussion at this stage is simply to point out some of the more obvious connections between the seven texts which, recommend the pursuit of enjoyment, and material which immediately precedes or follows them. It is, however, possible that if pursued further this might shed light on the questions of structure and of the delimitation of literary units.

9. *naḥat* and *ʿāmāl* are adverbial accusatives (so Gordis, Hertzberg).

3. The theme of 3:1–15 is how man should behave in the light of his ignorance of the future. According to the series of short sayings in verses 1–8, the things which happen to a man (for example, birth and death) and the opportunities which are given to him (for example, planting and uprooting, keeping and throwing away) occur at the time (*ʿēt*) which God has determined: "he has made everything proper for its due time" (verse 11). But since God has also ordained that "man cannot comprehend (*yimṣāʾ*) the work which God has done," the question must be asked, "What profit does the doer (*hāʿōśēh*)[10] derive from his toil?" (verse 9). Man as doer cannot know, and so cannot alter, the divine ordinance. But once more the man who *accepts* what God *gives* finds happiness (verse 13). Qoheleth's concluding advice is quite positive: precisely because he is ignorant of what the future holds, man can and should recognize and make full use of what opportunities for joy God gives him in the here and now.

4. The theme of 3:16–22 is the fact of injustice in the world (verse 16). In addressing this problem Qoheleth first reaffirms the traditional belief that "God will judge the righteous and the wicked" (verse 17a).[11] But the difficulty is that man does not know *when* this will happen: "there is a proper time for everything" (verse 17b), and foreknowledge of that time, Qoheleth has explained elsewhere, is not given to man. Moreover God's judgment does not extend beyond the grave: at death "all go to the same place" regardless of their deserts. But out of this depressing state of affairs Qoheleth draws, once again, a positive conclusion: it is *because* "that is his lot" and because no one can "let him know what will happen to him next" that man should set himself to "enjoy his work" (verse 22).

5. The theme of 8:10–15 is somewhat similar to that of 3:16–22. Verse 10 is extremely difficult to translate and has been interpreted in a variety of ways;[12] but verse 11 expresses the heart of the problem:

10. That *hāʿōśēh* here should be translated by "the doer" and not by "the worker" is shown by the context. Verses 1–8 speak of human activities generally rather than specifically of work; and these activities are contrasted in verses 10–15 with God's activity by the use of the root *ʿāśāh:* the verb *ʿāśāh* with God as subject occurs three times in verses 10–15, and the noun *maʿaśēh*, referring to God's activity, once in verse 11. Qoheleth's conclusion in verse 9 that human activity is profitless is explained in verses 10–15; this is so because God's activity is hidden from man. See further Ginsburg, Galling, Lauha, D. Lys (*L'Ecclésiaste ou Que vaut la vie? Traduction, introduction générale, commentaire de 1/1 à 4/3*, Paris, 1977), Lohfink, Zimmerli.

11. It is unnecessary, with Galling, Lauha and Lohfink, to regard verse 17a as a gloss or an addition by a redactor, or, with Kroeber and Gordis, to suppose that here Qoheleth quoted an older wisdom saying but did not himself accept it. Qoheleth's view of "time" as hidden from man enabled him to maintain the traditional belief in divine judgment, although as a result the latter obviously lost much of its force as a deterrent (cf. 8:11).

12. See the commentaries. Some emendation is probably necessary. But however the verse is interpreted, the general sense is in accordance with Qoheleth's thought as expressed in verses 11 and 14 in its observation that the wicked are often highly honored, whether in life or death. If *wᵉyištakkᵉḥū* is left unemended (as against Gordis and Lauha) the verse also draws a contrast between the fortunes of the wicked and of the righteous, who receive no honour but are forgotten.

> It is because the sentence pronounced on a wicked action is not executed promptly that men's minds are so ready to act wickedly.

Qoheleth's answer, in verses 12b, 13, that it "will be well with those who fear God . . . but it will not be well with the wicked," which seem at first to contradict the following verse, is not an "orthodox" gloss or quotation but corresponds to Qoheleth's own statement in 3:17 about the time, of which men are ignorant, which God has appointed for judgment.[13] So the temptation to imitate the wicked should be resisted: and their fate can be safely left in God's hands. The conclusion in verse 15 is, then, that man would do best to take the opportunity given by God to eat and drink and enjoy his work.

6. 9:1–10 is concerned with two problems: man cannot know whether his actions will please God ("whether it is love or hatred," verse 1b); and death will come to all alike (verses 2, 3a). In verse 3b Qoheleth describes how men commonly react to these facts: "men's minds are filled with evil, or else it is madness which dominates their minds throughout their lives"—that is, they either embark on an evil life because there seems to be nothing to restrain them, or they fall prey to the madness of a frantic attempt to achieve something lasting by their own efforts. But Qoheleth offers a better way: life is God's most precious gift (verses 4–6), and one can enjoy life because the very fact that God has given the opportunity for enjoyment means that he "has already shewn his approval of your actions" (verse 7). In the final verses (8–10) Qoheleth repeats as additional reasons what he has already adduced elsewhere: the certainty and finality of death and the fact that toil is not a burden if one adopts the right attitude towards it: "Whatever you find it possible to do, do it with your might."

7. In 11:7–12:7 the advice to enjoy life comes at the beginning of the final section of the book and is followed by the famous description of old age culminating in death, which is expressed in a series of subordinate clauses severally introduced by ʿad ʾᵃšer, "before, until," which are dependent on the main imperative clause, "Remember your Creator in the days of your youth." That

---

13. The authenticity of verses 12b, 13 is defended by Hertzberg and Zimmerli as part of one of the so-called "Zwar . . . aber" arguments characteristic of Qoheleth, in which he accepts the truth of a traditional belief but only in a qualified sense. The argument of verses 10–15 as a whole may be set out as follows: Qoheleth has observed that the wicked are frequently honored, a circumstance which is due to the interval which sometimes elapses between wicked deeds and their punishment, and which unfortunately encourages others to behave like them (verses 10–11). Punishment will, however, eventually follow in God's good time (verses 12–13). Meanwhile injustice sometimes—though not always: note the use of yeš—appears to be done (verse 14). This is one of the "vanities" of life. But it cannot be put right by man, who ought therefore to leave the issue to God and accept joyfully God's positive gifts when they come (verse 15).

Qoheleth, by ending his book with a description of old age, and death, intended his readers to face rather than shrink from reality is clear; but the prevailing note, expressed in the imperatives, is a positive one. It *is* imperative to enjoy life, because that is the way to "remember your Creator," that is, to do his will.[14] The brevity of one's active life, which is itself also a gift of God ("until the spirit returns to God who gave it," 12:7) is an additional reason for enjoying it in the here and now.

In these seven sections of the book, then, Qoheleth posed seven problems of human life and drew practical and positive conclusions concerning the proper conduct of life. The problems are:

1. The vanity of toil and human effort (1:12–2:26).
2. The vanity of man's ignorance of the future (3:1–15).
3. The vanity of the presence of injustice in the world (3:16–22).
4. The vanity of the pursuit of wealth (5:9–19).
5. The vanity of unpunished wickedness (8:10–15).
6. The vanity of the fact that all men share a common fate (9:1–10).
7. The vanity of the brevity of human life (11:7–12:7).

Qoheleth not only did not deny the existence of these "vanities": he emphasized them so strongly that he has been supposed to be a teacher of unrelieved pessimism. But in spite of them, and even *from* them, he was able, as we have seen, to provide answers and to make recommendations which in some sense transcend the evils which the Creator has inscrutably allowed to exist in the world. His conclusions may be summarized as follows:

1. What good things God has given us are intended for our enjoyment, and in the giving of them he has shown his approval of our actions. To enjoy them is actually to do his will.
2. We must accept our ignorance of God's purposes and of the reasons why he has permitted evil to exist in the world: and we must take life as we find it and enjoy what we can, because

14. The verb "remember" (*zākar*) with God as its object is used in the Old Testament in several somewhat different senses (see B. S. Childs, *Memory and Tradition in Israel* (SBT 37). London, 1963, 45–65; H. Eising, art. *zākar* in *TWAT* II, 1977, 575–78). Here it probably includes obedience to God's will (cf. 11:9b and the references to the "fear of God" in 3:14; 5:6; 7:18; 8:12, 13; 9:2) and the due promise of religious duties (cf. 4:17–5:6); but the context shows that more is meant than this. God is to be remembered specifically as Creator (so only here in the Old Testament); and it is made clear that this "remembrance" can only be properly carried out in youth, "before the bad days come, and the years approach when you will say, 'I get no pleasure from them.'" This suggests that by remembering one's Creator Qoheleth means principally the enjoyment of the good things which the Creator has provided. This interpretation is in accordance with his statements that "to the man whom he favours he gives wisdom and knowledge and joy" (2:26) and that "God has already shown his approval of your actions" in providing those good things (9:7).

       a. we cannot change the fate which God has chosen for us;
       b. we cannot know what God has in store for us;
       c. life is short and death inevitable.
  3. The recognition that toil is part of what God has allotted to us in this
     life and that reliance on our own efforts is vain, enables us to find en-
     joyment even in our toil.

Are the conclusions drawn from the study of these seven passages borne out by the rest of the book? It seems to me that they are. Qoheleth, without a doubt, consistently expressed the view that human life is "a sorry business" (1:13) and that it is "vanity." However, he regarded this not as a contradiction of his positive teaching but as actually providing support for it. But did he not, as has been frequently asserted, go further in some passages and deny that life has any redeeming features? If it could be shown that he did, then the seven passages just considered would still be a problem: they would still be anomalous, incapable of reconciliation with a fundamentally pessimistic standpoint.

Some of the texts which have often been held to express a totally pessimistic view can easily be shown to do nothing of the kind, especially when considered in their contexts. Thus the famous phrase "So I hated life" in 2:17 proves on examination to be an expression not of Qoheleth's own teaching, but of the thoughts of the supposed Solomon, reflecting the disillusionment which he felt before he came to make the more mature reflections which culminate in the positive conclusion of 2:24–26. The reflection in 6:3–5 that it would have been preferable to be still-born than to survive into adulthood has similarly to be read in its context. Qoheleth is not making a general observation but is referring to the particular hypothetical case of a man who possesses every advantage that life can offer yet gives himself no chance to enjoy life because, contrary to Qoheleth's recommendations elsewhere, he can never be satisfied with what he has got.[15] Again, the statement in 7:1b that "the day

---

15. This is clear enough from the immediate context: Qoheleth's conclusion, "I say that the stillborn child is more fortunate than he" (verse 3b) is the apodosis of 3a: "If a man begets a hundred children and lives many years . . . , yet does not get satisfaction from his wealth. . . . " Verses 4–5 support the preceding statement, still within the context of the thought of the man who can never be satisfied, by describing the state of the still-born child. Verse 6 concludes the passage by once again stating the paradox of the dissatisfied miser in an exaggerated form ("even if he lives a thousand years twice over"). That the statement about the relative good fortune of the still-born infant is made solely in connection with the case of the man with an insatiable appetite for wealth (rather than referring to human life in general) is shown even more clearly by Qoheleth's use of the words "darkness" (ḥōšek) and "rest" (naḥat) in verses 4 and 5. The still-born child "comes into vanity and disappears into darkness (ḥōšek) . . . , yet it finds rest (naḥat) rather than he." Elsewhere Qoheleth remarks that the miser, who also will leave this world naked as he came from his mother's womb (5:15), and whose life is also "spent in the dark (baḥōšek)" (5:16) gets no rest (naḥat) (4:6: cf. 2:23). This seems to be an intentional play on words.

of death (is better) than the day of birth" belongs to a series of paradoxical statements intended to remind the reader that death "is the end of all men, and the living should take this to heart" (verse 2b). The ironical character of these sayings is clearly recognizable.[16]

The only passage which at first sight appears to reject life altogether is 4:2–3:

> So I counted the dead, those who have already died, happier than the living, those who are still alive; but the man who is still unborn, and has had no experience of the evil things that are done under the sun I counted happier than either.

This is indeed a sombre reflection, made by Qoheleth after contemplating some apparently hopeless cases: "the acts of oppression that are committed under the sun" (4:1). He was so deeply affected by what he had seen that, quite uncharacteristically, he abandoned his usual stance of the detached observer and was moved to break into a kind of lamentation:

> Behold, the tears of the oppressed,
>   with no one to comfort them!
> Power on the side of their oppressors,
>   but no one to comfort them!

The somber reflection of 4:2–3 is not unique in the Old Testament. Job, equally overwhelmed by the hopelessness of his situation (Job 3), and Jeremiah, in one of his blackest moods (Jer. 20:14–18), expressed themselves in similar terms. These parallels are instructive, particularly that of Jeremiah. Genuine and heartfelt though Jeremiah's expression of despair undoubtedly was, it is not characteristic of his fundamental attitude, which was one of trust in God. So also Qoheleth's expression of despair here, wrung from him by his contemplation of the apparently hopeless case of the oppressed classes of his time, should not be interpreted as his final conclusion about life but rather as the most extreme and poignant expression of his belief in the vanity of the world: that is, the somber background

---

16. See especially Lohfink, who points out the ironical and playful character of the whole passage, in which Qoheleth plays on the original meaning of familiar sayings, drawing new and unlooked for, and not wholly serious, conclusions from them. Thus—as has also been recognized by other commentators—Qoheleth argues in this verse that if, as the traditional saying has it, a good lasting reputation (šēm) is the most precious thing which a man can acquire (verse 1a), then the day of one's death must be more significant an event in this respect than the day of one's birth (verse 1b), since while a man has no reputation at all when he is born, only death can ensure that a man who has acquired a good reputation during his life does not spoil it by subsequent folly or wickedness! This twisted conclusion is not at all the same thing as saying that death—that is, the state of being dead—is preferable to life, or that life itself is an unmitigated misfortune.

against which he put forward his more positive advice.[17] That this is so is shown by such texts as 9:4, where he asserted in a similar context that "for anyone who is counted among the living there is still hope, for it is better to be a live dog than a dead lion," or 8:15, "So I praise joy." It is this latter sentiment, I submit, which is what Qoheleth above all wished to commend to his readers.

---

17. Lys also recognizes that verses 2–3, although they are expressed in general terms, refer in their context specifically to the victims of particular acts of injustice and cruelty.

13

GOD AND MAN IN ECCLESIASTES

Roy B. Zuck

Is Ecclesiastes a Misfit?

Through the centuries many people have questioned whether the Book of Ecclesiastes belongs in the biblical canon, and especially in the wisdom corpus. Since it seems to underscore the futility and uselessness of work, the triumph of evil, the limitations of wisdom, and the impermanence of life, Ecclesiastes appears to be a misfit.

Because it apparently contradicts other portions of Scripture and presents a pessimistic outlook on life, in a mood of existential despair, many have viewed it as running counter to the rest of Scripture or have concluded that it presents only man's reasoning apart from divine revelation. Smith wrote, "There is no spiritual uplift embodied within these pages. . . . Ecclesiastes . . . accomplishes only one thing, confusion. Reason is elevated throughout the whole work as the tool with which man may seek and find truth."[1] Scott affirms that the author of Ecclesiastes "is a rationalist, a skeptic, a pessimist, and

This chapter is adapted from Roy B. Zuck, "A Biblical Theology of the Wisdom Books and the Song of Songs," in *A Biblical Theology of the Old Testament* (Chicago: Moody, 1991). Used by permission.

1. L. Lowell Smith, "A Critical Evaluation of the Book of Ecclesiastes," *Journal of Bible and Religion* 21 (April 1953): 105.

a fatalist. . . . In most respects his view runs counter to his religious fellow Jews."[2] Crenshaw speaks of the "oppressiveness" of Ecclesiastes, which conveys the view "that life is profitless; totally absurd."[3] Since "virtue does not bring reward" and since God "stands distant, abandoning humanity to chance and death," this book, Crenshaw asserts, contrasts "radically with earlier teachings expressed in the book of Proverbs."[4] "Qoheleth discerns no moral order at all,"[5] for "life amounts to nothing."[6]

Elements in the book that supposedly suggest this outlook of secularist despair include (a) the repeated refrains, "everything is meaningless"[7] (1:2; 2:11, 17; 3:19; 12:8); "this too is meaningless" (2:15, 19, 21, 23, 26; 4:4, 8, 16; 5:10; 6:9; 7:6; 8:10);[8] "chasing after wind" (1:14, 17; 2:11, 17, 26; 4:4, 6, 16; 6:9); and "under the sun," which occurs 29 times; (b) death's finality which removes any advantage or gain man may have acquired in life (2:14, 16, 18; 3:2, 19–20; 4:2; 5:15; 6:6, 12; 7:1; 8:8; 9:2–5, 10; 11:7; 12:7); (c) the fleeting, transitory nature of life (6:12; 7:15; 9:9; 11:10); (d) life's inequities, including the frustrating nature of work (2:11, 18, 20, 22–23; 4:4), the uselessness of pleasure (1:17; 2:1–2), the inadequacies of wisdom (1:17–18; 2:14–17; 8:16–17; 9:13–16); and uncorrected injustices (4:1, 6, 8, 15–16; 6:2; 7:15; 8:19; 9:2, 11; 10:6–9); and (e) the puzzle of life with its many enigmas of unknowable elements (3:11, 22; 6:12; 7:14–24; 8:7, 17; 9:1, 12; 10:14; 11:2, 5–6).

Is this the total picture of the message of Ecclesiastes? Is it true that the book presents "no discernible principle of order"[9] in life? How does this skeptical approach square with statements (a) that life is a gift from God (2:24; 3:13; 5:19; 8:15; 9:7, 9); (b) that life is to be enjoyed (2:24–25; 3:12–13, 22; 5:18–20; 8:15; 9:7–9; 11:8–9); (c) that injustices *will* be corrected (3:17;

2. R. B. Y. Scott, *Proverbs, Ecclesiastes*, Anchor Bible (Garden City, NY: Doubleday & Co., 1965), p. 192.

3. James L. Crenshaw, *Ecclesiastes: A Commentary* (Philadelphia: Westminster Press, 1987), p. 23.

4. Ibid.

5. Ibid.

6. Ibid., p. 34.

7. "Meaningless" is the NIV's translation of הבל, literally "a vapor or breath." This suggests brevity or transience and emptiness of content. See *Theological Dictionary of the Old Testament*, ed. G. Johannes Botterweck and Helmer Ringgren (Grand Rapids: Wm. B. Eerdmans Publishing Co., 1978), s.v. "הבל," by K. Seybold, 3:313–20. Other Bible versions translate the word "vanity" or "futility." Ogden suggests that הבל can best be translated "enigma" or "mystery" (Graham S. Ogden, "'Vanity' It Certainly Is Not," *Bible Translator* 38 [July 1987]: 301–7). All Scripture quotations in this article are from the NIV unless noted otherwise.

8. "Meaningless" is also used in 2:1; 4:7; 5:7; 6:2, 4, 11–12; 7:15; 8:14; 9:9; 11:8, 10. More than half the Old Testament usages of this word הבל are in Ecclesiastes—38 of its 73 occurrences!

9. Crenshaw, *Ecclesiastes: A Commentary*, p. 28.

8:12–13; 11:9; 12:14); (d) that God is in control (3:14; 5:2; 7:14; 9:1); and (e) that man is challenged to please God (2:26), remember Him (12:1, 7), and fear Him (3:14; 5:7; 7:18; 8:12–13; 12:13)? Can one ignore these counterbalancing ideas? When Qohelet[10] *five times* enjoined his readers to fear God, does the Bible student do justice to the book's message to say that only man's reasoning is presented, that the book provides no answer to life's anomalies and enigmas? Is it adequate simply to view Ecclesiastes as presenting thoughts and counterthoughts that stand in unresolved tension,[11] or as stating contradictions without solving them so that life is viewed as absurd and irrational?[12] To conclude that Qohelet recommended enjoyment of life only to make existence endurable on one's "journey into nothingness"[13] fails to account for the positive side of the book.

Why then does Ecclesiastes paint a dark picture of life? Why does the writer present the gloom and doom of life? How can the seeming contradictory elements in the book be reconciled? Four answers may be given to these questions.

First, Qohelet was demonstrating that life without God has no meaning. He was demolishing confidence in man-based achievements and wisdom to show that earthly goals *"as ends in themselves* lead to dissatisfaction and emptiness."[14] Solomon recorded the futility and emptiness of his own experiences to make his readers desperate for God, to show that their quest for happiness cannot be fulfilled by man himself. Qohelet "shocks us into seeing life and death strictly from ground level, and into reaching the only conclusions from that standpoint that honesty will allow."[15]

---

10. "Qohelet" transliterates the Hebrew word rendered "teacher" or "preacher" in 1:1–2, 12. Stemming from the verb קָהַל, "to call an assembly," the noun קֹהֶלֶת suggests one who calls an assembly to address them. Some scholars argue that the anonymous author called himself "son of David, king in Jerusalem" (1:1; cf. vv. 12, 16; 2:9) to give his book a ring of authority as having been written in the tradition of Solomonic wisdom. Others, however, including this writer, argue that the author is indeed Solomon. For a discussion of the arguments on each side of this issue see Donald R. Glenn, "Ecclesiastes," in *The Bible Knowledge Commentary, Old Testament* (Wheaton, IL: Victor Books, 1988), pp. 975–76; Louis Goldberg, *Ecclesiastes*, Bible Study Commentary (Grand Rapids: Zondervan Publishing House, 1983), pp. 19–20; and Gleason L. Archer, "The Linguistic Evidence for the Date of 'Ecclesiastes,'" *Journal of the Evangelical Theological Society* 12 (1969): 167–81.

11. J. A. Loader, *Polar Structures in the Book of Qohelet* (Berlin: Walter de Gruyter, 1979); and idem, *Ecclesiastes: A Practical Commentary* (Grand Rapids: Wm. B. Eerdmans Publishing Co., 1986).

12. Michael V. Fox, *Qohelet and His Contradictions* (Sheffield: Almond Press, 1989).

13. James L. Crenshaw, *Old Testament Wisdom: An Introduction* (Atlanta: John Knox Press, 1981), p. 144.

14. Roy B. Laurin, "Ecclesiastes," in *The Wycliffe Bible Commentary*, ed. Charles F. Pfeiffer and Everett F. Harrison (Chicago: Moody Press, 1962), p. 585 (italics added).

15. Derek Kidner, *The Wisdom of Proverbs, Job, and Ecclesiastes* (Downers Grove, IL: Inter-Varsity Press, 1985), p. 94.

Second, Solomon was affirming that since much in life cannot be fully understood, we must live by faith, not by sight. Unexplained enigmas, unresolved anomalies, uncorrected injustices—life is full of much that man cannot comprehend nor control. Like the Book of Job, Ecclesiastes affirms both the finiteness of man and the fact that man must live with mystery. Life "under the sun," that is, down here on earth, "does not provide the key to life itself," for the world in itself "is bankrupt."[16] Man therefore must have more than a horizontal outlook; he must look upward to God, fearing and trusting Him. Enigmas and injustices must be left in His hands to resolve.

Third, Ecclesiastes and its realistic view of life counterbalances the unqualified optimism of traditional wisdom. According to Proverbs 13:4; "The desires of the diligent are fully satisfied," but Ecclesiastes 2:22–23 challenges whether this is always true. Proverbs 8:11 extols wisdom, whereas Ecclesiastes 2:15 questions its value. Proverbs 10:6 affirms that justice is meted to the righteous and the wicked, but Ecclesiastes 8:14 observes that this is not always the case.

Are these contradictions? No, because for one thing Proverbs usually looks at the opposites in life without noting exceptions. Ecclesiastes, however, points out that while a righteous order does exist, as affirmed in Proverbs, it is not always evident to man as he views life "under the sun" from his finite perspective. "God is in heaven and you are on earth" (Eccles. 5:2). Job and Ecclesiastes, both wisdom books, demonstrate exceptions to what Proverbs often states in black-and-white fashion. The books then are complementary, not contradictory. While the affirmations in Proverbs are normally true, exceptions, as observed in Job and Ecclesiastes, do exist. As Williams has well observed,

> Proverbs affirms by *faith* (not by sight as is commonly assumed) that a righteous order exists in the world, but Qohelet contends that righteous order cannot be discerned by *sight*. This latter premise, that even the wise cannot explain the apparent lack of order in the world, is simply Qohelet's way of expounding on the limitations of wisdom. But these limitations were even admitted by the sages: "Do you see a man wise in his own eyes? There is more hope for a fool than for him" (Prov. 26:12). . . . Ecclesiastes was intended to balance the optimism of faith with the realism of observation.[17]

Job and Ecclesiastes both present the frustrations and futilities of wise, wealthy men. Both books demonstrate that wealth does not provide lasting

---

16. J. Stafford Wright, "The Interpretation of Ecclesiastes," in *Classical Evangelical Essays in Old Testament Interpretation*, ed. Walter C. Kaiser, Jr. (Grand Rapids: Baker Book House, 1972), p. 142.

17. Neal D. Williams, "A Biblical Theology of Ecclesiastes" (ThD diss., Dallas Theological Seminary, 1984), pp. 85–86 (italics his).

satisfaction, that many people experience injustice, that death is inevitable, that man must live with the mystery of suffering.

Fourth, Ecclesiastes affirms that the only answer to the meaning of life is to fear God and enjoy one's lot in life. Qohelet showed that man, left to his own machinations, finds life empty, frustrating, and mysterious. The book, however, does not mean that life has no answer, that life is totally useless or meaningless. Meaning is found, he explained, in fearing God—a point that clearly justifies a place for Ecclesiastes in the Bible's wisdom literature—and in enjoying life. Accepting what God has given and rejoicing in those gifts brings substance to a life that otherwise would be viewed as one of hopelessness and despair. Frustrations can thus be replaced with contentment. While recognizing the vanity of empty human pursuits, Solomon went beyond them and affirmed that "there is a bigger truth to live by," that we should "set our hearts not on earthly vanities themselves but on our Creator."[18] True, life has its puzzles, but with God life *is* worth living. Life is fleeting and death is coming, but with God life can be accepted and enjoyed.

The Doctrine of God in Ecclesiastes

Forty times Ecclesiastes uses the word Elohim, and no other name, in speaking of God. As the transcendent God ("God is in heaven," 5:2), He is the Creator (12:1), "the Maker of all things" (11:5). His created works include man, giving him life (8:15; 9:9) and a spirit (3:21; 12:7), making him upright (7:29), and setting eternity in his heart (3:11).[19] In His sovereignty God has planned the timing of all things (3:1–8), which timing is beautiful (v. 13), though incomprehensible (v. 11; 8:17; 11:5) and unalterable by man (3:14; 7:13). The events and activities God has under His control include positive elements of life such as birth, planting, healing, upbuilding, joy, searching, keeping, mending, speaking, loving, and enjoying peace—and all their negative opposites (3:1–8). All of life is under divine appointment and timing. Qohelet was not approving man's killing, tearing, hating, or engaging

18. Kidner, *The Wisdom of Proverbs, Job, and Ecclesiastes*, p. 94.

19. That is, God has given man an awareness that he is an eternal creature. He has a God-given "longing to know the eternity of things . . . but, try as we will, we cannot see it. . . . That eternal WHY hangs over our lives" (Wright, "The Interpretation of Ecclesiastes," p. 141). This is "a deep-seated, compulsive desire to know the character, composition, beauty, meaning, purpose, and destiny of all created things" (Walter C. Kaiser, Jr., "Integrating Wisdom Theology into Old Testament Theology: Ecclesiastes 3:10–15," in *A Tribute to Gleason Archer*, ed. Walter C. Kaiser, Jr. and Ronald F. Youngblood [Chicago: Moody Press, 1986], p. 205). Others say the word עוֹלָם rendered "eternity" means (a) the world, or (b) ignorance (emending the word to be read אֶלֶם), or (c) darkness (from a related Ugaritic root). "Eternity," however, is preferable, in light of the reference to forever (עוֹלָם) in 3:14 and its contrast to time (3:1–17).

in war; he was simply affirming that these things occur in human experience (because of man's sin, 7:29) and that man cannot alter what God has planned.

God in His sovereignty and providence controls the rising and setting of the sun, the cyclic movements of the wind, the flowing of rivers, and the evaporation of water (1:5–7). He is called the Shepherd, a term used only a few times of God in the Old Testament (Gen. 48:15; 49:24; Pss. 23:1; 28:9; 80:1; Eccles. 12:11).

Ten times God is said to give and 10 times to do. Man's burden, because of God's finite wisdom, is given by God (1:13; 3:10). God gives man opportunity to enjoy food and work (2:24; 3:13; 5:19–20; 9:7), He gives man wisdom, knowledge, and happiness (2:26), and wealth, possessions, and honor (5:19; 6:2). God's work, which man cannot fully understand (11:6), includes both good and bad times (7:14). What He does has endurance (3:14) and cannot be altered (7:13).

Other divine attributes evident in Ecclesiastes include God's personality (He hears, 5:2; He despises, 5:2; He can be pleased, 2:26; 7:26; or angered, 5:26), goodness (2:24–26; 3:13; 5:18–19, 6:2), holiness (5:1–2), and inscrutability (3:11; 8:17; 9:1; 11:5). In addition His justice will be exercised against wickedness. Even His judging the righteous and the wicked is included in God's control of the timing of events (3:17). Though the punishment of the wicked may seem delayed, it will occur (8:13). Young people, challenged to enjoy the energy of their youthful days, should also be sobered by the fact that they are accountable for their actions under the scrutiny of God's judgment (11:9). In fact every act, whether overt or hidden, good or evil, will be judged by God (12:14) and either rewarded or punished.

Though God cannot be fully understood, some motives for His actions are mentioned. These motives include seeking to get people to fear Him (3:14) and testing man to show him his finiteness (v. 18). All these truths about God are consistent with the rest of Scripture, thus affirming the validity of the place of Ecclesiastes in the Bible.

The Doctrine of Man in Ecclesiastes

Man's Nature

Man's finiteness is seen in the fact that he is created (11:5; 12:1), earthbound (5:2), and subject to death (3:19–20; 6:6; 7:2; 9:5). He is a rational creature, for he can be guided by his mind (2:3), he can evaluate (v. 11), understand (1:17), investigate (v. 13), observe (v. 14; 2:12, 24; 3:10; 5:13; 6:1; 7:15; 8:9–10; 9:11, 13; 10:5, 7), reflect (1:16; 2:1, 12, 15; 8:9; 12:9), and draw conclusions (2:14, 17; 5:18).

Human emotions, according to Ecclesiastes, include joy (2:10; 9:7, 9; 11:9), love (9:1, 6, 9), hatred (2:17–18; 9:1, 6), contentment (4:8), despair (2:20), grief (v. 23), envy (4:4), anger (7:9), and sadness (v. 4).

Qohelet referred to the material part of man by the word בָּשָׂר, normally translated "flesh" or "body." The body can experience "troubles" (11:10) and weariness (12:12). It can also be cheered, figuratively speaking (2:3), or ruined (4:5), that is, dissipated. The NIV translators thought of בָּשָׂר in 2:3 and 4:5 as a metonymy (a part for the whole), for they translated it "myself" and "himself" in these verses respectively.

The immaterial part of man includes his soul (נֶפֶשׁ), spirit (רוּחַ), and heart (לֵב). The soul is the center of desires for fulfillment (6:2–3, 7, 9; see NASB), the seat of inner satisfaction (NIV's "find satisfaction in his work" in 2:24 is literally "causes his soul to see good in his labor") or joy ("depriving myself of enjoyment" in 4:8 is literally "depriving my soul of enjoyment"), or the seat of inner contemplation ("while I [lit. 'my soul'] was still searching," 7:28).

The spirit is used of mood or temperament ("patience" in 7:8 is literally "length of spirit," and "provoked in your spirit," 7:9, speaks of anger). "Spirit" also speaks of man's animating principle of life, which returns to God at death (3:19, 21; 12:7).[20]

Man's "heart" is referred to in Ecclesiastes more often than his soul or spirit. Consistent with its usage elsewhere in the Old Testament, "heart" represents the inner part of man, either his intellect, his emotions, or his will. The intellect is suggested in 1:13, 16–17, in which the NIV translates the Hebrew "I said in my heart" by the words "I applied myself" or "I devoted myself." The idea in these verses is inner determination to complete an intellectual pursuit. The NIV renders "heart" by "mind" in 7:25; 8:9, 16—verses that suggest an intellectual exercise. "Take this to heart" (7:2), "you know in your heart" (v. 22), and "the wise heart will know" (8:5) all suggest the intellect. "I reflected on all this" (9:1), another instance of the exercise of the mind, is literally "I have taken all this to heart."

"Heart" also speaks of the emotional side of the immaterial part of man, as seen in 5:2 ("do not be hasty in your heart"), 7:3 ("a sad face is good for the heart"), 7:4 ("The heart of the wise is in the house of mourning, but the heart

---

20. Ecclesiastes 3:19–20 affirms that all animate creation, including men and animals, face death. The bodies of each expire and disintegrate into the earth. The spirit (רוּחַ) is the life principle in both men and animals (Gen. 7:22). However, Ecclesiastes 3:21 indicates, by means of a question, that no one can observe what happens to the spirit of man, "which ascends upward" (NASB) and the spirit of animals "which descends downward" (NASB). The NIV rendering "who knows if the spirit of man . . . " casts doubt on whether man's spirit goes upward. It seems preferable to render the verse, "Who knows that the spirit of man goes upward," as suggested by Goldberg (*Ecclesiastes*, p. 69; cf. Michael A. Eaton, *Ecclesiastes: An Introduction and Commentary* [Downers Grove, IL: InterVarsity Press, 1983], p. 87). Understood in this way, the verse is pointing up the difference in the destiny of men and beasts. Because they are different, man's spirit goes upward to God and the animal's spirit does not. Only in man's nostrils did God directly breathe the breath of life (Gen. 2:7), and only man was made in God's image (1:26–27). Therefore the breath or animating principle of men and animals has different destinies, but, as Ecclesiastes 3:21 indicates, no one can *see* or observe where their spirits go.

of fools is in the house of pleasure"), 9:7 ("a cheerful heart"), 11:9 ("Follow the ways of your heart"), and 11:10 ("banish anxiety from your heart").

The willful aspect of the heart is seen in these verses: 7:7 ("a bribe corrupts the heart"), 7:26 ("the woman . . . whose heart is a trap"), 8:11 ("their hearts . . . are filled with schemes to do wrong"), 9:3 ("the hearts of men . . . are full of evil"), and 10:2 ("the heart of the wise inclines to the right, but the heart of the fool inclines to the left").

Man's Sin

Sin is universal (7:20) and inward (9:3, "full of evil"). Man's inner pull toward sin accelerates if he feels he, like others, can get away with sin without immediate punishment (8:11). The sinful nature shows itself in specific acts of sin. In Ecclesiastes these acts include oppression of the poor (4:1, 3; 5:8), envy (4:4), greed (v. 8; 5:10), insensitivity in worship (vv. 1–2), unfulfilled vows (vv. 4–5), uncontrolled talk (v. 6), a stranger benefiting from someone else's work (6:2), pride (7:8), anger (v. 9; 10:4), discontentment (7:10), sexual seduction and adultery (v. 26), and foolish talk (10:13). Man's injustice to others is decried several times (3:16; 4:1; 5:8; 7:7; 8:9, 14).

Ecclesiastes repeatedly underscores human finiteness by pointing to man's ignorance. He does not know God's ways (3:11; 8:17; 11:5) nor does he know the future (6:12; 7:14; 8:7; 9:1, 12; 10:14; 11:2, 6).

Sin has its consequences. It holds sinners in its grasp (8:8), it brings them trouble (v. 13), it can undo much good (2:26; 9:18; 10:1), and it can even lead to an untimely death (7:17; 8:13). After man dies, God will punish his sin (3:13; 11:9; 12:14).

Man's Work

The word עָמָל ("labor, trouble, turmoil, work") occurs frequently in Ecclesiastes.[21] No lasting profit (יִתְרוֹן, "gain or advantage" 1:3; 2:11, 13; 3:9; 5:8, 15; 7:12; 10:10–11) comes from one's labor or toil (1:3; 3:9). The fact that work brings pain (2:17, 23) is said to be הֶבֶל, that is, meaningless or enigmatic,[22] as is the fact that the results of one's labors must be left to someone else (2:19, 21, 26; 4:7–8). Many people find no end to the toils of life (2:22; 4:8; 8:16), sometimes because they are driven by envy of what others have (4:4). Though work may bring despair (2:20), it can be enjoyed (vv. 10, 24; 3:22; 5:18–19; 8:15; 9:9) when seen as a gift from God.

Man's Death

Life is fleeting ("few days," 2:2; 6:12), and death is certain. All will die (2:14–16; 3:18–20; 6:6) including sinners (8:10, 12–13; 9:2–3). Since God has ap-

---

21. The noun occurs 21 times, the verbal form 8 times, and the adjective 5 times.
22. See notes 7 and 8.

pointed the time of each person's death (3:2), man cannot influence when it will occur (8:8) or even know when it will occur (9:12). Nothing can be taken from this life when a person dies; his exit is like his entrance (5:15–16). The dead go to Sheol (9:10), that is, the grave,[23] where they have no more opportunity to participate in this life's activities (9:5–6). Death is final. To be dead is said to be preferable to a life of oppression (4:1 2) or to nonenjoyment of one's prosperity (6:3–5), and yet the living do have an advantage over the dead (9:4). The dead will eventually be forgotten (1:11; 2:16; 9:5). Old age brings physical problems (12:1–5)[24] and eventuates in death (vv. 6–7), in which a person's spirit goes to God (3:21; 12:7) and he enters eternal consciousness ("his eternal home," v. 7).

A number of truths about man in Ecclesiastes are consistent with truths elsewhere in Scripture, particularly the early chapters of Genesis. Man was originally created good (Gen. 1:31; Eccles. 7:29), but fell into sin (Gen. 3:1–19; Eccles. 3:16; 4:1; 7:29), with the consequence of toil (Gen. 3:14–19; Eccles. 1:3, 8, 18; 2:11, 17, 22) and death (Gen. 3:19, 24; 4:5, 8; Eccles. 2:14–16; 3:20; 4:2; 9:5; 12:6–7). Made from dust and breath (Gen. 2:7; 3:19; Eccles. 3:20; 12:7), man has limited knowledge (Gen. 2:17; Eccles. 8:7; 10:14; 11:5). He was created to live in companionship with others (Gen. 1:27; 2:21–25; Eccles. 4:9–12; 9:9).[25]

Man's Responsibilities

What responsibilities does man have in light of the futilities and mysteries of life? What actions did Qohelet say will aid man in his pursuit of life? At least six suggestions are given in the book.

1. *Be wise.* While wisdom has its drawbacks (1:18), it can be nullified by a little folly (10:1), is transitory (4:13–16; 9:13–16), and does not prevent death (2:12), it does have advantages. It is better to be wise than foolish (v. 13) or famous (4:13–16), for wisdom can help preserve life (7:11–12), gives strength (v. 19), causes one to reflect on the seriousness of life and death (v. 5), and can brighten a person's countenance (8:1). Mere human wisdom, wisdom acquired by intellectual pursuits, is inadequate, but divine wisdom enables man to rest in the sovereign ways of God and in His providential timing (8:5).

2. *Worship and please God.* Proper worship entails a sense of caution and apprehension in God's presence (5:1–2). Making a commitment to the Lord

---

23. See R. Laird Harris, "The Meaning of the Word Sheol as Shown by Parallels in Poetic Texts," *Bulletin of the Evangelical Theological Society* 4 (December 1961): 129–34.

24. Views on this passage include these four: (a) the decreasing health of organs of the body, (b) old age depicted by a Palestinian winter or approaching storm (Franz Delitzsch, *Commentary on the Song of Songs and Ecclesiastes* [reprint, Grand Rapids: Wm. B. Eerdmans Publishing Co., 1970], pp. 403–5, and Christian D. Ginsburg, *The Song of Songs and Coheleth* [1857; reprint, New York: KTAV Publishing House, 1970], p. 458), (c) old age depicted as the ruin of an estate (Robert Gordis, *Qoheleth—The Man and His World* [New York: Schocken Books, 1968], p. 329), or (d) a combination of these views.

25. C. C. Forman, "Koheleth's Use of Genesis," *Journal of Semitic Studies* 5 (1960): 256–63.

should be done thoughtfully and without haste, but once having made it the worshiper should follow through on his promise (vv. 4–6). Pleasing God should be man's deepest desire (2:26; 7:26).

3. *Remember God.* More than a mental exercise, this means to acknowledge His authority and respond with loyalty (12:1, 6) and obedience (v. 13, "keep His commandments").

4. *Fear God.* Fearing God stands at the heart of wisdom literature (Job 28:28; Ps. 111:10; Prov. 1:7; 9:10).[26] Hence it is no surprise that in Ecclesiastes man is commanded five times to fear God (3:14; 5:7; 7:18; 8:12–13; 12:13), to recognize who He is and to respond accordingly in worship, awe, love, trust, and obedience.

5. *Be diligent.* Life with its many uncertainties (9:11–12) means man knows comparatively little. "You do not know" is stated three times in six verses (11:2, 5–6) along with the words "you do not understand" (v. 5) to point up man's ignorance of which disasters may come and when, where the wind will blow, how the human embryo develops in the womb, or which enterprise or investment will be successful. This ignorance need not paralyze man or stifle him into laziness. Instead one should forget trying to change things that cannot be changed (v. 3) or trying to predict what cannot be known (vv. 4, 6), and should be hard at work all day (v. 6), working wholeheartedly (9:10) and leaving the results to the Lord. Laziness results in increased problems (e.g., sagging rafters and leaking roofs, 10:18).

6. *Enjoy life.* The fact that Solomon admonished his readers not to look for the answer to life in the pleasures of life itself did not rule out his encouraging them to accept their lot (חֵלֶק) in life and to be glad for the simple pleasures of life including food, warmth, marriage, and doing good. This theme occurs seven times in the book: 2:24–26; 3:12–13, 22; 5:18–20; 8:15; 9:7–9; 11:8–9. "These modest pleasures are not goals to live for, but bonuses or consolations to be gratefully accepted."[27] The fact that these pleasures are for man's joy and contentment rules out asceticism, and the fact that they are given by God rules out sinful hedonism.

Castellino well summarizes the message of Ecclesiastes: "Therefore: (a) set aside all anxious striving and labor (*ʿamal*); (b) avoid all speculations on God's ruling of the world and (c) be thankful to God for whatever satisfaction He gives you, valuing and measuring everything as a gift from Him and enjoying it, never forgetting that you shall have to render strict account to God Himself."[28]

---

26. In Job the verbal form for fearing God occurs in 1:1, 8–9; 2:3; 23:15; 37:24, and related nominal phrases occur in 6:14 and 31:23. Proverbs refers to the fear of the Lord in 1:7, 29; 2:5; 8:13; 9:10; 10:27; 14:27; 15:16, 33; 16:6; 19:23; 22:4; and 23:17. The command to fear the Lord occurs in Proverbs 3:7 and 24:21, and four times the verbal form "fears the Lord" occurs (14:2, 16, 26; 31:30). Fearing the Lord is associated with wisdom six times (Job 28:28; Prov. 1:7, 29; 2:5; 8:13; 15:33).

27. Kidner, *The Wisdom of Proverbs, Job, and Ecclesiastes,* p. 100.

28. George R. Castellino, "Qohelet and His Wisdom," *Catholic Biblical Quarterly* 30 (1968): 28.

14

PIETY
OR HERESY?

Kathleen A. Farmer

W hat will you find within the pages of this book called Ecclesiastes?
Will you encounter the confessions of a true believer or the blasphe-
mies of a heretic? Will your reading introduce you to a person steeped in cynicism
or one who courageously faces and accepts the world as it is? For almost two
thousand years faithful and well-informed interpreters have disagreed radically
over the nature and purpose of these relatively short twelve chapters of Scripture.

Depending upon whom you read, you might conclude that Ecclesiastes is
either "the quintessence of skepticism" or that it is "the quintessence of piety." Interpretive opinions range from the conviction that Qohelet's views
run counter to the dominant teachings of the rest of Scripture to the assertion
that they faithfully reflect the heart of the traditions and values of Israel.

How is it possible for one small book to generate such opposite and contradictory theories about its meaning? One important reason is the ambiguity

From Kathleen A. Farmer, *Who Knows What Is Good? A Commentary on the Books of Proverbs
and Ecclesiastes*, International Theological Commentary (Grand Rapids: Eerdmans, 1991), 142–
46. Reprinted by permission.

of the thematic word *hebel*, which the RSV translates as "vanity." *Hebel* occurs thirty-eight times in Ecclesiastes, compared to only thirty-five other uses in all of the rest of the OT. Any word repeated so often in such a short space must leave a lasting impression on its hearers. But what does *hebel* mean?

Everything Is a Puff of Air

In its simplest and most basic sense, *hebel* means "a puff of air," "a breath," or "a vapor." This sense of *hebel* can be seen in the RSV in Isa. 57:13: "The wind will carry them off, a *breath* (*hebel*) will take them away." R. B. Y. Scott's translation of Ecclesiastes in the Anchor Bible preserves this concrete, basic sense of *hebel* when he renders Eccles. 1:2 as "Breath of a breath! . . . The slightest breath! All is a breath!" (*Proverbs–Ecclesiastes*, 209). This translation enables English readers to see that the phrase "all is *hebel*" is actually a metaphor. The thematic statement of the book is expressed as a figure of speech. Like all other metaphors, it invites its hearers to look for the qualities that two essentially unlike things have in common. Both the speaker and the hearer of a metaphor know that the two entities which are compared are alike in some ways and unlike in other ways. Thus, when the poet Carl Sandburg tells us that "the fog comes on little cat feet," we can appreciate the poet's insight into the quality of movement shared by fogs and cats without expecting the fog to purr or to leave paw prints. Similarly, when we find that in Ecclesiastes everything "under the sun" is compared to a puff of air, we ought to consider what points of similarity there might be between these two essentially unlike entities.

Metaphors are intentionally provocative figures of speech which can be understood in quite different ways. For instance in Luke 13:20–21 and 1 Cor. 5:6–7 "leaven" is used as a metaphor for both good influence and bad. It is possible, then, that *hebel* (meaning a puff of air) might be understood in either a positive or a negative sense. If the translation preserves the metaphor (as Scott does), the reader is forced to decide in what sense the comparison should be taken. In my opinion it is unfortunate that many modern versions of Ecclesiastes have chosen to take the decision away from the reader. Most translators obscure the metaphorical nature of the original statement and replace the concrete, nonjudgmental phrase ("breath" or "a puff of air") with various abstract terms—all of which have decidedly negative connotations in English. Even if a case could be made for replacing a metaphor with an adjective or a descriptive phrase, there are legitimate grounds for challenging the negative connotations of the words which many modern translators use to translate *hebel* in Ecclesiastes.

The Semantic Range of Hebel

In every language words have potential ranges of meaning, depending on how they are used in specific situations. When an ancient Near Eastern language such as Hebrew is translated into a modern Western language such as English, very few words can be said to cover exactly the same areas of meaning in both languages. Thus, if we examine every use of the word *hebel* in the OT, we find a variety of English words have been used to communicate the different meanings *hebel* seems to have expressed in different contexts. A number of Psalms use *hebel* to describe the brevity of human life and the transitory nature of human concerns compared to the eternity of God and the durability of God's concerns. The RSV translates this sense of *hebel* as "breath" in Ps. 39:5, 11; 62:9; 78:33; 94:11; 144:4; but as "nought" in Ps. 39:6 and as "vain" in Ps. 62:10. Job also uses *hebel* as a metaphor for the brevity of life; the RSV preserves this meaning of *hebel* in "my days are *a breath*" (Job 7:16). The plural of *hebel* is translated in the RSV as "idols" (Ps. 31:6; Jer. 8:19; 10:8; Jon. 2:8). Similarly, the RSV translates the singular forms used in the phrase "they went after *hebel* and became *hebel*" (which is usually understood to refer to idolatry) as "worthless(ness)" in Jer. 2:5 and as "false (idols)" in 2 Kings 17:15. Both the KJV and RSV use the words "vain" and "vanity" for less specific usages of *hebel*, as in Prov. 31:30 and in Ecclesiastes.

These traditional renderings were undoubtedly influenced by the precedent set by Jerome, whose translation of the Hebrew Scriptures into Latin functioned as the authorized OT text for the Roman Church from the 5th cent. C.E. into the modern era. In commenting on his translation, Jerome noted that several early Greek translators had understood *hebel* in the sense of "vapor." But Jerome himself chose to follow the LXX's interpretation. Thus, Jerome replaced the concrete Hebrew noun *hebel* with the abstract Latin noun *vanitas* and its corresponding adjective *vanus*. The Latin terms include within their semantic range the meanings of "unsubstantial" and "lacking in permanence" as well as "useless, futile, or illusory." However, the English words "vain" and "vanity" do not cover as wide a range of meaning as do their Latin predecessors. In modern English usage "vanity" has the basic sense of "lacking in value." That which is "vain" is useless, worthless, or futile. But this may not be the sense which was conveyed to the initial audience of the original statement "all is *hebel*."

Does Lack of Permanence Mean Lack of Value?

When we look closely at the ways in which the word is used in other parts of the OT, it becomes clear that the essential quality to which *hebel* refers is lack of permanence rather than lack of worth or value. A breath, after all, is of considerable value to the one who breathes it. However, it is not something one can hang on to for long. It is airlike, fleeting, transitory, and elusive rather than meaningless. Of course, if one tries to depend too heavily upon something which is essentially fleeting, one may suffer negative consequences. Thus Isaiah warns his contemporaries against depending too heavily upon

Egypt as an ally, "for Egypt's help is *hebel* ('fleeting') and empty" (Isa. 30:7). Similarly, one might say that to worship or to give ultimate value to anything which is transitory is the essence of idolatry. Thus idols are "airlike," transitory, and lacking in substance, and those who "go after" *hebel* ("transitoriness") will certainly "become *hebel*" ("transitory"). This sense of "ephemeral" or "fleeting" would fit very well in the passages in Psalms and Job discussed above. And in Prov. 31:30 the statement "beauty is *hebel*, but a woman who fears the LORD is to be praised" may very well mean that beauty simply is a less *enduring* quality to look for in a woman than piety.

Only one verse (the last verse in the book of Proverbs) separates Prov. 31:30 from Ecclesiastes in Christian Bibles. But ironically, some modern English versions (such as the NIV and NAB), which recognize that *hebel* means "fleeting" in Prov. 31:30 ("beauty is fleeting"), translate the same word two verses later (in Eccl. 1:2) as "meaningless" and "vain." It seems to me that this tradition of interpretation ignores the fact that in Ecclesiastes itself the word *hebel* is frequently paired with the word *ruah*, meaning "wind" or "spirit." In 1:14; 2:11, 17, 26; 4:4, 16; 6:9 *hebel* and *ruah* are virtually equated, lending a great deal of support to the supposition that the quality to which *hebel* refers is that of being like a puff of air, a breath.

In several of these verses (1:14; 2:11, 17) the pairing of *hebel* and *ruah* is also linked with the motif "under the sun," reinforcing the similarity between these statements in Ecclesiastes and the similar theme in the Psalms, where God's enduring qualities are contrasted to the impermanence of God's creatures.

Decide for Yourself!

Ecclesiastes has been understood in radically different ways by different readers in part because the thematic metaphor "all is *hebel*" is fundamentally ambiguous. Those who have taken *hebel* to mean "worthlessness, meaninglessness, or futility" have tended to see the author of the book as a man lacking in faith and piety and to see the book itself as an anomaly in the canon of Holy Scripture. Those who have understood *hebel* to refer to lack of duration ("transitoriness") have tended to see Ecclesiastes in a relatively positive light, especially when "fleetingness" is understood to apply to everything "under the sun" in contrast to the permanence of God.

Since most nonspecialists today must rely upon translations for access to the biblical texts, I would advise readers of the text in English to suspend judgment temporarily on the meaning of the metaphor and to substitute the phrase "breathlike" (or something similar) for every occurrence of the word "vanity" in the RSV. In this way they may allow the text to speak more clearly for itself before they draw interpretive conclusions about its meaning.

15

THE MEANING
OF THE
TERM *HEBEL*

Graham S. Ogden

That Qoheleth expresses a basically negative view of life in this world is a conclusion dependent upon assigning to the term *hebel* a meaning equivalent to "vanity." Our task here is to examine the specific manner in which Qoheleth used the term in order to discover more exactly what semantic value the word carries in this book.

Hebel occurs 38 times in Qoheleth, and is important not only for this fact of its frequency (this represents more than half of all OT examples), but also for the fact that it is employed as a key term in concluding statements which climax many smaller sections throughout the book (e.g. 2:11, 17, 23). Additionally, we note the significant use of the term, in a functional role, in 1:2 and 12:8; here the compound forms *hebēl habālîm . . . hebel* serve as the two inclusions which bracket the entire original work. For these reasons, we can appreciate how our understanding of the term will color our reading of Qoheleth and our assessment of his message.

It is a fact that in its occurrences outside Qoheleth, *hebel* means something equivalent to "vanity," "nothingness," "vapour." This is the sense we discover

From Graham S. Ogden, *Qoheleth* (Sheffield: JSOT Press, 1987), 17–22. Reproduced by permission of Sheffield Academic Press.

from its uses in Deut. 32:21; Isa. 57:13; Jer. 8:19; 10:8; 51:18; Prov. 13:11; 21:6; Ps. 78:33, and many others; it addresses the notion of the uselessness, the powerlessness of idols, and the fruitlessness of much human endeavor. Our question must then be "Does Qoheleth use *hebel* in this same manner?" So many scholars assume with R. Davidson (1983, pp. 187–89) that this is so, that it seems almost impolite to doubt this consensus.

James Barr[1] (1961, p. 171) has reminded us that words have meaning in specific contexts and in relation to the intention of those who use them. In a more modern context, we are all familiar with the way in which words assume new connotations and meaning with each generation, or with regional and geographical variations. This is so because language is a living and dynamic phenomenon, rather than something static and unchanging. Only by examining the way in which Qoheleth actually employs *hebel* (or any other key term) can we determine what meaning he gives to the term.

While it might be possible to infer from some examples of the *hebel*-phrase that human life is vain, there are at least three factors in Qoheleth which must be part of the equation by which we determine its meaning. They are:

1. the painful scenarios to which the *hebel*-phrase is added as a response;
2. the meaning of the parallel and complementary phrases, "striving after wind," "a sore affliction," and "an unhappy business";
3. the calls to enjoyment which punctuate the book at key points.

We shall consider representative examples of the *hebel*-phrase in order to arrive at a contextual definition of its meaning.

Scenarios Which Are Described as *Hebel*

a. 3:16–19. Qoheleth presents for reflection a human situation—corruption and evil are found in places where one would expect to find exemplary justice and righteousness. This general observation could refer to the legal system, the royal household, or to the religious world. It is the problem of pervasive evil. Qoheleth's response is two-fold. In v. 17 he offers an orthodox theological response. He affirms that God will at some point bring justice to bear; the "pus" will be cleansed from society, for all is under the control of a just deity. To introduce this "solution" Qoheleth has used the phrase, "I said in my heart (to myself) . . . " and it is the reiteration of this phrase at the head of v. 18 which indicates that the two comments in vv. 17 and 18 are actually parallel. Verse 18 thus represents another and equally valid response to the dilemma in v. 16. On this occasion, Qoheleth suggests that the pervasiveness of evil works as a form of testing, the purpose of which is to prove to humankind

---

1. *The Semantics of Biblical Language* (Oxford: Oxford University Press, 1961).

that on at least this level it is on a par with the animal world. Like the animals, even "sophisticated" humanity will die (Ps. 49). To denote his feelings about this, Qoheleth calls upon the term *hebel* (v. 19).

The specific socio-theological problem highlighted here is a very basic one. Qoheleth suggests that one approach to this issue is to affirm one's religious beliefs yet more strongly (v. 17), or alternatively to leave the question open (v. 18). In the latter case, God's justice often appears to come too late, if at all. Those trapped in unjust situations may die long before God's justice is seen to be done. So it is this scenario, and the apparently insoluble theological problem which it throws up, to which Qoheleth responds with the *hebel*-phrase.

Does this then mean that life is vacuous, or meaningless? Does the fact that there are no ready-made answers for the problem of v. 16 lead to the conclusion that therefore life is "vanity"? If God's justice were to intervene, as v. 17 confesses, then clearly the problem mentioned in v. 16 would be resolved, and "vanity" or "emptiness" would be thoroughly inappropriate as evaluations of the situation. On the other hand, if one were to die before actually seeing divine justice work itself out, would that strip life of its meaning? Surely not! The term *hebel* in this context is the vehicle chosen to draw attention to an enigmatic situation, a theological conundrum. Consistent with what is spelled out in more detail later in the book we find Qoheleth here impressing on his young readers the fact that we must live with many unanswered questions. It does not mean that life therefore is "vanity"; rather, it means the pain of faith's having to live with many questions unanswered.

b. 6.1–2. A theological problem of no small proportions is presented in the very brief case-study of 6:2. The author prefaces the description with comments about his feelings with regard to the situation (6:1): that is a *ra*ꜥ. (Throughout Qoheleth, *ra*ꜥ describes a painful or traumatic situation, rather than one which is morally corrupt or evil.)

Briefly, we are told of an individual to whom God has given material benefits. In the tradition of Deuteronomy (e.g. 7:12–15; 28:1–14) these benefits would be seen as unmistakable tokens of divine blessing and approval. Unfortunately, as Qoheleth describes the scene, this person is seen to lack the most important gift, the ability to enjoy those tokens. True, there is a bright side, in that these goods do bring joy to others, even if not to the person whose they are. This is a peculiar situation depicted by the word *hebel*. Would it then be correct to say that life was "vanity" or "empty" when from the Israelite perspective these goods were all tokens of God's pleasure? Those material benefits which are crucial to life cannot themselves make life meaningless. There is nonetheless a problem, an anomalous situation, brought about by the inability to enjoy what one has; it is an enigma, and Qoheleth does not offer any rationale for it. He merely opines that this kind of situation is *hebel*.

c. 4:7–8. A *hebel*-situation is the assessment which brackets the problem presented in these two verses. Pictured for us is the lonely workaholic, whose bank balance continues to rise as he climbs the corporate ladder. But to what purpose? He never stops to ask the important question: "for what purpose am I doing all this?" This failure to ask a most basic question is something which Qoheleth finds difficult to comprehend; it is *hebel*. It is clear that the man in question gains a great deal materially from his endeavors. He does acquire some "portion" (*ḥēleq*, 2:10 etc.), but to Qoheleth this is far from enough, so the situation represents yet another of life's ironies.

d. 8:14. Similar to the example provided in 3:16–18, this also draws attention to the anomalous dimension of life. Good things happen to bad people; bad things befall the good. Though not universal, this problem is sufficiently common to raise a serious theological question. Why does a just God allow this kind of thing to occur? We do not have the answer. Yet life does not thereby cease to have meaning, and become "vanity." In describing this scenario as *hebel*, Qoheleth's meaning is that life is enigmatic, and the sign of wisdom is that one can accept that.

Parallel and Complementary Phrases

Qoheleth on occasion adds several other phrases to the basic *hebel*-phrase, the purpose being to emphasize and to complement the thought of the central phrase. The most frequent of these additions is "a striving after wind" (RSV), *rᵉ ͨût rûaḥ* (1:14 etc.); but there are two others which deserve mention, "a sore affliction," *ḥŏlî rā ͨ*, and "an unhappy business," *ͨinyān ra ͨ*.

a. *rᵉ ͨût rûaḥ*. The root *r ͨh* describes the work of the shepherd as he pastors the flock. An alternative rendering of the phrase would be "shepherding the wind." What Qoheleth describes is the attempt to bring the wind under control, to make it blow in a certain direction according to the dictates of the shepherd. From this perspective we see it as a delightful idiomatic phrase for attempting the impossible. Qoheleth shares God's humor at any foolish attempt to control the environment, his breath (*rûaḥ*).
w

b. *ḥŏlî rā ͨ*. In 6:1 we meet a scenario which calls for much heart-searching. The way in which Qoheleth presents this particular problem suggests that God has a direct hand in the fact that the person concerned does not enjoy the material wealth accumulated. It is for this reason, more than for any other, that the sage feels pain. As a complementary expression, it suggests an interpretation for *hebel* which emphasizes the anomaly in the situation described.

c. *ʿinyān raʿ*. Descriptive of the sad soul frantically searching for wealth but neglecting the question of its purpose, this phrase again points to the fact that there are so many situations in life which defy our human comprehension, causing us painful moments of doubt.

It seems abundantly evident from the representative examples of *hebel* which we have investigated that Qoheleth does not mean to claim that life is empty, vain, and meaningless. As he addresses the next generation his point is simply that life is replete with situations to which even the sage, the philosopher theologian, has no answer. It is the word *hebel* that Qoheleth applies to describe these situations.

Qoheleth's Call to Enjoyment

There is yet a third factor which must play its part in our search for the meaning of the term *hebel* as used by Qoheleth. It lies in the reiterated calls to enjoy life.

Despite past difficulties in establishing the structure of the book as a whole, this commentary will give reasons for claims that the book does have a general structure, in the sense that it moves from programmatic question through response to advice grounded on the preceding evidence. That this pattern recurs throughout the first eight chapters allows us to claim that Qoheleth is searching for an answer to his question, and in light of what he finds, or has himself experienced, he offers his summarizing call to enjoy the life which God gives. This approach permits the conclusion that Qoheleth's purpose in writing is to be sought ultimately in the positive calls to his readers to receive thankfully from God the gift of life. This advice we find again in the discourse section 9:7–10, where Qoheleth urges the youth of Israel to enjoy the life and work which God apportions. These calls to enjoyment are actually theological statements of faith in a just and loving God, despite many signs which might appear contrary. Thus, from a structural standpoint, it is clear that Qoheleth's focus is upon an affirmative rather than a negative view of human life. Qoheleth comes to us as a realist, but one who never loses sight of the fact that life is God-given and for our benefit (see also Good, 1965, pp. 176–83; Polk, 1976).

For these reasons, it is important to state clearly once again, that the term *hebel* in Qoheleth has a distinctive function and meaning: it conveys the notion that life is enigmatic, and mysterious; that there are many unanswered and unanswerable questions. The person of faith recognizes this fact but moves forward positively to claim and enjoy the life and the work which God apportions.

16

ECCLESIASTES 1:5–7
AND THE
WONDERS
OF NATURE

R. N. Whybray

E ccles. 1:4–11 is generally understood[1] as expressing Qoheleth's characteristic view of the futility of human life, which he compares with the equally futile endless repetitions observable in nature. Undoubtedly certain repetitive processes in the natural world are described here (vv. 5–7), and the conclusion drawn that there is nothing new under the sun (v. 9).[2] But the view that Qoheleth regarded these natural phenomena as *futile* must be questioned.

From the *Journal for the Study of the Old Testament* 41 (1981): 105–12. Reproduced by permission of Sheffield Academic Press.
1. The principal commentaries consulted for this chapter are G. A. Barton (ICC), Edinburgh: T. & T. Clark, 1908; H. W. Hertzberg (KAT), Gütersloh: Gerd Mohn, 1963; R. Kroeber, Berlin: Akademie-Verlag, 1963; R. Gordis, New York: Schocken Books, 3rd edition, 1968; K. Galling (HAT), Tübingen: J. C. B. Mohr, 2nd edition, 1969; A. Lauha (BKAT), Neukirchen-Vluyn: Neukirchener Verlag, 1978; N. Lohfink (Die Neue Echter Bibel), Würzburg: Echter Verlag, 1980; W. Zimmerli (ATD), Göttingen: Vandenhoeck & Ruprecht, 3rd edition, 1980.
2. Verses 10–11, which are generally recognized as dealing with a possible objection to the conclusion drawn in v. 9, may be omitted from the present discussion.

It may be agreed that the purpose of vv. 5–7 is—at least in part—to set the human situation in a wider context by the use of these three analogies drawn from natural phenomena: the behavior of the sun, the wind and the rivers. It is with these verses that this chapter will be mainly concerned. It will be argued that these examples are not intended to show the futility of these phenomena, but only their regularity—or, more precisely, the limitations imposed on them by their allotted natures and functions, which necessitate their constant cyclical repetition. Not a word is said about their futility: on the contrary, the reader is implicitly invited to regard their activity with wonder and admiration.[3]

The common misinterpretation of these verses is due in part to a failure to understand the meaning of the verses themselves, but also to the ambiguity of certain words in vv. 4 and 8 and to uncertainty about the point at which the pericope begins.

The view that v. 4 is the continuation of v. 3[4] is due mainly to the assumption that *dôr* here denotes a human generation or life-span. If this were so, the verse would be a comment on the transitoriness of human lives as seen against the background of the continuing existence of the earth on which they play their fleeting roles. It would then be possible to see it as developing the thought that man's activities ultimately bring him no gain (*yitrôn*) by pointing out how soon his life is cut off by death, when all temporary gains must be surrendered. The connection thus envisaged between the two verses is not, however, a strong one, and it is more likely that v. 3 is editorial and is closely connected with v. 2, the two verses together forming an attempt by an editor to summarize Qoheleth's teaching as a whole.

The question of the authorship of v. 3 has been the subject of much discussion, and will not be further discussed here. But in the absence of proof that vv. 3 and 4 belong together, there is reason to doubt whether *dôr* in v. 4 refers, at least primarily, to the human life-span.

The word *dôr*, which has cognates in most of the Semitic languages, appears to have a cyclical connotation (cf. Heb. *dûr*, "circle"). In the Old Testament it frequently denotes a period of time measured by the length of the human life-cycle. But this association with human life is not essential to its meaning. A more general sense of "duration, age, period" is attested elsewhere, especially in Akkadian.[5] So also in the Old Testament: in many passages where *leʿdôr dôrîm*, *leʿdôr wādôr* and similar expressions are used there is reason to doubt whether the thought is of human generations. Indeed, in

---

3. Zimmerli and O. Loretz (*Qohelet und der Alte Orient* [Frieburg: Herder, 1964], pp. 193–94) among others recognize that the descriptions of nature in these verses should be reckoned as "nature poetry" comparable with the descriptions of natural processes in Job and elsewhere.

4. This view is held by most commentators but not by Galling and Lohfink.

5. See *TWAT*, II, cols. 181–84 (ET III, pp. 169–73); *THAT*, I, cols. 443–44.

some passages a human reference is improbable. Thus in Isa. 41:4, where Yahweh is represented as calling the *dōrôt* from the beginning; and in Isa. 51:9, where it was in the *dōrôt* *ʿōlāmîm* that Yahweh "cut Rahab in pieces and pierced the *tannîn*," it is most natural to suppose that the reference is to a primordial time before the appearance of the human race.[6]

From the way in which *dōr*—in the plural—frequently stands in parallelism with the singular *ʿōlām* it would seem that an unspecified multiplicity of such periods was thought to constitute time (past or future) in its entirety. This concept lies behind the use of the two words in the verse under consideration (4). Time (*ʿōlām*) consists of a succession of endlessly repeated cyclical processes in nature (*dōr . . . dôr*). Verses 5–7 then illustrate this statement, describing three such processes. The participial form of all the verbs in v. 4—*hōlēk, bāʾ, ʿōmādet*—stresses the unchanging nature of these phenomena.

In support of the view that *dôr* means "generation" here it has been pointed out that "go" and "come" are sometimes used as euphemisms for human death and birth: Qoheleth is believed to be saying that as each generation dies it is regularly replaced by a new one. It is true that "come" and "go" occur occasionally in the Old Testament in this sense, though only Qoheleth uses them as a pair (5:16 [EVV 15]; 6:4). In these two passages the reference is to individuals, and of their birth and death ("come" . . . "go") rather than of replacement ("go" . . . "come"). There is in fact no analogy for the collective use of these terms in v. 4 in the way suggested, and in the context it is more reasonable to suppose that the reference is to natural phenomena such as those which are about to be described in vv. 5–7. The verse is an introductory statement pointing out that these phenomena always providentially return even though they might seem to have vanished forever.

6. This is not the usual view. In the case of Isa. 41:4 the question turns upon the meaning of *mērōʾš* ("from the beginning"). In Isa. 40:21 this expression is parallel with *môsᵉdôt hāʾāreṣ* ("[from] the foundations of the earth"), and is clearly used in an absolute sense (so BDB and KB; cf. K. Elliger, BKAT 11/1 [1978], p. 83 n. 1), and this may also be true of its other occurrences in Deutero-Isaiah (41:26; 48:16). Certainly in Prov. 8:23, where it is parallel with *mēʿōlām, mērōʾš* must refer to a time before the creation of the world, "before the beginning of the earth." Wisdom there claims to have come into existence before any of the acts of creation was performed (vv. 24–30). So similarly in Isa. 41:4 the context ("I, Yahweh, the first . . . ") strongly suggests that the calling of the *dōrôt* "from the beginning" refers to Yahweh's control not merely of human history but of the whole creation: it is Deutero-Isaiah's argument that it is this universal sovereignty which makes it credible that he should also have performed such a lesser act as the summoning of Cyrus to do his work.

Isa. 51:9, where *dōrôt ʿōlāmîm* is parallel with *yᵉmê qedem* (cf. *mērōʾš miqqadᵉmê-ʾāreṣ* in Prov. 8:23), is, as is generally recognized, part of a passage (vv. 9–10) in which the thought moves from the mythological or primordial to the historical (the Exodus). But the pivotal point of the passage is verse 10a, which may refer to either or both. In v. 9 the primary reference is clearly to the former: the *dōrôt ʿōlāmîm* in which Yahweh destroyed Rahab and the *tannîn* are not human generations but primordial eras.

The interpretation of *dôr* suggested above may be thought to be, in itself, not susceptible of absolute proof. But the main cause of the mis-interpretation of the passage does not lie here. It lies in a failure to understand v. 8, and in particular the word *yᵉgēʿîm*. This word is almost universally translated as either "weary" or "wearisome." The latter rendering is patently quite unjustified: to be weary (tired) and to be wearisome (tiring) are two quite different things, and there is no evidence whatever for the latter meaning.

But, further, it is by no means established that *yāgēaʿ* means "weary." It is true that it has that sense in the only two other passages in which it occurs in the Old Testament (Deut. 25:18; 2 Sam. 17:2), where it is used, as it is not here, of human beings; but two examples out of a total of three are insufficient to determine the meaning of the third, especially in view of the fact that both the cognate noun *yᵉgîaʿ* and the verb *yāgēaʿ*, which occur much more frequently, have other meanings. *yāgēaʿ* frequently means to labor, while *yᵉgîaʿ* significantly never has the connotation of weariness but always means either labor[7] or the product of labor: produce, wealth, property.[8] The notion of purposeful or effective *activity* is thus a strong possibility here, and one which is particularly appropriate in this context: "all things are constantly in activity"[9] perfectly sums up the catalogue of activity in nature described in the preceding verses.[10] The remainder of the verse then makes good sense as stressing the marvelous nature of this activity as observed by man: man is rendered speechless when he contemplates it, and his eye and ear are incapable of taking it all in.[11]

We now turn to the descriptions of natural phenomena in vv. 5–7.

In v. 5 the daily and nightly course of the *sun* is described. After it has set in the west it returns swiftly by an underground route (the earth being regarded as a flat disc) to the east where it is to rise again—a cosmological concept shared by a number of ancient peoples including the Egyptians.[12] The

---

7. Gen. 31:42; Job 39:11, 16.

8. Deut. 28:33; Neh. 5:13; Job 10:3; Pss. 78:46; 109:11; 128:2; Isa. 45:14; 55:2; Jer. 3:24; 20:5; Ezek. 23:29; Hos. 12:9 (EVV 8); Hag. 1:11. All the occurrences are accounted for here.

9. An alternative translation of *kol-haddᵉbārîm* as "all words" or "all speech" is supported by Hertzberg, Galling, Lauha and Zimmerli, mainly on three grounds: that elsewhere in the book *dābār* always means "word" and not "thing"; that speaking, seeing and hearing form an appropriate series; and that *lᵉdabbēr*, "to speak," occurs later in the verse. None of these arguments, however, is conclusive, and the other commentaries take the opposite view. Since either "words" or "things" is equally possible as a translation of *dᵉbārîm*, the decision must depend mainly on the interpretation of the verse as a whole. My interpretation of *yᵉgēʿîm* rules out the possibility of "words" or "speech" here.

10. Lohfink has "Alle Dinge sind rastlos tätig."

11. *ŝābaʿ* and *mlʾ* (Niph.) are here used, as in 4:8 (also with the eye as subject) and 6:7 respectively and elsewhere in the Old Testament to denote the complete realization of something desired. However often one observes these phenomena, they remain beyond one's comprehension, and so leave one at a loss for words (*lōʾ yûkal ʾîš lᵉdabbēr*).

12. See S. Morenz, *Egyptian Religion* [London: Methuen, 1973], pp. 207–8.

verb šāʾap means to gasp or pant, sometimes through weakness or pain (e.g. Isa. 42:14; Jer. 14:6) but elsewhere with eagerness or desire (e.g. Ps. 119:131; Job 7:2). The positive sense is the more appropriate here: the sun pants eagerly like one running a race on the way to its next appearance. We may compare Ps. 19:6 (EVV 5), where, although its nightly subterranean passage is not specifically mentioned, the sun's daily passage through the heavens is presented as the joyful progress of a hero and as one of the glories of God's creation. Both in that passage and in Egyptian thought that progress is conceived in purposeful and triumphant terms.[13]

The changes in the direction of the *wind*, described in v. 6, might, in contrast to those of the sun, seem aimless; but it is not to this that Qoheleth is referring. As can be seen by comparing this verse with those which precede and follow it, his meaning is that the wind also has its own fixed circuit and can be relied on to remain within it, always returning (šāb) eventually to the direction from which it started: it "goes full circle," as NEB puts it.[14]

Verse 7 describes a similar cyclical movement in the case of the *rivers*: they—that is, their water—having flowed into the sea, return (šābîm) to their source to repeat the process.

This interpretation of the verse is not, however, universally accepted. This is due to ambiguities in the second half. še- (which is prefixed to hannᵉhālîm) may in this context mean either "from which" or "to which" ("where" is an unlikely meaning in a context referring to movement). šābîm lālāket is also ambiguous: šûb followed by an infinitive may either have its literal sense of "turn (back)," or may simply indicate the repetition of an action. The commentaries are consequently divided: some[15] render the sentence by "to the place from which the rivers flow they return," while others[16] render it by "to the place to which the rivers flow they continue to flow." In other words, the sentence has been thought either to refer to a process whereby the water which flows into the sea somehow returns to its source to resume its flow, or, alternatively, simply to the rivers' endless flow in the same direction to the sea.

The first alternative is supported by the fact that the entire passage up to this point (vv. 4–6) speaks of cyclical processes in nature. The introduction of a different kind of phenomenon here would be unnatural and would weaken the force of the argument. Further, the fact that šûb is one of a series of key words—the others are hālak (vv. 4 and 6 [twice]) and māqôm (vv. 5 and 7)—which bind these verses together strongly suggests that it should be accorded the same sense here as in v. 6: like the wind, the streams return on their circuit.

---

13. Cf. *ANET*, p. 33.

14. South and north serve here to represent all the points of the compass and were chosen because east and west had already been mentioned, by implication, in verse 5.

15. Toy, Galling, Lohfink; also NEB.

16. Gordis, Zimmerli, Hertzberg, Lauha, Kroeber.

The question how Qoheleth conceived of the cyclical motion in the case of water does not present serious difficulties. Among other suggestions, that of Ibn Ezra in his commentary on this verse that this is a reference to evaporation is probably correct.[17]

Against this interpretation it has been argued that on the cyclical view the phrase "but the sea is not full" has no point: that Qoheleth would hardly have drawn attention to this fact if he was about to give a rational explanation of it in the next sentence. In support of this objection the similarity of v. 7a to a line in Aristophanes' *Clouds* has been pointed out: "The sea, although all the rivers flow into it, does not increase in volume" (lines 1292–94). In making this somewhat commonplace observation the speaker, Strepsiades, was not referring to a theory of the cyclical motion of the water—though this had been mentioned earlier, in lines 1278–81—but simply using the phenomenon as an example of unprofitableness. But the image is capable of being applied in more than one way; and there is no reason, especially in view of the context, to suppose that Qoheleth used it for the same purpose as did Aristophanes. Qoheleth's observation that the sea is not full is simply part of his description of the cyclical flow of the water: *although* all the rivers flow into the sea, the sea does not overflow *because* the water returns to its source through evaporation.

Finally, the view that the flow of the water is here represented as in one direction only involves a dubious interpretation of *šābîm lālāket*. The normal connotations of the verb *šûb* are "turn, return, turn back." It is true that followed, as here, by an infinitive it may in certain circumstances signify the repetition of an action, as in Job's complaint *lōʾ tāšûb ʿênî lirʾôt ṭôb*, "my eye will not see good again" (7:7). But it must be pointed out that—as illustrated by the above quotation—this construction is used *only* of completed actions repeated *after an interval* and not of repeated actions forming a continuum like the continuous flow of water: the agent or subject *returns*, as it were, to perform the action a second time. *šābîm lālāket*, therefore, can hardly refer to a continuous flow of water in one direction.[18] *šābîm*, then, is to be taken in its literal sense of the return of the water to its source, and v. 7b should be rendered "to the place from which the streams flow they make their way back

---

17. "'The sea is not full, because there is a vapor (*ʾēd*) constantly rising from the sea to the sky, which forms the clouds, . . . and the vapor is converted into rain." This phenomenon, which may have been known to the author of the poem of Job (36:27–28), would be particularly noticeable in the case of the Dead Sea. The Targum, on the other hand, glosses the verse by referring to "subterranean channels" by which the water flows back to its source.

18. It could be argued that by using the word *naḥal,* which often denotes a torrent or *wadi* which flows only intermittently and during part of the year, Qoheleth intended to refer to the constantly repeated annual flow of the *wadis:* but *naḥal* does not always have that specialized meaning; and the use of the participle *hôlēk* here as the subject of *hannᵉḥālîm,* as in the previous verses, suggests continuously flowing rivers rather than *wadis* (see. P. Reymond, VT[S] 6 [1958], p. 111).

again." It is thus implied that, like the circuits of the sun and the wind, the cyclical movement of the water is not futile: its constant flow and distribution over the earth are a wonderful and beneficial phenomenon.

These verses, then, are concerned not with futility (*hebel*) but simply with the changing character of natural phenomena. Verses 5–7 illustrate the general statement of v. 4 and lead to the conclusion of v. 9a that "what has been will be again" and that consequently there is "nothing new under the sun." It is striking, in view of the frequency with which it occurs in the book, that the word *hebel* does not occur in vv. 4–11 at all. Nature is observed without such comment. Qoheleth's purpose here, in a passage placed at the beginning of his book, is to remind his readers of the cosmic setting within which human life, which is always his main concern, has to be lived. The only direct reference to human life—and it is an oblique one—occurs in the middle section of v. 9, where the observation that what has *been* (*hāyāh*) will *be* again is glossed by him with the further observation that what has been *done* (*na ʿăśeh*) will be *done* again: in other words, that human *actions*, like the natural phenomena, are part of what happens "under the sun" and so confined within fixed limits, unable to break out from these to achieve something radically new.

In v. 14, it is true, Qoheleth characterizes everything that is done under the sun as *hebel*. But this statement occurs in a new section of the book, in which no reference is made to the theme of vv. 4–11: indeed, the word *ḥādāš*, "new," does not occur in the book after v. 10. That Qoheleth regarded human life as in some sense cyclical cannot be denied: at death "the dust returns (*wᵉyāšōb*) to the earth as it was, and the spirit returns (*tāšûb*) to God, who gave it" (12:7). In his thought this procession from dust back to dust is undoubtedly one of the aspects of human existence which contribute to his sense of futility; but it would be wrong to read this judgment back into 1:4–11, which speak only of the *limits* within which nature—including human nature—must run its course.

Notes

I am indebted to Professor D. J. A. Clines for his helpful suggestions with regard to a number of points in this chapter.

17

NOTHING NEW UNDER THE SUN

ECCLESIASTES 1:4–11

James L. Crenshaw

This poem characterizes nature as an endless round of pointless movement, a rhythm that engulfs human generations as well. Oblivious to the relentless striving of heavenly and earthly bodies, the earth remains unchanged. The sun makes its rounds, as does the wind, and each one returns to start the process again. Streams flow to the ocean in a never-ending process, but they fail to fill the sea. Humans talk incessantly without fully expressing the wearisome nature of things. The eye always increases human desire, and the ear never hears enough. The past repeats itself ad infinitum, so that there is nothing new under the sun. Things only seem new because of a human tendency to forget the past.

[4]The prologue offers a justification for the pessimistic view of things expressed in 1:2–3. It emphasizes the ceaseless activity of the natural world (1:4–7), a constant movement that has no discernible purpose or result. But the prologue also hints that human actions (1:8–11) always fail to reach their goal.

Reprinted from *Ecclesiastes* in the Old Testament Libarary Series by James L. Crenshaw. © 1987 James L. Crenshaw. Used by permission of Westminster/ John Knox Press and SCM Press.

The initial unit (1:4–7) deals with the four elements of the universe as discussed by ancient philosophers: earth, air, fire, and water. The remaining unit (1:8–11) refers to the quality that distinguishes human beings from animals, the capacity for speech, and isolates two aspects of the affective dimension, sight and sound. The section concludes with a denial that novelty occurs anywhere and a bold assertion that everything is destined to oblivion.

The word *dôr*, an appropriate choice because of its ambiguity, suggests both nature and people. The primary sense here is probably the former: the generations of natural phenomena. But the other nuance must also be present, lending immense irony to the observation that the stage on which the human drama is played outlasts the actors themselves.

A traditional response to the earlier question about profit might have pointed to the quest for progeny: it is advantageous to have children, for one's name survives in them. Qohelet undercuts such an argument. Only the earth endures for long, he observes. With these Qal participles for the passing of one generation (*hōlēk*) and the coming of another (*bāʾ*) a significant feature of the book, antithesis,[1] first comes to expression. In this instance the same word is modified by contrasting ideas. One generation dies and another is born.

The participles indicate continuous action; the dying and birthing happen again and again without end. Qohelet's use of *hōlēk* to specify death (cf. 3:20, "All go to one place; everything came from dust and everything returns to dust"; and 5:15, "And this is also a grievous injustice; precisely as he came so shall he depart, and what advantage did he possess that he toiled for the wind?") is an extension of the phrase "to go to his fathers." The verb *hālak* has the sense of dying in several biblical texts outside Ecclesiastes (Ps. 39:14 [13E]; Job 10:21; 14:20; 2 Sam. 12:23).

The sequence (death-birth) is striking, for one normally expects the opposite order. Both the anterior position and the repetition of *dôr* give this word a force equal to the weightier notions of dying and coming into being. But the twofold occurrence of *dôr* already offers a hint of things to come, the monotonous recurrence of purposeless activity. Like generations, which are ongoing and repetitious, nature moves ceaselessly in circuits that are monotonous and futile.[2]

Not everything is caught up in the endless process of going and coming. Whether the endurance of the earth is meant to be contrasted with the transience of generations, in the aggregate or separately, depends on the way one reads the conjunction *wᵉ*. It is possible to understand the verse to mean that a generation

---

1. Unless *yitrôn* in 1:3 contrasts with *hᵃbēl* in 1:2.

2. Elsewhere the perpetual cycle of generations was likened to a tree's shedding its leaves and putting on new ones (Sir. 14:18–19; cf. Homer, *Iliad* 6.146ff.). In anticipation of standing naked before God the blushing trees cast off their garments one by one, while the deity averts the all-comprehending glance until the naked are fully clothed once more.

always succeeds its predecessor, so that (or while) the earth continues for a long time. However, the w^e probably means "but." Despite continual departures and entries of separate generations, both human and natural, the earth stands intact. The feminine participle *ʿōmādet* denotes duration. Jerome perceived the irony in this observation about ephemerality and permanence. He wrote: "What is more vain than this vanity: that the earth, which was made for humans, stays—but humans themselves, the lords of the earth, suddenly dissolve into dust?"

How long did Qohelet think the earth would remain? The word *lᵉʿôlām* indicates continuity for a long time, although it lacks the modern sense of eternity, that is, time without end. The idea is that the earth will last as long as the mind can project into the future. Nevertheless, human beings realize no profit, for they pass from the scene forever.[3]

[5] Ancient Egyptians thought of the sun as conveyed on a ship during its nocturnal journey from west to east, and the Greeks pictured Helios driven by steeds on its daily circuit. According to Ps. 19:5 the sun leaves its chamber like a bridegroom and returns like a strong man, having run its course with joy. Qohelet's description lacks this mood of celebration and wonder. Instead of picturing a vigorous champion who easily makes the daily round, he thinks of strenuous panting to reach the destination. Having arrived, an exhausted sun must undertake the whole ordeal again.

Whereas Qohelet placed the subjects before the participles in 1:4, they follow the participles in 1:5. The repetition of the subject in each verse (*dôr* in 1:4; *haššemeš* in 1:5) achieves perfect symmetry in the first four words of these two verses. But the balancing of subject and participle is broken at the level of meaning, for the sense of *bāʾ* in 1:4 does not extend into 1:5, where the meaning of *bāʾ* approximates that of *hōlēk* (sets, dies). Furthermore, the extreme brevity of 1:4, which echoes the succinct form in 1:1–3, disappears. The additional phrase "there it rises" advances the thought from exhaustion after an arduous journey to monotonous repetition of drudgery.

Again participles call attention to the durative nature of the action. Although the first *zôrēaḥ* is pointed as a Qal perfect, the prefixed w^e poses a problem. In all probability the original participle (*zôrēaḥ*) lost its *waw* by metathesis, giving rise subsequently to its present pointing. The root *šāʾap* occurs in the sense of panting with anticipation (Ps. 119:131, "With open mouth I pant, because I long for thy commandments") and from exhaustion (Jer. 14:6, "The wild asses stand on the bare heights, they pant for air like jackals; the eyes fail because there is no herbage"; cf. Isa. 42:14, a woman gasping in travail; Job 7:2, a slave longing for a shadow). The accents separate *šôʾēp* from w^e*ʾel-mᵉqômô*, but this is undoubtedly a mistake.

---

3. The Instruction for Merikare has an interesting parallel: "While generation succeeds generation, God who knows characters is hidden; one can not oppose the lord of the land, He reaches all that the eyes can see."

Thus far the prologue has made two sweeping claims. Human beings and natural forces in their individuality and as an aggregate vanish from the scene on which the drama of life is played. The earth alone endures. Moreover, the most visible of the heavenly bodies is consigned to perpetual drudgery. The sun's task is not unlike the punishment imposed on Sisyphus, who was condemned to an eternity of rolling a boulder to the top of a hill only to have it return to the starting place over and over again.

The withholding of the subject is the most striking stylistic feature of [6] this verse. The subject was the opening word in 1:4 and the second word in 1:5, but 1:6 holds it in abeyance until five participles have made an appearance. The immediate effect is to create the illusion that the movement of the sun is still being described. The south-north direction of the wind corresponds to the east-west movement of the sun, thus completing the four points on the compass.

Another stylistic characteristic of this verse is the repeated use of two participles, *sôbēb* and *hôlēk*. The threefold occurrence of *sôbēb* and twofold use of *hôlēk* serve to simulate the feeling of restlessness generated by the constant blowing of the wind. This sense of being caught in a rut reaches its peak in three successive participles *sôbēb sôbēb hôlēk* just before the subject *hārûah* is introduced. Even the next clause returns to this relentless striving for sameness, for it repeats the subject *hārûah* and employs a form of the root *sbb*.[4]

Some interpreters have used this verse among others to argue for a Palestinian composition of the book as opposed to an Egyptian setting. The argument is based on the observation that the wind is more tranquil in the land of the Nile. However, a literalistic reading of the verse hardly supports the claim, for the prevailing winds in Israel are from the direction of the Mediterranean Sea, that is, from the west. Poetic imagery must not be pressed in so literalist a fashion. The author engages in a little exaggeration for maximum effect. In his view the relentless blowing of the wind was no more effectual than the sun's daily round or the passing and coming of countless generations.

[7] The fourth example of pointless activity concerns the remarkable fact that countless streams flow into the sea without filling it to overflowing. The Dead Sea offered a particularly striking instance of such a phenomenon, for this small body of water demonstrably had no outlet and still it remained unfilled. From this observable instance, the same conclusion could be reached

---

4. The translation "from its rounds" is based on general Semitic use, a point that Whitley (9–10) has made and for which he has given a number of examples: Esarhaddon ("loyal conduct was taken away from [*ʿeli*] my brothers"); the Ahiram Inscription ("And may tranquility flee from [*ʿali*] Gebal"); the Moabite stone ("And Chemosh said to me, Go, take Nebo from [*ʿal*] Israel, and I went by night"); Dan. 6:19 [18E] ("And his sleep fled from him" [*ʿaôhî*]); Ps. 16:2 ("I said O Yahweh thou art my God, my good is indeed from thee" [*ʿāleykā*]); the Mishnah ("But if they receive food from him" [*ʿālâw*], *Maas.* 3:1).

about other seas. Aristophanes perceived the same thing, writing that "the sea, though all the rivers flow to it, increaseth not in volume" (*The Clouds*, 1294).

This description of the insatiable sea continues the extravagant use of participles, particularly the repeated use of single images. By means of this poetic device, 1:6 reaches a crescendo with three instances of the participle *sōbēb* and another use of the root *sbb*; it now begins to subside in 1:7. But a new twist emerges to fill the gap; an infinitive with a prefixed *lamed* employs the verbal root that occurs in participial form two other times in the verse. The breadth of nuance is remarkable, for *hôlēk* yields the following senses: die (1:4), blow (1:6, twice), flow (1:7, twice).[5]

The rendering in the Septaugint and Vulgate imply that the point of the verse was not the continual flow of streams so much as their constant cycle. Such a view brings the verse into line with the preceding observation about the sun. The final clause can be translated: "and to the place whence the streams flowed, there they returned in order to flow (once more)," but this interpretation requires an assumption of haplography, a putative *mem* having been assimilated from the relative particle *šᵉ* to the preceding *mem*. Of course, this way of understanding the verse precipitated discussions about the function of underground streams, which served to convey the waters back to their place of origin.

[8] Like the wind, which may blow with incredible force, then subside to the point of imperceptibility, the poem has introduced tangible realities against a backdrop of wonders beyond apprehension. The generations of the universe, the sun running its daily round, the elusive wind—these phenomena lie outside human grasp. With rivers and the sea a rapid shift takes place, for the tiny rivulets, rushing streams, and surging deeps can be seen and touched in a manner that differs appreciably from the way the sun's rays or the breezes are experienced. With this verse the author internalizes ceaseless and pointless movement. What can be observed about nature is also true on the human scene.

The translation "words" may be too restrictive, for Qohelet frequently uses vocabulary that connotes two different meanings at the same time. The translation of "things" provides a fine transition from nature, summarizing what has gone before and anticipating the meaning of the root *dbr* in the rest of the verse. The argument that all other uses of the plural *haddᵉbārîm* in Ecclesiastes (5:1, 2, 6 [2, 3, 7E]; 6:11; 7:21; 9:16; 10:12, 13, 14) connote "words" and therefore this one does too is persuasive only for interpreters who posit absolute consistency of linguistic usage to the author.

This focus on the human arena concentrates on the faculties of speech, sight, and hearing. The sequence is reminiscent of that represented by the

---

5. Three times counting the infinitive *lālāket*.

generations, the sun, and the wind.[6] One hears the constant talking of endless generations, beholds the sun in the heavens, and listens to the sound of the wind. In the case of the waves, both sight and hearing come into play. The observations about natural phenomena have vacillated between the themes of relentless movement and ineffectual activity. Both ideas continue in the comments on speech, if *haddᵉbārîm* carries this meaning. The insatiable aspect of seeing and hearing is prominent as well; moreover, this endless looking and listening invariably falls short of its goal.

Does Qohelet launch an attack on traditional wisdom at this point? The choice of illustrations certainly fits such an interpretation. The quest for the right word for the occasion is futile, the observations that arise from experience are incomplete, and the "hearing" is insufficient.[7]

[9] An obvious consequence of successive generations, the sun's relentless pursuit of its daily rounds, the cyclical blowing of the wind, and the endless flow of streams to the sea is predictability. The sages before Qohelet had exulted in the universe's orderly pattern. Qohelet does not. His startling conclusion divests the orderly universe, so dear to the sages, of its positive dimensions. The search for analogies between natural phenomena and human conduct retains its validity, but the insights that emerge do not enable the discoverers to extricate themselves from a paralyzing repetition of the past. Individuals are destined to lives that never achieve fulfillment. Existence under the sun is marked by inadequate speech, insatiable eyes, and partial hearing.

For persons who exalted eloquence—a sense of timeliness, restraint, integrity, persuasiveness—to the status of supreme virtue, the denial that speech can ever be adequate would undercut the entire wisdom enterprise. Furthermore, observation, the technique by which insights into reality were discovered, is judged faulty. But the most burdensome claim must surely have been the assertion that teaching failed to achieve its goal. The hearer did not embody the transmitted teaching, a problem that Egyptian Instructions take into account (cf. Ptahhotep and Ani).

In the view of this poet, present and future are so closely bound with the past that nothing new ever bursts forth. Unlike those who posited golden ages at both ends of the historical time line, Qohelet rejects the thesis that paradise is both a memory and a hope, a past accomplishment and a future possibility. A myth of eternal return does not lurk beneath Qohelet's reminder

6. If, that is, one understands *dôr* as deliberately ambiguous. According to Ps. 19:2–4 even natural phenomena are credited with unusual communicative powers, speech that dispenses with words.

7. The evocative employment of ʿayin ("eye," recalling the solar disc?) and *ʾōzen* is not matched by a comparable expression for speech (cf. 8:2, *pî-melek*). *ʾîš* may be chosen to contrast with *ʾādām* in 1:3, hence a specific individual rather than humankind in general.

that the past repeats itself. Rather, the emphasis falls on the burdensome monotony of everything in nature and among human beings.

Modern linguists may differ with Qohelet about novelty, for the use of the interrogative *māh*, coupled with the shortened relative *š*^{e},[8] itself departs from earlier usage, causing difficulty for the translators of the Septaugint and Vulgate. This late feature of the Hebrew language occurs often in Ecclesiastes (1:9; 3:15, 22; 6:10; 7:24; 8:7; 10:14) and is equivalent to Aramaic *māh-dî* (Dan. 2:28–29) and *māh-zî* in early extrabiblical Aramaic documents. The Mishnah uses *māh-š*^{e} as an indefinite pronoun just as Qohelet does (*Abot* 5:7, "concerning what he has not heard"; and *B. Bat.* 6:7, "whatever he gave, he gave"). Occasionally, *māh* serves as an indefinite substantive (1 Sam. 19:3, "and if I see anything I will tell you"; 2 Sam. 18:22, "and whatever happens I will run"), and occasionally as a relative (1 Chron. 15:13, "for that which was at first" [Whitley 1979a, 10–11]; 2 Chron. 30:3, "to what was sufficient"; Esth. 9:26, "what they saw").

Some biblical authors also believed new things came to pass. They announced that God was about to institute a new covenant and a new exodus, or they envisioned Israel as the grateful recipient of a new heart.

[10] Sages commonly introduced a striking observation by the particle *yēš*.[9] Qohelet uses this protasis often (1:10; 2:21; 4:8, 9; 5:12; 6:1, 11; 7:15; 8:14 [3 times]; 10:5). The Hebrew particle of existence takes on an ironic dimension in his hands, for it calls attention to bogus claims. The labeling of something as new, like the modern fashion, particularly in the arts, of freely bestowing the adjective "creative," is stripped of its cogency. Qohelet's argument rests on the identity of past and present, a point emphasized by illustrations from nature and human history.

The particle *hinnēh* often signals a shift in point of view.[10] Here Qohelet uses *r*^{e}*ʾēh* in a similar manner. Countering the claim to newness, he places the adverb *k*^{e}*bār* (already) in the emphatic position. This word, which seems to indicate duration, occurs in the Massoretic Text only in Ecclesiastes (2:12, 16; 3:15 [twice]; 4:2; 6:10; 9:6, 7). The plural *l*^{e}*ʿōlāmîm* is governed by a singular verb here and occasionally outside Ecclesiastes (Whitley lists Isa. 26:4; 45:17; and Dan. 9:24 [1979a, 11; all subsequent references will be to this volume]).

[11] Qohelet ascribes claims of newness to a colossal ignorance of the past, a failed memory.[11] Previous generations are quickly forgotten, and future

---

8. The twofold repetition of *mah-š*^{e} and *hûʾš*^{e} reinforces the claim of recurrent phenomena.

9. Prov. 12:18; 14:12; 15:10; 16:25; 18:24; 20:15; 26:12; 30:11–14. The juxtaposition of the particle of existence and that of nonexistence (*ʾên* in 1:9, *yēš* in 1:10) is especially effective.

10. The accentuation requires a translation such as: "Look at this! It is new" (Adele Berlin, *Poetics and Interpretation of Biblical Narrative*; Eisenbrauns, 1983).

11. The unusual form *zikrôn* is a construct before the preposition *l*^{e} rather than an absolute (which occurs as *zikkārôn* in the second half of the verse). Gordis lists the following examples of *zikrôn* before *l*^{e}: Hos. 9:6; Ps. 58:5; Prov. 24:9; 1 Chron. 23:28; Isa. 9:1; Ps. 2:12; *Abot* 5:14.

generations will fare no differently. Although some interpreters relate the *ri'šōnîm* and *'aḥᵃrōnîm* to things, particularly to the *ʿōlāmîm* (ages) in 1:10, the usual impersonal form is feminine plural. Therefore, it is better to understand the words as indicating generations past and future.

In this prologue Qohelet has laid down the grounds for reaching his conclusion that life is futile and that there is no profit from endless activity on earth. He supports the intellectual position by appealing to nature's ceaseless movement, which achieves no surplus, and by referring to human striving, which fails to reach its goal. The examples stress the monotony, repetition, and unfulfilled nature of constant activity. The prologue serves as a suitable introduction to the whole book, just as Prov. 1:2–7 introduces the initial collection (1–9), and perhaps the rest of the book as well.

18

THE SEARCH
FOR SATISFACTION
ECCLESIASTES 1:12–2:26

Derek Kidner

The Seeker

1:12 *I the Preacher have been king over Israel in Jerusalem.* [13] *And I applied my mind to seek and to search out by wisdom all that is done under heaven.*

The poem which we have just pondered set the tone of the book by its motto-theme and by its picture of a world endlessly busy and hopelessly inconclusive.

Now the focus sharpens. We turn from analogies and impressions to what we can know directly from experience. We are to scan a great spread of human pursuits, to ask whether anything on earth can be found which has lasting value. The author gets across to us the urgency of the search: we find ourselves involved in it. But his curious blend of titles for himself, "Qoheleth" and "King," alerts us to the dual character in which he is speaking, as we saw at the outset.[1]

Reprinted from *The Message of Ecclesiastes* by Derek Kidner. ©1976 by Derek Kidner. Used by permission of InterVarsity Press, P.O. Box 1400, Downers Grove, IL 60515.

1. See the comments on 1:1 (p. 21). With the expression in verse 12, "I was (or, became) king" (as it would most naturally be translated), compare Zech. 11:7ff.: "So I became the shepherd I

For the purpose of this passage the preacher has become a second Solomon, so that in our imagination we can do the same. Armed with such advantages, our search will be no circumscribed or tentative affair, but royal, exploring whatever the world can offer to a man of unlimited genius and wealth. In this line of country we can take his findings as definitive. To quote his words (2:12), "What can the man do who comes after the king?"

Perhaps, in passing, we can compare this roving reconnaissance with another passage written in the first person: the heart-searchings of Paul at the end of Romans 7. Each of these two confessions has a wider reference than to the one man who is speaking. Between them, Qoheleth and Paul explore for us man's outer and inner worlds: his search for meaning and his struggle for moral victory.

With his usual devastating candor Qoheleth is quick to tell us the worst. The search has come to nothing. To spare us the disappointment of our hopes, he warns us of the outcome (1:13b–15) before he takes us through his journey (1:16–2:11); finally he will share with us the conclusions he has reached (2:12–26).

The Summary

> 1:13 *It is an unhappy business that God has given to the sons of men to be busy with.* [14] *I have seen everything that is done under the sun; and behold, all is vanity and a striving after wind.*
> [15] *What is crooked cannot be made straight,*
> *and what is lacking cannot be numbered.*

Unobtrusively, but significantly, Qoheleth sums up his findings in terms which for a brief moment go right outside the secularist's field of vision. He sees the restlessness of life which any observer could report, but he traces it to the will of God. It is He who has *given* it to the sons of men. This may sound more like bitterness than faith, but in fact it drops a clue to something positive which will be picked up in the final chapters. At worst it would imply that there was sense, not the nonsense of chance, behind our situation, even if the sense were wholly daunting. But it can equally well chime in with the purposeful discipline which God imposed upon us as the sequel to the Fall. That was how Paul—with an evident glance at Ecclesiastes—was to interpret the travail of the world: "for the creation was subjected to futility (or, "vanity," AV) . . . by the will of him who subjected it *in hope*."[2]

---

destroyed the three shepherds . . . ," etc., which likewise uses autobiographical language, not to be taken literally, or with intent to deceive, but to present to us an illuminating sequence of events with much vividness.

2. Rom. 8:20.

That hope, however, lies quite beyond our own attaining, as the ensuing search will show. And verse 15 throws in two more reminders of our limitations, with the curtness of a proverb. TEV catches it well: "you can't straighten out what is crooked; you can't count things that aren't there." Whether this crookedness and this lack mean our own flaws of character or the circumstances that we can do nothing to alter,[3] we are faced again with the meagerness of what man can do. With this warning we now join Qoheleth in his series of experiments.

The Sampling of Life

1:16 *I said to myself, "I have acquired great wisdom, surpassing all who were over Jerusalem before me; and my mind has had great experience of wisdom and knowledge."*[17] *And I applied my mind to know wisdom and to know madness and folly. I perceived that this also is but a striving after wind.*
   [18] *For in much wisdom is much vexation,*
       and he who increases knowledge increases sorrow.
   2:1 *I said to myself, "Come now, I will make a test of pleasure; enjoy yourself." But behold, this also was vanity.* [2] *I said of laughter, "It is mad," and of pleasure, "What use is it?"* [3] *I searched with my mind how to cheer my body with wine—my mind still guiding me with wisdom—and how to lay hold on folly, till I might see what was good for the sons of men to do under heaven during the few days of their life.* [4] *I made great works; I built houses and planted vineyards for myself;* [5] *I made myself gardens and parks, and planted in them all kinds of fruit trees.* [6] *I made myself pools from which to water the forest of growing trees.* [7] *I bought male and female slaves, and had slaves who were born in my house; I had also great possessions of herds and flocks, more than any who had been before me in Jerusalem.* [8] *I also gathered for myself silver and gold and the treasure of kings and provinces; I got singers, both men and women, and many concubines, man's delight.*
   [9] *So I became great and surpassed all who were before me in Jerusalem; also my wisdom remained with me.* [10] *And whatever my eyes desired I did not keep from them; I kept my heart from no pleasure, for my heart found pleasure in all my toil, and this was my reward for all my toil.* [11] *Then I considered all that my hands had done and the toil I had spent in doing it, and behold, all was vanity and a striving after wind, and there was nothing to be gained under the sun.*

For so famous a thinker the search must naturally begin with wisdom, the quality most highly praised in his circle. But he says nothing of its first principle, the fear of the Lord, and we can assume that the wisdom he speaks of is (as his method demands) the best thinking that man can do on his own. It is splendid, as far as it goes; nothing else can compare with it (2:13); yet it has no answer to our misgivings about life. It only sharpens them by its clarity.

---

3. The second alternative seems the more likely, in view of 7:13 with 7:29, which speak of God as the author of "crooked" things, in the sense of awkward and obstinate facts, but not of moral evil.

So Qoheleth is taking wisdom with proper seriousness, as a discipline concerned with ultimate questions, not simply a tool for getting things done. If that were all, we should ask no more of it than worldy success. But wisdom is concerned with truth, and truth compels us to admit that success can go bad on us, and that nothing on earth has any permanence. He will have more to say on this; meanwhile his first point of rest has given way.

So he will plunge into frivolity. But part of him stands back from it all—*my mind still guiding me with wisdom*—to see what frivolity as a life-style implies, and what it does to a man. He notes at once the "paradox of hedonism," that the more you hunt for pleasure, the less of it you find. In any case, he is looking for something beyond it and through it, for this is more than simple indulgence. It is a deliberate flight from rationality, to get at some secret of life to which reason may be blocking the way. This is the force of verse 3b (which RSV translates more faithfully than, e.g., NEB or TEV): "how to lay hold on folly, till I might see what was good for the sons of men . . . "

Here we are brought very near to our own times with their cult of the irrational in its various forms, from romanticism down to the addict's craving for strange states of consciousness; and down still further into the nihilism which cultivates the ugly, the obscene and the absurd, not as a frolic but as an attack on reasonable values. While nothing as developed as this appears in Qoheleth, his assessment of his experiment with folly shows that he is disturbed as well as disappointed. The mild disparagement of pleasure, "*What use is it?*", is supplemented by the sharper verdict on laughter, "*It is mad*"; and in Scripture both "madness" and "folly" imply moral perversity rather than mental oddity.[4] To earn such rebuke, the laughter that goes with this way of life must be cynical and destructive. If so, we are not far from our own black comedy and sick humor.

As if he had over-reacted in turning to the futile pleasures, he now gives himself to the joys of creativity. He bends his energies to a project worthy of his aesthetic gifts, his grasp of skills and sciences, and his ability to command a great establishment. He creates a little world within a world: multiform, harmonious, exquisite: a secular Garden of Eden, full of civilized and agreeably uncivilized delights (8),[5] with no forbidden fruits—or none that he regards as such (10). He has had the sense, for all this, to avoid the rich man's boredom by strenuous activity, enjoyed and valued for its own sake (10); and he

4. E.g., in 9:3 "madness" is partnered by "evil," and in 10:13 the present word for "folly" is seen as a step towards "wicked madness." Likewise, to act foolishly (using the related verb to "folly") usually implies a fatally headstrong attitude: cf. 1 Sam. 13:13; 26:21; 2 Sam. 24:10.

5. The word *šiddâ*, occurring only here, is taken to mean "musical instrument" in AV. But in a letter from Pharaoh Amenophis III to Milkilu prince of Gezer (translation in *ANET*, p. 487a), demanding 40 concubines, the Egyptian word for concubine is accompanied by an explanatory Canaanite word akin to *šiddâ*. Although NEB prefers to make no conjecture, and JB offers the word "chests" (i.e., treasure-chests), RSV seems likely to be right with "concubines," as in RV (cf. TEV, "women").

has kept an appraising eye on his projects, even while in full pursuit of them. "*My wisdom,*" he tells us, "*remained with me*" (9). He has not lost sight of the quest, the search for meaning, which was the mainspring of it all.

In the end, what has it yielded? A less exacting mind than Qoheleth's would have found a great deal to report with satisfaction. The achievements had been brilliant. On the material level, the farmer's perennial ambition to make (in our phrase) "two blades of grass grow where one had grown before" had been overwhelmingly fulfilled; while aesthetically he had produced a connoisseur's paradise. If "a thing of beauty is a joy for ever," he had not searched in vain for what is timeless and absolute.

So we tend to think.

Qoheleth will have none of it. To call such things eternal is no more than rhetoric, and nothing perishable will satisfy him. In the brutally colloquial terms of Today's English Version, his report is, "I realized that it didn't mean a thing. It was like chasing the wind."

The Assessment

2:12 *So I turned to consider wisdom and madness and folly; for what can the man do who comes after the king? Only what he has already done.* [13] *Then I saw that wisdom excels folly as light excels darkness.* [14] *The wise man has his eyes in his head, but the fool walks in darkness; and yet I perceived that one fate comes to all of them.* [15] *Then I said to myself, "What befalls the fool will befall me also; why then have I been so very wise?" And I said to myself that this also is vanity.* [16] *For of the wise man as of the fool there is no enduring remembrance, seeing that in the days to come all will have been long forgotten. How the wise man dies just like the fool!* [17] *So I hated life, because what is done under the sun was grievous to me; for all is vanity and a striving after wind.*

[18] *I hated all my toil in which I had toiled under the sun, seeing that I must leave it to the man who will come after me;* [19] *and who knows whether he will be a wise man or a fool? Yet he will be master of all for which I toiled and used my wisdom under the sun. This also is vanity.* [20] *So I turned about and gave my heart up to despair over all the toil of my labors under the sun,* [21] *because sometimes a man who has toiled with wisdom and knowledge and skill must leave all to be enjoyed by a man who did not toil for it. This also is vanity and a great evil.* [22] *What has a man from all the toil and strain with which he toils beneath the sun?* [23] *For all his days are full of pain, and his work is a vexation; even in the night his mind does not rest. This also is vanity.*

[24] *There is nothing better for a man than that he should eat and drink, and find enjoyment in his toil. This also, I saw, is from the hand of God;* [25] *for apart from him who can eat or who can have enjoyment?* [26] *For to the man who pleases him God gives wisdom and knowledge and joy; but to the sinner he gives the work of gathering and heaping, only to give to one who pleases God. This also is vanity and a striving after wind.*

The brief and blunt verdict of verse 11 needed some spelling out, for in delving into life's possibilities Qoheleth was not acting purely on his own account. If he of all people has come back empty-handed, even in the mantle of Solomon, what hope has anyone else (12)?[6] So he goes back to the great alternatives, wisdom and folly, to compare them and then to assess them radically. Has either of them an answer to this search for something final? They were the two ways of life he had been testing in the experiments of 1:17–2:10—for he includes in "folly" not only the "madness" of self-indulgence and cynicism but the pursuit of pleasure at any level, even the highest, as an escape from painful thoughts that should be faced. This was clear enough from the sequel to 1:18, where it was the comment, "he who increases knowledge increases sorrow," which led to the brisk resolve, "Come now, I will make a test of pleasure; enjoy yourself."

The bare comparison of wisdom and folly is simple, but the final assessment is shattering. Nothing could be more obvious than that the two compare with one another as light with darkness (13, 14a); but Qoheleth has the wit to remember that they are abstractions and we are men. It is little use commending to us the ultimate worth of wisdom, if in the end none of us will be around to exercise it, let alone to value it. This of course is why the purely human achievements which we call lasting are nothing of the kind. As men of the world we may revere them in this way, but only for lack of Qoheleth's honesty in seeing that *in the days to come all will have been long forgotten* (16). He has no illusions, though by rights it is we who should have none—we who have heard from the secularists themselves that our very planet is dying.

So, for the first time in the book but by no means the last, the fact of death brings the search to a sudden stop. If *one fate comes to all,* and that fate is extinction, it robs every man of his dignity and every project of its point. We look at these two results in turn in verses 14–17 and 18–23.

As to man's dignity, what is so mortifying (an appropriate word!) about death's final leveling of wise men and fools—to which we could add, "good men and bad," "saints and sadists," and every other pair of opposites—is that if it is true, it allows the last word to a brute fact which tramples on every value-judgment we can make. Everything may tell us that wisdom is *not* on a par with folly, nor goodness with evil; but no matter: if death is the end of the road, the contention that there is nothing to choose between them will get the last word. The choices that we positively knew to be significant will be brushed aside as finally irrelevant.

So I hated life. If there is a lie at the centre of existence, and nonsense at the end of it, who has the heart to make anything of it? If, as we might put it,

---

6. TEV tampers with the meaning of verse 12 by reversing the order of its two main clauses and translating 12b (its own 12a) as ". . . a king can only do what previous kings have done"—which is manifestly untrue. NEB resorts to a different transposition, removing 12b to the end of verse 18.

every card in our hand will be trumped, does it matter how we play? Why treat a king with more respect than a knave?

Incidentally, this bitter reaction is a witness to our ability to stand clear of our condition and to weigh it up. To be outraged at what is universal and unavoidable suggests something of a divine discontent, a hint of what the great saying in 3:11 will call "eternity" in man's mind. In fact our verse 16 uses that word to lament the lack of any *enduring* remembrance of the wise.

Verses 18–23 look at a smaller grief, but one which can sap the spirit in its own way; the frustrating uncertainty of all our enterprises once they slip from our control, as sooner or later they must. On his own principles, the man of the world should hardly object to this, provided they last his time; yet he does mind, for he shares our inbuilt longing for what is permanent. The more he has toiled at his life's work (and verses 22f. show how obsessive this toil can be), the more galling will be the thought of its fruits falling into other hands—and as likely as not, the wrong hands. This is yet another blow to the hope, glimpsed earlier in the chapter, of finding fulfilment in hard work and high attainment. Their very success will accentuate the anticlimax.

At last a more cheerful note breaks in. Perhaps we have been trying too hard. The compulsive worker of verses 22f., overloading his days with toil and his nights with worry, has missed the simple joys that God was holding out to him. The real issue for him was not between work and rest but, had he known it, between meaningless and meaningful activity. As verse 24 points out, the very toil that tyrannized him was potentially a joyful gift of God (and joy itself is another, 25),[7] if only he had had the grace to take it as such.

Here is the other side to the "unhappy business that God has given to the sons of men" (1:13), for in themselves, and rightly used, the basic things of life are sweet and good. Food, drink and work are samples of them, and Qoheleth will remind us of others.[8] What spoils them is our hunger to get out of them more than they can give; a symptom of the longing which differentiates us from the beasts, but whose misdirection is the underlying theme of this book.

So, for a moment, the veil is lifted in verse 26, to show us something other than futility. The book will end strongly on this positive note, but meanwhile we are shown enough in such glimpses to assure us that there is an answer, and that the author is no defeatist. He disillusions us to bring us to reality.

What he is saying in this final verse could be carelessly read as an escape-clause for God's favorites, sparing them the material risks which have just been described. Today's English Version goes out of its way to give this im-

---

7. The words, *apart from him* (25) are an emendation, supported by LXX. The MT has "apart from me," which would make good sense only if God were speaking in the first person. AV, RV, "more than I," is intelligible, but scarcely a possible translation.

8. Cf. 9:7–10; 11:7–10.

pression by removing the word "sinner" (for no reason) and by describing those who please God merely as "those he likes" or "likes better" than others. But even without that gratuitous distortion it would be easy to overlook the vital contrast in this verse, which is between the satisfying spiritual gifts of God (wisdom, knowledge, joy), which only those who please Him can desire or receive, and the frustrating business[9] of amassing what cannot be kept, a business which is the chosen lot of those who reject Him. The fact that in the end the sinner's hoard will go to the righteous is only a crowning irony to what was in any case *vanity and a striving after wind*. And for the righteous it is a crowning vindication, but no more. Like the meek, who are promised the earth, their treasure is elsewhere and of another kind.

---

9. *Work*, in this verse, is the same word as "business" in the phrase of 1:13, "it is an unhappy business that God has given to the sons of men to be busy with." TEV creates a further misleading contrast, namely between those to whom God gives His gifts and those who have to work for what they get.

19

THE GRIP OF TIME

ECCLESIASTES 3:1–9

J. A. Loader

This passage is one of the most ingenious parts of the Old Testament. Its beauty lies in the absolute symmetry of the entire poem and the precise balance of every pronouncement. This precision is not hard to understand—the Preacher can say grand things simply.

The first and last verses are obviously not cast in the same mold that the rest of the poem is. In verses 2–8 every line has two pronouncements concerning "a time for *x* and a time for *y*." Verse 1, which is more general in content, therefore has to be the heading that gives a summary of the theme of the passage. Verse 9 has a totally different form and has to be the conclusion in which the Preacher, in his own characteristic way, uses a question to posit a thesis. So our attention is directed especially toward the fourteen parallel lines in between.

Each of the Bible verses consists of two poetic verses or lines. Each of these lines consists of two halves, the one half stating the opposite of the other (e.g., planting versus uprooting, killing versus healing), and the two lines that occur together in one Bible verse run parallel to each other. Each statement concerns a "favorable" or an "unfavorable" matter. Now the Preacher so arranges

From J. A. Loader, *Ecclesiastes: A Practical Commentary,* Text and Interpretation (Grand Rapids: Eerdmans, 1986), 33–38. Reprinted by permission.

the favorable and the unfavorable pronouncements that they continually relate to each other in an X-pattern (chiasmus). The lines of verse 2 begin, for example, with two favorable pronouncements ("to be born" and "to plant") and end with two unfavorable ones ("to die" and "to pluck up"). But in verse 3 the order is reversed: two unfavorable matters ("to kill" and "to break down") are followed each time by a favorable one ("to heal" and "to build up"). The poem continues and we get the following pattern (F: Favorable, U: Unfavorable):

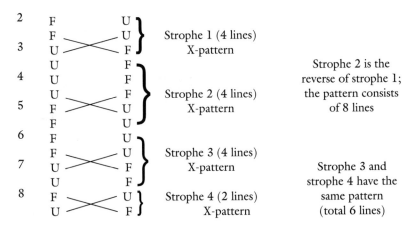

This elaborate pattern makes the poem resemble a modern sonnet. The sonnet also consists of fourteen lines, of which the first eight (octave) comprise two quatrains (strophes of four lines each), and the last six, a quatrain and a couplet (strophe of two lines). It pays to note the precise attention to detail that marks the work of the Preacher, for that shows the penetration of his thought. This passage recounts 28 phenomena, which could be a dull list; this is prevented by the interesting way in which they are arranged. The meticulous attention to the X-pattern, however, has still another function: it emphasizes that things are put in positions of tension with each other.

This poem is one of the very few parts of the book of Ecclesiastes that are generally known. But very often it is misunderstood, too. As a rule, the error arises from mistaking these pronouncements for prescriptions. That the Preacher does not *pre*scribe but only *de*scribes is readily apparent when we look at some of those pronouncements. How could he possibly command a woman to give birth to a child at a given time? Or say that, from a moral point of view, the time has come to die? What sense does it make to tell ordinary people to see to it that war will break out? Thus we see that the Preacher is not saying what people ought to do; he is simply describing the situations they end up in. The entire poem, from verse 1 to verse 9, can be understood on this assumption.

The heading, both in form and content, is most appropriate. Here, too, the X-pattern surfaces (all, time; time, all); the Preacher says there is a time for everything. This cannot mean that there is a correct time to do everything, so the only alternative is that the word *time* has to mean something else. The word can in fact mean "occasion"; then the point at issue is not time as such but the content that fills time. For everything under heaven (everything that happens) there is then a specific occasion. When the occasion arrives, the event that fits it occurs. That is a deterministic view according to which fate has fixed all things in advance and there is nothing anyone can do about it. In harmony with this view is the regular repetition of the word *time* that occurs 28 more times; it sounds like a clock that, inexorably and independent of the wishes of people, keeps ticking and striking. Whatever happens happens, and there is nothing you can do about it.

The Preacher starts his list with those events within which human life is enclosed—birth and death. At a predetermined moment life begins; and when a man's time has come, death takes over. A person has no more choice at death than he or she had at the time of birth. This idea is further qualified by the parallel line in verse 2. The actions of planting and uprooting refer to agriculture. Planting parallels life beginning; uprooting parallels life ending.

Similarly, there is a time at which people kill each other and another time at which they do the precise opposite and devote themselves to healing the sick. Since the Preacher is not saying what people ought to do, we need not worry our heads over the question whether verse 3a concerns murder or "lawful" manslaughter, say in wartime or as part of a judicial procedure. The text does not concern itself with it. Again, a parallel follows in verse 3b. There comes a time in which people tear down and a time in which they build. This may refer to the demolition of houses and their construction; it may also be figurative. In the Old Testament the words for tearing down and building up are often used with reference to the destruction and building up of a human life (see Job 16:14; Gen. 16:2). In that case the first line in verse 3 is expanded by the second.

In verse 4 we have a clear example of how the pronouncements of the first line are made more intense by the second. Sometimes there is occasion for people to weep, and sometimes there is occasion for people to laugh. Weeping represents sorrow, and laughter represents joy; but sometimes sorrow becomes intense and joy exuberant. At the time of a death there is occasion for people to mourn and wail; when other circumstances come their way, people are so happy that they not only laugh but even dance for joy (cf. Ps. 114:4, 6 where the same verb occurs).

What is meant by casting stones and gathering stones (v. 5)? People have thought the reference was to pebbles used by merchants for adding up accounts, stones used in slings, the accumulation or removal of stones on fields, and even to certain funeral practices. But there is another interpretation that does justice to the entire context in which the statement occurs. There is an age-old Jewish interpretation of the book that correctly reports that "casting away stones" refers to sexual intercourse. Gathering stones then means that a man abstains from intercourse with a woman. In each instance the imagery is clear [cf. "the time for making love and the time for not making love," TEV]. Corresponding to this meaning is the mention in the next line of the embrace, which is used as a toned down expression for the same thing (which in fact was the case in the ancient East). So the parallelism between the two lines of a verse, a parallelism maintained throughout the poem, is kept. It would have been odd if it had not been. But the casting away of stones has to have a favorable meaning, unless the finely spun net of the poem was ignored, which would be equally strange. And in fact it was true that abstinence from sexual intercourse took place in times of mourning, hence in unfavorable circumstances (cf. 2 Sam. 12:24 and 1 Chron. 7:21–23). So the opposite situation was a favorable time in which normal relations could again take place. This explanation also fits well after verse 4, where the reference is to the time of mourning and its opposite.

In verse 6 the positive pronouncements again come first and the negative second, as was the case in the first strophe. As in all the other lines, the opposites are mutually exclusive: seeking is the opposite of giving up, and keeping is the opposite of throwing away. The words of the second pair again imply an intensification of the first: "keeping" as compared with "seeking," "throwing away" as compared with "giving up."

At first glance the two lines of verse 7 seem unconnected, but in reality they also parallel each other. The beginning words of each line relate to mourning practices. When in the time of the Old Testament people mourned the death of a loved one, they tore their clothing (cf. Gen. 37:29; 2 Sam. 1:11) and kept silent (cf. Lev. 10:1–3; 2 Kings 2:3, 5; Job 2:13). When the period of mourning was over, clothes could be mended, and the ordinary conversations of the day could continue. So the unfavorable occasions are contrasted with favorable ones. People act in conformity with these occasions but cannot do anything about the caprice with which they come.

In conclusion there is the couplet of verse 8. Here love and peace are placed in a cross pattern, as are hate and war. And again we observe the parallel. The concurrence of these words indicates that the love intended here is nonerotic and general. The other member of the pair, peace, means not only the absence of war but also perfect harmony. On the other hand, war is an intense form of hatred.

This, then, is what human life looks like. On one side is the pole of life and well-being (F) and on the other the pole of death and loss (U). Just as the poem continually moves like a shuttle from one extreme to the other, so the contrasting occasions of life simply befall the people who are subject to them. The Preacher does not advise the reader how people can leap, as it were, from one favorable occasion to the other. And so he ends with the question to which he expects a negative answer: the worker does not profit from all his labor because favorable or unfavorable occasions come over him as a result of fate, quite regardless of his wisdom. By making this point the Preacher again attacks the very core of the prevailing wisdom. The aim of wisdom teachers throughout their working lives was to exclude the negative poles, as it were, by teaching their disciples to make smart choices. But according to the Preacher this attempt to control life was hopeless.

Summary

Thought:	Life, well-being
Counterthought:	Death, loss
Tension:	Abandoning defenseless humanity to the happenstances of life

In this regard we can again be in agreement with the Preacher. No matter how advanced the development of human capacities, science, and technology may be, man cannot guarantee his own happiness. But there is also something very unsatisfactory about the poem. There is a restlessness like that of a weaver's shuttle in it, a persistent uncertainty in the back-and-forth movement of its ideas. It is a restless and unfathomable sea in which the human lifeboat tosses about. Rest is possible only at anchor—and that is what the gospel of Christ offers.

From this perspective the negative experiences of life gain another dimension. According to the Preacher the arbitrariness of God is responsible for the disasters and troubles of human life. But if God is love he does not cause times of hatred, suffering, and war. True, he permits them—we do not know why, any more than Job did—but he is not their cause or author. He is a mighty fortress and refuge especially for the people who threaten to go under in the tensions of life.

20

TIME AND TOIL
ECCLESIASTES 3

Warren W. Wiersbe

Ponder these quotations from two famous professors: "Why shouldn't things be largely absurd, futile, and transitory? They are so, and we are so, and they and we go very well together." That's from philosopher George Santayana, who taught at Harvard from 1889 to 1912.

"There is no reason to suppose that a man's life has any more meaning than the life of the humblest insect that crawls from one annihilation to another." That was written by Joseph Wood Krutch, professor of English at Columbia University from 1937 to 1952.

Both of these men were brilliant in their fields, but most of us would not agree with what they wrote. We believe that something grander is involved in human life than mere transitory existence. We are *not* like insects. Surely Dr. Krutch knew that insects have *life cycles*, but men and women have *histories*. One bee is pretty much like another bee, but people are unique and no two

Reprinted from *Be Satisfied*, by Warren W. Wiersbe, published by Victor Books, 1990, SP Publications, Inc., Wheaton, IL 60187.

stories are the same. You can write *The Life of the Bee*, but you can't write *The Life of the Man* or *The Life of the Woman*.

If we as individuals are not unique, then we are not important; if we are not important, then life has no meaning. If life has no meaning, life isn't worth living. We might as well follow the Epicurean philosophy: "Let us eat and drink, for tomorrow we die."

Solomon has presented four arguments proving that life was nothing but grasping broken soap bubbles and chasing after the wind. But he was too wise a man to let his own arguments go unchallenged, so in Ecclesiastes 3–10, he reexamined each of them carefully. His first argument was *the monotony of life* (1:4–11), and he examined it in Ecclesiastes 3:1–5:9. He discovered four factors that must be considered before you can say that life is monotonous and meaningless.

First, he saw something *above* man, a God who was in control of time and who balanced life's experiences (3:1–8). Then he saw something *within* man that linked him to God—eternity in his heart (3:9–14). Third, Solomon saw something *ahead of* man—the certainty of death (3:15–22). Finally, he saw something *around* man—the problems and burdens of life (4:1–5:9).

So, the Preacher asked his listeners to look up, to look within, to look ahead, and to look around, and to take into consideration time, eternity, death, and suffering. These are the four factors God uses to keep our lives from becoming monotonous and meaningless. We will consider three of these factors in this chapter. . . .

Look Up: God Orders Time (Eccles. 3:1–8)

You don't have to be a philosopher or a scientist to know that "times and seasons" are a regular part of life, no matter where you live. Were it not for the dependability of God-ordained "natural laws," both science and daily life would be chaotic, if not impossible. Not only are there times and seasons in this world, but there is also an overruling providence in our lives. From before our birth to the moment of our death, God is accomplishing His divine purposes, even though we may not always understand what He is doing.

In fourteen statements, Solomon affirmed that God is at work in our individual lives, seeking to accomplish His will. All of these events come from God and they are good *in their time*. The inference is plain: if we cooperate with God's timing, life will not be meaningless. Everything will be "beautiful in His time" (v. 11), even the most difficult experiences of life. Most of these statements are easy to understand, so we will examine only those that may need special explanation.

Birth and death (v. 2). Things like abortion, birth control, mercy killing, and surrogate parenthood make it look as though man is in control of birth and death, but Solomon said otherwise. Birth and death are not human accidents; they are divine appointments, for God is in control. (Read Gen. 29:31–30:24 and 33:5; Josh. 24:3; 1 Sam. 1:9–20; Pss. 113:9 and 127; Jer. 1:4–5; Luke 1:5–25; Gal. 1:15 and 4:4.) Psalm 139:13–16 states that God so wove us in the womb that our genetic structure is perfect for the work He has prepared for us to do (Eph. 2:10). We may foolishly hasten our death, but we cannot prevent it when our time comes, unless God so wills it (Isa. 38). "All the days ordained for me were written in Your book" (Ps. 139:16, NIV).

Planting and plucking (v. 2). Being an agricultural people, the Jews appreciated the seasons. In fact, their religious calendar was based on the agricultural year (Lev. 23). Men may plow and sow, but only God can give the increase (Ps. 65:9–13). "Plucking" may refer either to reaping or to pulling up unproductive plants. A successful farmer knows that nature works for him only if he works with nature. This is also the secret of a successful life: learn God's principles and cooperate with them.

Killing and healing (v. 3). This probably refers, not to war (v. 8) or self-defense, but to the results of sickness and plague in the land (1 Sam. 2:6). God permits some to die while others are healed. This does not imply that we should refuse medical aid, for God can use both means and miracles to accomplish His purposes (Isa. 38).

Casting away stones and gathering stones (v. 5). Tour guides in Israel will tell you that God gave stones to an angel and told him to distribute them across the world—and he tripped right over Palestine! It is indeed a rocky land and farmers must clear their fields before they can plow and plant. If you wanted to hurt an enemy, you filled up his field with stones (2 Kings 3:19, 25). People also gathered stones for building walls and houses. Stones are neither good nor bad; it all depends on what you do with them. If your enemy fills your land with rocks, don't throw them back. Build something out of them!

Embracing and refraining from embracing (v. 5). People in the Near East openly show their affections, kissing and hugging when they meet and when they part. So, you could paraphrase this, "A time to say hello and a time to say good-bye." This might also refer to the relationship of a husband and wife (Lev. 15:19–31; and see 1 Cor. 7:5).

Getting and losing (v. 6). "A time to search and a time to give it up for lost" is another translation. The next phrase gives biblical authority for garage sales: a time to keep and a time to clean house!

Tearing and mending (v. 7). This probably refers to the Jewish practice of tearing one's garments during a time of grief or repentance (2 Sam. 13:31; Ezra 9:5). God expects us to sorrow during bereavement, but not like unbelievers (1 Thess. 4:13–18). There comes a time when we must get out the needle and thread and start sewing things up!

Loving and hating (v. 8). Are God's people allowed to hate? The fact that the next phrase mentions "war and peace" suggests that Solomon may have had the nation primarily in mind. However, there are some things that even Christians ought to hate (2 Chron. 19:2; Ps. 97:10; Prov. 6:16–19; Rev. 2:6, 15).

Life is something like a doctor's prescription: taken alone, the ingredients might kill you; but properly blended, they bring healing. God is sovereignly in control and has a time and a purpose for everything (Rom. 8:28). This is not fatalism, nor does it rob us of freedom or responsibility. It is the wise providence of a loving Father Who does all things well and promises to make everything work for good.

Look Within: Eternity Is in Your Heart (Eccles. 3:9–14)

The Preacher adjusted his sights and no longer looked at life *only* "under the sun." He brought God into the picture and this gave him a new perspective. In verse 9, he repeated the opening question of 1:3, "Is all this labor really worth it?" In the light of "new evidence," Solomon gave three answers to the question.

First, *man's life is a gift from God* (v. 10). In view of the travail that we experience from day to day, life may seem like a strange gift, but it is God's gift just the same. We "exercise" ourselves in trying to explain life's enigmas, but we don't always succeed. If we believingly accept life as a gift, and thank God for it, we will have a better attitude toward the burdens that come our way. If we grudgingly accept life as a burden, then we will miss the gifts that come our way. Outlook helps to determine outcome.

Second, *man's life is linked to eternity* (v. 11). Man was created in the image of God, and was given dominion over creation (Gen. 1:26–28); therefore, he is different from the rest of creation. He has "eternity ["the world," KJV] in his heart" and is linked to heaven. This explains why nobody (including Solomon) can be satisfied with his or her endeavors and achievements, or is able to explain the enigmas of life (1:12–2:11). God accomplishes His purposes in His time, but it will not be until we enter eternity that we will begin to comprehend His total plan.

Third, *man's life can be enjoyable now* (vv. 12–14). The Preacher hinted at this in 2:24 and was careful to say that this enjoyment of life is the gift of God (see 3:13; 6:2; and 1 Tim. 6:17). "The enjoyment of life" is an important theme in Ecclesiastes and is mentioned in each of the four sections of chapters 3–10. . . . Solomon is encouraging not pagan hedonism, but rather the practice of enjoying God's gifts as the fruit of one's labor, no matter how difficult life may be. Life appears to be transitory, but whatever God does is forever, so when we live for Him and let Him have His way, life is meaningful and manageable. Instead of complaining about what we don't have, let's enjoy what we do have and thank God for it.

When the well-known British Methodist preacher William Sangster learned that he had progressive muscular atrophy and could not get well, he made four resolutions and kept them to the end: (1) I will never complain; (2) I will keep the home bright; (3) I will count my blessings; (4) I will try to turn it to gain. This is the approach to life that Solomon wants us to take.

However, we must note that Solomon is not saying, "Don't worry—be happy!" He is promoting faith in God, not "faith in faith" or "pie in the sky by and by." Faith is only as good as the *object* of faith, and the greatest object of faith is the Lord. He can be trusted.

How can life be meaningless and monotonous for you when God has made you a part of His eternal plan? You are not an insignificant insect, crawling from one sad annihilation to another. If you have trusted Jesus Christ, you are a child of God being prepared for an eternal home (John 14:1–6; 2 Cor. 4). The Puritan pastor Thomas Watson said, "Eternity to the godly is a day that has no sunset; eternity to the wicked is a night that has no sunrise."

The proper attitude for us is the fear of the Lord (v. 14), which is not the cringing of a slave before a cruel master, but the submission of an obedient child to a loving parent. (See 5:7; 7:18; 8:12–13; and 12:13.) If we fear God, we need not fear anything else for He is in control.

Look Ahead: Death Is Coming to All (Eccles. 3:15–22)

Solomon already mentioned the certainty of death in 2:12–23, and he will bring the subject up several times before he ends his book (4:8; 5:15–16; 6:6; 8:8; 9:2–3, 12; 12:7–8). Life, death, time, and eternity: these are the "ingredients" that make up our brief experience in this world, and they must not be ignored.

Verse 15 helps us recall 1:9–11 and gives us the assurance that God is in control of the "cycle of life." The past seems to repeat itself so that "there is no new thing under the sun" (1:9), but God can break into history and do what He pleases. His many miracles are evidence that the "cycle" is a pattern and not a prison. His own Son broke into human life through a miraculous birth. He then died on a cross and rose again, thus conquering the "life-death cycle." Because Jesus Christ broke the "vicious circle," He can make us a part of a new creation that overcomes time and death (2 Cor. 5:17–21).

Solomon added a new thought here: "and God will call the past to account" (v. 15, NIV). Scholars have a difficult time agreeing on the translation of this phrase. It literally says "God seeks what hurries along." Solomon seems to say that time goes by swiftly and gets away from us; but God keeps track of it and will, at the end of time, call into account what we have done with time (12:14). This ties in with verses 16–17 where Solomon witnessed the injustices of his day and wondered why divine judgment was delayed.

"How can God be in control when there is so much evil in our world, with the wicked prospering in their sin and the righteous suffering in their obedience?" Solomon was not the first to raise that question, nor will he be the last. But once again, he comforted himself with two assurances: God has a time for everything, including judgment (see 8:6, 11); and God is working out His eternal purposes in and through the deeds of men, even the deeds of the wicked.

Yes, God will judge when history has run its course, *but God is judging now* (v. 18). In the experiences of life, God is testing man. (The word is "manifest" in the KJV. The Hebrew word means "to sift, to winnow.") God is revealing what man is really like; He is sifting man. For, when man leaves God out of his life, he becomes like an animal. (See Ps. 32:9; Prov. 7; 2 Pet. 2:19–20.) He lives like a beast and dies like a beast.

We must be careful not to misinterpret verses 19–20 and draw the erroneous conclusion that there is no difference between men and animals. Solomon merely pointed out that men and beasts have two things in common: they both die and their bodies return to the dust (Gen. 2:7; 3:19). Being made in the image of God, man has a definite advantage over animals as far as life is concerned; but when it comes to the fact of death, man has no special advantage: he too turns to dust. Of course, people who are saved through faith in Christ will one day be resurrected to have glorified bodies suitable for the new heavenly home (1 Cor. 15:35ff.).

The Bible says that death occurs when the spirit leaves the body (James 2:26, and see Gen. 35:18 and Luke 8:55). In verse 21, Solomon indicates that men and animals do not have the same experience at death, even though they both turn to dust after death. Man's spirit goes to God (see 12:7), while the spirit of a beast simply ceases to exist. You find a similar contrast expressed in Psalm 49.

The Preacher closed this section by reminding us again to accept life from God's hand and enjoy it while we can (v. 22). Nobody knows what the future holds; and even if we did know, we can't return to life after we have died and start to enjoy it again. (See 6:12; 7:14; 9:3.) Knowing that God is in sovereign control of life (3:1), we can submit to Him and be at peace.

> God holds the key of all unknown,
>   And I am glad;
> If other hands should hold the key,
> Or if He trusted it to me,
>   I might be sad.
>
> I cannot read His future plans,
>   But this I know:
> I have the smiling of His face,
> And all the refuge of His grace,
>   While here below.
>
>   (J. Parker)

Faith learns to live with seeming inconsistencies and absurdities, for we live by promises and not by explanations. We can't explain life, but we must experience life, either enduring it or enjoying it.

Solomon calls us to accept life, enjoy it a day at a time, and be satisfied. *We must never be satisfied with ourselves,* but we must be satisfied with what God gives to us in this life. If we grow in character and godliness, and if we live by faith, then we will be able to say with Paul, "I have learned to be content whatever the circumstances" (Phil. 4:11, NIV).

21

THE FUTILITY OF INJUSTICE

ECCLESIASTES 4

R. N. Whybray

The Plight of the Oppressed
4:1–3

In this passage the theme of injustice, which was introduced in 3:16 and led to reflections about the human situation and how it should be faced, is taken up again. But the two passages are otherwise unrelated. These three verses have a character of their own: a common theme is not enough to justify the attempts which have been made to attach them either to the preceding or to the following verses. (Ogden's argument [1984], on the basis of the occurrence of the word *šᵉnêhem* (**both**) in v. 3 to treat the passage as the first of a series of "numerical sayings," is forced.) The structure is quite simple: a brief general statement about the oppression of the weak by the strong is followed (v. 1, from **And behold**) by a poignant comment on this situation in terms of human misery, and this in turn by a reflection which questions the positive value—in such circumstances—of human life.

1. Again I saw: literally, "And I returned and saw." The same phrase recurs at the beginning of v. 7. The threefold repetition of the same root in **oppres-**

From R. N. Whybray, *Ecclesiastes*, The New Century Bible Commentary (Grand Rapids: Eerdmans, 1989), 81–91. Reprinted by permission.

sions . . . **oppressed** . . . **oppressors**, the use of the dramatic **behold** and of emotive words like **tears** and **comfort**, the change from prose to poetical form and the repetition of **and they had/there was no one to comfort them** (a repetition which RSV has obscured by translating the same phrase in two different ways): all these features combine to produce an effect of emotional intensity which is rare in Qoheleth. Despite his generalization (**all the oppressions . . . under the sun**) he was clearly writing about what he himself had seen. **to comfort** (*mᵉnaḥēm*): it is not just soothing words which are meant here but active assistance (cf. Ps. 23:4; 71:21; 86:17). Qoheleth has been criticized for contenting himself with pointing out the existence of injustice without taking or proposing action to put it right, as had the prophets of earlier times; but such a judgment is anachronistic and unrealistic.

2–3. It is commonly stated that these verses constitute a calculated attack on a traditional wisdom attitude which regarded life as the most absolutely desirable of all good things (so, e.g., Zimmerli). But this is to misrepresent what was meant in the older wisdom teaching by "life." The Book of Proverbs, for example, does not equate "life" with bare existence. Its authors, who frequently refer to the poor and their misery (e.g. Prov. 14:20; 18:23; 19:4, 7) and were aware of the oppression of the weak by the strong (e.g. Prov. 28:15–16), did not regard such persons as possessing "life" in the sense of that fullness of life which was the goal and the reward of those who followed the counsels of wisdom (e.g. Prov. 3:2, 22; 4:22; 16:22). Qoheleth's comments here, therefore, are less revolutionary than has often been supposed. For those who have failed to "find life" (Prov. 8:35–36) Qoheleth feels, in his present mood, that death or non-existence would be preferable to their suffering. This view is not far removed from that of Proverbs; and it has to be taken in conjunction with other statements of Qoheleth about the positive aspects of life (see on 2:17).

2. **thought . . . more fortunate:** these words are represented in the Hebrew by a single verb *šbḥ* (Piel), which always means "to praise" except in this book, and always with God (or, in two Aramaic passages in Daniel, 5:4, 23, "the gods") as its object. This is also its meaning in later Hebrew. In this book, where it occurs twice (also in 8:15) it clearly has somewhat different connotations; and here RSV's rendering is the only one which makes good sense: it is clearly used in a sense similar to that of *ṭôb*, **better**—that is, "(more) fortunate"—in v. 3.

In form, *šabbēaḥ* is almost certainly the infinitive absolute used in place of the finite verb, though its use with the subject following it as here (*ᵃnî*) is rare (GK § 113gg).

3. Qoheleth now offers a third item for comparison. Death is better than life for those for whom life has consisted mainly of suffering, since it brings that suffering to an end (v. 2). But it now appears that those not yet born are

more fortunate (*ṭôb*) still, since they have no knowledge at all of what happens in the world. The argument is tortuous. First, it is not clear why Qoheleth could not have made his point more simply. Possibly he thought that this step-by-step way of proceeding was more effective rhetorically. In any case he seems to have generally been unwilling to admit that anything was either black or white (cf. 2:13–14; 4:13–16; 9:13–16). Secondly, the point of the "yet" in **not yet been** is not clear. Its presence shows that Qoheleth is not here referring—as in 6:3–5 and in Job 3:11–19—to children who are stillborn or who die soon after birth, but to all those who will be born in the future; but since presumably these will cease to be fortunate when they enter the world and see **the evil deeds which are done under the sun**, the comparison does not appear to be a felicitous one. Possibly the insertion of the **yet** is due to Qoheleth's reluctance, mentioned above, to attribute unqualified good to anything at all.

he who: the Hebrew *ʾēt ʾᵃšer* normally denotes the object of a sentence (i.e. "him who") rather than the subject. The question whether it can on occasion denote the latter has been much debated (see Blau, 1954; Saydon, 1964; Macdonald, 1964). Here it may be simplest to take the phrase as either the object of *šabbēaḥ* in v. 2, or of a similar verb implied but not expressed: so, e.g., "but *I called* him who has not yet been . . . more fortunate." The latter possibility is supported by Vulg., which has such a verb, viz. *iudicavi*. LXX and Pesh., however, treat the phrase as a nominative. The general sense is not affected.

The Folly of Overwork
4:4–6

This passage appears to be unrelated to vv. 1–3. It does, however, share a common topic with vv. 7–12, though attempts to find a literary unity in vv. 4–12 are somewhat forced. The common subject is "toil" (*ʿāmāl*, vv. 4, 6, 8, 9).

In vv. 4–6 Qoheleth reverts to the theme of the *futility* of toil and effort which was a major theme of 1:12–2:26. As in 2:22–23 he points out the folly of making work an end rather than a means and of ruining one's life by straining too hard to make money.

4. It is questionable whether RSV's translation of this verse renders its sense correctly. First, **skill in work** (*kišrôn hammaʿᵃśeh*) would be better rendered by "success" or "achievement" (so NEB)—cf. 5:11 (MT 10), where *kišrôn* refers to something gained or achieved, and the meaning of the verb *kšr* in 11:6 and possibly also 10:10. Secondly, *qînāh* (RSV, **envy**) here probably means "rivalry" or "competition": this meaning is found in the Talmud (*Baba Bathra* 21a), and in a positive sense: "Rivalry (*qnʾt*) among scribes increases wisdom." Thirdly, Qoheleth does not say that toil and success **come from**—that is, are motivated by—the desire to compete with others, but rather that, according to his own observations (**I saw**), they are inseparable from it (literally, they are the same thing: **come from** has no equivalent in the Hebrew).

What Qoheleth is saying here, then, is that in his experience man appears to be incapable of working or achieving anything without striving frantically to do better than others. This is probably a reflection of the entrepreneurial rivalries of his time. It was for such waste of effort that he reserved the expression **vanity and a striving after wind** (cf. 1:14; 2:11, 17, 26; 4:6; 6:9). It was not his intention to put forward the absurd proposition that toil is in itself totally valueless. This is clear from the following verse and also from other passages (e.g. 2:10; 3:13).

5–6. The negative judgement on work expressed in v. 4 needs further explanation and qualification if it is to be relevant to the circumstances of real life. Verses 5–6 provide this, in a manner characteristic of Qoheleth: the complexity of the question is brought out by judicious quotation of traditional wisdom sayings. Often—as in 2:12–17—the saying quoted is reinterpreted and its assertion relativized by its being placed in a context consisting of Qoheleth's own reflections; here, however, Qoheleth achieves the same result by juxtaposing *two* such sayings which qualify one another (for this practice in earlier wisdom literature see Prov. 26:4–5; and for a discussion of these verses see Whybray, 1981, pp. 439–40, 449–50).

5. In every respect—language, form and theme—this verse is indistinguishable from many sayings in Proverbs. Nothing in it suggests that it is Qoheleth's work, and the commentaries agree that it is a quotation. That laziness leads to want is a frequent wisdom theme (e.g. Prov. 6:9–11; 10:4; 12:24; 19:15; 20:13; 24:30–34). In two of those passages (6:10; 24:33) the same expression (*ḥbq yādayim*, **folds his hands**) is used as here to denote aversion to work.

The precise connotation of **eats his own flesh** is unknown (Driver, 1954, p. 228). Certain other passages (Ps. 27:2 [see RSV margin]; Isa. 49:26; Mic. 3:3; Prov. 30:14) have been cited as shedding light on the phrase, but these are not really comparable (see Whybray, 1981, p. 440, n. 9). One or two commentaries, notably Lohfink, give the phrase a positive meaning (i.e., fools still have flesh [meat] to eat despite their idleness), but this meaning is very forced. Some unpleasant fate, probably starvation, is demanded by the context. Qoheleth used the saying to put his adverse comments on work (v. 4) into proper perspective: although work is frustrating because it leads to senseless rivalry, it would be a fool who thought that he could do without it altogether. The meaning would have been clearer if he had been able to use the modern device of quotation marks, or if he had introduced v. 5 with a phrase such as "But don't forget the saying that . . . "; but, like other biblical writers, he preferred simple juxtaposition, leaving his readers to work out the implications for themselves (cf. again Prov. 26:4–5).

6. By means of this second quotation, also of the same type as is found in Proverbs, Qoheleth draws his conclusion: it is better to be satisfied with a little and live a peaceful life than to acquire a fortune, for ambition to achieve the latter inevitably entails so much toil and effort that it brings no true enjoyment. The final words, **and a striving after wind**, a phrase peculiar to Qoheleth (see on 1:14) are, as the poetical metre shows, an addition made by Qoheleth himself to reinforce the conclusion.

Like v. 4, this saying has parallels in earlier wisdom, of which one strand emphasized the value of **quietness**, that is, a life free from jealousy or rivalry (Prov. 14:30, where *qin'āh* [RSV, "passion"] is used; cf. v. 4 above) or disputes (Prov. 17:1). In the present context these hindrances to contentment are specifically linked with **toil**. The conclusion is an adverse judgement on the assumption of Qoheleth's contemporaries that the drive to make more and more money (**two hands full**) is well worthwhile even at the cost of mental strain. A tranquil life is more conducive to happiness even at the expense of wealth.

A handful of quietness; two hands full: the meaning is "a handful *with* quietness" and "two handfuls *acquired by* toil." On this adverbial use of the noun see GK § 131 p, r.

The Miser
4:7–8

Most commentators treat these verses as a part of a larger section vv. 7–12, interpreted as an exposition of the need for companionship and of the futility and danger of trying to manage one's life on one's own. But while there is some similarity at least between vv. 7–8 and 9–10, vv. 7–8 are much more closely linked thematically with vv. 4–6 and may reasonably be interpreted as illustrating the truth of the impersonal and generalizing assertion of v. 6 by presenting a particular case of a man who in toiling for his own personal gain is depriving himself of pleasure. Yet the repetition of the phrase **Again, I saw** (which occurs nowhere else but here and in v. 1 and, with a slight variation, in 9:11) suggests that v. 7 begins a new section. The difficulty of determining where the original literary units in the book begin and end is nowhere better illustrated than here. But it may reasonably be asked whether this question is really important for the understanding of the book, since each individual thought of Qoheleth's needs to be interpreted in the light of other passages irrespective of their proximity to it.

8. The case cited here is that of a rich man who sacrifices all the pleasures that he might get out of life in order to labor at amassing greater and greater wealth, never satisfied with what he has already got: in other words, a miser. Presumably such cases were commonplace in Qoheleth's world. The case is similar to that of 2:18–23, but with one difference: this man has neither a partner (**no one**: literally, "no second person") nor relations with whom he can share his wealth or to whom he can leave it at his death. Qoheleth puts his finger on the stupidity of such behavior by putting onto his mouth the question which such people never ask: what is the point of it all? The truth of the matter has already been succinctly stated in v. 6.

The words **so that he never asks** have no equivalent in the Hebrew. They have been added by the translators (following Gordis) in order to supply a link which would not have been needed by the original readers. The putting of this question in the first person singular—a device frequently used by Qoheleth in expounding his own thoughts—adds vividness to the picture. There is no reason to suppose, as some commentators have done, that it conceals an autobiographical confession on the part of Qoheleth himself. This device, of telling a moral tale in a fictional first person singular, was widely practiced in the wisdom literature: cf. Prov. 7:6–23; 24:30–34; Ps. 37:35–36.

his eyes: the singular verb requires the singular "eye," which is the reading of *Qere* and many MSS. *Kethibh* has the plural.

Two Are Better Than One
4:9–12

These verses have a common theme: it is dangerous and unwise for the individual to attempt to face life alone, and simple common sense to seek the co-operation of others in all that one does (v. 9). This is illustrated by three examples, all of which concern the dangers of travel, but are also meant to be taken metaphorically: falling into a pit (v. 10), perishing with cold at night (v. 11) and attack by robbers (v. 12). The section is rounded off—somewhat incongruously—with a proverb which seems to suggest that two are not sufficient after all, and that real security can only be obtained if the company consists of three! The addition of this sentence may be due to the influence of the "numerical proverb" with its pattern of ascending numbers (see [G.] Sauer [Die Sprüche Agurs], 1963, p. 70 and note 5).

There is thus a superficial connection between these verses and vv. 7–8: a progress from the "one, who has no second one" of v. 7 to the **Two are better than one** of v. 9, and finally to the **threefold cord** of v. 12. But—despite the views of most commentators—there is no *thematic* continuity here: vv. 7–8 are about a self-made man who makes a success—in worldly terms—entirely on his own without the need for co-operation with others; his solitariness has nothing to do with his achievement but is mentioned only in connection with a question about its ultimate purpose. The theme of vv. 9–12 is totally different: the need for co-operation if an enterprise is to meet with success. The connection between the two passages is probably editorial.

9. a good reward for their toil: better, "a good outcome from their trouble." The word *śākār*, frequently "monetary payment" for work done, here has the wider meaning of a satisfactory or pleasant outcome, as in 9:5 (cf. Ps. 127:3; Isa. 40:10 and other passages where it is simply a gift from God). Similarly ʿāmāl here can hardly mean "toil," but rather, as frequently in the Old Testament, "trouble." It is not *toil* which rescues these men from danger, but the fact that, being two together, they can *help* one another.

Two; one: the article before these two words serves to specify the persons referred to in the examples which follow (GK § 126g, q, r).

10. There is no doubt about the meaning of this verse, although some commentators find the Hebrew unsatisfactory and propose emendations partly based on some of the Versions. In the first half the correctness of the plural verb **they fall** has been questioned, since clearly the kind of incident envisaged is one in which only *one* of the travelers falls or slips. However, GK (§ 1240) is probably correct in seeing the verb here as a plural denoting an indefinite singular: that is, the plural is used because such incidents may occur not just once but an indefinite number of times involving one or other of the persons. If this is correct, the phrase may be rendered "if one of them falls," and no emendation is necessary (see Gordis).

11. lie together: the reference is still to the two travelers, not to husband and wife. Huddling together to keep warm during the cold nights which occur in Palestine was a matter of common sense or even necessity (cf. Exod. 22:26–27 [MT 25–26]; Luke 17:34).

12. And though ... alone: the Hebrew is somewhat obscure; but the meaning is probably "And though someone could overpower him (who is) alone." The rest of the sentence then forms the apodosis: "(the) two would be able to resist him." The verb *tāqap* (RSV, **prevail**) is late and rare in the Old Testament but occurs again in 6:10. Its subject here ("someone") is not expressed but is impersonal (GK § 144d). On the unusual suffix (-ô for -ēhû), see GK § 60d. The imperfect *yaʿamᵉdû*, **might prevail**, is potential ("would be able to")—see Driver, §37.

The final sentence has the characteristics of a popular proverb rather than of a learned wisdom saying: cf. 1 Sam. 24:13 (MT 14); Ezek. 18:2; 16:44. Qoheleth uses it in its original sense: it applies the common practical experience that only a three-stranded rope can be relied on not to snap by implied analogy to the human sphere.

The Hazards of Power
4:13–16

This passage, which is unrelated both to those which precede and those which follow it, is one of the most difficult in the book, and has been interpreted in a variety of ways. The short saying (**Better ... king**) with which it begins is a typical encomium of wisdom in the traditional manner; but the remainder of the passage is a rather complicated series of reflections about the realities of political power, cast in the form of an anecdote (cf. 4:7–8; 9:13–16), the details of which are unfortunately difficult to follow, but which in any case greatly qualify the original statement. Various attempts have been made to find here (as also in 9:13–16 and 10:16–17) an allusion to historical events; but it is now agreed by most commentators that all these episodes, although quite plausible in terms of the political realities of Qoheleth's time, are examples of the fictional story or "parable" which was one of the devices commonly employed by the wisdom writers (cf. also the "Solomonic fiction" of chapters 1–2).

13. The initial saying (**Better . . . king**) has the same form as many similar sayings in Proverbs and elsewhere. It may be a quotation, though the use of the word *miskēn* (**poor**), which is a late word found elsewhere in the Old Testament only in this book (9:15–16), suggests that it cannot have been composed much before Qoheleth's time. The remainder of the verse, which is in prose, enlarges upon the initial saying, attributing the old king's folly to senility (**no longer**). **take advice:** this verb (*zhr*, Niphal) occurs in the Old Testament only in relatively late books, but is frequent in later Hebrew. It has a similar meaning in 12:12 ("beware"). The pairing of **wise** with **youth** and of **old** with **foolish** is a remarkable reversal of traditional views.

14. The serious difficulties of the interpretation of this passage begin here. In this verse the main problems are the identity of the person referred to (**he**): and the meaning of the initial word *kî* (RSV, **even though**).

At first sight it might seem natural to take **he** as referring to the old king, who is the subject of the previous clause. But in the initial saying in v. 13 it is clearly not he but the poor young man who is singled out for attention; and the repetition of the reference to poverty in v. 14 (even though different words for **poor** are used) confirms the view that it is the latter who is referred to in v. 14.

But the point of the account of the young man's earlier experiences in this verse is not at all clear, and many different explanations have been given. The word *kî* has many meanings and is often difficult to interpret. RSV's **even though** is supported by some commentaries, but it is difficult to see why the young man's rule should be preferable *despite* the way in which he attained to the throne. It may be that the clue lies in the meaning of the word **Better** (*ṭôb*) in v. 13. In this kind of comparative saying "better" usually has a universal sense: it means what is more advantageous to anyone at all. But earlier in this chapter Qoheleth uses *ṭôb* in the sense of "(more) fortunate" with regard to particular persons (4:3; cf. 9:4) or even of "(more) effective" (4:9). If *kî* means "because," or possibly "in that," here, the sense may be that the young man who has surmounted so many initial disadvantages and achieved the supreme goal of kingship should *for that reason* be considered more fortunate— or more successful—than the old king who has occupied that position for many years but whose judgment is now failing.

If this interpretation is correct, *bᵉmalkûtô* (RSV, **in his own kingdom**) can more naturally be rendered "under his—i.e. the old king's—rule." The young man in the story has evidently supplanted—presumably by revolution or at least a change of dynasty—the very king under whose rule he himself had been born in poverty.

or: this expression (*kî gam*) means "although." RSV has rendered it in this way because of its translation of the earlier *kî* as **even though**. The verse may now be translated as follows: "in that he came from prison to the kingship, and despite his having been born in poverty under his (i.e. his predecessor's) rule."

prison: this word *hāsûrîm* is an abbreviated form of *hāᵃsûrîm*, literally "fetters" (see GK § 35d).

15. The major problem of this verse has been concealed by RSV, which has omitted the most crucial word—"the *second* (youth)"—from its translation, relegating it to the margin and replacing it by **that**. By this omission RSV has identified the young man (**youth**) of this verse with the young man of vv. 13 and 14. In fact there is no reason to delete the word. Commentaries are, however, divided as to the identity of this "second" young man. There are two main possible interpretations: first, if the young man is the same as in the previous verse, "second" may refer to his position in government: he is "the youth who holds the second position (in the kingdom)," that is, he is the heir to the throne. This would rule out the interpretation of v. 14 given above, that he supplanted the old king in a revolutionary coup. Alternatively, the "second young man" is an entirely new character, a third person who supplants the previous usurper. The latter explanation is the most probable: it seems unlikely that the heir to the throne should be a nobody recently released from prison, while a usurper might well be such a person.

The rendering of RSV is unconvincing in other ways as well. A more probable translation might be: "I saw that all the living who live their lives under the sun were supporting (*ᶜim*, literally '(were) with' [RSV, **as well as**] a second young man (for the use of the article here see GK § 126q, r) who would take his place" (i.e. that of the first usurper; see GK § 107k for this use of the imperfect).

In other words, Qoheleth, in his role of the wise man telling his moral tale (**I saw**), has reached the "second act" of the drama: the first young usurper is about to be supplanted in his turn by a second, who is equally (or even more) a "wise"—i.e., clever—young man (see v. 13) who has succeeded in gaining universal popular support. **all the living who move about under the sun** is simply an ironical exaggeration like the English expression "all the world and his wife."

16. there was no end of all the people: *ᶜam* here means a throng of people: the new ruler enjoyed universal popularity on his succession to the throne. But the commentators are divided on the question whether this ruler is the same as in v. 15. RSV clearly takes this view: **he** (i.e. the young man previously mentioned) **was over all of them**. But this phrase is susceptible of more than one interpretation. The Hebrew has a relative clause here: literally, "all those before whom he was." Some commentators take the word "before" (*lip^{e}nê*) as referring either to political leadership (as RSV) or, more literally, as marching at the head of an adoring crowd of people, for example on coronation day. Others, however (Galling, Zimmerli, Lauha, Lohfink) take the whole verse as a general comment on the fickleness of the crowd's attitude towards *any* ruler: there is boundless support from the crowd for anyone when he attains supreme power, but . . . (Gordis improbably takes "before" in a temporal sense and translates: "there is no end to the people who lived before both.")

Whichever of these interpretations is correct, the verse is a concluding comment on the disenchantment of political power. Political regimes succeed one another, and each ruler may attain to the throne on a wave of popular enthusiasm; but as the reign wears on **those who come later** will become disillusioned and find little cause for rejoicing.

The conclusion, then, is that political power is yet another example of futility (on this final phrase see on 1:14). The form of the argument is characteristic of Qoheleth (compare, e.g., 2:13–17). The truth of the initial saying that a poor man who is clever is an improvement on an old king who is foolish is not totally denied; but the anecdote which follows qualifies it almost to the point of nullity. However hopefully a new reign or regime may begin, in the end there is little to choose between one king and another, and little satisfaction either for ruler or ruled. It is also possible to regard the passage as a further example of the questionable value of wisdom: it is the young man's intelligence which supposedly gives him an advantage, but this has now been shown to be no real advantage at all.

22

WORSHIP, OFFICIALS, WEALTH AND ITS UNCERTAINTIES

ECCLESIASTES 5:1–6:9

Roland E. Murphy

Form/Structure/Setting

This section can be divided into an instruction concerning cultic conduct, with particular emphasis on sacrifice, prayer, and vows (4:17–5:6[7]), followed by a short instruction concerning officials (5:7–8[8–9]) and a reflection about possessions (5:9[10]–6:9).

Admonitions make their first appearance in the book, and Qoheleth warns particularly against the conduct of fools (כסיל, a catch word in 4:17, 5:2–3[3–4]; cf. the use of כסל/סכל in 10:1–3, 6, 12–14). The admonition about speech ends in 5:2(3) with what appears to be a traditional saying. There follows a treatment concerning vows, which ends with a text that seems somewhat garbled (5:6[7]). However, the imperative, "fear God!" at the conclusion is the key attitude that he wants to inculcate. This basic reverence for the numinous, the distance from the Wholly Other (5:1[2]), informs the entire instruction.

The admonition concerning officials (5:7–8[8–9], a rather obscure text), serves as a transition to the topic of riches, the subject of a lengthy reflection

281

in 5:9(10)–6:9. Possessions are seen as deceitful because of the insatiable appetite that humans have (5:9–11[10–12]), or because they can be lost (5:12–16[13–17], a kind of story), or simply because they fail to bring happiness. Although they are a gift of God, they are inadequate compensation for human existence, serving only as a distraction from life's difficulties (5:17–19[18–20]). Moreover, riches are uncertain: God can give them to another to enjoy (6:1–2, perhaps another example story). Finally, even the stillborn is better off than the one whose desire for possessions is unfulfilled (6:3–6). The conclusion (6:7–9) returns to the topic of the human appetite (5:9–11[10–12]; cf. 4:8). The verdict of "vanity and a chase after wind" closes off the section and makes its final appearance in the book.

This final section (5:9[10]–6:9) has been subjected to a careful structural analysis by D. C. Fredericks. He has rightly remarked (*JBL* 108 [1989] 17–35) that its unity "is seen by many commentators, who with different titles distinguish it clearly from the surrounding materials" (18). He pursues his point (see the outline on p. 29 of his article) by indicating the parallel structure of 5:9–18(10–19) and 6:1–9 (to simplify this exposition only the Hebrew verse numbering will be used). While the parallelism is not perfect (5:9–11 is separated out as an introduction), the structural parallelism is quite clear: (1) the evil of having and losing riches (5:12b–13a and 6:1–2b); (2) begetting when one has nothing, along with the theme of coming and going (5:13b–15a and 6:3a–6); (3) what advantage from toil? none, but there is some contentment (5:15b–19 and 6:7a–9). I think that the parallelism breaks down at the point of contentment, which is claimed for 6:9, but for the rest the parallelism is remarkable. Furthermore he notes that the four main concerns of 5:9–6:9 can be detected: "(1) wealth or poverty (5:9, 10, 11, 12, 13, 14, 18; 6:2); (2) satisfaction, rest, or enjoyment—or not (5:9, 10, 11, 12, 16, 17, 18; 6:2, 3, 5, 6, 7, 9); (3) breath, transience (5:9, 13; 6:2, 3, 6, 9); (4) What advantage? (5:10, 15; 6:8)" (20). One may not agree on the chiastic precision which is presupposed (see Fredericks' diagram on p. 19), but the structure of 5:9–6:9 has been laid bare by his analysis.

Comment

17(5:1) Qoheleth's admonition (surprisingly?) fits well into traditional Israelite wisdom (Prov. 15:8; 21:3, 27). The stance of the wise man more or less comes down to that of the prophet: obedience is better than sacrifice (1 Sam. 15:22; see L. Perdue, *Wisdom and Cult*, 182). The linguistic expression is characteristic of the sage: "listen." This has been interpreted narrowly in the sense of hearing a specific temple teaching (E. Podechard, H. Hertzberg). In the light of 5:2, W. Zimmerli prefers to understand listening in opposition to talking (James 1:19), and he goes on to see a preference for passive acceptance of the word over the life-securing activity of the cult. This seems like over-interpretation. Qoheleth manifests in 4:17–5:6(5:1–7) a cautious but reverent attitude to the cult that is not essentially different from the usual critique of cultic abuses.

The translation of v. 17b is uncertain . . . , and the line is given various interpretations. Our translation leaves open the possibility that this is a sarcastic remark, or else that it gives a reason for the ineptitude of fools, who count on ritual excuses (5:5[6]) to cover their irreverence. According to N. Lohfink (ZDMGSup 5 [1983] 113–20), the fool makes sin out to be a harmless violation by offering a שגגה sacrifice that is for involuntary wrongdoing (Eccles. 5:5[6]). This is tantamount to "being unable to sin," since they are without guilt.

1(2) Precipitate action is warned against in traditional wisdom (Prov. 19:2b). When applied to speech, as here, the usual result of thoughtless activity will be just words, and often too many of them (see Eccles. 10:14a). The wise person exercises restraint in speech (Prov. 10:19). But the motivation provided by Qoheleth is unique: the difference between God and humans. As Ps. 115:3 (and cf. Ps. 115:16) says, "Our God is in heaven; whatever he wills, he does." The emphasis is upon the supremacy of God, not upon his indifference. It is a mistake to characterize Qoheleth's God as a "distant despot" (A. Lauha); rather, this God cannot be manipulated (5:5[6]). See Matt. 6:7. The conclusion is in the form of an admonition.

2(3) This verse has the air of a wisdom saying. Loquacity stultifies the speech of the fool, just as weighty concerns cause dreams. In context it serves as another motivation for v. 1(2). See also 10:12–14.

3–4(4–5) The transition from verbosity to rash vows is an easy one, and here Qoheleth restates the law of Deut. 23:22–24. A. Lauha points out a subtle difference between Deuteronomy and Ecclesiastes. In the former the emphasis is on making vows, rather than in not making them; while in Ecclesiastes it is the other way around: the preference is not to make them lest they be unfulfilled. The same concern for the fulfillment of vows is evidenced in Prov. 20:25 and Sir. 18:21–23. The perspective would seem to be that of the wisdom teacher rather than of the priest. But the end result is the same. The prohibition is reformulated in typical wisdom style by the "better" saying in v. 4.

5(6) The background for this verse is Num. 15:22–31 (cf. Lev. 4:2ff.), which legislates about sins of inadvertence (שגגה). Qoheleth speaks out against alleging inadvertence as an excuse before the מלאך or priest (certainly not God, as LXX inferred). The precise wrongdoing is not clear, except that it is a sin of the tongue. This could be understood in context as continuing the topic of vows. H. Hertzberg argues that the שגגה cannot be understood as a vow; it refers to commission of a sin, and in this case, a sin in which the tongue is involved. In any case Qoheleth warns against wrongdoing, under the threat of divine wrath and ensuing punishment (v. 5b[6b]). The presumption behind vv. 4–5(5–6) is that God hears what humans say, and that God reacts. There is no sign of the "deed-consequence" mentality here. In short, God judges and even punishes. Qoheleth never denies that there is a divine judgment, even if it remains a mystery to him (cf. 11:5, 9b). It is not a satisfactory answer to claim (with Michel, *Eigenart*, 257) that 5:5(6) is not from Qoheleth but is a later orthodox insertion.

6(7) The text of v. 6a seems to be corrupt . . . , and perhaps the original reading was similar to 5:2 (NAB deletes these words as a dittography of 5:2). In any translation the line seems flat and repetitious, and it hardly leads into the imperious command in v. 6b(7b).

The imperative, "fear God!" comes as a conclusion to Qoheleth's observations about ritual practice (4:17ff.). It is at the heart of his religious attitude. . . .

7(8) This admonition has no relationship to the previous lines. Qoheleth sees no cause for wonder at injustice, because of the hierarchy of officials, one over another. In itself, this reason is ambiguous. The hierarchy of powers could provide reassurance that one need not be concerned. After all, there is some supervision. The verb, תמה, can be understood in two senses: either "wonder" or "fear." On the other hand, Qoheleth is more probably making an ironic observation about dishonest bureaucracy—that one should not expect anything better from such operators. They look out (שמר, "keep watch") for each other.

It is not likely that this statement should be seen as a defense of Providence, as though the גבהים, "powerful," were a plural of majesty referring to God, who would be able to correct the injustice. Nowhere does Qoheleth narrate an actual divine intervention that would correct injustice, although God remains a judge (3:17; 5:4–5[5–6]).

8(9) Any interpretation of this verse hinges on the translation, on which there is no consensus. . . . Hence commentators diverge widely. Our translation may be interpreted thus: in the context of v. 7, the mention of the king seems to be a kind of corrective to the situation of villainous officials. His rule is seen as somehow an advantage for the farmers. How this is achieved, whether through stability or a better tax system, etc., is simply not stated (cf. N. Lohfink, *Bib* 62 [1982] 535–43 for an attempt to spell out the situation in the Ptolemaic period).

9(10) A series of reflections on the topic of riches begins at this point. The meaning of v. 9a(10a) is clear: the person who is greedy for money will never be satisfied. The more one has, the more one wants. Qoheleth has already anticipated this notion in 1:8 (eyes not satisfied with seeing) and in 4:8 (eyes not satisfied by riches). This is not the same as the frequent warning against the deceitfulness of riches (Prov. 11:28; Job 31:24; Ps. 49:7). The saying stresses the subjective element, the self-destroying and self-defeating nature of greed. It seems best to understand v. 9b(10b) as strictly parallel to v. 9a(10a). . . . E. Podechard prefers to tie this verse with v. 10(11) in such a way that the lack of income is caused by those dependents, or others, who will consume it. In any case, there is no moral reproof about insatiable greed in v. 10(11); it is an insight into a basic human trait: money will not answer (but see also 10:19).

10(11) Qoheleth now turns to the specific troubles that riches give rise to. They involve the care of several persons dependent on the master. The relation is symbiotic; the master will be dependent upon them also for his riches, since the workers labor for his profit. In addition there is the inevitable attempt on the part of others to partake of these riches (cf. Prov. 14:20; 19:4, 6). V. 10b(11b) points out that since the actual use of the riches is limited, they are no more than a sop to one's greed, something merely for the eyes to feast on, without any other profit. Just as wisdom begets trouble (1:18), so also do riches, and the next verse continues this theme.

11(12) Qoheleth contrasts favorably the laborer with the rich insomniac. The concerns occasioned by riches (rather than by a full stomach . . .), do not allow one to sleep. It is as if the riches that the eyes contemplated so avidly (v. 10b[11b]) now keep them from being closed in sleep. Qoheleth had already pointed out a similar result as stemming from one's toil (2:23; cf. 5:2[3]; 8:16). The theme appears also in Sir. 31:1–2 (an uncertain text).

12(13) V. 12 initiates the discussion of a particular case (שׁ, "there is"), which extends down to v. 16(17). Vv. 12–15 (13–16) are bound together by the repetition of "grievous evil." What is this evil? It is not only that riches have to be guarded by a person and thus give trouble (vv. 9–11[10–12]), but the loss of these riches (vv. 12b–13a[13b–14a], with the repetition of עשׁר, "riches," and רע, "evil") is also a possibility. Qoheleth has just described a bad effect of wealth; it allows the possessor no sleep (v. 11[12]). His hoarding, his concerned watching over possessions (v. 12[13]), is to his own hurt. When the mainstay of his life disappears, the evil is compounded. The wealthy man is suddenly poor, indeed naked (v. 14[15]).

13(14) The loss of riches is further aggravated by the motif of the birth of a son (contrast 2:18–23). A child is born, and the unfortunate man has "nothing to hand" (v. 13[14]; note the repetition of מאומה בירו in v. 14[15]).

14(15) This verse appears to be a description of the destitution of the rich person in terms of the nakedness of a babe (cf. Job 1:21). In this case the subject of the verbs (יצא, ישׁוב, בא) would be the adult; at the end of his life he is as poor as the day he was born, with nothing to show for it all. "Naked" (ערום, which appears only once) dominates the preceding and the following words, and the final "as he came" resumes the initial "as he came forth from the womb of his mother." One is naked at both birth and death, and the earth is seen to be a mother. The parallelism of womb and earth appears elsewhere: Job 1:21; Ps. 139:15; Sir. 40:1cd. The theme that "you can't take it with you" is prominent in Ps. 49.

R. Gordis argues that the child is the subject in v. 14(15). There may be a deliberate ambiguity in v. 14a(15a), but it disappears in v. 14b(15b) where the subject must be the adult since "toil" is mentioned.

15(16) This verse repeats the formula of v. 12(13) ("grievous evil") and also the theme of coming and going of v. 14(15). There is no profit for all one's toil (עמל *ʿāmāl*; cf. also v. 14b[15b]).

16(17) Although v. 16 is textually uncertain . . . , the general idea concerning the unhappy life of the rich person is clear. The vaunted possessions are now darkness, sickness, and wrath.

17(18) Vv. 17–19(18–20) are reminiscent of the resigned conclusion already drawn in 2:24–26 and 3:12–13, 22. However, in the present context the case of the unfortunate rich person (vv. 12–16[13–17]) serves as a contrast with vv. 17–19(18–20), in which God enables a person actually to enjoy (ראה טובה, "see good"; cf. 2:1, 24) riches and not to lose them. That this can happen is solely God's doing.

Qoheleth introduces his conclusion rather solemnly . . . : good and beautiful appear together. In 3:11 God is said to have made everything beautiful in its time; now what is beautiful is the "portion" (חלק *ḥēleq*, 2:10; 3:22) that comes to a person as a divine gift.

18(19) The key words of v. 17(18) (give, portion, toil) are repeated in this affirmation of the divine (although arbitrary) gift.

19(20) The usual explanation of the verse . . . is that the gift of joy keeps a person from thinking much about life and its brevity (cf. v. 17[18]). It could be merely an accurate summary of what the divine gift achieves, at least for some people. Obviously this was not true for Qoheleth, whatever his personal "portion" may have been, since he never ceases to think about "the days of his life." Rather than being a "consoling conclusion" (L. di Fonzo), this verse sounds a sardonic note. The implication can be drawn that the God-given joys ultimately distract humans (rather than satisfy them) from the misery of their short lives that must end in death; they fail to keep their minds on the weighty problems that occupy Qoheleth.

But if one translates by "answer" instead of "occupy" . . . , then joy is affirmed as a divine gift (as in Eccles. 3:13), and a more benign and positive interpretation is possible (so Lohfink, *CBQ* 52 [1990] 625–35, but not D. Michel, *Eigenart*, 190–91). Now humans will not brood (the meaning of זכר in the context?) over the shortness of life, since God "answers" a human being by revealing joy.

6:1 The formula (יש, "there is"; see D. Michel, *Eigenart*, 190–93—how riches can be an evil) that introduces another instance of vanity is reminiscent of 5:12(13), 15(16); cf. also 8:6. While this is a different case, it can be seen as having some continuity with the "evil" described in 5:12–16(13–17). See also 2:18 and 4:8.

2 The first complaint (vv. 1–2) is about a rich person who has all his desires fulfilled but is prevented by God from enjoying his riches (the contrast with 5:18[19] is deliberate; "the power to partake of"). No detail is given on how this happens (perhaps sickness or some hindrance). The point would seem to be that it would have been better not to have had the riches rather than to have them and yield them to a stranger without ever partaking of them. The "stranger" cannot be identified; it does not necessarily mean a non-Jew (K. Galling claims that this is a Ptolemaic official in Jerusalem). Whereas in 2:18 Qoheleth complained about inheritance within the family, this verse envisions a harsher situation: the rich person failed to enjoy the wealth, and now a stranger takes over!

3 It is not clear whether vv. 3–6 are meant to be taken with the previous case that concluded in v. 2 with "evil" (רע), echoing the "evil" (רעה) of v. 1. They can be considered an extension or an intensification of vv. 1–2 in that the failure to enjoy one's possessions and to fulfill one's desires (cf. נפש in vv. 2–3) remains the problem. A large progeny and a long life are typical ideals of divine blessing (Gen. 25:8; 35:9; Job 42:17). But they cannot offset the absence of good things (echoed by "good" in v. 6) in this life. Qoheleth's verdict is not simply negative; it is sharpened by a comparison with the stillborn (cf. also 4:3). Even though the stillborn receives no burial (see note 3.c.), it is better off than the long-lived person whose desires remain unsatisfied. The importance of proper burial is obvious from such passages as 2 Kings 9:33–37; Isa. 14:19; Jer. 22:18–19.

4–5 Qoheleth heightens his conclusion by elaborating on the awful fate of the stillborn (cf. Job 3:16), but favoring it over that of the long-lived person. He gives no explicit reason why the fate of the stillborn is superior, but one may infer that its affliction is negative in that it is in darkness (contrast 5:16[17]) without vision or knowledge, whereas the affliction of the rich is positive in that they have been thwarted. They have no enjoyment in life, only futile desire. Covering the name with darkness (v. 4) is idiomatic for nonexistence or death; the name is the person. In 6:10 giving the name means to call into existence, to create (cf. the opening lines of *Enuma Elish*: "Lahmu and Lahamu were brought forth, by name they were called" (*ANET*, 50–51; see also Isa. 40:26; Ps. 47:4).

6 The theme of long life is taken up from v. 3, and with heightened emphasis; not even the patriarchs before the flood attained such an age. But what good is extension in time "without experiencing good," if one cannot escape the dark "place" to which all must go (cf. the "going" in 3:20; 5:14[15]); 9:10)? The concrete examples of misfortune discussed since 5:12(13) come to an end here, to be followed by some loosely associated sayings.

7 Vv. 7–9 seem to have little connection with the preceding, but D. Michel (*Eigenart*, 137) has pointed out that four of the seven occurrences of נפש,

"soul," "appetite," in the book are to be found in 6:1–12. The two occurrences in vv. 7 and 9 may serve as catch words to give a certain unity. This verse has the ring of a proverbial saying (cf. 1:8). The thought is that the appetite (נפשׁ), although at the root of human activity, is never really satisfied. This saying does not reflect upon the immediate context. . . . It can be taken as loosely connected with v. 3 (ונפשׁו, "his desire"; cf. also 6:2b).

8 The first half of the verse repeats a favorite idea: the wise man has no advantage over the fool (cf. 2:14–16). The meaning of v. 8b is uncertain. . . . The parallelism of wise and poor (v. 8b) is striking despite the fact that the terms occur (in contrast) in 4:13 and 9:15. The Bible does not usually associate wisdom and poverty. The second half of the verse seems to say that the poor man has no advantage either, despite being able to cope with life. According to the biblical ideal, the poor should be favored by God on whom they rely. But their situation is also futile.

9 Strictly speaking, the comparison in this "better" saying is not between objects but between actions. The object seen/desired is not the issue. Seeing is superior to desire because it implies some kind of possession. Vision is a kind of possession (cf. 11:9), a state of rest in contrast to insatiable desire (cf. 5:9–11[10–12]; 6:3, 7). In 5:10(11) Qoheleth scored the vanity of feasting one's eyes on riches (which also permit no sleep!). Now the point has shifted. The saying concentrates on what is available, what can be "seen." The one who sees something has an object in view, whereas the one who is locked into desire, by definition, has not attained the desired.

As the succeeding comment ("vanity") shows, Qoheleth rejects this "better" saying. He gives no reason, but one may infer that such traditional wisdom fails to take into account the voracious appetite of human beings, already expressed in 1:8 (eye, ear). The full vanity formula (v. 9b) appears here for the last time in the book. It is justified by the cases discussed earlier and is applicable to the sayings in vv. 7–9.

Explanation

It has already been indicated that several topics are to be found in this section, and most commentators treat them separately. Following the lead of "vanity and chase after wind" (6:9) as a section divider, all have been included here under the term "varia." Division is of relatively little import, provided that the course of Qoheleth's thought is correctly indicated: words before God (Temple presence; 4:17–5:6[5:1–7]), observations on government (5:7–8[8–9]), considerations about wealth (5:9–11[10–12]), a case of a rich person who loses possessions (5:12–16[13–17]), another of Qoheleth's frequent conclusions about enjoyment of life (5:17–19[18–20]). Finally, the uncertainty of riches and the futility of desires (6:1–9) close off the narrative.

This sequence seems reasonable enough but many questions remain. The ending of 4:17(5:1) is not clear. N. Lohfink has proposed that it be taken with 5:5(6), in which Qoheleth condemns a false excuse; it is only by such a ruse that it can be said that fools have no knowledge of doing evil (cf. ZDMGSup 5 [1983] 113–20). D. Michel (*Eigenart*, 254) prefers to see here a lack of knowledge that stems from not knowing the one to whom the sacrifice is offered: the God who cannot be influenced by sacrifice. Fools are therefore ignorant. Their sacrifices are "bad" in that they are senseless. Michel (258) refuses to acknowledge that 4:17(5:1)–5:5(6) reflects typical OT tradition. In any case, the command to fear God 5:6(7) is to be considered as a final comment on the liturgical instructions that have just been given.

The social conditions behind the seemingly cynical observations in 5:6–7(7–8) are not exactly known. Oppression (cf. 4:1–2) has never been lacking in human existence. Although we do not know the details of Qoheleth's period, there must have been many opportunities for exploitation (by way of taxes; see N. Lohfink for details). D. Michel interprets the passage as thoroughly pessimistic. He claims that "profit" is never used in a positive sense through the book, much less in v. 7(8). He construes these lines as a quotation that suggests a changed political situation would be an improvement—and this is answered by v. 9, denying such a possibility because of the destructive factor of human greed (*Eigenart*, 110).

The ambiguity, if not the harm, of riches (5:9–11[10–12]) is sharpened by the events related in vv. 12–16(13–17). D. Michel (*Eigenart*, 187–90) recognizes here a "limit situation" or *Grenzfall*, introduced by ש, "there is"; it shows that wealth of itself is no guarantee of happiness. A bad business venture leads to a pauper's death. As indicated . . . , N. Lohfink (*VT* 39 [1989] 488–93) builds upon the "evil turn" suffered by the rich person. Many recognize it as some kind of business venture that turned out badly. Lohfink, on the strength of an idiomatic usage of ביד ("in the hand," or "charged to one's account" . . .) interprets it of a bank failure of some kind. In that case, v. 14(15) does not speak of death. Rather, it compares the change in life style to the helplessness (and lack of possessions) of a newborn babe. Instead of enjoying the riches that had been saved up, that person has to begin again; vv. 16–17(17–18) describe the dim prospects for the future. This interpretation is in harmony with the general understanding that commentators have reached about the passage, but it makes the "evil turn" very specific—an unsuccessful bank deal. This specification is possible, but not compelling.

More important is the interpretation of 5:17–19(18–20) proposed by N. Lohfink (*CBQ* 52 [1990] 625–35), following the lead of L. Levy. The first two verses are typical of the conclusions that Qoheleth puts forth many times in the book: eating and drinking are a joyous portion of life, the gift of God. Then v. 19(20) reflects upon this divine "generosity." Everything hinges on the meaning of עָנָה ("to occupy, keep busy"—or "to answer, reveal" . . .). Lohfink claims that God reveals self in a positive way by the joys of the heart that are provided to humans. There are three objections to this view. First, a "revelation" of God is an unusual idea for Qoheleth, and especially a revelation through "joy." While this joy is a divine gift, it remains arbitrary and given at divine pleasure. Hence one is to enjoy while one can. Second, "revelation" is a strained extension of the root meaning, "answer." L. Levy proposed this (99, *offenbart*) and referred to Gen. 41:16; 1 Sam. 9:17; and especially Job 33:12–13 (in 33:13 "speak" seems to mean "reveal," but the word is דבר). Not every response is revelation. Third, the tone of v. 19a(20a) suggests that a divine strategy is at work: God uses "joy" to distract humans from the awful reality of their short lives. Of this verse M. Fox remarks, perhaps too strongly: "Pleasure is an anodyne to the pain of consciousness" (*Qohelet*, 73).

23

SUFFERING AND SIN

ECCLESIASTES 7:1–8:1

Michael A. Eaton

The proverbial units of this section deal with aspects of life that anger or infuriate. The early proverbs deal with death or suffering (7:1–4, 7, 10, 14). Seven proverbs (in 7:1–3, 5, 8, 10) are comparisons involving the words "better than," a common proverbial style. Since the Preacher was a collector of proverbs (12:9f.), these may be a fragmentary collection of "Better than" proverbs, though the subject-matter provides a fundamental unity.

First the reader is shown the possible instructiveness of sufferings (1–6), then the dangers of trials, compromise, impatience, anger, discontent (7–10). Wisdom is indispensable (11f.); life is under the hand of God (13f.). Thus the first half of ch. 7 follows up the theme of Ecclesiastes as a whole with the question: Will the life of faith survive hard and troublesome times when the "good old days" have gone and the "days of adversity" come? The second half of the chapter moves from the crookedness of life (13) to that of mankind (29). Basic questions touching the origin, universality, inequity and perverseness of evil are posed in a mixture of factual statement and exhortation, urging also

Reprinted from *Ecclesiastes* (TOTC) by Michael Eaton. ©1983 by Michael A. Eaton.   Used by permission of InterVarsity Press, P.O. Box 1400, Downers Grove, IL 60515.

the need for wisdom which is so rare and remote (19, 23f.) and concluding in 8:1 with a further appeal for wisdom.

Instruction from sufferings (7:1–6). 1. There is no need to hold that the first half of v. 1 is "a proverbial phrase which has no relation to the context" (Barton), or a conventional proverb followed by an unconventional deduction (Gordis). We may translate: "*As* a name is better than oil, *so* the day of death is better than the day of birth," thus avoiding the anomaly of a dangling irrelevance. The first half may well have been a popular saying; if so, the Preacher is comparing his point (1b) with a well-known distinction (1a; cf. Song 1:3). Hebrew comparisons often put two statements alongside each other leaving out "As . . . so" (cf. Pr. 17:3). The word-play of *name* (*šēm*) and *oil* (*šemen*) is preserved in Williams' "Better is name than nard" and Martin's "Fair fame is better than fine perfume."[1]

In Israel a *name* was no mere label but intended to express an underlying nature. What is in view is not simply *a good name* (which may be undeserved), but a reputation which flows from character. Such a name was highly valued; even God at the time of the exodus "got himself a name" (Neh. 9:10).[2]

As inner character is more crucial than outer fragrance, so it is the funeral, not the rowdy birthday party, that poses the ultimate questions about life the Preacher is pressing. This severe statement arises not from despondency but from sheer realism.

2. A further surprise comes and the explanation follows: *the living lay it to heart.* Death brings us to think about life (cf. Ps. 90:12), especially since mourning was taken very seriously (cf. Gen. 50:10). A party has no such effect. Every funeral anticipates our own.

3. That *the heart* ". . . may be put right" or ". . . is put right" is the appropriate translation (better than *made glad*), for it means that the inner life may be "better situated" for making right judgments and estimations, "put right" in one's approach to life (cf. NIV). A man who has looked death in the face may have his inner life transformed for the better,—not, however, that there is any automatic effect of suffering.

4. The *heart* (NEB *thoughts*) is amongst other things the center of a man's attention (Exod. 7:23), thought (Deut. 7:17), understanding (1 Kings 3:9) and memory (Deut. 4:9). One's *heart* being in *the house of mourning* means that death is the object of the wise man's reflections; he allows it to rouse him to thought and concern. The *fool* (*kᵉsîl*), on the other hand, is blind to spiritual issues (Eccles. 2:14), yet content in his blindness (Prov. 1:22), verbose yet empty-headed (Prov. 18:2), a menace to society (Prov. 14:7). Not surpris-

---

1. G. C. Martin, *Proverbs, Ecclesiastes, and Song of Songs* (1908), p. 253.
2. See further art. "Name," *IBD*, pp. 1050–53; J. A. Motyer, *The Revelation of the Divine Name* (1959).

ingly his preoccupation is with *the house of feasting*, presumably a place where men indulge in festivity, perhaps a rowdy party.

5. It has been maintained that *the song of fools* means "the song of praise and flattery," "the compliments showed by fools" (cf. GNB, NEB). But since the word *song* (*šîr*) is always used of quite literal songs (more than seventy times in the Old Testament), it is more likely that the reference is to the songs of jubilation in the house of festivity.[3] The *rebuke of the wise* is exemplified in 2 Samuel 12:1–12; the song of the fool in Amos 6:5f.

6. The pun "Like the sound of *sîrîm* (thorns) under the *sîr* (pot, cauldron)" is caught by Moffatt's *Like nettles crackling under kettles*. Thorns were a rapidly burning, easily extinguishable fuel in the ancient world (Ps. 58:9). Thus fools' laughter is a sudden flame, a fine display of sparks, accompanied by plenty of noise, but soon spent and easily put out. The last phrase notes that the superficiality of the *fool* is part of life's *vanity*, which elsewhere is said to characterize both the environment of man (1:2ff.) and man himself (6:12).

Four dangers (7:7–10). 7. The opening word in the Hebrew (*kî*) has been taken as an explanation ("For . . . ," cf. Leupold), but this does not seem to explain v. 6, whose concluding phrase appears to end a paragraph. More probably the word introduces a strong assertion, *Surely . . .* (as in most translations).[4] Thus vv. 7–10 introduce the less beneficial effects of trials. Oppression "makes a man mad" and may cause even a wise man to lose his head (cf. Deut. 28:33f.). Similarly the whole inner life of man may be brought to spiritual ruin by the temptations that belong to an oppressive regime.

To secure a perfect parallelism some have understood *oppression* (NIV *extortion*) to refer to the exercise of it rather than the suffering under it (JB *laughter . . . merriment* follows an amended text). The Preacher would thus be urging that the "very exercise of oppression tends to infatuate and bewilder" (Wardlaw; so too Aalders). Alternatively the Hebrew word (*ʿōšeq*) has been taken to mean "bribe" (Gordis, following M. Seidel) or "slander" (the ancient versions, understanding it as an Aramaism; they are followed by G. R. Driver);[5]

---

3. This statement is reversed in Jones, but no evidence is cited. Old Testament usage seems to support the statement above.

4. Because of the slight difficulty the *kî* has been regarded as a textual slip (for it seems to have no equivalent in ancient translations). Others (e.g. Lauha) think some words have fallen out between vv. 6 and 7. Others think that the last phrase of v. 6 belongs to v. 7 ("and even this is vanity, for . . . "). Hertzberg thinks vv. 11 and 12 should be between vv. 6 and 7. Yet others regard the whole verses as a gloss. None of these expedients is necessary; an emphatic *kî* is well attested. (Cf. R. Gordis, "The Asseverative Kaph in Ugaritic and Hebrew," *JAOS*, 63, 1943, pp. 176–78.) The RSV translates *kî* as asseverative in, e.g., Job 5:2; 28:1; Prov. 30:2; Amos 3:7 as well as in Eccles. 7:7.

5. VT, 4, 1954, p. 229. Driver also suggests *mattānāh* be amended to *mᵉṭānāh* or *moṭnōh* and translates "and it (a false accusation) destroys his stout heart." The combination of a hypothetical word and a speculative reading makes this at best doubtful.

this secures a synonymous parallelism. Verses 1–14, however, deal with the suffering of oppression, not its exercise. It is better, therefore, to see here not synonymous parallelism (expressing the same thought) but synthetic parallelism (taking the thought further). The first line, then, speaks of a pressure which oppression may exert on the faithful; the second goes further and provides an example of how a wise man may be "made mad" by another kind of folly. AV *gift* is literal; NIV, RSV *bribe* catches the sense.

8. The second warning concerns patience. NAB *end of speech* takes a Hebrew word (*dābār*) in its other meaning, but *end of a thing* fits better and has the assent of most translators. In a number of passages *end* has the sense of "outcome," "end-product"[6] (cf. Prov. 14:12) and this is suitable here. The proverb implies that times of trial may be purposeful, that they are confined to limited seasons, that the end-product makes them worth while (cf. James 1:2–4). Thus the reader is invited to grasp the hope of an "outcome" to trials and to face them accordingly. This will enable him to overcome premature complaint, boasting or arrogance and thus be *patient in spirit*. The antithesis *patient . . . proud* suggests that patience is an aspect of humility and impatience a proud irritation at God's ways with men (Prov. 16:5).

9. *Anger* (Heb. *kaʿas*) is anger tinged with exasperation and elsewhere indicates "indignation" over idolatry (1 Kings 15:30) or unmerited treatment (1 Sam. 1:6, 16), "exasperation" over an erring child (Prov. 17:25) and "resentment" of a nagging wife (Prov. 27:3). In Ecclesiastes it expresses the exasperation at the perplexities of life (1:18; 2:23), the bitter grief of bereavement (7:3), and here the resentment roused by unjust persecution. It is stronger than Dahood's "care"[7] or NAB *discontent*. If tolerated, resentment makes its permanent home in the personality of the fool (cf. Heb. 12:15), for *bosom* (AV, RSV) indicates the innermost part of something (1 Kings 22:35).

10. Each age has its particular difficulties and opportunities. "The night will come when no man can work," said Jesus (John 9:4), but the Preacher holds that it is no part of wisdom to herald its arrival prematurely. Wright illustrates the point from the gloom of the older generation at the building of the second temple (Ezra 3:12–13); the day of small things (Zech. 4:10) was in fact a step towards the coming of Christ. Ginsburg points to the Israelites' longing for Egypt (Exod. 16:3; Num. 11:5–6; 14:1–4). To evaluate the times may be needful; to ask specifically for days gone by is wrong and foolish. One cannot face the difficulties of one age by pining for another.

The need of wisdom (7:11–12). 11. The previous verses again highlight the need of *wisdom*. The *inheritance* was the land belonging supremely to the LORD but allocated among his people (Exod. 15:17; Num. 26:53). It could

---

6. Cf. study of *aḥᵃrît* in G. Vos, *The Pauline Eschatology* (1953), pp. 1–7.
7. M. Dahood, "Hebrew-Ugaritic Lexicography III," *Bib*, 46, 1965, p. 330.

not pass out of the tribe or the family (Num. 27:8–11; 36:7–9).[8] The Hebrew could be translated "Wisdom is good *with* an inheritance" or ". . . as good as an inheritance" (Heb. *'im* meaning "in common with," "like," "as . . . as" is found in Ps. 73:5b; Eccles. 2:16 and elsewhere). In the first case the thought is that family wealth is desirable—the Bible never sees any inherent blessing in poverty—but unaccompanied by wisdom it will not sustain in times of adversity. If "as . . . as" is the right translation, wisdom is being compared to an inheritance: it comes supremely from the LORD (cf. Deut. 4:21), is greatly to be desired (cf. Prov. 3:13–18), and should be the inalienable possession of the people of God.

12. This should be translated: "To be in the shadow of wisdom is like being in the shadow of[9] silver; and knowledge is an advantage; wisdom keeps the life[10] of him who has it." To be "in the shadow of silver"[11] refers to the protective power of wealth. Like riches, knowledge and wisdom protect, but at a deeper level. If J. Gray[12] is right in believing that the Hebrew (*ṣēl*) may mean (i) protection or (ii) glitter (cf. Ugaritic *ẓl ksp*, "glitter of silver"), there is a play on words here.

Life under the hand of God (7:13–14). 13. This echoes 1:15; the crookedness of the world, which is being expounded throughout, is not mere "fate." It is subject to God's will (cf. Rom. 8:20). We may wish to quarrel with it, but we can effect no change in the basic structure of things.

14. Both *prosperity* and *adversity* have their uses. One leads to joy, the other draws attention to the realities of life and leads (if so allowed) to a life of faith in a sovereign God. Both are subject to God's will and part of his providence. The constant fluctuation between them keeps us dependent not on our own guess-work, but on God who "holds the key to all unknown."[13]

Dangers along the way (7:15–18). 15. *My vain life* is that dominated by the problems expounded in 1:2–11. The introduction of a vertical perspective does not nullify the overall problem: life remains subject to vanity. The

---

8. See further art. "Inheritance," *IBD*, pp. 691f.

9. In the MT the two *beth*'s are used in much the same way as two *kaph*'s would be used in a comparison (cf. Gen. 18:25; Hos. 4:9). Some scholars wish to emend the text to *kᵉṣēl . . . kᵉṣēl* (as was read apparently by most ancient translations) or to *bᵉṣēl . . . kᵉṣēl*. Others (e.g. Aalders, Gordis) defend the MT and think the usage is akin to the *beth essentiae*. The present writer is inclined to read *bᵉṣēl . . . kᵉṣēl*; but if MT is correct, the second *bᵉṣēl* is still to be translated "like being in the shadow of." Dahood wishes to drop the second *beth* altogether (CPIQ, p. 209).

10. W. Crosser ("The Meaning of 'Life' (Hayyim) in Proverbs, Job and Ecclesiastes," *Transactions of Glasgow University Oriental Society*, 15, 1953–4, pp. 48–53) points out that "life" in the Old Testament often refers to more than "the trivial round and common task" and indicates a satisfying and God-orientated life (cf. Prov. 2:19; 10:11, etc). He translates "shall have life indeed."

11. For the bearing of this phrase upon translation hypotheses, cf. CPIQ, p. 209.

12. J. Gray, *The Legacy of Canaan* (1965), p. 285.

13. NAB *so that man cannot find fault with him* (God) *in anything* is an unlikely translation.

Preacher aims neither to abolish nor even to explain life's anomalies, but to enable one to live with them. It is a simple fact that the *righteous* may, like Naboth (1 Kings 21:13), *perish in his righteousness,* whereas the wickedness of a Jezebel (1 Kings 18–19; 21) may persist. The anomaly frequently perplexed the devout Israelite (cf. Job; Pss. 37; 73; Hab. 1:13–17). The blunt statement with no explanation (except perhaps 7:29) demands simply that the believer face life in this world as it really is. Forewarned is forearmed (cf. 1 Pet. 4:12).

16. The Preacher warns against two opposing moral dangers. The first some interpreters take as indifference to morality (cf. Barton) or a pagan "moderation in all things." Others feel that the emphasis is on legalistic righteousness and means "Do not strive too hard in legalistic observances." R. N. Whybray on the other hand argues persuasively that what is discouraged is not excessive righteousness but self-righteousness.[14] The Preacher holds that there is no righteous man (7:20). "Do not be greatly righteous" must be taken ironically and must refer to the way a person thinks about himself and presents himself. The translation *too* or *overmuch* goes somewhat beyond the Hebrew, which means "greatly" and does not express the judgment implicit in "too great" or "overmuch." This view is confirmed in the next line where the Hebrew for *Do not make yourself overwise* (RSV) contains a Hebrew hithpael which may mean "to play the wise man" (cf. Num. 16:13 "play the part of a prince"; and 2 Sam. 13:5 "pretend to be ill"). Play-acting righteousness delights in the reputation of wisdom (cf. Matt. 23:7).

17. The contrary danger is capitulation to evil. *Greatly* (RSV *overmuch*) does not imply that wickedness in moderation is acceptable! To have omitted *overmuch,* apart from breaking the parallel with v. 16, would have contradicted vv. 20, 29. The Preacher recognizes wickedness as a fact of human experience. The right life walks the path between two extremes, shunning self-righteousness, but not allowing one's native wickedness to run its own course. The end-product of wickedness run riot may be an untimely death (Ps. 55:23).

18. *The one . . . the other* refers back to the two dangers of which vv. 16f. warned. The righteous person must see both clearly and walk between them, motivated by reverence towards God: it is *he who fears God* that *shall come forth from them all.* The Hebrew *all* is sometimes used when only two items are in view; it should then be translated "both."[15] This awe-inspired

---

14. Whybray relates this to the form of the verb which is *'al-tᵉhî ṣaddîq,* not *'al tiṣdaq,* suggesting that the longer construction combined with the hithpael of the next line points to an interpretation along the line of that suggested above. Cf. "Qoheleth the Immoralist? Qoh. 7:16–17," *Israelite Wisdom: Samuel Terrian Festschrift* (ed. J. G. Gammie et al., 1978), pp. 191–204.

15. In later Hebrew "to come forth" may mean "to do one's duty"; thus Gordis translates "he who reverences God will do his duty by both." But it is better to take the verb as meaning "escape," as in 1 Sam. 14:41.

regard for God is the beginning of knowledge and wisdom (Prov. 1:7; 9:10) and serves as one of the many links between Old and New Covenants (cf. Rev. 15:4).

The need of wisdom (7:19–22). 19. Both general attitude (*fear*) and detailed application (*wisdom*) are required if the right path between moral legalism and moral indifference is to be maintained. It is difficult to decide whether *ten rulers in a city* uses ten as an indefinite number (Jones; cf. Gen. 31:7) or refers to the number of a city council (Gordis, citing Josephus' *Antiquities* 20.8.11; *Vita* 13 and 57). Either way, the meaning is that wisdom in the fear of God may be greater than the collective wisdom of a group of experienced leaders. Power from within is needed, more than advice from without.

20. The argument of vv. 16–19 is brought to a climax, echoing Solomon's words in 1 Kings 8:46. It is put emphatically (with the Heb. emphatic *kî, surely*); it is a universal truth (*not a righteous man on earth*); it covers sins of omission (*does good*) and commission (*never sins*).

21. Human sinfulness is seen particularly in unreliability of speech (cf. James 3:2). The corollary is that we are not to pay unnecessary attention to the vindictiveness of others (cf. 1 Sam. 24:9), for it will unsettle our tranquility.

22. Our own experience is sufficient proof that vindictiveness arises from human sinfulness and is frequently inaccurate.

The inaccessibility of wisdom (7:23–24). 23. Having explored the problems of life by his God-given (2:26) wisdom, the Preacher has realized that wisdom cannot answer the ultimate questions (cf. 1:17f.), particularly death (2:15f.). It is this "ultimate" wisdom, the Preacher says, that was *far from me*.

24. The argument of Ecclesiastes demands that we refer *That which is* not only to all that exists (Gordis' "all that is come into being"), but also to the very way in which it is constituted by God. It is all that exists as God controls and decrees it that is beyond the Preacher's comprehension. God appoints man's life and environment (cf. 1:13; 3:10f., *etc.*). As Moffatt puts it: *Reality is beyond my grasp*, says the Preacher. *Who can find . . . ?* is a rhetorical question. No one can grasp God's plan and purpose.

The sinfulness of man (7:25–29). 25. The Preacher's realization of the limits of his wisdom drives him to ponder further the character of man. RSV *the sum of things* derives from a word meaning "to reckon" in both the mathematical and intellectual sense, and translates it as "thought" in 9:10. Here the point is that the Preacher has pondered long and hard the enigmas of human character. What did it all amount to? The welter of intellectual and moral terms, *know . . . search . . . seek, wisdom . . . reason, wickedness . . . folly . . . foolishness . . . madness*, again emphasizes his point and indicates his thoroughness.

26. The Preacher sets out his conclusions; first, about a particular kind of woman. She is *more bitter than death*, her personality (*heart*) is dominated by the instincts of the hunter (*snares and nets*), and she is forceful in her attentions (*hands* as *prison fetters*). The wisdom to perceive the snares and traps is given only to one *who pleases God* (cf. 2:26). Any accusation of misogyny misses the Preacher's point, as we see from the contrasting picture of married love in 9:9.

27–28. The Preacher then sets out his conclusions about men and women in general. Mathematical imagery still pervades this section. The Preacher wants to know what the sinfulness of man adds up to. The passage is still dealing with wisdom (cf. vv. 23, 25); this is in his mind when he draws a distinction between the sexes. Wisdom, he says, is rare in men, but rarer in women. Such a statement is not unique to Ecclesiastes (cf. 2 Tim. 3:6); he need not be thought a bachelor (Gordis) or one disappointed in love (Plumptre). The statement is historical, unlike the generalized statement of v. 29. Emphasis is not on what the Preacher found, but on what he found lacking. In either sex wisdom is rare; "he finds men only one-tenth of one percent better than women!" (Gordis). Ancient Near Eastern literature contains more extreme statements (e.g. "Woman is an iron dagger—a sharp one, which cuts a man's neck")[16] which find no parallel in Ecclesiastes.

29. This verse presents the Preacher's conclusions about the whole human race. The first Hebrew word (*lᵉḇaḏ*) means "above" or "by itself,"[17] and the opening words may be literally translated "on its own (*lᵉḇaḏ*), see, this I found. . . ." The Preacher is driven to a single point which is the source of the calamities previously described (vv. 15–28): here is the grand total of his spiritual calculations. The blame for the rarity of wisdom is attributed to no one but mankind himself. He was created neither sinful, nor neutral, but *upright*, a word used of the state of the heart which is disposed to faithfulness or obedience (cf. 2 Kings 10:15, Heb.; Ps. 7:11).[18] Despite an original uprightness, sin has "entered in" (cf. Gen. 3:1–7; Rom. 5:12). Man's sin is perverse (AV *invention* means a deliberate contrivance for overcoming what would otherwise be expected), deliberate (*sought* indicates something positive and persistent), universal (*they* individualizes *man* mentioned earlier; cf. 1 Kings 8:46; Rom. 3:23), multiform (*many* points to the variety of manifestations of sin: "every one to his own way," Isa. 53:6). Kidner points to the contrast with a passage in the *Babylonian Theodicy* where the gods are blamed for man's wickedness: "With lies, and not truth, they endowed them for ever."[19] *Behold* draws attention to the fact and assures us it is there for all to see. *This I found* shows that the Preacher's theology was confirmed by life itself.

16. *ANET*, p. 425.
17. Cf. BDB, p. 94.
18. Cf. D. J. Wiseman, "Law and Order in Old Testament Times," *Vox Evangelica*, 8, 1973, pp. 5–21, esp. pp. 5f.
19. Kidner, p. 73; cf. Lambert, p. 89.

Who is really wise? (8:1). This verse belongs more to what precedes than to what follows, for it forms a fitting conclusion to proverbs which have appealed for wisdom in relation to suffering and sin; it is reminiscent of a similar final challenge at the end of Hosea (14:9). The Hebrew word translated *like* sometimes speaks of exact likeness to an ideal. It could be translated "Who is really wise . . . ?" *Interpretation (pēser)* is the word well-known to students of the Qumran scrolls, where it is used of the distinctive out-of-context interpretations of the Old Testament by the Qumran community. Another form of the word (*pitrôn*) is used in Genesis of the interpretation of dreams (Gen. 40:5). Where, asks the Preacher, is the man who discerns his way through the problems detailed in 7:1–29, and who will interpret aright the mysteries of providence? The shining *face* generally speaks of favor (cf. Num. 6:25). Here it speaks of the wise man who is visibly gracious in his demeanor, and (as the next phrase says) whose gentleness is obvious in his facial expression (contrast Deut. 28:50; Dan. 8:23).[20]

20. Gordis and others who take the verse with Eccles. 8:2ff. understand it to refer to discretion at court. NEB follows an emended text to give . . . *make a man hated* (cf. also NAB).

24

RIGHTEOUSNESS
AND WICKEDNESS
IN ECCLESIASTES 7:15–18

Wayne A. Brindle

G ood and evil, righteousness and wickedness, virtue and vice—
these are common subjects in the Scriptures. The poetical books,
especially, are much concerned with the acts of righteous and unrighteous
persons. Qoheleth, in Ecclesiastes, declares that "there is nothing better . . .
than to rejoice and to do good in one's lifetime" (3:12, NASB). In fact, he
concludes the book with the warning that "God will bring every act to judgement, everything which is hidden, whether it is good or evil" (12:14).

But how righteous should one try to be, and for what purpose? Qoheleth
sets forth what appears to be a strange answer in Eccles. 7:15–18:

> I have seen everything during my lifetime of futility; there is a righteous man who
> perishes in his righteousness, and there is a wicked man who prolongs his life in his
> wickedness. Do not be excessively righteous, and do not be overly wise. Why should
> you ruin yourself? Do not be excessively wicked, and do not be a fool. Why should

From *Andrews University Seminary Studies* 23 (1985): 243–57. Reprinted by permission.

you die before your time? It is good that you grasp one thing, and also not let go of the other; for the one who fears God comes forth with both of them. (NASB)

Common Interpretations of Ecclesiastes 7:15–18

Walter C. Kaiser contends that "few verses in Ecclesiastes are more susceptible to incorrect interpretations than 7:16–18."[1] In fact, interpreters of Ecclesiastes tend to view the argument of 7:15–18 in a variety of ways, depending upon whether they are willing to attribute to the author a sense of relativity and "moderation" in moral conduct.[2]

The Golden Mean

Kaiser has also observed that "for many, Solomon's advice is the so-called golden mean; it is as if he had said: 'Don't be too holy and don't be too wicked. Sin to a moderate degree!'"[3] Indeed, almost every commentator speaks directly or indirectly of Qoheleth's "doctrine of the golden mean."[4] Those commentators who understand the author of Ecclesiastes to be advocating the idea of this sort of "golden mean" between virtue and vice usually date the book quite late, since the concept of a "mean" by which to guide one's life is thought to have gained popularity during the time of Aristotle, or even of the Stoics.[5]

To many, Qoheleth's apparent failure to exhort his readers to totally righteous behavior seems to leave him open to the charge of teaching immorality and misconduct.[6] They believe that he was advocating a "middle way" between righteousness and wickedness, because, as stated by R. N. Whybray,

1. Walter C. Kaiser, Jr., *Ecclesiastes: Total Life* (Chicago, 1979), p. 85.

2. The Jewish Targum seems to interpret the word "righteous" here in a technical sense as an admonition to judges not to be too severe in their judgments but this is a minority view and is certainly not consistent with the context; cf. A. D. Power, *Ecclesiastes or The Preacher* (London, Eng., 1952), p. 94; Christian D. Ginsburg, *Coheleth* (1861; reprint, New York, 1970), p. 379.

3. Kaiser, p. 85; the arguments and conclusions presented here are valid regardless of one's view of the authorship of Ecclesiastes, as long as one accepts the unity and positive perspective of the book; this latter problem is important, but cannot be discussed in this chapter.

4. R. N. Whybray, "Qoheleth the Immoralist? (Qoh. 7:16–17)," in *Israelite Wisdom: Theological and Literary Essays in Honor of Samuel Terrien*, ed. John G. Gammie (New York, 1978), p. 203, n. 4.

5. See n. 2, above; cf. Robert Gordis, *Koheleth: The Man and His World*, 3d ed. (New York, 1968), pp. 178, 276. Aristotle said, "Virtue lies in a mean between opposite extremes" (*Nicomachean Ethics*, 2.6.7), a golden mean that was constantly advocated by Greek and Latin writers (see Power, pp. 94–95). Confucius also advocated a type of "common sense" which resembled the Aristotelian mean (see Harold H. Watts, *The Modern Reader's Guide to Religions* [New York, 1964], p. 540). Buddha recommended his "Middle Way," which sought to avoid the two extremes of self-indulgence and self-mortification; this "Middle Way" involves an eightfold path toward detachment from life, the elimination of desire, and thus the cessation of suffering (see Watts, p. 480; and J. N. D. Anderson, *The World's Religions* [Chicago, 1950], p. 121).

6. Whybray, p. 191.

"(i) his [Qoheleth's] experience had taught him that neither necessarily has any effect on men's fortunes in terms of divinely imposed reward or punishment"; and "(ii) it had also taught him that extremes of any kind are in practice more likely to lead to disaster than is moderation."[7]

Is this what Qoheleth is urging? Is he suggesting that since personal righteousness is no guarantee of long life or happiness (7:15), the reader should become "amoral,"[8] steering a middle course between right and wrong? Or is he warning against becoming "too goody-goody or too impossibly naughty"?[9]

G. A. Barton, who concludes that Qoheleth's warning against "extreme righteousness" is a reproof of the excessive legal observances of the "*Chasidim*," states further that "some interpreters . . . hesitate to admit that Qoheleth really implies that one may sin to a moderate degree. That, however, is what he undoubtedly implies."[10]

Loyal Young takes the meaning of the passage to be that if "one would avoid premature death, let him be neither too righteous nor too wicked"; he refers to a number of Hebrew and Christian martyrs, on the one hand, and to the inhabitants of Sodom and Gomorrah, on the other hand, and then concludes: "The first class were too righteous for their own safety:—the last class were too wicked to be spared. This seems to be the only *satisfactory* explanation of the verses."[11] He adds, however, that "every man, judging for himself, is consoled in his short-comings by the supposition that those more godly or more moral than he are too righteous," and that the true explanation seems to be that "if there is no future world, let us make the best we can of this, avoiding the extremes of too much zeal for God, and too much wickedness."[12]

Some commentators who recognize the "golden mean" in Eccles. 7:15–18 do so because they believe that the author is speaking as a mere "man under the sun." Samuel Cox, for example, concludes that the author permits a "temperate indulgence both in virtue and in vice, carrying neither to excess (ver. 18)—a doctrine still very dear to the mere man of the world."[13]

J. N. Coleman suggests that the word "saying" belongs at the end of 7:15, so that the passage should read: "And there is a wicked man who prolongs his life through his iniquity (saying), 'Be not righteous overmuch, neither make

7. Ibid.

8. Ibid., p. 102, n. 3.

9. Power, p. 95.

10. George A. Barton, *A Critical and Exegetical Commentary on the Book of Ecclesiastes*, ICC (New York, 1908), p. 144.

11. Loyal Young, *A Commentary on the Book of Ecclesiastes* (Philadelphia, 1865), p. 170.

12. Ibid., p. 171.

13. Samuel Cox, *The Book of Ecclesiastes*, The Expositors' Bible, ed. W. Robertson Nicoll (New York, n.d.), p. 200.

yourself overwise; why should you destroy yourself?'"[14] Coleman thus declares that "this worldly maxim is the counsel of the wicked man, not the maxim or teaching of Solomon"; and consequently, the inspired reply of Solomon, then, is at v. 17: "Do not be overmuch wicked"—that is, do not add to original sin actual rejection of God and his will.[15]

R. B. Y. Scott contends that the "mean" of 7:16–17 follows from the assertion in 7:15 that "men do not receive their just deserts." It is therefore "as unprofitable for men to exhaust themselves in struggling for moral perfection as it is to hasten their demise through folly"; and while wisdom is important, he says, no one can be perfect.[16] On the other hand, Robert Gordis interprets the passage as a warning that "both extremes of saintliness and wickedness lead to unhappiness"; what is best is a moderate course between both extremes.[17]

According to C. D. Ginsburg, it is impossible to make the passage conform to orthodoxy.[18] The author teaches that one should be "as moderate in the indulgence of sin" as he should be "temperate in the practice of virtue."[19] Ginsburg adds, however, that this viewpoint is not the final opinion of the author; that opinion comes later, at the end of the book, and it should not be anticipated in this passage.[20]

Fanaticism and Legalism

Other commentators, while perhaps acknowledging an exhortation to moderation in Eccles. 7:15–18, see the author as warning especially against fanaticism. Edgar Jones, for instance, says that the passage is "reporting that the fanatical extremist does run into trouble."[21] And Franz Delitzsch holds a somewhat similar opinion, declaring that the author teaches that one should not exaggerate righteousness; for "if it occurs that a righteous man, in spite of his righteousness, perishes, this happens, at earliest, in the case in which, in the practice of righteousness, he goes beyond the right measure and limit."[22]

Certain other commentators see in all of this a reference to the legalism of the Pharisees. A. D. Power, for example, suggests that possibly "reli-

14. John N. Coleman, *Ecclesiastes* (Edinburgh, 1867), p. 37.

15. Ibid., p. 38.

16. R. B. Y. Scott, *Proverbs, Ecclesiastes* AB (Garden City, N.Y., 1965), p. 237. He attributes the Greek maxim, "nothing too much," to Solon (ca. 600 B.C.).

17. Gordis, p. 179.

18. Ginsburg, p. 379.

19. Ibid., p. 380.

20. Ibid.

21. Edgar Jones, *Proverbs and Ecclesiastes*, Torch Bible Commentaries (New York, 1961), pp. 319–320.

22. Franz Delitzsch, *Commentary on the Song of Songs and Ecclesiastes* (Grand Rapids, Mich., 1950), p. 324.

gious" would be a better understanding of the word "righteous" here, "for K. might have been thinking of the Pharisees who paid tithe of mint and anise and cummin, but overlooked such matters as judgment, mercy and faith (cf. Matt. 23:33), so perhaps the writer here meant religious or ritualistic, like the Pharisees who strained at a gnat and swallowed a camel. . . ."[23]

This view understands the words of Qoheleth to refer to an excessive concentration on legal observance or pious practices. H. C. Leupold describes them as referring to "a righteousness that is beginning to go to seed, a righteousness that will flourish in its most distorted form in the days of Jesus, in regard to which Jesus will be moved to say: 'Except your righteousness shall exceed the righteousness of the scribes and Pharisees, etc.' (Matt. 5:20)."[24]

Whybray states that scholars have suggested two possible reasons for the giving of such advice:

> (i) Such striving after perfection is not a virtue, but rather a sin: that of pride or blasphemy. (ii) Such excessive behavior is not required by God, and is to be avoided: for on the one hand its goal is beyond man's capacity and so it can achieve nothing; and on the other hand it makes life joyless, leading to narrowness and bigotry. So, in one way or another, the striving after perfection produces misery.[25]

Overreaction to Truth

R. W. DeHaan and Herbert Vander Lugt explain Eccles. 7:16–17 as a warning against overreactions to the truth of 7:15:

> First, some conclude that everyone who goes to an early grave somehow must have fallen short of doing what pleases the Lord. Therefore they set about to make up this lack in their own lives by extreme legalism, ascetic practices, or some other form of works-righteousness. . . .
> The second wrong reaction is that of going down the road of lustful living, giving oneself over to unbridled sensuality. . . . Many who see apparently good people suffer adversity or die young go down the pathway of a false and artificial works-religion while others go down the road of unrestrained wickedness. Both courses will lead to disaster.[26]

This viewpoint explains the context (both 7:15 and 7:18) and is in concord with the rest of Scripture. The command not to be "overly wise" (7:16) would be interpreted similarly, as a possible overreaction to the failure of wis-

---

23. Power, p. 95.
24. H. C. Leupold, *Exposition of Ecclesiastes* (Columbus, Ohio, 1952), p. 164.
25. Whybray, p. 191.
26. Richard W. DeHaan and Herbert Vander Lugt, *The Art of Staying Off Dead-end Streets* (Wheaton, Ill., 1974), pp. 107–8.

dom to provide the full answer to life (do not devote yourself fully to wisdom as if it *were* the only solution to life, but do not reject it to become a fool either).

Self-Righteousness

An increasingly common interpretation has been to see in the word "righteous" a reference to hypocrisy, and to understand the author to be referring to "self-righteousness" rather than genuine righteousness.[27] As Power puts it: "It may be he [Qoheleth] had in mind those excessively religious people who spend all their time seeking out wickedness in others and have no time for real religion themselves; another translation therefore might read as an injunction not to be self-righteous."[28]

According to Kaiser, what most commentators miss is that "verses 16–17 are not cautioning against possessing too much real righteousness." Rather, the danger is that men might delude themselves and others through "a multiplicity of pseudoreligious acts of sanctimoniousness; ostentatious showmanship in the art of worship; a spirit of hypercriticism against minor deviations from one's own cultural norms, which are equated with God's righteousness; and a disgusting conceit and supercilious, holier-than-thou attitude veneered over the whole mess."[29] He states, further, that the real clue to this passage is that the second verb in 7:16 ("to be wise") must be rendered reflexively, as "to think oneself to be furnished with wisdom."[30]

G. R. Castellino, in a careful analysis of the Hebrew forms, comes to a similar conclusion: namely, that 7:16 refers to "passing oneself off as righteous" (self-righteousness) and "passing oneself off as wise" (intellectualization). Vs. 18 then urges the reader to "grasp true wisdom" and not to let go of "the avoidance of foolishness," both of which are achieved through the fear of God.[31]

Whybray argues from the structure, grammar, and meaning of the passage as a whole that what is in view is "the state of mind which claims actually to have achieved righteousness or perfection."[32] He advances the following arguments:

1. In 7:16 the use of the construction *haya* + adjective (*ʾal-tĕhî ṣaddiq*—"do not be overly righteous") instead of the cognate verb *ʾal-tiṣdāq* is not due to chance or to purely stylistic considerations, but has a deliberate purpose: in order to give some special meaning to the word *ṣaddiq* which could not be conveyed by the use of the verb. The phrase "refers to the self-righteous man,

27. A. F. Harper, "Ecclesiastes," in the *Beacon Bible Commentary* (Kansas City, Mo., 1967), 3:575.

28. Power, p. 95.

29. Kaiser, pp. 85–86.

30. Ibid., p. 86.

31. George R. Castellino, "Qoheleth and His Wisdom," *CBQ* 30 (1968): 24.

32. Whybray, p. 191.

the would-be *ṣaddîq*, the man who claims to be, or sees himself as, exceptionally righteous."[33]

2. The word *ṣaddîq* ("righteous") has an ethical sense, and the author recognizes that in the strict sense there is no *ṣaddîq* in existence (7:20). He does not distinguish between "righteous" and "perfect," but uses the same term for both. Whybray concludes, therefore, that in 7:16 he must be using the term in an ironical sense: "Do not be a self-styled *ṣaddîq*."[34]

3. The word *harbēh* (7:16) always means "much, many, greatly, very," etc., and does not express any value-judgment such as "too great, or too much." The word is best taken as qualifying the whole preceding phrase. Qoheleth thus "uses the qualifying adverb *harbēh* to indicate that he recognizes a tendency in human nature towards self-righteousness." His meaning is "Do not allow self-righteousness to become your dominating characteristic." It is "a gentle warning which takes account of human weakness."[35]

4. In 7:16b the phrase "be overly wise" is simply the hithpael of the verb *ḥkm*. Whybray contends that of the meanings generally attributed to the hithpael, only three would make any sense at all here: "to conduct oneself in a particular way"; "to imagine/set oneself up to be"; or "to pretend to be." The first possibility would mean "Do not act with great wisdom," which cannot be what the author is saying. The last two options have a similar meaning: "Having first warned his readers against setting themselves up to be, or pretending to be, absolutely righteous, Qoheleth now warns them against similar pretensions to wisdom."[36]

5. Vs. 17 states, "Do not be very wicked." Here again the word *harbēh* is a concession to human frailty. Qoheleth adds a warning not to go to the other extreme and throw off all restraints and all striving towards these virtues, abandoning oneself to a life of folly. But "he knows that one cannot entirely avoid either wickedness or folly (cf. v. 20), and so he adds the word *harbēh*: what is to be avoided is the carrying of them to extremes." It is not an encouragement to immorality, but merely a recognition of the frailty and inherent sinfulness of man.[37]

Charles Bridges likewise understands Qoheleth's words as a warning against self-righteousness: "To whom then, and to what, does the admonition apply? We have seen that it does not warn us against true righteousness. But it is a wholesome caution against the 'vain affectation of it.' Every right principle has its counterfeit."[38]

33. Ibid., pp. 192–95.
34. Ibid., p. 195.
35. Ibid., p. 196.
36. Ibid.
37. Ibid., p. 197.
38. Charles Bridges, *An Exposition of the Book of Ecclesiastes* (London, Eng., 1960), p. 163.

Exegesis of Ecclesiastes 7:15–18

In Eccles. 6:8, Qoheleth introduces the question, "What advantage does the wise man have over the fool?" Throughout the second half of the book, he deals with the futility, benefits, and limitations of *wisdom*, focusing especially on the issue, "Who knows what is good for a man during his lifetime?" (6:12).

In chap. 7, the author points out that no one can really understand the work or the ways of God, or of the future. "Who is able to straighten what He has bent?" he asks (7:13b). God has made adversity as well as prosperity, and both must be accepted from him (7:14). Human beings cannot *really* know for certain what the future holds for them during their lifetime.

What Qoheleth Has Seen—7:15

At this point a question surely enters Qoheleth's mind: "I have already said that in place of righteousness there is wickedness [3:16], and that man can expect both prosperity and adversity from God [7:14]. What, then, of the age-old principle that righteousness brings blessing [prosperity], and wickedness brings cursing [adversity]? Is that principle invalid?"

This question clearly relates closely to the central problems of the Book of Job. Qoheleth has neither the problem with God's justice that Job had, nor the faulty view of reality that Job's friends demonstrated. He sees clearly (with Job) that the principle of righteousness–prosperity is only a general principle and has many exceptions. Qoheleth thus states from his experience: "There is a righteous man who perishes in his righteousness, and there is a wicked man who prolongs (אֲרִךְ—"lengthen," "prolong"] his life in his wickedness" (7:15). *In spite of* their righteous character, some men die young. And *in spite of* their wickedness, some evil men live long, prosperous lives.

The Law stated time after time that those who obeyed God and lived righteously would "prolong" (אֲרִךְ) their days and receive blessing (Deut. 4:26, 40; 5:16, 33; 6:2; 11:9; 17:20; 25:15; 30:18; 32:47). Solomon in his wisdom had also made similar promises (cf. Prov. 28:16). But the problem of exceptions persisted.

Job recognized the same problem when he asked, "Why do the wicked still live, continue on, also become very powerful?" (Job 21:7). They have many children, safe houses, prosperity, and many days of rejoicing (21:8–12). "They spend their days in prosperity," Job complains (21:13), while many righteous men are suffering or dying.

The psalmist also "saw the prosperity of the wicked" (Ps. 73:3), and it nearly caused him to stumble (73:2). He complains: "Behold, these are the wicked; and always at ease, they have increased by wealth. Surely in vain I have kept my heart pure, and washed my hands in innocence" (Ps. 73:12–13). This was very "troublesome" to him (73:16), until he went to God's sanctuary and finally understood the end of the wicked (73:17). God would destroy them, sooner or later (73:18–20). The psalmist's solution is to focus all his desires on God: "Whom have I in heaven but thee? And besides Thee, I desire nothing on earth. . . . God is the strength of my heart and my portion forever . . . as for me, the nearness of God is my good" (Ps. 73:25–28; cf. Matt. 6:33).

Qoheleth himself explains the problem and its principle more in detail in the following chapter (Eccles. 8). The general principle is valid, he says, that "it will not be well for the evil man and he will not lengthen his days like a shadow, because he does not fear God" (8:13). And, on the other side, it is still true generally that "it will be well for those who fear God, who fear Him openly" (8:12).

However, judgment for evil does not come quickly; and because of that, many are inclined to give themselves over to do evil (8:11). Qoheleth declares further that "there are righteous men to whom it happens according to the deeds of the wicked," and, on the other hand, "there are evil men to whom it happens according to the deeds of the righteous. I say that this too is futility" (8:14).

This is the same problem that he relates in 7:15. Righteousness does not *necessarily* bring prosperity, and wickedness does not *necessarily* bring suffering and death.

Qoheleth's Advice—7:16–17

The following two verses must therefore be understood as Qoheleth's counsel in the light of v. 15. It is here that the two major exegetical problems of the passage arise: (1) Do the expressions "excessively righteous" and "overly wise" really refer to self-righteousness and pretended wisdom, as Kaiser, Whybray, Castellino, and others contend? Or do these expressions imply, instead, an exaggerated "striving after" righteousness and wisdom? (2) Does Qoheleth in 7:16–17 intend to warn against a possible overreaction (on the part of some) to the statement in 7:15 that righteousness does not guarantee prosperity, nor wickedness death (i.e., deciding to strive fanatically for perfection or to slide cynically into foolish immorality)? Or does he instead begin a new, unrelated section, discussing the nature of true righteousness and true wisdom, in order that the reader might be able to evaluate inner character?

Before embarking on a detailed consideration of these questions, the unusual structure of this passage must be noted:

7:16a   אַל־תְּהִי צַדִּיק הַרְבֵּה
do not be excessively righteous

7:16b   וְאַל־תִּתְחַכַּם יוֹתֵר
and do not be wise to excess

7:16c   לָמָּה תִּשּׁוֹמֵם
why should you cause yourself desolation?

7:17a אַל־תִּרְשַׁע הַרְבֵּה
do not be excessively wicked

7:17b וְאַל־תְּהִי סָכָל
and do not be a fool

7:17c לָמָּה תָמוּת בְּלֹא עִתֶּךָ
why should you die before your time?

Each verse consists of three parts, each of which begins with the same word: אַל, וְאַל, and לָמָּה, respectively. Each verse begins with a *pair* of negative warnings ("do not"), these four warnings generally containing a negative particle (אַל), a verb or verbal clause, and an adverb (the adverb is lacking in 7:17b). The *third* part of each verse consists of an interrogative sentence introduced by the word לָמָּה followed by a verb. And in each case, the interrogative sentence implies a positive concept or result.[39]

At this point, several of the more controversial words in the passage must be defined. Lexically, the word צַדִּיק in 7:16a means "just" or "righteous" in conduct and character, either toward God or, ethically, toward others. Nothing more than this can be read into the statement from the term itself. The form הַרְבֵּה is the hiphil infinitive absolute of the verb רָבָה ("to be many, much, great"), and is here used adverbially to mean "greatly," "exceedingly."[40] It is used, for instance, in Neh. 2:2: "Then I was *very much* afraid." In Eccles. 7:16a, this word modifies the adjective "righteous," so that the sentence should read, "Do not be exceedingly righteous." The meaning of the statement will depend on the nuance which the context gives to the expressions "exceedingly" and "righteous." If "righteous" refers to inward character, then an inordinate striving for perfection may be in view. If, however, "righteous" refers to outward conduct, then the warning probably has to do with excessive occupation with some sort of Pharisaic externalism.

In 7:16b, תִּתְחַכַּם is the hithpael form of the verb חָכַם ("to be wise"), and, according to Whybray, means "to pretend to be wise" or "to make great pretensions to wisdom."[41] In the Brown-Driver-Briggs *Lexicon*, it is rendered as "make or show thyself wise."[42] A. B. Davidson states that the hithpael is reflexive of piel[43] (in this case, "to make wise," "to teach wisdom"). Thus, the

---

39. Whybray, p. 192. Another interesting aspect of this structure is the fact that there is a 3:2:2 decrescendo in the meter of v. 16, followed by a 2:2:4 crescendo in the meter of v. 17, indicating, perhaps, the comprehensive, yet parallel, nature of the passage.

40. Francis Brown, S. R. Driver, and C. A. Briggs, eds., *A Hebrew and English Lexicon of the Old Testament* (Oxford, 1906), s.v. רָבָה, p. 915. (This title hereinafter cited as BDB.)

41. Whybray, pp. 196–97.

42. BDB, s.v. חָכַם, p. 314.

43. A. B. Davidson, *An Introductory Hebrew Grammar*, 25th ed. (Edinburgh, 1962), p. 107.

hithpael would mean "to make oneself wise" or "to teach oneself wisdom." But Davidson adds that "it very often implies that one shows himself as, or gives himself out as, performing the action of the simple verb."[44] In this case, the verb in Eccles. 7:16b could mean "to show oneself to be wise," or perhaps even "to pretend to be wise."

Several factors argue against the latter meaning of the word in the passage at hand. First, there is absolutely no reason from the context to understand the verb as a reference to pretense. Second, grammatically the hithpael form may just as easily mean "to make oneself wise" or "to teach oneself wisdom," as noted above. Third, the only other use of the hithpael of חָכַם is in Exod. 1:10, where it refers to wise conduct—"Let us deal wisely with this people"—and there is no reason to treat it in any other way in Eccles. 7:16. (The appeal made by some exegetes to Prov. 3:7 ["Do not be wise in your own eyes"] is invalid, since the reference there has the modifying expression ["in your own eyes"] spelled out; and, moreover, the verb is not hithpael, but rather "to be" with an adjective.)

The word יוֹתֵר (Eccles. 7:16b) is common in Ecclesiastes, usually meaning "superiority," "advantage," or "excess."[45] As an adverb it means "to excess," or perhaps "to a superior degree." It is used in Eccles. 2:15, where Qoheleth asks himself, "Why then have I been extremely wise?" In 7:16b, he is apparently saying that there is no need for anyone to try to become the wisest person on earth. It is not worth the trouble.

In 7:16c, the verb תִּשּׁוֹמֵם is the hithpael form of שָׁמֵם which means "to be desolated." As a reflexive, the word means "to cause oneself desolation or ruin."[46] Qoheleth asks, "Why should you cause yourself ruin by such extreme reactions?" This cannot refer primarily to either a divine judgment or societal sanctions, as Whybray suggests,[47] since the reflexive makes the ruin self-caused.

The verb תִּרְשַׁע in 7:17a is simply the Qal imperfect of the verb רָשַׁע ("to be wicked," "to act wickedly"). It is important to note that on this negative side of the coin, no process is in view (such as was the case with "make yourself excessively wise"). The word simply looks on the actions of wickedness.

It is perhaps obvious by now that Whybray's interpretation of the passage depends almost entirely upon a highly questionable meaning of *one word* in the passage: תִּתְחַכַּם(7:16b). Having concluded that this word refers to "pretensions of wisdom," he reasons that 7:16a is parallel and that it should therefore read, "Do not pretend to be righteous" or "Do not be self-righteous." This is an unwarranted leap.

44. Ibid.; Ginsburg, p. 380, notes, however, that the wisdom under consideration must be real, since the antithesis speaks of real, not affected, foolishness. He thus concludes that the piety referred to is also sincere and genuine piety.

45. BDB, s.v. יוֹתֵר, p. 452.

46. BDB, s.v. שָׁמֵם, p. 1030.

47. Whybray, p. 198.

Whybray's solution fits neither the context nor the details of the passage. He is forced to conclude that 7:15 is totally disconnected from 7:16, and that 7:16–17 in *no* way provides counsel for the problem of 7:15.[48] He is also forced to treat the questions of 7:16c and 7:17c as extremely vague references to a possible future calamity, and in the process he violates his own explanation of the hithpael/hithpoel form. In addition, Whybray completely boxes in 7:16–18 as a separate passage almost totally unrelated to the rest of the chapter,[49] since he has divorced himself from any sort of correct contextual meaning.

What, then, is the conclusion of the matter? (1) The expressions "excessively righteous" and "make yourself overly wise" are best understood as an exaggerated striving and seeking after perfection and super-wisdom. Qoheleth's point is that these things are not *really* of value; he had discovered that himself—both experientially and through observation. (2) Vv. 16 and 17, therefore, have a very close relationship to v. 15. As DeHaan and Vander Lugt suggest, if the principle that righteousness brings prosperity does not always hold (7:14–15), and if wisdom cannot really discover everything that man needs to know for his life (6:10–7:14), many people would have one of two types of reaction: (a) They might decide that if they could reach perfection in character and knowledge, their problems would be solved; or (b) they might decide that God is unfair and simply devote themselves to immorality and foolish living as the best they can get out of life. Qoheleth warns them against both of these options, since both of them lead to disaster. The best life, he says, depends on the fear of God.

The Spiritual Conclusion—7:18

Following the negative admonitions of 7:16–17, Qoheleth now describes positively a "good" in life. Though neither righteousness nor wisdom can guarantee prosperity or unlock the mystery of the future, they are nevertheless good and necessary. It is good to hold on to righteousness, and not to let go of wisdom. Both wickedness and foolishness lead to disaster.

Both righteousness and wisdom are achieved through the *fear of God*. It is through trust in, and obedience to, God that righteousness and wisdom can actually be balanced and made worthwhile.

Conclusion

In Eccles. 7:15–18, Qoheleth discusses the problem of the value and balance of *righteousness* and *wisdom*. He has concluded that human wisdom cannot really explain all of life nor the future (6:10–7:14), and that even the principle that righteousness brings prosperity has many exceptions (7:14–15).

48. Ibid., p. 202.
49. Ibid.

Thus, he notes in 7:15 that some righteous people die *in spite of* their righteousness, and some wicked people live long lives *in spite of* their wickedness.

How would a concerned human react to this admission of reality? Many would tend to overreact either toward striving harder, or toward ending all efforts and slipping into identity with those who do not know God. Qoheleth offers some helpful counsel: Do not strive for exaggerated righteousness or try to make yourself the wisest person on earth, for these are not really worthwhile goals; and in the end, such striving will ruin your life. Likewise, do not turn to immorality or act like a fool, since God's principles do still operate and you will put yourself in danger of premature death. God is still in control.

What then of righteousness and wisdom? What good are they? Qoheleth answers that they are both of great benefit. Grasp them both. If you learn to *fear God* (which is the important thing), you will come out right in both areas.

25

HOW MUCH CAN WE REALLY KNOW?

ECCLESIASTES 7:23–8:1

Louis Goldberg

A s the Teacher pauses after looking back at what he has declared in the past several verses about finding a balance between excesses and acknowledging that wisdom is better (7:12, 19), he has to admit that he has not attained an ultimate wisdom. He has examined a number of specific instances where wisdom has taught him well, but like Job (28:12ff.), he continues searching for fundamental wisdom in spite of life's limitations. All who are sensitive to the will of God recognize this endeavor amidst life's pressures and joys to find ultimate answers. But unbelievers likewise struggle with the same difficulties in seeking basic wisdom and answers to life.

The Teacher begins with "all this" (v. 23); he perhaps was referring to the rules of conduct already discussed in chapter 7, but there is also a sharp anticipation of what he wants to learn concerning a fundamental wisdom. With his declaration, "I tested by wisdom," he continues with his honest search to find out the essence of things that are. Previously he declared that men "cannot fathom what God has done from beginning to end" (3:11), but this fact does not hinder him as he continues to look, even as we do in our day. He insists that "I am determined to be wise," that is, he wants to fully know this basic wisdom so he can explain the mysteries of time and answer questions that trouble mankind. But he has to admit that what he is searching for always seems so elusive. He learns some facets of wisdom but does not attain its fundamental aspect.

The Teacher is not questioning the fact that ultimate wisdom actually exists; he is sure that this wisdom has being (v. 24). However, he must confess that it is far off in its ultimate sense and very deep, a Hebrew compound that emphasizes it in a superlative way. He raises the question concerning who can reach it, discover it, in an intellectual sense. In many ways he is a wisdom teacher, but he discovers his limitations to find the essence of wisdom even though he can teach a number of specific, concrete lessons.

All this discussion is only a general observation concerning what we can know, but the Teacher does have something specific in mind about this matter of fundamental wisdom (v. 25). He turns his mind (Hebrew, heart; see 2:20 for a similar occasion of turning) to a number of areas of investigation. With his whole heart he wants to be involved in his search and not do it in a superficial manner. His deepest desire is to understand (know) in an intellectual sense, to investigate (explore), and to search out (seek out) wisdom and the scheme (explanation) of things. He has dedicated himself to a careful study and will not be deterred. He is involved in a noble effort.

In addition the Teacher also wants to understand (know) the stupidity of wickedness. The reference to wickedness describes the choices that lead a person to turn away from God and from the Word that is designed to teach him to do good. A lifestyle of wickedness is stupid, and the person who makes the wrong choices hates knowledge (Prov. 1:22), takes no pleasure in understanding (Prov. 18:2), and finds pleasure in evil conduct (Prov. 10:23). In his search for knowledge the Teacher also seeks to discover the horror of the madness of folly. Interestingly, folly comes from the same verb as stupidity; once again we see how folly, or stupidity, is sheer madness and causes ungodly men to be blind to wisdom and to rage in their wicked behavior. But how can we know in an ultimate sense, and do we even want to know, all the ways of wickedness and folly man takes?

With these specific questions, was the Teacher able to attain to ultimate wisdom? No. His answers provide only the particulars of knowledge, but they are very important because they will lead him to discern between good and evil. He does not completely despair in his search since he at least is finding out pertinent and extremely useful information. The effort expended in his search for wisdom will help him build a fund of knowledge to make even more helpful pronouncements for a godly lifestyle.

The Teacher describes the woman who ensnares man (v. 26) but goes even further to declare that he has not found one upright woman among a thousand (v. 28)! From today's viewpoint the implications are devastating. Does he mean to say that not one good woman can be found? If this is his thought, then he is in trouble with many of our women's movements today! Various explanations have been offered to avoid these implications: 1) the woman spoken of in deprecation is heathen philosophy that detracts from the real wisdom (Leupold, p. 173); and 2) the woman, and man who also falls short (v. 29), is interpreted to be civilization at large (Gordis, p. 283). As difficult as the text is, we have to probe it for the real meaning.

The Teacher found an experience more bitter than death (v. 26). What is it that could be worse than the heartwrenching experience of the death of a loved one or close friend? It is the woman who is a snare, the same word used for the hunting net in which birds are caught (9:12) and huge siegeworks used for blockading (9:14). Why should a woman be described in this sense, and what had she done for men to be warned to keep away from her?

The woman under consideration has a heart like a trap or fishing net in which her victims are caught; her hands are like chains, holding her victim as a prisoner with vise-like clutches. When we are later told that the man who pleases God will escape from her, we are not left to imagine too much as to what is in mind. The wisdom of Proverbs 5 is reflected here where two women are contrasted—the legitimate wife and the adulterous woman. In Proverbs 7 wisdom is the true sister while the adulteress is to be avoided like the plague. It appears without question that the wise man is talking about the loose woman who can take hold of the unsuspecting man and entrap him (Prov. 7:13). The Teacher clearly warns that if a man holds God as the object of his love, then he will escape the adulteress. The sheltering hands of a loving God are more to be desired than all the illicit love in this world.

However, the Teacher is not content to leave the matter. He emphasizes the point that we should look with him, see, and understand well what he has discovered (vv. 27–29). We started out in verse 23 by observing that the Teacher wanted with all his heart to know ultimate wisdom and continued to add one thing to another to discover or find out the scheme of things, that is, a well-grounded and established knowledge. While he indicates that he is not able to find this ultimate knowledge, he does get into a discussion concerning what can be disagreeable to men and women. He found only one upright man among a thousand, but not one woman was among the same number! Is he saying this with tongue in cheek? Certainly he does respect a wife when he tells a man to "enjoy life with your wife, whom you love" (9:9), and he has only praise for marital fidelity with no questions raised regarding the wife. In Proverbs the wise Teacher praises the wife in many ways (i.e., 12:4; 14:1; 18:22; 19:14; 31:10–31).

Taking the focus off the woman for the moment, the search among a thousand human beings could reveal only one man as he *ought to be*. (The word "upright" does not appear in the Hebrew text.) The point is that the Teacher was looking for the ideal, righteous, wise person who might serve as his model; but the search was disheartening.

Why, however, in the search among an equal number of people, could there not be found a woman who could fit the model of the ideal, righteous, and wise? (Again, the words "one" and "upright" concerning the woman are not in the Hebrew text.) We might ask, "Where was the Teacher looking?" If he was searching among his harem (700 wives and 300 concubines, 1 Kings 11:3), it is doubtful that he would find a woman as she ought to be among the pagan women who had turned his heart from God. Unacceptable also is the view that because no ideal woman could be found among a thousand, therefore not one woman was honored to author a book of the Bible, a task given only to the chosen few among men. Neither is it fair to throw in a crumb to say that certain godly women have written sacred songs in Scripture—Miriam, Deborah, Hannah, and Mary (Leupold, p. 177). This position seems so unfair, but we are still left with the problem as to why he *seemingly* deprecated the woman.

Perhaps it is safest to say that since he has in only rare moments found an ideal righteous man searching for ultimate wisdom, and even fewer woman, that he therefore proceeds to his final observation. He introduces his conclusion with "this only have I found" (v. 29). He states that God made mankind, or the world of all human beings, upright. Adam *and* Eve, both human, were made originally upright in a state of innocence. After the Fall, mankind was characterized by a fallen nature but not totally unaware of the difference between good and evil. Both a man and a woman, because of their common fallen nature, can make wrong moral choices and indulge in sinful practices. With this nature both often exhibit how far they have strayed from the ideal.

In considering biblical history, however, it was Eve who tempted man to sin, being the first to be deceived, and then enticing her husband to follow her choices. In the pronouncements by God concerning Adam and Eve after the Fall, both of them are under the curse. Eve, and all women afterward, are to bring forth their children in pain. Man is to earn his food and whatever else by the sweat of his brow (Gen. 3:16, 19). But God did add a further restriction concerning the woman in that she is to serve her husband, and the husband is to exercise rulership over his wife. In no way does this deprecate the woman because she can provide as much input within the family relationship as she desires, but in the headship the man has his responsibility to exercise the leadership in the family.

In the ancient world, among pagan nations and even from selected sources in the Jewish traditions, the fundamental makeup of a woman with her desires and actions was not held in high esteem; and it was deplorable if the woman asserted any kind of leadership, such as Vashti's action in the Persian court (Esth. 1:17b). The Teacher does not go as far as this statement; but perhaps he somehow, because of the pronouncements by God after the Fall, reflected generally the concern of headship whereby man is to take the leadership in matters of the spiritual realm. This fact does not mean that in specific instances a woman cannot be wise so as to provide acceptable advice and expertise in many areas in both the family and society. But the role of the wise and ideal teacher will be in areas of spiritual leadership, and therefore we see the guidance in 7:28.

The Teacher has had a long, hard struggle with the problem of attaining the essence of wisdom (8:1). In his long experience he also indicated the futility of making this search the *only* goal of his life (1:12ff.). But he has learned already in his search for ultimate wisdom that there is no one who can equal the wise man, and no one likewise can know or understand the explanation or foundation of things like the wise person. He is not being one-sided, but he has lived long enough to realize that a godly wisdom is indispensable to "make it" in this world and to get at the "whys" of so many of life's experiences.

The last two lines of verse 1 are a popular proverb indicating what wisdom from God and His Word can do for a person when he takes it to heart. His face is brightened, even as the psalmist declared in Psalm 119:130 and 19:8; the gloom is taken away; and joy and peace are very evident on the countenance. The fourth line of the verse follows as a matter of course whereby godly wisdom takes away a man's hard appearance. The word "hard" is rendered "impudent" in BDB (p. 739), but here the meaning is reflected by the description of the "fierce-looking nation" (Deut. 28:50) or the "stern-faced king" (Dan. 8:23). The entrance of godly wisdom has the power to change the hard appearance of a person's face and make it shine with the glory of God; and only a believer can know this experience firsthand. As a result, he finds life and receives favor from the Lord (Prov. 8:35). Certainly we are not talking about mere intellectual wisdom but that which comes from God, enabling a person to become a believer when he learns to fear the Lord.

While the Teacher has not arrived with an ultimate wisdom, yet he does not give up on acquiring its specifics that enable him to live in the push and pull of everyday life. As he piles up the specifics, perhaps the real essence of wisdom will be revealed.

26

MANKIND'S IGNORANCE
ECCLESIASTES 8:1–10:11

Donald R. Glenn

Man's Ignorance of the Enigma of Divine Retribution (chap. 8)

The key to interpreting this chapter properly is seeing how its two parts are related. The chapter begins with a question and a statement that magnify the value of wisdom (v. 1) and closes with an acknowledgment of wisdom's limitations (v. 17). Wisdom enables a wise man to avoid the king's wrath (vv. 2–9), but not even a wise man can figure out the enigmas in God's distribution of justice (vv. 10–17).

A Wise Man Can Avoid the King's Wrath (8:1–9)

The background for this section is the recognition of the absolute authority of the king (cf. Prov. 24:21–22) and the need for proper decorum to avert his wrath (cf. Prov. 14:35; 16:14; 20:2).

(1) A wise man knows the proper decorum. **8:1.** A **wise man** is able to practice proper decorum. In two rhetorical questions Solomon affirmed that only a wise man can size up situations properly and act accordingly. Only he

Reprinted from *The Bible Knowledge Commentary, Old Testament,* edited by John F. Walvoord and Roy B. Zuck, published by Victor Books, 1985, SP Publications, Inc., Wheaton, IL 60187.

knows the explanation (*pēšer*) **of things.** The noun *pēšer* occurs only here in Hebrew. In the Aramaic in Daniel it refers to the interpretation of dreams (cf. Dan. 5:12). Here it is applied to the Hebrew word *dāḇār* ("matter, affair," trans. "things" in the NIV). Because of his wisdom a wise person knows how to act graciously and avoid brash behavior which would lead to his harm (cf. Prov. 14:35). For the two figures of speech (in the last two lines of Eccles. 8:1) where behavior is reflected in one's **face** or **appearance**, see Numbers 6:25 and Proverbs 7:13.

(2) Obedience to the king is of paramount importance. **8:2–4.** Solomon then set forth examples of proper decorum before a king. A king has great authority: he *can* (not **will** as in the NIV) **do whatever he pleases, his word is supreme,** and no one **can say to him, What are you doing?** (Cf. Job 9:12; Isa. 45:9 where the same idea is applied to God.) Therefore people should **obey** the king, maintain allegiance to him (**do not be in a hurry to leave** his **presence,** i.e., as suggested by the Heb. to resign from his service; cf. 10:4), and not be rebellious toward him by standing **up for a bad cause.**

(3) Proper decorum averts harm (8:5–9). **8:5–7.** Affirming that obedience to a king's **command** would avert **harm,** Solomon commended the value of wisdom, saying that **the wise** person would **know** the best course of action and when to apply it (**the proper time and procedure,** lit., "time and judgment"). Such wisdom is necessary, according to Solomon, because people (*ʾāḏām* is generic, referring to people in general) suffer harm (**a man's misery weighs heavily upon him**). The word for "misery" (*rāʿāh*) is related to the word for "harm" (*rāʿ*) in verse 5. This misery comes because people are ignorant of "what will happen" and "when it will happen" (v. 7, NASB; not **what is to come** as in the NIV for the Heb. word means "when," not "what").

8:8–9. The reason for such misery is the inescapable consequences of wickedness that arise from such ignorance; just as **no man** can control **the wind** (cf. Prov. 27:16), postpone **the day of his death,** or be **discharged** while in the midst of battle, so **no** man can escape the consequences of his **wickedness.** The first three clauses in Ecclesiastes 8:8 are parallel in Hebrew and are comparative to the last clause. Solomon observed these things as he **applied** his **mind** (cf. 1:17; 8:16) to what was **done under the sun** (cf. comments on 1:3).

The consequences Solomon had in view here resulted from a ruler's anger (the harm a wise man can escape by proper decorum; cf. 8:1) as is clear from verse 9 where Solomon referred to a ruler lording **it over others to** their **hurt.** (The NIV marg., "to their hurt," is preferred to "to his own hurt." The pronoun refers back to "others," which is lit., *ʾāḏām*, "men.")

Even a Wise Man Cannot Understand God's Judgment (8:10–17)

This section is often misunderstood because verses 16–17 are often separated from it and placed with 9:1–11:6 (cf., e.g., Christian D. Ginsburg, *The Song of Songs and Coheleth*, p. 406). However, the recurrence of the divider phrase "cannot discover" (8:17; cf. 7:14, 28) argues for the inclusion of verses 16–17 with verses 10–15. This is also supported by the bracketing effects of verse 1 ("the wise man . . . knows") and verse 17 ("man cannot discover" and "a wise man . . . cannot really comprehend"). Verses 16–17 thus refer in particular to the enigma of God's work of divine judgment.

(1) Failure to punish wickedness is a great enigma (8.10–14). **8:10–12a.** Solomon had noted that wickedness is not always punished (cf. 3:16; 4:1). He had seen that **the wicked** have access to **the holy place** (i.e., the temple), die, are **buried**, and even are praised **in the city where they** practiced wickedness. Affirming that such a contradiction of the doctrine of retribution was **meaningless** (*hebel*; cf. 1:2) or enigmatic, Solomon lamented the fact that **a wicked man** could sin with impunity (i.e., commit **100 crimes and** live **a long time,** 8:12). According to Solomon, man's failure to carry out retribution (e.g., to punish **a crime . . . quickly,** v. 11) often leads to more wrongdoing: then **the hearts of the people are filled with schemes to do wrong** (cf. 7:29).

8:12b–14. These verses are one long sentence in the Hebrew. Verse 14 is the main clause of a subordinate clause consisting of verses 12b–13 and introduced by the Hebrew particle *gam* (meaning "though," not "still" or "yet" as in NASB, KJV; not trans. in NIV) before the words I **know.** Solomon firmly believed in the doctrine of retribution: life is **better** for **God-fearing** people (cf. 3:14; 5:7; 7:18; 12:13) but does **not go well** for **the wicked** whose lives will be shortened (cf. Prov. 2:22; 10:27; 29:1). Yet Solomon had observed contradictions to retribution. He had seen the **righteous . . . get what the wicked deserve and** the **wicked . . . get what the righteous deserve.** Solomon affirmed emphatically that such a contradiction in the distributing of divine justice is enigmatic or **meaningless** (cf. Eccles. 8:10; "meaningless" occurs as a bracket at the beginning and the end of v. 14).

(2) Enjoy the life God gives. **8:15.** Having shown that there are enigmatic contradictions in the doctrine of retribution—righteousness is not always rewarded and wickedness is not always punished, and sometimes the wicked prosper and the righteous meet with disaster—Solomon again recommended **the enjoyment of life.** He said that life's best is to enjoy the fruits of one's labor (i.e., **to eat and drink;** cf. 2:24; 3:13; 5:18) **and** "to rejoice" or **be glad** (cf. 3:12; 5:19). Also he noted that this **joy** would enliven one's labor (i.e., it would **accompany him in his work**). As is obvious from earlier occurrences of this theme (cf. 2:24–26; 3:12, 22; 5:18–20), this is not Epicurean hedonism based on despair but is a note of submission. Man cannot control or predict adversity or prosperity; however, each day's joys should be received as gifts from God's hand and be savored as **God** permits (3:13; 5:19). All this is to be while one is **under the sun** (twice in 8:15; cf. comments on 1:3).

(3) No man can comprehend God's providence. **8:16–17.** Solomon closed his treatment of the enigma of contradictions in divine retribution much as he

had concluded his discussions on the significance of adversity and prosperity (7:1–14) and on the significance of righteousness and wisdom (7:15–29), namely, by acknowledging man's ignorance of God's ways (cf. 7:14b, 28a). After searching diligently (**I applied my mind**; cf. 1:17; 8:9) **to gain wisdom** and observing **man's** many activities, he concluded that man is ignorant of God's work (the phrases **all that God has done** and **what goes on under the sun** are synonymous). In emphatic terms, repeating the negative three times (v. 17) and the verb "comprehend" twice—**no one can comprehend . . . man cannot discover . . . he cannot really comprehend**—Solomon said that no one can understand God's ways (3:11; cf. Isa. 55:9; Rom. 11:33) **even if** he expended all his energies or were **wise** and claimed he could.

Man Does Not Know What Will Happen (9:1–11:6)

This section is characterized by the repetition of the phrase "no man knows" (cf. 9:1, 12; 10:14) and "you do not know" (cf. 11:2, 6). It deals with man's inability to predict what will happen to him, whether good or bad (cf. 9:1), or whether his work will fail or succeed (cf. 9:11–12; 11:2, 6). Contrary to the writings of some, this formula ("no man knows" and "you do not know") serve to *introduce* the subsections, not *conclude* them, as is evident from their occurrences in 9:1 and 11:2.

No One Knows What Will Happen to Him (9:1–10)

Summary: No One Knows What Awaits Him (9:1)

9:1. This verse closely relates verses 2–10 to the preceding section, as indicated in the NIV translation, **So I reflected on all this and concluded that the righteous and the wise and what they do are in God's hands.** The "all this" that Solomon "reflected on" is human ignorance of the significance of righteousness and wickedness in God's sovereign disposition of adversity and prosperity (chaps. 7–8). Solomon "concluded" (lit., "my heart saw") from his prior reflections "on all this" that people are not masters of their own fate; people and "what they do" are subject to God's sovereign will (i.e., they "are in God's hands"; cf. Prov. 21:1 for a similar use of this figure). Since one does not know God's providence, neither does he know whether he will experience prosperity or adversity, or **whether** he will be the object of **love** or **hate** (for a similar use of these two nouns, cf. Mal. 1:2–3).

All People Are Subject to the Same Fate (9:2–3)

9:2–3. Solomon supported the statement that nobody knows what awaits him (v. 1) by stating that **all** people **share** the same fate or **common destiny**. However, there is some ambiguity as to the nature of that fate because of a common failure to relate the beginning of verse 2 to the end of verse 1. The same fate or destiny relates to the "love or hate," adversity or prosperity, referred to in verse 1. The Hebrew is literally, "whether it will be love or hate, no man knows"; both (i.e., love and hate—for this use of *kōl*; cf. 2:14; 3:19; 7:18) are before them (i.e., the righteous and the wise, 9:1). Both love and hate are experienced by everyone, there is one fate (or destiny) for **the righteous and the wicked.** This commonality of fate applies to **the good and the bad,** those who are ritually **clean** as well as those who are ritually **unclean, those who offer sacrifices** as well as **those who do not.** . . . **those who are afraid to take** God's name in **oaths** (cf. Exod. 20:7, "misuse the name of the LORD") as well as **those who** are not afraid to do so. **The same destiny** befalls **all** these. The bad part of all this (i.e., **the evil in everything that happens under the sun**), Solomon wrote, is that this common fate causes people to be rampant in sin (people's **hearts . . . are full of evil and . . . madness**; cf. Eccles. 8:11). Solomon added that not only does everybody (including the righteous and the wise, 9:1) share this same inscrutable distribution of adversity and prosperity *during* life, but they also share the same ultimate fate *after* life; **they** all **join the dead.**

Life Is Preferable to Death (9:4–6)

9:4–6. However, despite the fact that all people, both righteous and wicked, are subject to the same inscrutable distribution of adversity and prosperity and ultimately join one another in death, they should not despair of life. Life has advantages over death. Comparing the lot of a **live dog** with that of **a dead lion,** Solomon affirmed that it is better to be alive and dishonored (cf. 1 Sam. 17:43; the dog was the most despised animal) than to be honored and dead (cf. Prov. 30:30; the lion was the most honored beast). **The living** at least have consciousness and **hope,** things they can look forward to enjoying. But **the dead** have no consciousness (they **know nothing**) or hope of **reward** or enjoyment. Moreover, their passions—**their love, their hate, and their jealousy**—are stilled. As Ginsburg has noted, the concepts of consciousness and unconsciousness here are not in their barest forms as though these verses taught soul sleep. Instead they should be understood in the context of enjoying life (Eccles. 9:7–9) and possessing the capacities for enjoyment; the living have those capabilities but the dead do not (*The Song of Songs and Coheleth,* pp. 414–5). Thus the living have opportunities and capacities for fruitful labor but the dead do not (v. 10). The living have opportunities for reward from that labor, but the dead do not (v. 5; the word trans. "reward" refers to wages or earnings). The living have capacities for enjoyment (vv. 7–9), but the dead do not (v. 6). Solomon was not describing what the state of the dead *is*; he was stating what it is *not*. He did this to emphasize the lost opportunities of this present life, opportunities for serving God and enjoying His gifts (cf. Isa. 38:11, 18–19 for similar ideas). Solomon added that the dead **never again . . . have a part in anything that happens under the sun** (cf. . . . Eccles. 1:3).

The word for "part" (*ḥēleq*, "lot, portion, allotment") is the word he used elsewhere of life and its enjoyments (3:22; 5:18–19; 9:9).

Some commentators see a contradiction between 9:4–6 and 4:2–3 ("the dead . . . are happier than the living"). However, no real contradiction is here because Solomon was stating that a person who experiences the pressures of oppression (4:1) may feel that death is preferable. On the other hand in 9:4–6 (and in vv. 7–10) Solomon stressed that when a person is dead opportunities for enjoying life are gone. The two passages view life and death from different perspectives.

Enjoy Life as God Enables (9:7–9)

9:7–9. In view of the uncertainties of what the future may bring, whether adversity or prosperity (vv. 1–3), and in view of the certainty of death with the loss of all opportunity for enjoyment (vv. 4–6), Solomon again recommended enjoying life as God's good gift (cf. 2:24–26; 3:12–13, 22; 5:18–19). Solomon here spelled out in greater detail than elsewhere some of the aspects of life which would be enjoyed: **food** (lit., "bread"), **wine** which sustain life and make it merry (cf. Ps. 104:15), fine clothes and pleasant lotions (cf. 2 Sam. 12:20 where they are the opposites of mournful grief), enjoyment of **life with** one's **wife** (cf. Prov. 18:22). In short, these include both the basic necessities of life and some luxuries God bestows as His gifts (cf. Eccles. 5:19). Solomon underlined the need to enjoy these gifts by emphasizing life's brevity. He did this by almost repeating a phrase, **all the days of this meaningless life** and **all your meaningless days.** "Meaningless" here (*ḥebel*) should be rendered "fleeting" (cf. . . . 3:19; 6:12; 7:15).

Affirming that **this is** one's **lot** (*ḥēleq*; cf. 3:22; 5:18–19 and contrast 9:6 where the same word is trans. "part") **in life** and **labor under the sun** (cf. comments on 1:3), Solomon encouraged his readers to enjoy life because it is God's will for them to do so. He stated, "God has already approved your works" (NASB; preferred over NIV's **God favors what you do**). By this he summarized what he had previously said about the enjoyment of life: (a) wealth and possessions, which stem from one's "labor," ultimately are gifts of God (5:18–19), (b) only God gives the ability to enjoy the fruits of one's labor (cf. 2:24; 3:13; 5:18), and (c) the ability to enjoy those things depends on whether one pleases God (2:26). So the statement "God has already approved your works" means that possessing God's gifts and the ability to enjoy them evidence God's prior approval that one can do so; if God had not so approved the gifts, one could not enjoy them.

Labor Diligently While You Can (9:10)

9:10. Besides encouraging his readers to enjoy life as God enabled them, Solomon also encouraged them to work diligently. The idiom **whatever your hand finds to do** means "whatever you are able to do" (cf. 1 Sam. 10:7). Whatever a person is able to do, he should **do it with all** his **might,** that is, expend all his energies. The reason for this advice is that when death comes all opportunities for work and service will cease. In death a person will have no further energies or abilities to work; there will be **neither working nor planning nor knowledge nor wisdom.** (This does not suggest soul sleep; see comments on Eccles. 9:5.)

No One Knows Whether His Wisdom Will Succeed (9:11–10:11)

The preceding section (9:1–10) began with a statement that the righteous and the wise are subject to the same uncertain future as anyone else (9:1). Then in 9:2–10 Solomon discussed this fact with regard to the *righteous* (in contrast with the wicked), and now (in 9:11–10:11) he showed that the wise are also subject to an uncertain future.

Introduction:
Wisdom Is Subject to the Uncertainty of the Future (9:11–12)

9:11–12. The fact that wisdom is subject to the future's uncertainty is introduced by a series of five human abilities, each of which fails to succeed. The last three relate to a wise person: **the wise . . . the brilliant . . . the learned.** As a **race** is not always won by the swiftest runner, or a victory in a **battle** always won by the mightiest soldiers, so also the wise do not always earn a living (i.e., gain **food,** lit., "bread"), get rich, or acquire a great reputation (gain **favor**).

The reason for such failures is that **all** people are subject to times of misfortune (**time and chance** is another example of a hendiadys; cf. comments on 7:25) which no man is able to predict (9:12, **no man knows . . . his hour;** lit., "his time"). This refers back to times of misfortune (v. 11), not merely to death. Comparing such times of misfortune to a **net** and a **snare** by which **birds** and **fish** are **caught,** Solomon said that such **evil times** come suddenly and **unexpectedly upon them,** thus nullifying their abilities.

Wisdom May Be Unrewarded Because of Negligence (9:13–16)

9:13–16. An **example of wisdom** not being rewarded (v. 11) is a **poor** wise **man** who had delivered a **small,** poorly defended **city** from a siege by a **powerful king.** But the **poor man's wisdom** went unrewarded because **nobody remembered** him (also in 1 Sam. 25:31 "remember" conveys the idea of "reward"). Solomon said this example **greatly impressed** him, that is, it was significant to him (lit., "it was great to me" in the light of his previous discussion, Eccles. 9:11–12). Though **wisdom** had proven **better than strength,** that is, military might (cf. 7:11–12; 9:18; Prov. 21:22), that **poor** wise man received no benefit from his wisdom. His **wisdom** was **despised and his words** were not **heeded,** and he remained poor and unremembered (i.e., unrewarded with wealth or social esteem; cf. Eccles. 9:11).

Wisdom's Value May Be Nullified by a Little Folly (9:17–10:1)

9:17–10:1. After giving the example of the poor wise man whose wisdom did not benefit him (9:13–16) Solomon warned that though wisdom deserves attention, its value can be nullified by a little folly. Alluding to his previous example, Solomon said **The quiet words of the wise are more to be heeded than the shouts of a ruler of fools** because **wisdom is better than weapons of war** (cf. 7:19; 9:16). Playing on the word "good" or "better"—the same Hebrew word *tôḇâh*—and the contrast between "one" and "much," Solomon said that **one sinner destroys much good.** In other words, **a little folly** can destroy the great value of **wisdom**, as **dead flies** in **perfume** ruin it by giving it **a bad smell.** The use of the Hebrew words for **outweighs** and **honor** is another interesting wordplay, for both words are used for weight or value and social esteem.

Wisdom's Value May Be Nullified by a Ruler's Caprice (10:2–7)

Speaking of "errors," literally "sin" (v. 4; cf. "sinner," 9:18), "fool," and "fools" (10:3, 6; cf. "folly," v. 1), Solomon gave another example of how a little folly nullifies the great value of wisdom. Though wisdom suggests ways to maintain one's position at court (vv. 2–4), that position may be subverted by an error of some leader.

10:2–4. Solomon set forth the value of wisdom by stating that a **wise** person has the quality of **heart** and mind that will protect him from danger (cf. 7:12). This is stated in the words **inclines to the right**, which are literally "is at his right hand" (as in the KJV); as is well known, the right hand was the place of protection (cf. Pss. 16:8; 110:5; 121:5). Conversely a **fool lacks** such **sense** which is evidenced by his foolish behavior. Using a common figure for moral behavior—walking in the way (1 Sam. 8:3; 2 Kings 21:21)—Solomon said that **even as he walks along the road, the fool shows everyone how stupid he is.**

Solomon then gave an example of how wisdom can protect one who possesses it. With a deliberate wordplay on the double sense of the Hebrew verb *nûaḥ*, meaning "to leave or abandon" or "to give rest to," Solomon advised that the wisest course when confronted with a king's **anger** is not to **leave** (*tannaḥ*) one's **post** (i.e., not to resign his office; cf. Eccles. 8:3) because calm and cool composure (cf. Prov. 14:30 for a somewhat similar use of the noun "calmness") could **lay great errors** (lit., "sins"; actually it is the anger caused by such sins, a metonymy of cause for effect) **to rest** (*yanniaḥ*; cf. Prov. 16:14 for a similar idea).

10:5–7. Though Solomon affirmed that a wise man's good sense might suggest ways to maintain his position before an angry king (v. 4), he also noted that one's position or job is not always awarded on the basis of merit. The Hebrew word for "errors" in verse 4 means sins, but the word for "error" in verse 5 means an inadvertent mistake, something done without proper consideration (cf. 5:6 where the same word is trans. "mistake"). The word for "ruler" in 10:5 differs from "ruler's" in verse 4. In verse 4 the word for ruler's (*môšēl*) emphasizes one's dominion or reign, whereas in verse 5 the word for ruler (*šallîṭ*) emphasizes one's sovereignty or domineering mastery (the same root is in 8:4 [*šilṭôn*, "supreme"] and 8:9 [*šallaṭ*, "lords it over"]). Solomon stated that he had seen an evil *ra'āh*; cf. 5:13, 16; 6:1) **under the sun** (cf. . . . on 1:3), the sort of error that arises from a ruler, that is, the kind of reversal of roles that results from a ruler's caprice. Solomon had seen **fools** occupying **high positions while the rich** (who were supposedly therefore wise; cf. Prov. 14:24; 19:10) occupied **the low** positions. He also had seen **slaves** riding **on horseback**, a position of honor (cf. Jer. 7:25), **while princes** went **on foot like slaves.** Thus since position was not assigned on the basis of merit but on the basis of a ruler's caprice, the value of wisdom was often nullified.

Wisdom's Value May Be Nullified by Improper Timing (10:8–11)

10:8–9. Verses 8–11, whose figurative language and proverbial character have occasioned a great variety of interpretation, are carefully related to one another. Thus the repetition of the words **snake** and **bitten** at the beginning (v. 8) and "snake bites" at the end (v. 11) forms a bracketing effect (an *inclusio*). Also Solomon repeated the Hebrew word *yiṭrôn* ("profit"; cf. . . . 1:3) in 10:10–11 (rendered "advantage" in v. 10 by NASB and not rendered at all in NIV). Though wisdom has advantages, that gain can be lost when wisdom is not applied or is applied too late.

Moreover, the reference to "ax" (v. 10) serves as a bridge between verse 9b, the last of four proverbs in verses 8–9, and the two contrasting proverbs in verses 10–11. Solomon strung together four proverbs that set forth the potential dangers inherent in representative daily tasks—digging **a pit,** tearing down **a wall,** quarrying **stones,** splitting **logs**—dangers which could only be averted by applying wisdom or prudence.

10:10–11. In log-splitting (v. 9) a man can either use wisdom and sharpen his **ax** or leave it **unsharpened** and exert **more** energy. Applying wisdom to using an ax makes it easier to succeed. "Wisdom has the advantage of giving success" (NASB).

However, in a contrasting proverb (v. 11) Solomon noted that a man's wisdom or skill has **no profit** if it is not applied at the proper time; **if a snake bites before it is charmed,** the **charmer** is in trouble. Thus Solomon showed in this series of proverbs that though wisdom is valuable in dangerous and difficult tasks, its value can be nullified by improper timing.

27

VARIATIONS ON THE THEME OF WISDOM'S STRENGTH AND VULNERABILITY

ECCLESIASTES 9:17–10:20

Graham S. Ogden

Thought Units in Qoheleth 9–10

The task of delimiting units of thought in Qoheleth has been, and remains, notoriously difficult,[1] and this difficulty is felt acutely in the case of chapters 9–10. To review the entire range of opinion on these chapters would consume an inordinate amount of space, but one can reduce the basic issue to that of determining some thematic arrangement of the material, in contrast to a miscellaneous collection of proverbial matter largely devoid of cohesion. A consideration of representative views is called for.

H. L. Ginsberg locates chapters 9–10 in the larger context of 6:10–12:8 in which "the inscrutability of the future" is the theme.[2] More precisely, in 8:16–

From *Vetus Testamentum* 30 (1980): 27–37. Used by permission.

1. O. Eissfeldt, *Einleitung in das Alte Testament* (3rd edn, Tübingen, 1964), p. 669 = E. Tr. *The Old Testament. An Introduction* (Oxford, 1965), p. 494; W. Zimmerli, *Der Prediger* (2nd edn, Göttingen, 1967), p. 131.

2. "The Structure and Contents of the Book of Koheleth," in M. Noth and D. Winton Thomas (ed.), *Wisdom in Israel and in the Ancient Near East, Supplements to VT* 3 (1955), pp. 138–49.

9:16 he sees the certainty of death impelling one to enjoy worldly goods (9:7–10) because success is either illusory (9:11–12) or unattainable (9:13–16). However, the material in 9:17–10:19 is merely "a block of associative digressions" (p. 142, n. 3). Another recent attempt to put these chapters in a wider context comes from A. G. Wright[3] for whom, like Ginsberg, 9:1 develops the theme of man's inability to know the future outlined in 6:10–12. He identifies 9:13–10:15 as a pericope within that larger complex. Thus both Ginsberg and Wright share the identification of a theme for chapters 6–12, as well as agreeing in general terms on the internal division which carry this message, at least as far as 9:16. Their treatment of chapter 10 finds them in disagreement, Ginsberg claiming 9:17–10:19 is digressionary, and Wright seeing them as originally independent but now serving the wider theme. There is much to commend both these attempts to identify a theme in these chapters, although one should note in criticism that man's inability to know his future is an idea implicit in the earlier chapters of the book, for example in 1:17, 2:21, and 3:11, and in the rhetorical questions of 2:19, 3:21, and 4:8. Furthermore, although the stated theme occurs in 9:1, 12 and 10:14, it is no more central to these chapters than in the beginning of the book—the problem posed in 6:10 is raised previously in 1:9–11, 3:15, 22. Indeed, the wide variety of material, in terms of both form and content, in chapters 9–10 makes their precise relationship to the theme "man does not know" difficult to define closely. This is undoubtedly why Ginsberg makes an exception of 9:17–10:14a, 15–19.

The second group of opinions coheres around the view that most of the material in chapters 9–10 consists primarily of collected sayings with only a strictly localized thematic connection. Although there is some overlap with Ginsberg, this view does not seek to identify chapters 9–10 with any particular theme from the wider context. K. Galling[4] is perhaps the best known exponent of the disconnected nature of Qoheleth's material, but more representative is W. Zimmerli[5] whose views are better able to do justice to the varied material before us.

For Zimmerli, 9:1–10 relates to the inevitability of death and the consequent need to seek pleasure while one is able; 9:11–12 shows how human wisdom and strength are at times powerless within the vagaries of human existence. Both comments arise from the inscrutability of God's acts (8:16–17). A change of theme is registered in 9:13–10:3 where wisdom is seen to be vulnerable to small misfortune, while 10:4–20 consists of various individual say-

3. "The Riddle of the Sphinx: The Structure of the Book of Qoheleth," *CBQ* 30 (1968), pp. 313–34; see also G. Castellino, "Qohelet and His Wisdom," *CBQ* 30 (1968), pp. 15–28.

4. "Kohelet-Studien," *ZAW* 50 (1932), pp. 276–99; "Stande und Aufgabe der Kohelet-Forschung," *ThR* 6 (1934), p. 360.

5. *Prediger*, pp. 221–38; "Das Buch Kohelet-Traktat oder Sentenzen-sammlung?" *VT* 24 (1974), pp. 221–30.

ings lacking any common theme. Similar views are held by O. S. Rankin[6] who suggests two separate sections, 1:1–16 and 9:17–10:20. He argues for at least some semblance of order in the material to 9:16 but none at all in 9:17–10:20. R. Gordis[7] suggests that there is a "lack of logical organization" in 10:2–11:6, and O. Eissfeldt (p. 669; E. Tr., p. 494) is left wondering why the collection 9:17–10:20 is placed where it is when it could well have been included anywhere else in the book.

It becomes clear that the latter part of chapter 9 and chapter 10 constitute a difficulty at the level both of delimiting the extent of the larger unit of thought and of defining relationships internally and externally.

A catalogue of suggested limits to thought units in these chapters is informative:

(i)   Castellino (p. 20), 9:11–11:6; J. F. Genung,[8] 9:11–11:6; E. Glasser,[9] 9:11–12:7; E. Podechard,[10] 9:11–11:6.

(ii) Galling,[11] 9:13–16, 9:17–10:3, 10:4–7, 8–11, 12–15, 16–17, 18–20; Gordis (pp. 309–33), 9:13–10:1, 10:2–11:6; W. Johnstone,[12] 9:13–10:4, 10:5–21:7; J. Pedersen,[13] 9:13–10:20; R. B. Y. Scott,[14] 9:13–10:1, 10:2–11:6; Wright (p. 332) 9:13–10:15; Zimmerli,[15] 9:13–15, 9:16–10:3, 10:4–20.

(iii) G. A. Barton,[16] 9:17–10:3, 10:4–20; Eissfeldt (p. 669; E. Tr., p. 494), 10:17–10:20; Ginsberg (p. 142, n. 3), 9:17–10:19; Rankin (p. 77), 9:17–10:20; Zimmerli,[17] 9:17–10:20.

Thus 9:11, 9:13, and 9:17 have been suggested as points at which a new section commences, with the possibility of secondary or sub-units beginning at 10:2, 10:4, and 10:5. A wider variety of concluding points has been suggested—10:15, 10:19, 10:20, 11:6, 12:7.

The difficulty in defining the limits of Qoheleth's thought units is partly related to the question of relationships between the various sub-units, which themselves at times are not easily isolated, and to an overall theme.

6. "The Book of Ecclesiastes," *Interpreter's Bible* 5 (New York and Nashville, 1956), p. 77.
7. *Koheleth: The Man and His World* (3rd edn, New York, 1968), p. 317.
8. *Words of Koheleth* (Boston, 1904), pp. 175–90.
9. *Le Procès du bonheur par Qohelet* (Paris, 1970), pp. 179–87.
10. *L'Ecclésiaste* (Paris, 1912), pp. 142–70.
11. "Kohelet-Studien," pp. 282–97.
12. "'The Preacher' as Scientist," *SJT* 20 (1967), p. 216, n. 1.
13. "Scepticisme israélite," *RHPR* 10 (1930), p. 326.
14. *Proverbs, Ecclesiastes* (Garden City, New York, 1965), pp. 247–52.
15. *Prediger*, pp. 229–38.
16. *The Book of Ecclesiastes* (Edinburgh, 1908), pp. 165–79.
17. "Traktat oder Sentenzensammlung?" p. 228. Note that in this later article he has apparently altered his assessment of the thought unit.

If such an overarching theme as suggested by Ginsberg and Wright is not present, then that potential guide is not operative. However, relationships between sub-units can be ascertained quite well on the basis of local thematic connections expressed in phrases, vocabulary, and a variety of rhetorical features.

If one looks at the suggestion that a major thought unit begins at 9:11 and seeks to identify features which might help delimit the unit as a whole, one is left with little evidence for extending the unit as far as 12:7 as, for example, Glasser does. The poem 12:1–7 is clearly lacking in specific references and other formal criteria which could tie it in with material before 11:8. However, the view that a unit beginning in 9:11 extends as far as 11:6 has some merit in view of the theme of man's lack of knowledge (9:11–12, 10:14, 11:2, 5, 6). If this theme were to be regarded as an important *inclusio*, then we should have one criterion for insisting that these are the limits of the thought unit. Our problem with *inclusio* as a sole criterion (as it would be in this case, for the intervening material is quite disparate in form and content) is that it does not necessarily inform us about the relatedness of statements within those limits. The further apart the *inclusiones* are, the less useful they become as criteria for establishing the limits of a unit. This is well illustrated by the book of Qoheleth as a whole, for it opens and closes with the theme of vanity (1:2 and 12:8), and although the theme is reiterated throughout, it provides little guide to the relationships between the details embraced within those limits. On such a broad scale, therefore, one is forced to generalize about content, and this certainly holds true for 9:11–11:6.

If the longer unit were to begin at 9:11, one would then have to account for the considerable transition in mood and content in 9:13–16. Not only does it have a formal introduction often used elsewhere to mark a change in thought direction (3:10, 16, 4:1, 4, 7, 6:1, 8:10, 9:11); it cites an example similar to another identifiably independent unit in 4:13–16. The task of 9:13–16 is to exemplify wisdom's power, not man's limited knowledge as in 9:11–12. Qoheleth's observation concludes with v. 16 and the view that, even though wisdom may be dismissed by some as of no value, it does have a power of its own which is superior to military force. Zimmerli's decision to conclude the unit at 9:15 and to begin anew at v. 16 because of the first person verb forms[18] ignores the function of v. 16 as a conclusion based on the observation in vv. 13–15. Using the *inclusio ḥokmâh* as a criterion, Wright wishes to include 10:1 in the unit beginning at 9:13 (p. 332). The problem with Wright's position is the importance of the root *ḥkm* in 9:17, 18, 10:1, 2, 10, 12. That is to say, *ḥkm*, if it is an *inclusio*, cannot be restricted to 9:13–10:1, for it extends well into chapter 10.

18. *Prediger*, p. 230.

In my article "The 'Better'-Proverb (*Ṭôb-Spruch*), Rhetorical Criticism and Qoheleth" *JBL* 96 (1977), pp. 489–505, I have sought to establish the importance of the *Ṭôb-Spruch* (T-S) as a rhetorical device in Qoheleth, and to demonstrate the significance of its function as an introductory and concluding element in thought units throughout the book. Thus the T-S of 9:16 expresses the conclusion Qoheleth draws from the observation in vv. 13–15. Using the criteria of content, of introductory and concluding devices, of contrast throughout between "little" and "much/great," and the dominant position given to wisdom, we have a more adequate basis for identifying 9:13–16 as an independent pericope.

The concluding verses of chapter 9 bring together two other T-S (9:17–18). The similarity of 9:16 and 18 with the *inclusiones dbr, ṭwb, smᶜ, ḥkm*, plus the "little-much" contrast, may suggest that the three T-S belong together. However, while the values of the T-S in 9:16 were upheld by Qoheleth against their popular rejection, those same values are made subject to a contrary condition in 9:18 by the adversative *waw*. This suggests that 9:17–18 is not fundamentally linked with the preceding. It certainly does not arise from the observation in 9:13–15, though one should observe that its similarity in other respects with 9:16 is the most likely explanation for its juxtaposition to it. What 9:17 does is to move the discussion in quite a new direction—it upholds the value of wisdom together with its vulnerability to even a small measure of folly. This latter is a theme not met before in quite this way. The reference to folly in 9:17 brings in a theme which does not occur in the previous part of chapter 9 (except at 9:3, *hll*). Indeed, the keywords *ḥokmâh/ḥākām* and *kᵉsîl* are basic both to the T-S in vv. 17–18 and to the verses which follow (cf. *ḥkm*—9:17, 18, 10:1, 2, 10, 12; *ksl*—9:17, 10:2, 12, 15; *skl*—10:1, 3, 6, 13, 14). These factors, together with the rhetorical function of the T-S as an introductory device, require that 9:17–18 be seen as introductory statements of the thesis to be expanded upon in the ensuing material.

The contention in this chapter is that the thesis of wisdom's strength and vulnerability in 9:17–18 is demonstrated by a set of variations on that theme in 10:1–4, 5–7, 8–11, 12–15, 16–20.

Qoheleth 9:17–10:20

In 9:17 Qoheleth draws a comparison between wise words heard in quiet (*dibrê ḥᵃkāmîm bᵉnaḥat nišmāᶜîm*) and a ruler's outburst among fools (*zaᶜᵃqat môšēl bakkᵉsîlîm*), affirming that the former is better. The adverbial elements *bᵉnaḥat* and *bakkᵉsîlîm*, which accompany each of the compared items, heighten the contrast between them and reinforce the claim for wisdom's superiority. The second T-S (*ṭôbâh ḥokmâh mikkᵉlê qᵉrāb*) elevates wisdom above weapons, but an appended clause (*wᵉḥôṭeʾ ʾeḥād yᵉʾabbēd ṭôbâh harbēh*) modifies the values contained within it.[19] Although wisdom is so powerful, it is also vulnerable, for even one sinner (= fool) is able to jeopardize a great deal of good (= wisdom). The two T-S represent a tension—wisdom's superiority is maintained and its limitations acknowledged. The thesis herein contained is then worked out in chapter 10.

The illustration with which chapter 10 opens is of a small insect, a fly, which falls into and contaminates a container of expensive oil. By analogy, says Qoheleth, a little folly may destroy wisdom and honor.[20] Wisdom's vulnerability is set forth again with "one" and "little" contrasting with "much good" and "wisdom and honor."

In 10:2–3 the contrast between the sage and the fool is noted, with the plight of the fool (v. 2b, introduced by the conjunction *w*) further elaborated (v. 3, introduced by *w^egam*). Apart from the contrasts between *ḥkm* and *skl/ksl*, *yāmîn* and *š^emō'l*, the keyword *lēb*, provides an additional link between both verses. It is clear that in the comparison the superiority of the wise is maintained. The fool's conduct proclaims his lack of sense. By upholding this set of values, Qoheleth illustrates the thesis of 9:17.

The following verse (10:4) gives an example of wise conduct as distinct from that of the fool. An irate, and thus foolish, ruler turns upon one of his subjects to whom Qoheleth's advice is that he stand firm, for such prudent action (*marpē'*) will make amends for (*nwḥ*) great sins.

We are now in a position to appreciate the structure and rhetorical features present in these verses which indicate the relationship between 9:17–18 and 10:1–4. They are:

> *Inclusiones*—*nwḥ* (9:17a, 10:4b twice), *mšl* (9:17b, 10:4a), *ḥṭ'* (9:18, 10:4c).
> *Chiasmus*—wisdom's superiority (9:17, 10:2–4), folly's power (9:18b, 10:1).
> *Contrast*—*ḥôṭe' 'eḥād* and *tôbâh harbēh*, *siklût m^e'āṭ* and *ḥokmâh mikkabôd*, *marpē'*, and *ḥ^aṭā'îm g^edôlîm*.
> *Keyword*—*lēb* (10:2–3).

These features allow the conclusion that the delicate balance between wisdom and folly in 9:17–18 is illustrated in 10:1–4, but with the point being made by way of antithesis that even though wisdom is vulnerable (10:1b) it can overcome much folly (= great offences, 10:4). This structure is more than a mere literary device; it in fact brackets the sub-unit, thus supporting the thesis of wisdom's superiority. To do as Zimmerli does[21] and break the unit at 10:3

---

19. G. E. Bryce, "'Better'-Proverbs: An Historical and Structural Study," L. C. McGaughy (ed.), *Book of Seminar Papers* 2 (Missoula, 1972), p. 349.

20. An apparent unwillingness on the part of the versions to accept this text has led to their attempt to preserve wisdom's position unsullied. Compare the LXX, "a little wisdom is more precious than great glory or folly."

21. *Prediger*, pp. 230–32; so also G. A. Barton, p. 169.

cannot be justified on the basis of the range of rhetorical features identified above. Furthermore, to link v. 4 with the succeeding verses is problematic in view of the change from *mšl* to *šlṭ*, and the introductory formula of v. 5 which elsewhere (5:13, 6:1) marks a point of transition. The vocabulary of vv. 5–7 is also quite distinctive within the limits of chapters 9–10. Apart from *skl* in v. 6 and *ḥlk*[22] in v. 7, this distinctiveness and the *inclusio r'ḥ* in vv. 5–7 calls for their isolation as a clearly definable sub-unit.

The evil which Qoheleth identifies (v. 5) is set out in parallel statements in vv. 6–7:

folly		in high places	
	rich		in a low place
slaves		on horseback	
	princes		on the ground

The expected order of wise leadership is here reversed and, in lieu, slaves (= fools) are in positions of authority. This situation is likened in v. 5b to a mistake made by a ruler, and the simile[23] provides an important clue to the meaning of the passage. The use of *š^egāgāh* indicates that the ruler has committed an *unintentional* error. Though a person in a position of authority ought to be wise, *even he* is prone to mistakes (= folly) on occasion, and with drastic consequences, for a fool may take his place. The reversal which constitutes the "evil" here—folly in high places—illustrates the thesis of 9:18, the vulnerability of the wise.

The change in subject matter and form suggests that vv. 8–11 constitute another sub-unit. The formal change is that of a series of four participial phrases which share in general their subject matter to the extent that they have to do with the use of metal tools in digging or cutting. This subject matter occasions distinctive vocabulary with *ḥokmāh* the only word shared with the rest of the chapter. In each example an imperfect verb form denotes a potential danger in the activity specified. Verses 10–11 are two conditional clauses related by their contrast between *yitrôn* (v. 10) and *'ên yitrôn* (v. 11). These verses are not an isolated pair for they are bound to vv. 8–9 by two rhetorical features: the *inclusiones nḥš* and *nšk* in 10:8, 11, and the bridge reference to the iron tool (*barzel*) in v. 10 which is also implicit in vv. 8–9. Wright's suggestion (p. 332) that there is a chiasmus in what he identifies as six pictures of the unexpected in vv. 8–11 cannot be sustained.

---

22. A. G. Wright (p. 332) suggests *ḥlk* is an *inclusio* in v. 3 and v. 7. Its function as *inclusio* needs further supportive evidence for the suggestion to be taken seriously.

23. Gordis (p. 319) denies that the *kaph* is other than asseverative. His contention that the clause is otherwise meaningless is here disputed.

The structure of this sub-unit is important in setting forward the theme of vulnerability. Although wisdom does help one to succeed (10:10b), the predominant message of the unit is of the constant danger to which one is exposed. The balance for the moment tilts toward the thesis of 9:18b, and in doing so provides a sub-unit which offsets the superiority of wisdom in 10:2–4. Furthermore, 10:8–11 continues the motif of 10:1 in which a small creature has power to threaten the well-being of something much larger. Wisdom's vulnerability is thus forcefully portrayed.

The pendulum swings back again in vv. 12–15. As was the case in 10:2–3 the wise is briefly but favourably presented in contrast to the fool whose negative position is set forth in some detail. Thus 10:2a parallels 10:12a and 10:2b–3 is aligned with 10:12b–15. Whereas in 10:2–3 *lēb* was a keyword, here *dābār* and *peh* have that function. Throughout, the purpose is to show the priority of wisdom over folly as in 9:17 and the introductory *dibrê-ḥᵃkā-mîm* and *dibrê-pî-ḥākām* cement the relationship. Additionally, the motif of a "little" being more powerful than "much" (9:18, 10:1, 4, 10) is implicit in 10:14 with the use of the Hiphil of *rbh*. Within the larger unit as defined in this chapter, the theme of man's inability to know is not present apart from this particular sub-unit where it is reiterated in 10:14, 15. Yet we note that here the context is of the fool who is *unaware* that knowledge of the future is hidden from mankind. This is slightly different from the more general affirmation that man cannot know the future, the theme of 9:1, 12. Wright's suggestion (p. 332) that *ʿîr* is an *inclusio* in 9:14 and 10:15 may be of significance in accounting for the location of 10:12–15 in the vicinity of 9:13–16, but it cannot have great value within the limits of 9:17–10:20.

The remaining verses of chapter 10 present us with a difficulty in that the various criteria which have been available to us thus far to tie the sub-units together and to the thesis of 9:17–18 are not so evident. The subject matter of 10:16–20 differs from the surrounding material and thus the connections at the level of vocabulary are not present (though some vocabulary in 10:16–20 is found in 9:11–12—*lḥm*, *ʿîr*, *ʿēt*). The frequent use of *ḥākām/ḥokmâh*, *sākāl* and *kᵉsîl* in 9:17–10:15 does not typify 10:16–20, though wise and foolish actions are described.

The major rhetorical feature available as a criterion is the motif already encountered in 10:1a, 11—that of the small animal or insect representing a potential source of danger. On this basis we are able to see how a *motif* has been used as the *inclusio* for the whole chapter; the fly in v. 1, the serpent in vv. 8, 11, and the bird in v. 20.

More than in any other sub-unit in this chapter, 10:16–20 consists of material marked by a variety of form and content, and interpretation of its component parts is amongst the most contested in the book. Thus it is difficult to define precise relationships within the unit apart from verses which are structurally parallel.[24]

_____

24. Zimmerli, *Prediger*, p. 237.

The Woe-form and its antithesis in vv. 16–17 differ in structure from those known in prophetic material, lacking the participial phrases which are a regular feature in that context (cf. also Prov. 8:34, 14:21, 16:20, 28:14, 29:18). The structure of both verses is identical:

ʾî-lāk	*ʾereṣ šemmalkēk nāʿar*	*wᵉśarayik babbōqer*	*yōʾkēlû*
ʾašrayik	*ʾereṣ šemmalkēk ben-ḥôrîm*	*wᵉśārayik bāʿēt*	*yōʾkēlû*

This structural identity heightens the contrast being drawn between the two situations envisaged. Implicit in v. 16 is foolish action on the part of one king, over against the more appropriate action (= wisdom) of another king and his administration. While there may be some sociological overtones[25] in these contrasting sentences, the juxtaposition of the two is co-ordinated with the contrast in 9:17 between wise and foolish behavior. The folly or laziness of those in v. 16 is picked up in a traditional saying in v. 18 (cf. Prov. 10:4). Its use in this context is to demonstrate that laziness or folly brings dire consequences and thus constitutes a threat or danger to wisdom (cf. 9:18), as the king in both clauses is expected to act responsibly and thus wisely.

If there were a way of establishing more positively that vv. 16, 18 were thematically connected—the danger of folly—we might posit that vv. 17, 19 were similarly related to show the value of wisdom. The question whether v. 19[26] ought to be understood as a negative assessment (so Wright, p. 332, Barton, p. 175, Rankin, p. 80) or in a more positive manner appears insoluble owing to the lack of criteria. However, in the light of the thesis that 9:17–18 provides the framework of thought for 10:1–20, there is nothing in v. 19 which would demand its attachment to the theme of folly's threat to wisdom. At the very least we must allow its neutral position[27] and thus favor its alliance with v. 17 (*ʾašrê* accords well with *śḥq* and *śmḥ* of v. 19). Thus, the good things of life which God provides (5:19) are to be enjoyed appropriately.

Chapter 10 concludes with an injunction against cursing the king. The precise connection between this verse and vv. 16–19 is uncertain, though Zimmerli suggests (*Prediger*, p. 238) that it concludes vv. 16–17. In its wisdom context, as distinct from its legal context (Exod. 22:28), a motive clause accompanies the injunction and informs our understanding of it. Cursing the

25. Gordis, p. 327; R. B. Y. Scott, p. 251, suggests a similar class-conscious comment in 10:5–7.

26. The problems in the interpretation of this verse are notorious and are reflected in the translation attempts of the versions. The issue focuses particularly about the verb *ʿānâh* and its various meanings ("answer, obey, submit, hear, testify").

27. Zimmerli, *Prediger*, p. 238.

king or wealthy person, even when done in secret,[28] is a risky business because one is apt to be discovered and duly punished. Thus cursing the ruler becomes folly, and the principle is illustrated by way of a reference to a bird carrying the message to the king (4 Ezra 5:6, Ahiqar 7:96–99), the motif providing the *inclusio* which binds the chapter together.

It would appear that a measure of irony is present in this the concluding statement of chapter 10, for in 9:17 Qoheleth has given priority to the words of the wise heard in quiet (*b^enahat*). This concluding verse powerfully portrays wisdom's vulnerability, for the secret cursing of a ruler, a critical and thus foolish word spoken *quietly*, even during one's sleep, may well prove to be one's undoing. Further factors tie 10:20 to the preceding. In 10:12 the *dibrê-pî-hākām*, which provides a bridge back to 9:17 and *dibrê-h^akākmîm*, also provides a bridge forward to 10:20 by virtue of the keyword *dbr* (9:17, 10:12, 13, 14, 20). In addition, these same points exhibit a thematic connection with each other in the potential destruction of even the wise man should he utter a foolish word.

By means of the *inclusiones* 10:1, 8–11, 20, material which appears at first to be disparate and unconnected is held together. The theme of wisdom's vulnerability resident in the *inclusio* stands over against and balances the power of wisdom, these being the themes of the T-S in 9:17, 18 with which the unit began. Each of the sub-units, 10:1–4, 5–7, 8–11, 12–15, 16–20, relates in a quite individual way to the thesis of 9:17–18 portraying wisdom as that indisputably powerful force which at times finds itself so vulnerable to even a small amount of folly. The irony of this situation is poignantly brought out by using such examples as the fly, snake, or small bird in contrast to a human wisdom which under normal circumstances is more powerful than military hardware. There is, therefore, a clearly discernible relationship internal to 9:17–10:20, appreciation of which takes us some way further in understanding Qoheleth's method of presenting his material.

---

28. O. Loretz, *Qohelet und der alte Orient* (Freiburg, Basel and Vienna, 1964), p. 25, n. 31.

28

PRINCIPLES OF FINANCIAL INVESTMENT
ECCLESIASTES 11:1–8

David A. Hubbard

P ut in a nutshell the *theme* of the passage is this: we should use wisdom boldly and carefully, cannily yet humbly, taking joy from life while remembering that our days of joy are limited by the certainty of death. The structure and movement of the text can be analyzed as follows:

Admonitions to diversity in investments and other activities	1–2
Take the risk	1a
Expect a return	1b
Divide the risk	2a
Hedge against disaster	2b
Examples of lessons learned from observation	3–4
Clouds	3a
Trees	3b
Wind	4a
Clouds	4b

Reprinted from *Ecclesiastes, Song of Solomon,* Communicator's Commentary, David A. Hubbard, 1991, Word, Inc., Dallas, Texas. Used with permission.

Make the most of what you have, counseled the wise man, and you will find *the path to prosperity.* His first proverb that illustrated this is familiar yet often misunderstood:

> Cast your bread upon the waters,
> For you will find it after many days.
>
> *Eccles. 11:1*

The misunderstanding is that we usually take this casting of bread as a picture of charity. "Do good deeds and you will be rewarded" is a customary interpretation.

But the Preacher's practical shrewdness and the context within the book suggest something else—namely, advice not about charity but about wise investment. Where did one gain the highest return on one's money? In investments overseas: in the rich export and import business of the Mediterranean ports like Tyre and Sidon. "*Bread upon the waters*" that you will "*find*" "*after many days*" was Ecclesiastes' way of describing investment in those lucrative mercantile enterprises where fortunes were to be made.

There was risk involved, of course, and in the second admonition, the Teacher urged his students to diversify their investments to hedge against such risk:

> Give a serving to seven, and also to eight,
> For you do not know what evil will be on the earth.
>
> *Eccles. 11:2*

Misfortune and calamity (here as usual in Ecclesiastes called "*evil*"; see. . . 2:21) are part of life. Who knows what crop will fail, what ship will be seized by coastal pirates, what merchant will abscond with the profits? Spread your investments ("*serving*" is lit. "lot" or "portion"; Heb. *ḥēleq,* see at 2:10) widely—to seven or eight places—so that no one or two tragedies can wipe you out. That advice was crucial to the path to prosperity.

"*Seven or eight*" is a Hebrew numerical formula called x, x + 1. It occurs frequently in Proverbs (chaps. 6, 30) and in the first two chapters of Amos. Here it is not to be taken literally but means "plenty and more than plenty," "the widest possible diversification within the guidelines of prudence. . . ." Seven means "plenty," and eight means, "Go a bit beyond that."

Close observation as well as wise investment was what the Preacher pre scribed as part of his formula for fruitfulness (vv. 3–4). Although some of his countrymen may have been paying too much attention to the actions of the "*wind*" and the "*clouds*"—not as observers of the weather, but as practitioners of magic, Koheleth believed that certain observable trends in the patterns of wind and rain had to be right for them to do their work successfully, especially their sowing and reaping (v. 4).

Learn to watch the weather, Koheleth commanded. It is God's work. He will do his work on schedule, and you must seek to understand it.

> If the clouds are full of rain,
> They empty themselves on the earth;
> And if a tree falls to the south or to the north,
> In the place where the tree falls, there it shall lie.
>
> *Eccles. 11:3*

The processes of creation go on without your worry, and you could not change them if you tried. So keep your eye on those processes and get on with your work, Ecclesiastes urged.

Contemplation of the right time or the suitable season will result in hedging against costly mistakes that come when one harvests ("*reaps*") or "*sows*" at the wrong time.

> He who observes the wind will not sow;
> And he who regards the clouds will not reap.
>
> *Eccles. 11:4*

The wrong "*wind*" will blow away the seed; misgauging the possibility of rain ("*clouds*") can either make us hurry the harvest prematurely or tarry to the point where we miss its peak. *Rain* is the key here as in other semidesert parts of the world. Its importance in these verses is signaled by the fact that "*clouds*" are mentioned at the beginning and end. The passage is literally enveloped in "*clouds*" (vv. 3–4).

As much as wisdom drawn from observation helped them learn important things, there were other things that wisdom could not tell them. These limits were drummed home in the triple beat of "*you do not know*" (vv. 5–6). Koheleth warned his pupils not to try to guess at *all* of God's ways, just because patterns in creation taught them *some*. They are as mysterious as the act of conception:

> As you do not know what is the way of the wind
> Or how the bones grow in the womb of her who is with child,
> So you do not know the works of God who makes everything.

Eccles. 11:5

The chief question here is whether Koheleth was listing two or just one unknowable reality. The two (so NKJV, NIV, JB, NASB) are the "*way of the wind*"—what causes it, why it blows sometimes and not others, and what determines its force and direction—and "*how the bones grow in the womb*" of a pregnant woman ("*bones*" stand for embryo, the unborn child; see Isa. 66:14 and Prov. 14:30 where "*bones*" describe the whole person). If just one unknowable reality is in view, it would be the question of how the "life-spirit" (so Crenshaw and Fox) "comes to the bones in the womb of a woman with child" (RSV). To choose between the two options is almost impossible. If the double-mystery interpretation is adopted, "*everything*" should probably be read "*both*," as frequently in Koheleth (see 2:14). The combined mystery of wind (or spirit; Heb. *rú^{a}ḥ* can mean either) anticipates Jesus' word to Nicodemus:

> "The wind blows where it wishes, and you hear the sound of it, but cannot tell where it comes from and where it goes. So is everyone who is born of the Spirit."

John 3:8

Let God take care of his mysteries and you take care of your work, was the Preacher's conclusion:

> In the morning sow your seed,
> And in the evening do not withhold your hand;
> For you do not know which will prosper,
> Either this or that,
> Or whether both alike will be good.

Eccles. 11:6

"*Morning*" and "*evening*" seem to be a *merism*, embracing the whole day. "*Sow your seed*" diligently and abundantly is the gist of this admonition. The reason for the diligence ("*for*") is that the mystery of which seed grows and how it does ("*prospers*"; Heb. *kāshēr*, see 10:10; Esth. 8:5, means lit. to be right or proper and is the root of the familiar Jewish word *kōsher*) is in God's hands and cannot be known to us. The limits of our wisdom are a catalyst to industry not despair. Verse 6 is the counterpart to verses 1–2: both speak of hedging against the ups and downs of life that we "*do not know*" about and cannot control. The sphere of activity in the beginning verses seems to be mercantile investment in export and import overseas; the final verse uses the language of agriculture. We cannot be certain of the literalness of either. The points are boldness, diversification, and hard work—a common sense that applies to almost every field of endeavor.

So alongside the path to prosperity, the wise Preacher lined out *the road to joy.* Find the beauty in every day, was his simple advice in the conclusion to this remarkable passage:

> Truly the light is sweet,
> And it is pleasant for the eyes to behold the sun.
>
> *Eccles. 11:7*

Reminded of life's fragility and the limits of our understanding of it, he encouraged his friends to celebrate every hour of daylight. "*Sweet*" is a strong word picturing the exquisite joy that each new day can bring: joy like the taste of honey (Judg. 14:18), like a kiss (Song of Sol. 2:3), or like the attraction of God's word (Ps. 19:10). "*Pleasant*" (lit. "good") depicts the blessings that the gift of each day of sunlight offers.

There is an urgency to this celebration, noted the wise Professor, because *death is coming* and lasts so long:

> But if a man lives many years,
> And rejoices in them all,
> Yet let him remember the days of darkness,
> For they will be many.
> All that is coming is vanity.
>
> *Eccles. 11:8*

Enjoy the tasks at hand; savor each bit of food and drink; share your joys with the wife of your youth. Make the most of what you have, Ecclesiastes has urged, because the "*days of darkness*" are coming when your enjoyment will cease. Death will pull the blinds and black out the light of life.

These words on prudent investment, dedicated labor, and daily joy reprise the final alternative conclusion of 9:7–10, where the closing admonition urges its hearers to give themselves wholeheartedly to life's varied labors: "Whatever your hand finds to do, do it with your might" (9:10). The reason for the command is the one given in 11:8: the rate of unemployment in the grave is precisely 100 percent.

DEATH,
AN IMPETUS FOR LIFE
ECCLESIASTES 12:1–8

Barry C. Davis

In the Book of Ecclesiastes the author described his search for the key to the meaning of life. That search, however, became an exercise in futility because the more he sought for the answers to life, the more he discovered that life itself is unfair, that human wisdom is woefully insufficient, and that death continually laughed in his face. Furthermore he realized that of those three barriers—injustice, ignorance, and death—death by far is the most devastating. As Fuerst wrote, "Death is clearly the major problem, which intensifies and exacerbates all others; the spectre of death mocks the brave plans of the living. Man cannot argue with this spectre, and cannot combat it. It will win in the end."[1]

Death has a voracious, insatiable appetite. Much like a vicious animal, it silently stalks its prey and then strikes with great fury and often little warning. It tears asunder hopes and dreams, and declares that life itself is "vanity,"

From *Bibliotheca Sacra* 148 (1991): 298–318. Used by permission.

1. Wesley J. Fuerst, *The Books of Ruth, Esther, Ecclesiastes, The Song of Songs, Lamentations: The Five Scrolls* (Cambridge: Cambridge University Press, 1975), p. 151.

"futility," "meaninglessness," or emptiness" (הֶבֶל). Thus death "can make a man hate life, not because he wants to die, but because it renders life so futile."[2]

Since death cannot be circumvented, Solomon argued that the key to life and living is to be found in facing death and dying. Going to a wake will help one become awake to the realities of life (7:2, 4). Perhaps to his surprise, Solomon discovered that the meaning of life can be found only by facing the inevitable reality of death.

Ecclesiastes includes numerous references to death and dying.[3] The most thorough treatment on the process and finality of death is in 12:1–8, a passage that graphically depicts the decay of life with its frailty, fear, and ultimately its finality. Before discussing this passage six principles on death and life will be presented.

Principles on the Death-Life Phenomenon

Principle One: All die (2:14–16; 3:19–22; 9:3). There is an inescapable finality to death; "the inclusiveness of the grave [is] universal."[4] Whether human or animal, wise or foolish, righteous or unrighteous, clean or unclean, sacrificer or nonsacrificer, good or bad, swearer or the one who refuses to swear oaths, each one must face the fate of death. Being a human may have its advantages over being an animal, and being wise may have its advantages over being foolish in being able to live longer. Yet ultimately death functions as the great equalizer. Thus the one certainty of life is death.[5]

Principle Two: Death has certain advantages over life (4:1–3; 7:1–2; 26). In life, wickedness abounds; in death, there is no suffering and there are no snares to entrap a person. In life, there is constant oppression, often with none to offer comfort; in death, there is a sense of escape. For the living, there is seldom relief—the innocent are unable to "throw off an oppressive yoke, and in the absence of hope, life becomes intolerable."[6] Contemplating these

---

2. J. Stafford Wright, "The Interpretation of Ecclesiastes," in *Classical Evangelical Essays in Old Testament Interpretation,* ed. Walter C. Kaiser, Jr. (Grand Rapids: Baker Book House, 1972), p. 143.

3. 2:14–16; 3:2, 19–22; 4:1–3; 5:15–16; 6:3–4, 6; 7:1–2, 4, 17, 26; 8:8, 10, 12–13; 9:2–3, 4–6, 10–12; 12:1–7.

4. J. Barton Payne, *The Theology of the Older Testament* (Grand Rapids: Zondervan Publishing House, 1971), p. 453.

5. Ecclesiastes does not soften the harsh reality of death. In fact little by way of a theology of the afterlife is presented, leaving it to be understood primarily as a mystery. Moreover, when the subject of the afterlife is addressed (9:5–6, 10), it is presented as a contrasting existence to the present life, as a place where all earthly experiences cease (Michael A. Eaton, *Ecclesiastes: An Introduction and Commentary* [Downers Grove, IL: InterVarsity Press, 1983], p. 129). Furthermore even though at death the human spirit returns to God (12:7), no one is able to show what that existence will be like (3:21).

6. James L. Crenshaw, "The Shadow of Death in Qoheleth," in *Israelite Wisdom,* ed. John G. Gammie et al. (Missoula, MT: Scholars Press, 1978), p. 208.

truths, Solomon concluded that death is to be preferred to life and nonexistence to either death or life.[7] The quest to find meaning to life by investigating life itself, therefore, becomes a hopeless and vain effort.[8]

Principle Three: Death cannot be avoided, but it is best not to act foolishly and to rush it (3:2; 6:6; 7.17; 8:8, 12–13; 9:11–12). Humans desire to control death and, to a limited extent, they are able to forestall it. They are capable of acting in ways that would seem to hasten death on the one hand or to extend life on the other (7:17; 8:12–13). Yet typically death happens without regard to people's plans. In the ultimate sense, it is controlled by God (3:2; 9:11–12).

Remarkably, despite principle two (that death has certain advantages over life), the author of Ecclesiastes never encouraged the shortening of life, by either unintentional or intentional means. To the contrary, he urged people to refrain from wickedness or foolishness which conceivably could hasten the end of their lives (7:17). Furthermore he avoided offering suicide as an option—a lure which "would seem irresistible for one who hates life and falls into despair's vise-like grip."[9] Avoiding such extremes, he offered principles four and five as positive affirmations of life in the face of death.

Principle Four: Studying the reality of death can be instructive on how to live life to the fullest (7:4; 12:1–7). "The mind of the wise is in the house of mourning" rather than in "the house of pleasure" (7:4). Such a perspective forces the individual to face the reality of death toward which all life inevitably points. A soberness or an attitude of reflection thereby is thrust on the individual. "Sorrow penetrates the heart, draws the thought upwards, purifies, transforms."[10] By advocating the study of death, Qohelet challenged his readers to face life in light of their mortality. Also he urged them to consider their fate early in life (12:1) while there is still time to make a difference in how they live. The longer the delay, the more old age will rob them of the ability to make changes necessary to live life to the fullest to the glory of God (vv. 1–5).

---

7. Qohelet's conclusion regarding the preference of nonexistence over present existence appears on the surface to be at variance with the Old Testament Israelite's aversion to Sheol, the place of the dead. Knudson states that "the Israelites looked forward to it [Sheol] with unconcealed dread. Almost any kind of earthly existence was to be preferred to it" (Albert C. Knudson, *The Religious Teaching of the Old Testament* [New York: Abingdon Press, 1918], p. 390). Qohelet, however, did not embrace the place of the dead as the place to be. Rather, he preferred nonsuffering as the "place" to be. The dead and the never-alive do not face the miseries of this life. Their fate, moreover, is not a question mark but a reality; it is not something to be feared by the child of God but something to be experienced. (Compare principle five in which Qohelet argued that there are advantages to being alive when compared to being dead.)

8. J. Coert Rylaarsdam, *The Proverbs, Ecclesiastes, The Song of Solomon,* The Layman's Bible Commentary (Richmond, VA: John Knox Press, 1908), p. 110. See Ecclesiastes 1:13–2:11.

9. Crenshaw, "The Shadow of Death in Qoheleth," p. 210.

10. Franz Delitzsch, *Commentary on the Song of Songs and Ecclesiastes,* Biblical Commentary on the Old Testament, trans. M. C. Easton (Grand Rapids: Zondervan Publishing House, 1988), p. 315.

Principle Five: Life has certain advantages over death (9:4–6, 10). While one is alive, there is a hope of finding meaning to life and the possibility of attaining success in life that carries beyond the grave. Qohelet illustrated this truth by maintaining that even the lowest of the low (i.e., the dog)[11] that is alive is better off than the greatest of the great (i.e., the lion)[12] that is dead (9:4). By this contrast he reinforced the superiority of life to death. Whereas life offers hope, death shatters all dreams. Death allows no further opportunity for obtaining any reward in this life or the next.

Principle Six: Living solely for this life is meaningless (5:15–16; 6:3–5; 8:10). Securing all possible physical possessions (wealth, health, and family) and religious credits does nothing to ensure an enduring reward or a meaningful existence after the grave. Riches in fact deceive the individual who places his or her trust in them (5:13–16). They are inherently unsatisfying—they are never enough; someone always desires to take them away; and they produce worry and misery in this life. Riches also are temporary—they provide no true security. They cannot be taken into the next life; they are as fleeting as the wind.

Having a long life with many descendants (6:3–5) does not guarantee earthly satisfaction, much less eternal rewards. The joy of children's laughter may fade through the years and children's love for their father may turn to resentment or apathy—the resultant tragedy being that none of a man's children may care enough even to save face by giving him a decent burial.[13] Such a man, as Kidner states, would "have the things men dream of—which in Old Testament terms meant children by the score, and years of life by the thousand—and still depart unnoticed, unlamented and unfulfilled."[14]

These tragic situations are compounded by the fact that even if an individual is religious, he is quickly forgotten after he dies (8:10).[15] The seemingly solid permanence of this life fades quickly into the shadowy, elusive specter of the next.

---

11. Crenshaw describes the Hebrew view of "dog" as follows: "The lowly cur [9:4b], restricted to a life of scavenging on the perimeters of human existence, functioned as a term of opprobrium. The epithet 'dog,' was hurled in the faces of male prostitutes, who belonged, in the speaker's opinion, outside the domain of human beings (Deut. 23:18–19). The term also became a means of self-abnegation, particularly in the presence of nobility (1 Sam. 24:14)" ("The Shadow of Death in Qoheleth," p. 209).

12. In direct contrast to the dog, which was despised by the Hebrews, the lion enjoyed an exalted status. "To the Jews the lion was the mightiest of beasts, having a king's regal bearing (Prov. 30:29–31). Thus it symbolized leadership (Gen. 49:9, 10; Num. 24:9)" (Walter A. Elwell, ed. *Baker Encyclopedia of the Bible*, 2 vols. [Grand Rapids: Baker Book House, 1988], 1:107–8).

13. Eichrodt argues that the Israelites attached much significance to having a proper burial. He states that they saw a direct relationship between the absence or inadequacy of a burial and the realization of a less desirable position in the afterlife (Walther Eichrodt, *Theology of the Old Testament*, trans. J. A. Baker, 2 vols. [Philadelphia: Westminster Press, 1961, 1967], 2:212).

14. Derek Kidner, *The Message of Ecclesiastes* (Downers Grove, IL: InterVarsity Press, 1976), p. 59.

15. This verse may be understood either as focusing solely on the wicked who in some way make a pretense of being religious or as presenting the wicked in the first half and the righteous

An Introduction to 12:1–8 on Death and Life

Many attempts have been made to unify Ecclesiastes 12:1–8 under one analogical scheme.[16] Some scholars have advocated that the passage describes physiological changes. Others have suggested that it pictures a funeral, and still others have indicated that it depicts a ruined house. The wisest approach seems to be that suggested by Gordis who maintains that "most plausibly, old age is pictured here without one line of thought being maintained throughout."[17] Fuerst concurs, stating that "it is better not to insist on . . . the presence of just one dominant figure of speech."[18] Perhaps Solomon saw death and dying as such debilitating and devastating events that he determined to portray them through a multiplicity of analogies with great rapidity to ensure that the thrust of his message was clearly understood.

Because of the diversity of illustrative material in the passage, it is necessary to analyze each of the images separately to determine its specific point of reference.[19] In doing so, the various conundrums will be clarified and the integrity of the passage maintained.[20]

The passage is framed by references to God as the Originator of life. Despite the inequities of life and the terrors of death, God is ever the Creator of both the living (v. 1)[21] and the dead (v. 7). God's sovereignty is thus recognized as a regulating element in all human activities. If God is present at the beginning and the ending of life, He most certainly is there throughout the totality of life. God thus can give meaning to an otherwise meaningless existence; He can even help individuals make sense out of the senselessness of death.

To aid the flow of thought through the passage, Qohelet employed three times the temporal marker עַד אֲשֶׁר ("before") (vv. 1–2, 6) to denote the transitions between the temporal-psychological shifts in the passage. While signaling a new thought, the words also recall the command of verse 1, "Remember also your Creator." The primary activity to undertake throughout all phases of life is to consider God and His involvement in the life-death phenomenon.

---

in the second half. For a discussion of these two positions see Delitzsch, *Commentary on the Song of Songs and Ecclesiastes*, pp. 345–47, and Crenshaw, *Ecclesiastes: A Commentary* (Philadelphia: Westminster Press, 1987), p. 154.

16. For a discussion of some of the more common approaches toward unification, see Delitzsch, *Commentary on the Song of Songs and Ecclesiastes*, and Robert Gordis, *Koheleth—The Man and His World* (New York: Schocken Books, 1968).

17. Gordis, *Koheleth—The Man and His World*, p. 339.

18. Fuerst, *The Books of Ruth, Esther, Ecclesiastes, The Song of Songs, Lamentations: The Five Scrolls*, p. 152.

19. R. N. Whybray, *Ecclesiastes*, The New Century Bible Commentary (Grand Rapids: Wm. B. Eerdmans Publishing Co., 1989), pp. 163–64.

20. Kidner, *The Message of Ecclesiastes*, p. 101.

21. See below for a discussion of the arguments for and against בּוֹרְאֶיךָ as a reference to God as Creator.

The Days before the End (12:1)

"Remember also" (וּזְכֹר) provides a transition from the injunction to live life to the fullest because it is short and the future is uncertain (11:1–10) to a serious enjoinder to live life wisely precisely because it is short and the future is certain (12:1–7). That future certainty is the fact that every individual will die. Furthermore the process of dying is an experience filled not with pleasure but with sorrow.

"Remember" (זְכֹר) is the most appropriate choice for this solemn religious adjuration.[22] Though the *Qal* form of this verb normally refers "to inner mental acts, either with or without reference to concomitant external acts,"[23] the context of this passage (and of the entire book) implies that action subsequent to the mental activity must be undertaken. Readers are challenged to remember, not for the sake of reminiscing but for the purpose of revolutionizing their lives, bringing them into conformity with God's eternal and sovereign plan.

Various commentators have sought to emend בּוֹרְאֶיךָ ("your Creator") in the Masoretic Text to read "your well" or "your cistern"—euphemistic terms for one's wife.[24] These commentators argue that the verse is recommending "the enjoyment of marital relations."[25] Others have suggested "your pit" as a possible alternative, thereby implying the grave. Still others have offered "your vigor, well-being."[26] These options are similar in phonics but not in orthography.[27]

Though there is no textual support for these alternative readings,[28] those who recommend an emended text do so because they believe that an "allusion to God the Creator ill fits this context."[29] However, strong arguments based on the context may be made in favor of the reading "your Creator." First, in 11:5, God is first mentioned since 9:7. Then the Person of God is kept before the minds of the readers in the concluding verses of the book (11:5, 9; 12:1, 7, 13–14). Second, the reference to God provides an effective inclusio to the discussion of death, picturing God both as the One from whom life comes (v. 1) and as the One to whom life returns (v. 7). Third,

---

22. Gordis, *Koheleth—The Man and His World*, p. 340.

23. Theological Wordbook of the Old Testament, ed. R. Laird Harris, Gleason L. Archer, Jr., and Bruce K. Waltke, 2 vols. (Chicago: Moody Press, 1980), s.v. "זָכַר," by Andrew Bowling, 1:241.

24. Proverbs 5:15, 18 presents this euphemistic use of the term בְּאֵרֶךָ.

25. Both Whybray and Gordis discuss and reject this view that requires an emended text (Whybray, *Ecclesiastes*, p. 163, and Gordis, *Koheleth—The Man and His World*, p. 340).

26. Crenshaw discusses these various alternatives and selects "your wife" as his preferred translation (*Ecclesiastes: A Commentary*, pp. 184–85).

27. Kidner, *The Message of Ecclesiastes*, p. 100.

28. Eaton, *Ecclesiastes: An Introduction and Commentary*, p. 148.

29. Crenshaw, *Ecclesiastes: A Commentary*, p. 184.

though in 11:9–10 Qohelet urged his readers to enjoy the pleasures of life, he counterbalanced that charge by a solemn warning to remember the judgment of God. To shift away from that God-oriented perspective in 12:1 to encourage the embracing of one's wife would be contrary to his argument.[30] Fourth, remembering one's "grave" or one's "well-being" might be shown to fit the context of 12:1–7, but their use would weaken the impact of the text.

In contrast to the alternative renderings, the term בּוֹרְאֶיךָ, a probable plural of majesty,[31] is highly appropriate in this context. Since the theme of 12:1–8 is death, the end of physical life, what better way is there for expressing the nonfinality of that death than to remind the readers that God is Creator? Death is pictured not as the end but rather as the beginning of an everlasting existence.

Readers are to remember God early in their lives ("in the days of your youth")[32] "because childhood and the prime of life are fleeting" (11:10). As the days of one's youth pass quickly, the onset of the aging process brings with it a decline that impacts the vigor and drive of one's life.[33] Pleasure and hope are inversely proportional to age. Thus people ought to turn to God while there is still time to discover the meaning of life and alter the course of their lives.[34] Goldberg suggests the intent behind Qohelet's concern as follows: "We are encouraged . . . to commit ourselves to our Creator while we have our wits about us, while we can still enjoy life, and before we lose the fullest capacity to even think of God's purposes and desires."[35]

In verse 1 the first of the three עַד אֲשֶׁר ("before") temporal clauses, "before the evil days come," highlights the time of life before the onslaught of death's decay is noticeable. This summarizes in an overview fashion what is described in detail in verses 2–7, namely, that in his dying the individual will have no delight.

---

30. Qohelet commended spousal love-making in 9:9 in a somewhat less somber context. To reintroduce it here would be an unnecessary (and incongruous) redundancy.

31. Whybray suggests that בּוֹרְאֶיךָ is a plural of majesty (*Ecclesiastes*, p. 163); Gesenius says that the singular should be read (*Gesenius' Hebrew Grammar*, ed. E. Kautzsch and A. E. Cowley, 2d Eng. ed. [Oxford: Clarendon Press, 1910], p. 399).

32. Qohelet did not define the age of "youth," except as a contrast to what follows (12:2–5). Furthermore he did not indicate that an older person cannot or should not remember his God, but rather he seems to imply that the older an individual becomes, the more difficult it is to change his life when he does remember.

33. Eaton, *Ecclesiastes: An Introduction and Commentary*, p. 148.

34. Interestingly Qohelet did not suggest that the act of "remembering" God acts either as a deterrent to or as a cosmetic against the ravages of old age; it is not an elixir from the mythical fountain of youth. The assumption is that everyone who lives long enough will experience the natural debilitating effects of the aging process.

35. Louis Goldberg, *Ecclesiastes*, Bible Study Commentary (Grand Rapids: Zondervan Publishing House, 1983), p. 132.

To what do "the evil days" refer? Rather than being a reference to moral perversion[36] or the darkness of Sheol,[37] as some suggest, "evil days" is synonymous with "old age, in which there is no pleasure."[38] Such a view is contextually appropriate because of its contrast to "in the days of your youth" and because of its continuation of the argument (11:6–10) that the early years of life provide opportunities for enjoyment whereas the later years do not.

Furthermore the closing chapter of one's life reduces dramatically the opportunity for accomplishing the desires of one's heart. They are in fact times of "no delight"—times in which there is an absence or impossibility[39] (אֵין) of delight. This "delight" (חֵפֶץ) is an emotion-laden word that implies an attraction to some object, hence a "desire" or a "longing" for something.[40] It conveys the idea of "delight" or "pleasure" and may be used "in reference to a person's great interest."[41]

The fact that an individual will lose his delight in life seems to indicate that he may tend to focus too much on his infirmities to the detriment of enjoying what God has created.[42] He will have lost the proper perspective on life and will have run counter to the commands to rejoice while growing up, to follow the impulses of one's heart and the desires of one's eyes, and to enjoy life with one's own spouse (9:9; 11:9). As Hengstenberg perceptively summarizes this message: "How mournful a thing must it be to pass into the ranks of those who are here described, without having tasted of the feast of joys prepared by the Creator for all those who remember Him."[43]

The Days of the Ending (12:2–5)

The second thematic marker (עַד אֲשֶׁר, "before") shifts the reader's thinking from that time of life before the individual is fully aware of the aging process to that time when he is painfully aware of his personal decay. Verses 2–5 include a series of metaphors that reveal that the signs forewarning old age are no longer mere warnings; they have become realities.

The beginning metaphor is that "the sun, the light, the moon, and the stars are darkened" (v. 2). Because the passage speaks of aging and the dying pro-

---

36. Eaton, Ecclesiastes: An Introduction and Commentary, p. 148.

37. George A. Barton, A Critical and Exegetical Commentary on the Book of Ecclesiastes, International Critical Commentary (Edinburgh: T. & T. Clark, 1908), pp. 185–86.

38. Gordis, Koheleth—The Man and His World, p. 341.

39. Theological Wordbook of the Old Testament, s.v. "אַיִן," by Jack B. Scott, 1:37.

40. Francis Brown, S. R. Driver, and Charles A. Briggs, A Hebrew and English Lexicon of the Old Testament (Oxford: Clarendon Press, 1955), p. 343.

41. Theological Wordbook of the Old Testament, s.v. "חָפֵץ," by Leon J. Wood, 1:311.

42. H. C. Leupold, Exposition of Ecclesiastes (Grand Rapids: Baker Book House, 1968), p. 274.

43. Ernest W. Hengstenberg, A Commentary on Ecclesiastes (reprint, Minneapolis: James and Klock, 1977), p. 245.

cess, this verse should not be thought of as referring to the future cosmic judgment in which the sun, moon, and stars will be destroyed (Rev. 6:12–13). In addition, this clause should not be considered a reference to the loss of one's family, drawing on the symbolism of Genesis 37:9–10 (i.e., the sun meaning father, the moon meaning mother, and the stars meaning brothers). Rather, it should be understood as being generically suggestive of one or more of the following: "a time of affliction and sadness,"[44] "the fading capacity for joy,"[45] "the more general desolations of old age,"[46] or the failing of one's eyesight "so that the lights of all sorts become dim."[47] Most simply,[48] the clause is expressing metaphorically the loss of joy and excitement in life.[49]

Solomon next pictured old age as clouds that return after[50] the rain. Delitzsch succinctly describes the Hebrew concept of the cloud image when he states, "A cloudy day is = a day of misfortune, Joel ii. 2, Zeph. i. 15; an overflowing rain is a scourge of God, Ezek. xiii. 13, xxxviii. 22."[51] Ecclesiastes 12:2 may have in mind a Middle Eastern winter rainstorm, which is normally followed by blue skies that promise good weather. However, "the unexpected return of the clouds soon after a storm, once more shutting out the light, is a

44. J. M. Fuller, ed., *Proverbs–Ezekiel*, The Bible Commentary (Grand Rapids: Baker Book House, 1972), p. 111.

45. Eaton, *Ecclesiastes: An Introduction and Commentary*, p. 148.

46. Kidner, *The Message of Ecclesiastes*, p. 101.

47. Barton, *A Critical and Exegetical Commentary on the Book of Ecclesiastes*, p. 186.

48. Simplicity and caution are perhaps the best guides in attempting to understand these and the following analogies regarding old age. Kidner agrees: "If some obscurities in these lines can be clarified, so much the better for kindling our imagination; but so much the worse if they tempt us into treating this graceful poem as a laboured cryptogram, or forcing every detail into a single rigid scheme" (*The Message of Ecclesiastes*, p. 101).

Furthermore stepping beyond the bounds of simplicity and caution may lead to an allegorical hermeneutic. The reader must be wary of commentators who pull from these analogies more than can be justifiably proven. For example Plumptre states that "the sun may be the Spirit, the Divine light of the body, the moon as the Reason that reflects the light, the stars as the senses that give but a dim light in the absence of the sun and moon" (E. H. Plumptre, *Ecclesiastes: or the Preacher, with Notes and Introduction* [Cambridge: Cambridge University Press, 1881], p. 214). Delitzsch, though decrying various attempts at interpreting these figures and calling those attempts "wholly or for the most part unfortunate," also oversteps the bounds of careful hermeneutics. He suggests that the sun, light, moon, and stars may be understood as alluding, respectively, to the spirit, the light of self-examination, the soul, and the five senses (*Commentary on the Song of Songs and Ecclesiastes*, pp. 403–5).

49. Leupold states, "in the Scriptures 'light' is quite generally a symbol of joy and, when it is sent by God, a token of favor. Just as clearly the Scriptures let darkness be synonymous with judgment and punishment, cf. Joel 3:4; 2:10; Amos 8:9; Isa. 13:10; 5:3; Jer. 4:33; Ezek. 32:7; Rev. 6:12" (*Exposition of Ecclesiastes*, pp. 476–77).

50. Eaton suggests that אַחַר ("after") may mean "with," though he recognizes that such a translation is not normally associated with אַחַר (*Ecclesiastes: An Introduction and Commentary*, p. 148, n.).

51. Delitzsch, *Commentary on the Song of Songs and Ecclesiastes*, p. 405.

bad sign and brings gloom, both literally and psychologically."[52] This imagery is not depicting gradually failing eyesight or the onset of glaucoma,[53] but rather the repetitive gloom into which the elderly may be prone to fall as they encounter setback after setback in the final years of their lives. Much as an elderly person recovers from one injury or illness only to be subjected to another, the individual's hopes and dreams are continually being dashed. Thus as Kidner comments, "the clouds will always gather again, and time will no longer heal, but kill."[54]

The metaphors in verse 3 have been variously interpreted by some as "a household falling into decay or house struck by a violent storm."[55] Other commentators understand the verses to be picturing the deterioration of the human body as it ages[56]—the watchmen representing the arms, the mighty men the legs, the grinding ones the teeth, and those at the window the eyes.[57] The uncertainties in these images, therefore, result in a general lack of agreement among scholars regarding how best to depict each individual image.[58]

What can be noted, however, is that Qohelet did not play favorites. He did not picture the decaying process of old age as solely the lot of one sex as opposed to the other. In fact, of the four metaphors in this verse, he relates two of them to the male population and the other two to females. Thus the terrors associated with dying are a reality of life for all people.

"The watchmen of the house" who "tremble" are those who preserve, protect, and guard the house. Their function is to ensure that everyone within the house is safe and secure. Yet these men "tremble," "quake," are "in terror," or "quiver."[59] What might cause this trembling is the degen-

---

52. Whybray, *Ecclesiastes,* p. 164.

53. Crenshaw, *Ecclesiastes: A Commentary,* p. 185.

54. Kidner, *The Message of Ecclesiastes,* p. 102. Fredericks suggests that the returning clouds are representative of "the despair and terror of imminent death" that the individual faces "at the close of those miserable years" (Daniel C. Fredericks, "Life's Rise and Demise in Ecclesiastes 11:1–12:8," paper presented to the Evangelical Theological Society, San Diego, CA, November 18, 1989, p. 19).

55. Whybray, *Ecclesiastes,* p. 164.

56. The words found in the Egyptian Ptah-hotep's preface to his *Instruction* to his son may be of interest at this point. He wrote, "Feebleness has arrived; dotage is coming. . . . The eyes are weak, the ears are deaf, the strength is disappearing. . . . The heart is forgetful. . . . All taste is gone" (cited by R. B. Y. Scott, *Proverbs, Ecclesiastes,* The Anchor Bible [Garden City, NY: Doubleday & Co., 1965], p. 255). See also 2 Samuel 19:35 for Barzillai's description of his physical deterioration at the age of 80.

57. Fuller, *Proverbs–Ezekiel,* p. 11, and Rylaarsdam, *The Proverbs, Ecclesiastes, The Song of Solomon,* p. 132.

58. Crenshaw, *Ecclesiastes: A Commentary,* p. 186.

59. Brown, Driver, and Briggs, *A Hebrew and English Lexicon of the Old Testament,* p. 266; and *Theological Wordbook of the Old Testament,* s.v. "זוע‎," by Andrew Bowling, 1:238.

eration of the nervous and muscular system of the body[60] or a powerful outside force that greatly intimidates the watchmen, causing them to cower in fear.

What then is the impact on the house? What is the impact on the elderly when the guardians tremble? Protection against a dreaded enemy decreases. Vulnerability to attack increases and there is a subsequent increase in the potential for catastrophe or ultimate destruction to occur.

The second of the two male-oriented metaphors is that "mighty men stoop." Because חַיִל ("mighty") has a broad semantic range including strength, efficiency, ability, wealth, force, army, and virtue,[61] determining exactly who these men are is difficult. They undoubtedly are men of high standing, at least in the house, if not in the city. Whybray indicates that they "may be masters, but are probably the stalwart men-servants."[62]

Why would such honorable (and perhaps strong) men stoop? Are they doing so because of old age or are they bending over in abject submission to some outside force? The verb עָוַת ("stoop," here in the *Hithpael* form) is best translated "bend themselves,"[63] and therefore would seem to favor the latter position. They are not naturally bent over nor do they choose to be, but rather forces working contrary to their will impose conditions to which they finally succumb.

The next metaphor states that "the grinding ones [feminine form] stand idle because they are few." An often held view of this metaphor argues that "the grinding ones" (הַטֹּחֲנוֹת) are teeth. If this is true, then Delitzsch is correct when he states that "they [the teeth] stand no longer in a row; they are isolated, and (as is to be supposed) are also in themselves defective."[64] This view, however, does not seem to fit the pattern of development in this verse. The other three metaphors in the verse are more easily understood as references to actual people rather than as references to body parts.

A second view of this metaphor presents "the grinding ones" as women (i.e., female servants) who make flour for the household's bread.[65] This metaphor thus suggests that the women are no longer able to complete their work because they are few in number and apparently need a full complement of laborers to function properly.[66] Though this view is plausible, it has one

---

60. Plumptre suggests that the trembling may be caused by "the unsteady gait of age, perhaps even of paralysis" (*Ecclesiastes: or The Preacher, Notes and Introduction*, pp. 214–15).

61. Brown, Driver, and Briggs, *A Hebrew and English Lexicon of the Old Testament*, pp. 298–99; and *Theological Wordbook of the Old Testament*, s.v. "חוּל," by Carl Phillip Weber, 1:271–72.

62. Whybray, *Ecclesiastes*, p. 164.

63. Brown, Driver, and Briggs, *A Hebrew and English Lexicon of the Old Testament*, p. 736.

64. Delitzsch, *Commentary on the Song of Songs and Ecclesiastes*, p. 407.

65. Whybray, *Ecclesiastes*, p. 164.

66. Hengstenberg, *A Commentary on Ecclesiastes*, p. 246.

major weakness, as Crenshaw points out. Would not one expect the grinders to work even more diligently if they are few in number, unless the implication is that the residents of the house are also few in number and have little need for food?[67]

If Crenshaw's implication is correct, then the metaphor changes its focus from the visible grinders to an unspecified group of people in the house who no longer possess the wherewithal to support a flourishing household. Whereas such a shift of focus is possible, it would seem to lessen the impact of the metaphor, making the reference to the aging process indirect rather than direct.

An alternative suggestion is that the grinders themselves have become few through attrition due to old age, incapacitation, or death. Under such conditions, there would be much sadness among the remaining grinders because so many of their friends are no longer around to make their work a joy. So the remaining grinders, themselves too weary to carry on, have just given up.

The fourth metaphor in this verse (and the second one directed toward women) states that "those who look through windows grow dim." Most commentators agree that "those who look through windows" is a reference to the women of the household who, according to Middle Eastern custom, were not allowed to mingle with the men in the business of the household and so they peered through the lattice-work of the house.[68] That they "grow dim" means either (a) that others outside the house have a more difficult time seeing them in the windows because they go to the windows no more,[69] (b) that it has become dark,[70] or (c) that they themselves have a harder time seeing, for their eyes have lost their brilliance.[71] In each case, the women are becoming progressively isolated from the outside world, shut off from whatever joys and pleasures they once knew.

The writer continued this isolation-fear imagery as he began verse 4 by stating that for the aging person "the doors on the street are shut." Immediately the reader grasps the idea that life is not as it once was or as it should be. What once allowed people or objects to go in or out no longer does so. The doors are closed—perhaps through fear, perhaps through inattentiveness or a lack of care by those responsible for opening them, or perhaps through their own inability to be opened any more.

"Doors" (דְלָתַיִם) is a dual form meaning "literally 'double doors,' only found at the entrance to cities, temples and exceptionally grand houses,"[72]

67. Crenshaw, *Ecclesiastes: A Commentary*, p. 186.
68. Gordis, *Koheleth—The Man and His World*, p. 342.
69. Ibid., p. 343.
70. Delitzsch, *Commentary on the Song of Songs and Ecclesiastes*, p. 405.
71. Barton, *A Critical and Exegetical Commentary on the Book of Ecclesiastes*, p. 188.
72. Whybray, *Ecclesiastes*, p. 165.

most houses apparently having had only one door.[73] The doors may remain shut as a picture of a self-enclosed, self-isolated group of people or may refer symbolically, as many suggest, to the lips or the ears.[74]

"The sound of the grinding mill is low" because few people are working there (cf. v. 3). Such a condition would be discouraging to the elderly because what they remember as a cheerful indicator of the exciting activities of business is now more and more being shut out of their lives. They in turn find themselves "increasingly cut off from the hum of daily life."[75]

The Hebrew of 12:4, however, does not isolate the metaphor of the grinding mill from the previous metaphor of the doors on the street being shut. Rather, it uses the sound of the mill being low to explain why the doors are closed. The בְ in בִּשְׁפַל ("as . . . low") functions as a temporal preposition indicating that the doors on the street are shut "when" or "at the same time as" the activity of the grinding mill decreases dramatically. If the grinders in verse 3 are understood as a reference to teeth, then that lends credibility to the view that "doors" here refer to lips. On the other hand if the grinders in verse 3 are women who prepare flour for bread, then the house imagery better fits the closing of the doors in this verse. This latter view seems preferable.

Having completed what Fredericks observes is a chiasm beginning with verse 3b and ending with verse 4a,[76] the symbolism shifts to picture death from still another angle, the chirping of birds—"one will arise at the sound of the bird." Whybray offers two possible interpretations for this illustration: "either that the elderly get up early in the morning . . . or that their voice becomes high like that of a bird."[77] What is so discouraging or sad about arising when birds sing or about the pitch of one's voice being elevated? The latter would be merely a statement of fact and therefore not necessarily a source of worry, but simply rather a reminder that one has aged. The former (rising when birds sing) only becomes a matter of dread if it implies that one is awak-

73. Crenshaw, *Ecclesiastes: A Commentary*, p. 186.

74. Fuller, *Proverbs–Ezekiel*, p. 111. Those who accept the lips or ears metaphor do so because of the dual nature of those organs. The closure of the lips would imply that little is ingested in the way of food or that little is allowed to pass out in the way of speech. The shutting of all of the ears, of course, would suggest that the hearing of the older person has diminished greatly. Those who favor the lips and ears metaphor here in 12:4 tend also to argue for the eyes symbolism of verse 3 in reference to "those who look through windows grow dim." Hence they do not understand "doors" to be eyes despite what might seem to be a logical metaphoric relationship due to the dualism of the doors and the dual nature of the eyes (or of the eyelids).

75. Eaton, *Ecclesiastes: An Introduction and Commentary*, p. 149.

76. Fredericks states that in 12:3b and 12:4a "a chiasm is formed by two comments on the limited milling (either ceasing or its sound is decreasing) which frame the comments about the openings in the houses of the millers ('windows' and 'doors')" ("Life's Rise and Demise in Ecclesiastes 11:1–12:8," p. 21).

77. Whybray, *Ecclesiastes*, p. 165. See also Crenshaw, *Ecclesiastes: A Commentary*, pp. 186–87.

ened by every little sound. Kidner points out, however, that if the previous metaphors imply that deafness accompanies old age, then the elderly person would "hardly be wakened or startled by the sparrow."[78]

The music metaphor is continued in the final portion of verse 4: "all the daughters of song will sing softly." This may refer to female singers, to song birds, or to musical notes.[79] That they "will sing softly" may mean that the sound is faint to the ears of the elderly,[80] that for the elderly "all singing as well as all appreciation of singing is a thing of the past,"[81] or that the singers themselves have lost the ability to sing.[82] A further possible interpretation is that the singers sing softly for fear of waking the elderly who have difficulty sleeping and who arouse easily, even at the sound of the birds chirping. No matter which view is correct, the disheartening fact is that those who have aged in this way are no longer able to enjoy what was once a pleasure to them.

The quiet sadness of the metaphors in verse 4 changes in verse 5 into what Crenshaw terms "a full measure of existential Angst."[83] Fear now runs rampant. Those who have grown old "are afraid of a high place and of terrors on the road." A straightforward rendering of these two pictures of fear best expresses their meaning. To a person who is old, feeble, and defenseless, the world looms as a place of great risks and physical dangers. Delitzsch equates this fear to that of the sluggard of Proverbs 22:13.

> As the sluggard says: there is a lion in the way, and under this pretence remains slothfully at home . . . so old men do not venture out; for to them a damp road appears like a very morass; a gravelly path, as full of neck-breaking hillocks; an undulating path, as fearfully steep and precipitious; that which is not shaded, as oppressively hot and exhausting—they want strength and courage to overcome difficulties, and their anxiety pictures out dangers before them where there are none.[84]

78. Kidner, *The Message of Ecclesiastes*, p. 102, n. Kidner suggests that the phrase may simply be "a note of time, like our 'up with the lark.'" Such a view again would seem to present merely a statement of fact rather than a condition of sadness related to old age. Perhaps the tragedy is to be explained by a realization that in an agricultural society everyone who works is expected to rise at the break of dawn. The elderly person who is no longer required to work and thus has the privilege of sleeping later in the morning than others finds it impossible, however, to enjoy that luxury because his sleep is disturbed by the slightest sound.

79. *Gesenius' Hebrew Grammar*, p. 418, and Whybray, *Ecclesiastes*, p. 165.

80. Fuller, *Proverbs–Ezekiel*, p. 112.

81. Leupold, *Exposition of Ecclesiastes*, p. 280.

82. Whybray, *Ecclesiastes*, p. 165.

83. Crenshaw, "The Shadow of Death in Qohelet," p. 207. Actually Crenshaw makes this statement regarding Qohelet's overall view of death as observed throughout the Book of Ecclesiastes. Crenshaw's words, however, seem especially appropriate here.

84. Delitzsch, *Commentary on the Song of Songs and Ecclesiastes*, pp. 411–12.

The remaining three metaphors in Ecclesiastes 12:5 are difficult to interpret. The two primary views are that the imagery symbolizes either the rapid growth of spring or the deterioration of the human body. The former contrasts the downfall of a house which will never rise again with the fresh renewal of nature which offers a wellspring of hope. The latter understands that the words focus on the gradual encroachments of old age.[85]

Regarding the first of these three images—"the almond tree blossoms"—most commentators say the symbolism refers to the white hair of an elderly person. This view is favored because the almond blossom, which exhibits a pink color when it blooms in January, very soon thereafter becomes white at the tip, only to fall to the ground later like white snowflakes.[86]

Hengstenberg, however, offers a different perspective. He contends that both the context and the etymology of the word for almond tree (שָׁקֵד) support the notion that the tree is "a symbol of that watchfulness with which old age is visited."[87] The word for almond tree is similar to the verb "be watchful" (שָׁקַד).

For the second of the three metaphors—"the grasshopper drags himself along"—the following views are most often suggested: (a) the stiffness of the joints; (b) the bent figure of an old person, (c) the enormous appetite of the locust which, becoming weighted down by its full stomach, moves awkwardly, (d) the inability of the male sex organ to function as it should in old age, and (e) an emblem of smallness, indicating that even the smallest object is a burden to carry.[88]

The first two explanations (stiffness and being hunched over) and possibly the fifth suggestion (difficulty in burden-bearing) offer the more reasonable suggestions of the meaning of the grasshopper illustration. The overeating view (view c) functions at cross purposes to imagery regarding the elderly's loss of ability to eat (if grinders in verses 3–4 refer to teeth) and to the picture of the elderly's loss of a desire to eat in the caperberry metaphor below. Furthermore the diminished sexual capacity view (view d) requires that a double entendre be understood—a suggestion about the grasshopper not observed elsewhere in Scripture.[89]

85. Crenshaw, *Ecclesiastes: A Commentary*, p. 187.

86. Delitzsch, *Commentary on the Song of Songs and Ecclesiastes*, p. 413; Gordis, *Koheleth—The Man and His World*, p. 345; and Whybray, Ecclesiastes, p. 166.

87. Hengstenberg, *A Commentary on Ecclesiastes*, p. 248.

88. Barton, *A Critical and Exegetical Commentary on the Book of Ecclesiastes*, p. 190; Gordis, *Koheleth—The Man and His World*, p. 345; and Whybray, *Ecclesiastes*, p. 166.

89. The word used here for grasshopper (חָגָב) is used only four other times in Scripture: Leviticus 11:22; Numbers 13:33; 2 Chronicles 7:13; and Isaiah 40:22. In Leviticus it is said to be an edible food, whereas in 2 Chronicles it becomes an instrument of God's plague against the people of Israel. In the remaining two passages it indicates the small stature of people compared to the Nephilim giants of the land (Num. 13:33) and to God (Isa. 40:22).

The third metaphor in verse 5, "the caperberry is ineffective," is easier to interpret than the other two. Caperberries were used in ancient times as a "provocative to appetite."[90] This implies, therefore, that in old age, not even an artificial stimulant can move the individual to do what in years gone by would have been done with gusto and relish.[91]

Verse 5 concludes with a straightforward presentation of the fact of death: "For man goes to his eternal home while mourners go about in the street." The verb הָלַךְ ("goes") is used euphemistically in typical Hebrew fashion to express the concept of dying.[92] "To his eternal home" indicates that the end of that "going" is the individual's final resting place.

As a common designator of the grave,[93] the "eternal home" is "a 'home' for successive generations of a family [that] spans an endless period of time."[94] It should not be thought of as expressing anything more than the grave, nor should it be assumed that it introduces the nascent underpinnings of a theology of the afterlife. As Youngblood states, "OT references to the afterlife are, for the most part, shrouded in darkness when compared to the fuller revelation of the NT."[95]

The final clause of this section, "while mourners go about in the street," reveals one last insult that the dying process has in store for the aged. The irony of the clause should not be missed. While the man dies, and even before he is dead, professional mourners gather around in front of the dying man's house seeking employment to engage in the practice of mourning (cf. Jer. 9:16–20; Amos 5:16). Little thought, if any, is given to the one who has suffered the mockery and misery of death. As Gordis concludes, the tragedy of this man's death "constitutes merely one more professional routine for the hired mourners—the vanity of life is climaxed by the vanity of death!"[96]

---

90. Fuller, *Proverbs–Ezekiel*, p. 112.

91. Some such as Crenshaw have suggested that the caperberry was used as an aphrodisiac, and thus the caperberry metaphor is a reference to dwindling sexual desire in old age (*Ecclesiastes: A Commentary*, p. 188). Delitzsch and Whybray, however, find no records from antiquity (the earliest being from the Middle Ages) that support such a usage for the caperberry (Delitzsch, *Commentary on the Song of Songs and Ecclesiastes*, p. 416, and Whybray, *Ecclesiastes*, pp. 166–67).

92. Nicholas J. Tromp, *Primitive Conceptions of Death and the Netherworld in the Old Testament* (Rome: Pontifical Biblical Institute, 1969), p. 167.

93. Whybray, *Ecclesiastes*, p. 167; and Gordis, *Koheleth—The Man and His World*, p. 347. Youngblood provides a thorough treatment of the phrase אֶל־בֵּית עוֹלָמוֹ ("to his eternal home"). Analyzing contemporary uses from Mesopotamian, Ugaritic, and Phoenician sources on the one hand, and Egyptian sources on the other, he concludes that בֵּית עוֹלָמוֹ should be translated as "his dark house" rather than as "his eternal home" (Ronald F. Youngblood, "Qoheleth's 'Dark House' [Eccl. 12:5]," *Journal of the Evangelical Theological Society* 29 [December 1986]: 383–410).

94. Tromp, *Primitive Conceptions of Death and the Netherworld in the Old Testament*, p. 78.

95. Youngblood, "Qoheleth's 'Dark House' (Eccl. 12:5)," p. 410.

96. Gordis, *Koheleth—The Man and His World*, p. 347.

The End of Days (12:6–8)

The beginning of this final analysis of death again employs the temporal marker עַד אֲשֶׁר ("before"), the third such usage of this Hebrew phrase in the verses under study.[97] The first (v. 1) places the individual under the indictment of death but seemingly (though not actually) far removed from it. The second (v. 2) dramatically portrays the rapidly deteriorating conditions of life and the fast approach of death. Finally, here, the last act of life (i.e., death) is played out. There is no timidity about death when it comes and there is no escape for the individual whom death attacks. Ultimately what is discovered is that both the body and the spirit of the dead man return to their place of origin—the body to the ground and the spirit to God (v. 7).

In verse 6, Qohelet portrayed the end of life by three graphic metaphors: the crushing of a lamp, the shattering of a jar, and the breaking of a wheel. Each presents an irreversible destruction, symbolizing the suddenness and finality of death. Furthermore each picture may be thought of as suggestive of a different type of life that is taken in death. The rich imagery of the lamp made up of the cord and bowl appears to reflect the fact that even the wealthy do not escape death. The pitcher illustration, by contrast, seems to show that those who are fragile and helpless also do not escape death. And the wheel at the cistern pictures apparently the strong, utilitarian type of person as still another category of individuals who are unable to avoid death.

The two metaphors—the silver cord being broken and the golden bowl being crushed—are in reality only one,[98] for the cord and the bowl are parts of one lamp. Once the cord is cut, the bowl drops to the ground and is irreparably damaged. So too, when the cord of life is cut, the individual falls to the ground never to rise again.

The final two images in this verse—the pitcher and the wheel—may also, according to certain commentators, be two components of one metaphor. Gordis suggests that Levy is correct when he states, "One end of the cord has a pitcher, the other a metal ball . . . as a counterweight. When the cord is torn, ball, pitcher and wheel all fall to the bottom and are broken."[99]

Other commentators, however, view the two as separate metaphors.[100] The fragile, easily broken pitcher suggests the fragile life of the elderly. It, like they, needs only to be struck once and then it is of no use to those who are

97. Delitzsch, *Commentary on the Song of Songs and Ecclesiastes,* p. 419.

98. Barton, *A Critical and Exegetical Commentary on the Book of Ecclesiastes,* p. 192; and Whybray, *Ecclesiastes,* p. 167.

99. Gordis and Crenshaw also espouse this view (Gordis, *Koheleth—The Man and His World,* p. 348, and Crenshaw, *Ecclesiastes: A Commentary,* p. 188).

100. Barton, *A Critical and Exegetical Commentary on the Book of Ecclesiastes,* p. 192; Eaton, *Ecclesiastes: An Introduction and Commentary,* p. 150; Kidner, *The Message of Ecclesiastes,* p. 103; and Leupold, *Exposition of Ecclesiastes,* pp. 283–84.

under the sun.[101] Likewise, the crushing of the wheel is assumed to symbolize the total destruction of life at the point of death.

Concluding these dramatic illustrations of devastation, Solomon moves from what to many has been a series of indistinct metaphors in verses 2–6 to a picture that is unmistakably clear in verse 7. Death, simply and finally, is the separation of body and spirit.

An important point to note, however, is that the purpose in verse 7 (and throughout the Book of Ecclesiastes) is not to present a theology of the afterlife. The goal was not to have readers understand the details of life after death, but rather to have them recognize the fact of the existence of an afterlife so that they might live eternally purposeful lives here and now. Wright states this thesis in this way:

> The dead have run their course. They are waiting in Sheol for the judgment. They do not, like the living, know what is happening on the earth. They have no further opportunities of earning the Master's reward. Their bodies, the vehicles of the emotions of love and hatred and envy, have gone to dust, and no more can they share in life under the sun.[102]

Verse 7 begins by stating that "the dust will return to the earth as it was." "Dust" (עָפָר) refers symbolically to the physical nature of the individual. This is a favorite term employed by Old Testament writers to remind the reader of his or her "earthly origin (Gen. 2:7; 3:19; Job 10:9) and physical weakness (Ps. 103:14)."[103] The human body, being in essence dust, returns to dust when the individual dies.[104] Fuerst presents the perspective of life and death in Ecclesiastes as follows: "Migration from dust to dust, with a brief moment for wisdom and striving and reflection, is the fate of man."[105]

Verse 7 ends by differentiating the disposition of the human spirit from the dissolution of the human body. Despite the interplay between the two during life, there is no absorption of the one by the other in death. Each has a separate destiny. Whereas the body goes back to the earth as dust, the spirit returns to God who gave it.

To his credit, though he understands the finality of death to be a tragic disruption of human life, Solomon neither condemns that fact nor reproaches God for making life "a temporary gift which God would one day withdraw."[106]

101. Leupold, *Exposition of Ecclesiastes*, p. 285.

102. Wright, "The Interpretation of Ecclesiastes," p. 147.

103. Eaton, *Ecclesiastes: An Introduction and Commentary*, p. 150.

104. Carl Shank, "Qoheleth's World and Life View as Seen in His Recurring Phrases," *Westminster Theological Journal* 37 (1974–75): 62.

105. Fuerst, *The Books of Ruth, Esther, Ecclesiastes, The Song of Songs, Lamentations: The Five Scrolls*, p. 153.

106. Whybray, *Ecclesiastes*, p. 168.

As the body and spirit of the dead person return to their origins (v. 7), so the author in verse 8 returns to his original remarks in 1:2: "'Vanity of vanities,' says the Preacher, 'all is vanity!'" These words seemingly declare that all in life and in death is "futile"[107] (הֶבֶל). Crenshaw is led to assert that "one cannot imagine such a conclusion if the allusion to breath's return to God contained the slightest grounds for hope. In truth, divine support of life has vanished for Qoheleth."[108] Crenshaw's pessimistic position, however, fails to recognize that the statement "all is futile," is thoroughly steeped in Qohelet's positive understanding of the significance of life as he presents it throughout the book.

In line with this view of life and in light of the reality of death, individuals are challenged to live to the fullest and at the same time to be ever mindful of the transitory nature of life and of the sudden, irreversible coming of death. Qohelet urged individuals, moreover, to remember their Creator in the days of their youth (12:1) and to "fear God and keep His commandments" throughout all the days of their lives (v. 13). This therefore presents a balanced picture of life: "Man should enjoy what he can, be circumspect and pious, and fear the Lord; but [at the same time recognize a sense] of helplessness because the inexorable round of life finally does come to an end."[109]

Conclusion

Based on this study of death and dying in Ecclesiastes, including an examination of 12:1–8, the final and most extensive passage in the book on the subject, several conclusions may be drawn about the life-death phenomenon.

1. Everyone must turn to God while there is still time, because the end of days will come swiftly.

2. The aging, dying process, though in no way to be considered beautiful, does post warning signs of impending doom—signs that need to be heeded to ensure a successful life now and a proper reward after death.

3. Laying up treasures in this world is futile, because death will come for the individual, and the world will continue on as though he or she never existed.

4. No matter how long one lives or how much preparation one makes for dying, death comes suddenly and without fail.

107. Though הֶבֶל may be used in a variety of ways depending on its context, the sense of "futile" seems to fit the present context best. Furthermore it completes the introductory remarks in 1:2 and gives structure to the entire Book of Ecclesiastes. For a discussion of the uses of הֶבֶל, see Theophile Meek, "Translating the Hebrew Bible," *Journal of Biblical Literature* 79 (1960): 331.

108. Crenshaw, "The Shadow of Death in Qoheleth," p. 210.

109. Goldberg, *Ecclesiastes*, p. 137.

5. Life after death does exist, and one needs to live now in such a way as to be ready to meet one's Maker.

Hengstenberg summarizes well this philosophy of life and death in Ecclesiastes.

> Since all things are vain, man, who is subject to vanity, should do all in his power to enter into a living relation to Him who is the true absolute Being, and through fellowship with Him to participate, himself, in a true eternal being. All being vanity, man should not further vex himself about a "handful of vanity"— he should not care much whether he have [*sic*] to suffer a little more or a little less, but [should] attach importance alone to that which either hinders or favours his fellowship with Him who is the true absolute, personal, Being.[110]

"Vanity of vanities, all is vanity"; yet with God there is hope.

---

110. Hengstenberg, *A Commentary on Ecclesiastes*, p. 257.

30

REMEMBER THY CREATOR
ECCLESIASTES 12:1–6

George A. Barton

1b. *While the evil days come not.* This is the continuation 11:10, from which it has been severed by the gloss inserted in 12:1a. Qoheleth urged:

> Put away vexation from thy heart
> And remove misery from thy flesh,—
> For youth and prime are vanity,—
> While the evil days come not, etc.

*T*he evil days*"* do not refer to the days of darkness in Sheol mentioned in 11:8, but to the period of old age which he now goes on to describe. They are "evil" in the sense of "miserable" because less full of pleasure than youth and prime. This is the meaning of *I have no pleasure in them.*

Vv. **2–6** have been variously interpreted. All have agreed that the passage is allegorical, but as to the details of the allegory there are wide differences of opinion. These opinions may be grouped in seven divisions. (1) The verses are believed to describe the failing of an old man's physical powers, the various

From George A. Barton, *A Critical and Exegetical Commentary on the Book of Ecclesiastes* (Edinburgh: T &T Clark, 1908), 185–93. Reprinted by permission.

367

figures referring to anatomical details. This was the view of early Jewish commentators beginning with Tobia ben Eliezer, and of many modern ones. (2)
The verses represent under the figure of a storm an old man's approaching
death. So, Umbreit, Ginsburg and Plumtre. (3) The approach of death is here
pictured under the fall of night. Thus, Michaelis, Spohn, Nachtigal and Delitzsch. (4) Marshall thinks it the closing of a house at the approach of a si-
rocco. (5) The passage is a literal picture of the gloom in a household when
the master has just died. So Taylor. (6) The verses are to be explained by the
"seven days of death," or days of cold wintry weather, which immediately precede a Palestinian springtime. These days are thus named because they are pe-
culiarly dangerous to aged and sickly persons. This is the view of Wetzstein
and Wright. (7) The verses are in general a picture of old age, but one line of
thought is not followed throughout. The metaphors change and intermingle
in accord with the richness of an Oriental imagination. This is the view of
McNeile. The last of these explanations is but a slight modification of the first.
It seeks to avoid, by the exercise of a little plain sense, the vagaries to which
excessive zeal for anatomical identification has led, and in so doing strikes the
right path. Green, *Expositor* (1895), p. 77ff., points out that in Icelandic poetry the parts of the body are often alluded to under similar figures, and that
such allusions are known as *kennings*.

   2. *While the sun be not darkened, nor the light and moon and stars.* This may
be taken in two ways: it may either refer to failing eye-sight, so that the lights
of all sorts become dim, or it may refer to the fact that, as age advances, the
brightness (i.e., the enjoyment) of life becomes less. The context both before
and after the phrase favors the latter view. The speaker says, "I have no pleasure in them," because the brightness of his joy is decreasing. The Talmud
(*Sabbath*, 152a) explained the "sun" as forehead, "light" as nose, "moon" as
soul, and "stars" as cheeks. Haupt explains them thus, "the sun is the sunshine
of childhood when everything seems bright and happy, the moon is symboli-
cal of the more tempered light of boyhood and early manhood, while the stars
indicate the sporadic moments of happiness in mature age." The anatomical
application is so far-fetched as to be absurd, Haupt's explanation seems too
esoteric to be probable, and it has the disadvantage of leaving "light" (which
Haupt does not erase from the text) unexplained. Earlier interpreters explained this "light" to be "twilight" or "dawn"—a period of light when none
of the orbs of light were visible. Such detailed explanations are, however, unnecessary. The poet is describing the lessening brightness of advancing life. Its
characteristic is fading light. To express his thought, he has with Oriental richness of imagination and carelessness in exact use of metaphor mingled "light"
and the various orbs of light in one figure.—*For the clouds return after rain.*
When clouds follow rain they cut off brightness. The frequency of gloomy
storms happily figures the increasing gloom of age. Vaihinger thought it re-

ferred to winter, as the rainy time or time of gloom, Palestine having but two seasons, winter and summer. In Palestine the "winter of life" might well be opposed to our "springtime of life."

3. *In the day when*, a fuller way of saying "when," cf. Song 8:8. From a general description of the darkening of life's joys in advancing age, the poet now passes on to picture the decay of the body under the picture of a house. The figure is loosely used, perhaps with no thought that all its details were to be literally applied to the members of the body, though the figure itself is, as a whole, appropriate and forcible. Whether the house is portrayed as undergoing the changes described, because of an approaching storm, or because night has come, is open to discussion. Those who favor the storm, find an argument for it in the "clouds" and the obscuring of all the heavenly bodies in v. 2. It is really unwise to press the figure too far, either as a description of the decay of the body, or the closing of a house. In speaking of the former in terms of the latter, the poet has mingled the features of the two in pleasing and suggestive imagery, which, though poetically vague in details, does not mislead.—*The keepers of the house shall tremble.* The "keepers" correspond, as Ginsburg saw, to the menials or guards of a palace. When we come to applications to definite parts of the body, there is more difficulty. Rashi thought it meant "ribs" and "loins," Plumtre the "legs," Delitzsch the "arms," Haupt the "hands." The last is probably right.—*The men of valor bend themselves.* In the figure, as Ginsburg saw, "men of valor" are the superiors of the house, each palace containing masters and servants. In applying the figure to the body, there are again differences. The Targum and Plumtre think of the "arms," Ra., Rashbam, AE., Knobel, Hitzig, Zöckler, Delitzsch, Wright and McNeile of the "legs," "knees," or "feet," Haupt of the "bones," especially the spinal column. The reference is probably to the legs. See the description of the feet of old men in 3 Macc. 4:5.—*The grinding maids shall cease because they are few.* It is generally agreed that this refers to the teeth, which are called "maids," because grinding in the East is usually done by women (cf. Isa. 47:2; Job 31:10; Matt. 24:41; *Odyssey* 20.105, 106).—*The ladies who look out of the windows.* These are with much unanimity taken to be the eyes. For the figure, cf. Jub. 5:28ff. The figures represent the two classes of women in a house—ladies and serving maids—just as the two classes of men were represented.—*Are darkened*, that is, the eyes lose their lustre and their sight.

4. *The doors on the street are shut.* In applying this part of the figure, there are again diversities of opinion. The Talmud, Ra. and Rashbam thought the pores of the skin were referred to, the Targum the feet, AE., Död., Ros., Kn., Ew., Hit., Vaih., Zö., Wr. and Sieg. the lips, which, when the teeth are gone, shut more closely; Kimchi, Grotius and Cleric thought of the literal shutting of the street door, so that the old man could not go out; Hengstenberg of the eyes, Lewis of the eyes and ears, Wildeboer of the ears, Haupt of the anus and bladder, the man beginning to suffer from retention (*ischuria*) and intestinal stenosis. It is probable that the reference is to the lips, the figure of a door being elsewhere applied to them (see Mic. 7:5; Ps. 141:3).—*When the sound of the mill is low.* Again there are differences of opinion. The Talmud, Ra., Rashbam and AE. and Haupt hold it to refer to the impaired digestion; the Targum, to the appetite; Grotius, Döderlein, Knobel and Hitzig to the voice of age, which is broken and quavering; Zöckler and Delitzsch to the rustle of the toothless mouth. The last is, perhaps, right.—*And he shall rise at the voice of the bird.* This phrase has been variously translated, and even more variously interpreted. Kn., Wr., Wild. and Ha. think that it means that the old man awakes early just as the birds begin to twitter, and so refers to the loss of sleep in old age; Ew., Hit., Heil., Zö., Del. and Pl. hold it to refer to the childish treble of age. Probably the first of these interpretations is the right one.—*The daughters of song are prostrate.* Kn. and Heil. thought that this refers to the failure of the old man's singing voice, which is lost, though Kn. held that possibly it might refer to the notes of birds, which the old man could not hear. Del., who is followed by Wr., Wild., McN. and Ha., interprets it by 2 Sam. 19:35, where the aged Barzillai can no longer hear the voice of singing men and singing women, and so takes the line to refer to the deafness of age. With this Ges.[k.] and Kö. seem to agree, for they show that "daughters of song" mean the various notes of music, these all seem low to the old man. The line accordingly refers to deafness.

5. *Also he is afraid of a height.* The figure of the house is now dropped, and four additional statements of growing incapacity are added. Interpreters generally agree that the reference here is to the shortness of breath which comes in old age, and makes the ascent of a height difficult. For the rendering "he fears" instead of "they fear," see critical note.—*And terror is on the road.* This is almost a synonym of the previous clause. A walk is full of terrors, because the old man's limbs are stiff and his breath short.—*And the almond-tree blooms.* According to Kn., Ew., Zö., Wr., Marsh., Gen., and Ha., it is poetical reference to the white hair of old age. The almond-tree blooms in January, and at the time it has no leaves. The blooms are pink at the base, but soon turn white at the tips, giving the tree a beautiful white appearance, which makes the landscape in January and February most attractive (see Post, in Hastings' DB., I, 67a). This, then, is a natural symbol of the gray-haired man. It is used allegorically by Philo, *Life of Moses*, 3.22. Probably this is the correct interpretation, though others are urged by some. Since the Hebrew word for almond-tree is derived from a stem which means "to waken," and that is the use made of it in Jer. 1:11ff. Hengstenberg and Plumtre take it to mean that "sleeplessness flourishes." De Jong, Wildeboer and McNeile render the verb "despised," and take it to refer to the old man's failing appetite, because "the almond is rejected" (see critical note). This view is not so probable.—*The* *grasshopper is burdensome.* The rendering "grasshopper" is disputed by some. Delitzsch and Wildeboer, following the Talmud, render it "hips" and the verb "drag themselves along," thinking the phrase a reference to an old man's walk. Kn. rendered "breath," making it refer to labored breathings. Graetz thought it a poetical reference to *coitus,* while Moore (JBL., X, 64) thinks that a melon instead of a grasshopper was intended. Of the interpreters who translate "grasshopper," Heiligstedt understands it to mean that the old man is too weak to cook and masticate the grasshopper for food (cf. Matt. 3:4), Zöckler that the old man's form is emaciated like that of a grasshopper, Plumtre that the grasshopper is an emblem of smallness (Isa. 40:22; Num. 13:33), so that the smallest thing becomes burdensome; Wetzstein and Wright, that the grasshopper springs up in the days when spring begins, i.e., just after the seven days of death (see above, after v. 1), and Genung takes it to refer to the halting walk of age—the old man like a grasshopper halts along. Biblical analogy would lead one to agree with Plumtre and take it as a symbol of smallness, though there is no reason to regard it, as he does, as a Greek symbol, and so to find an example of Greek influence here. The passage then means that the smallest weight is a burden, which the old man drags along.—*The caper-berry is made ineffectual.* The caper-berry was a plant used to excite sexual appetite. There can be little doubt that the Hebrew word here used refers to it, since it is the singular of the word which designates the same product in the Talmud (see Moore, JBL., X, 55ff., and James 5b). Most interpreters rightly take it to mean that stimulants to appetite are rendered ineffectual by the failing of vital power. Graetz, however, takes "caper-berry" as a figure for the *glans penis,* but, as Renan remarks, Qoheleth is never obscene. Wetzstein and Haupt, taking a hint from Σ, connect the word rendered "caper-berry" with the Hebrew root for "poor," and think it a figurative expression for the soul. Haupt renders the word for "grasshopper" "chrysalis," making "inert lies the chrysalis, till the soul emerges." This is very improbable, though beautiful. For the rendering "is made ineffectual," see critical note.—*The man goes to his eternal house.* Here first the writer speaks of death itself. "Eternal house" is a reference to the tomb; cf. Tobit 3:6 and the Talmudic and Coranic usage cited in crit. note.—*Mourners go around the street.* According to Hebrew custom, cf. Amos 5:16; Jer. 9:16–20.

6. *While* is a repetition of the opening word of v. 1b, and like it connects the thought with 11:10, urging the young man to enjoy himself.—*While the silver cord is not severed, nor the golden bowl broken.* This last is a poetic picture of death, to which the thought was led in v. 5b. The imagery by which this is expressed is, as several critics have seen (Pl., No., Wr., Wild. and McN.), borrowed from Zech. 4:2, 3, where a golden bowl is, with that richness of imagery common to the Orient (cf. Prov. 25:11), represented as hanging by a silver cord. The cord is severed, the lamp falls, the bowl is broken (or more literally crushed, the objection that a golden bowl cannot be broken, is without force), the oil lost and the light goes out—a fit emblem of the sudden dissolution of the body and the escape of the spirit. Probably Qoheleth used this imagery with poetic freedom without thinking of special applications of details, but it has been otherwise with his commentators. The Targum makes the silver cord, the tongue; the golden bowl, the head; Del. makes them, respectively, the soul and the head; Haupt, the spinal column and the brain.— *And the water-jar be shattered at the spring.* By another common figure life is likened to a fountain (cf. Ps. 36:9). That figure is now employed. The individual body is made the water-jar, such as women in the East still use in carrying water home (cf. Gen. 24:14, 17, 43; Jub. 7:16, 19, 20); when the jar is broken it can contain no more water, and so the life ends.—While this meaning is clear, some contend that the bucket does not represent the whole body, but some special organ, Del., Sieg. and Ha. think of the heart.—*The wheel broken at the cistern.* This is another application of the same figure. Some wells are fitted up with a wheel to assist in drawing water. Sometimes this is small and can be worked by hand, as that seen today at "Jacob's well," near Nablous, or on one of the wells at Beersheba, sometimes large enough to be worked by a camel or a donkey, like that pictured in Barton's *A Year's Wanderings in Bible Lands,* p. 205. When the wheel is broken, the water can no longer be drawn. The "wheel" in this line is again a metaphor for the whole body. Some, however, make a special application of the "wheel," Del. and Sieg. regarding it as symbolizing the breathing process. Haupt thinks its "breaking" refers to paralysis of the heart. All the symbols of the verse picture death as coming suddenly—the lamp is crushed, the jar shattered, or the wheel broken.—7. *The dust shall return to the earth as it was, and the spirit shall return to God who gave it.* As Tobia Ben Eleazar in the eleventh century and, in modern times, Plumtre and Wildeboer have noted, this is a definite reference to Gen. 2:7. Qoheleth pictures death as undoing what the creative act of God had accomplished. Siegfried holds that the first clause cannot come from Q^1,—the pessimist,—for he believed the spirit of a man to be no more immortal than that of a beast (3:19, 20); he therefore assigns 7a to Q^2; 7b he denies to Q^2 because that writer did not trouble himself about the dead, but rejoiced in life (5:17; 9:4, 7–12; 11:7ff.), and assigns it to Q^4, the *Chasid* glossator. Such an analysis makes no allowance, however, for the moods of human nature. No man's thought—especially the thought of an Oriental—is as clear-cut as Siegfried supposes. One may have his pessimistic moods in which he questions whether anybody knows whether a man's spirit differs from a beast's; he may hold that man's only good comes from enjoying the sunshine of this physical existence, brief though it be, and still, holding Qoheleth's idea of God (see e.g., on 9:1), write "the spirit shall return to God who gave it." Even a pessimist may quote Scripture without reading into it all the hopes of an optimist. Qoheleth's thought is not out of harmony with the later development of OT. Judaism on this subject (see Schwally, *Leben nach dem Tode*, 104ff.).—**8.** *Vanity of vanities.* The book concludes with the dirge with which it opened. Qoheleth's concluding sentence reiterates his opening declaration. He has, from his point of view, proved his thesis and closes by reiterating the sad words with which he began: *All is vanity.—Saith Qoheleth* is probably an insertion of the late editor, who added vv. 9, 10, and who praises Qoheleth.

31

THE MEANING
OF ECCLESIASTES 12:1–5

Michael Leahy

The opening verses of the 12th chapter of *Ecclesiastes* as they are
rendered from the Hebrew by many exegetes read:

1. And remember thy Creator in the days of thy youth, before the evil
   days come, and the years draw nigh of which thou shalt say: I have
   no pleasure in them;
2a. Before the sun be darkened and the light and the moon and the stars,
2b. and the clouds return after the rain,
3a. Namely, in the day that the keepers of the house tremble,
3b. and the strong men are bent,
3c. And the grinders are idle, because they are few,
3d. and those that look through the lattices are darkened,
4a. and the doors are shut in the street,
4b. When the sound of the mill-stone is low,
4c. and the voice of the bird is thin,
4d. and all the singers cease;

From *Irish Theological Quarterly* 19 (1952): 297–300. Reprinted by permission.

5a. When they fear that which is high,
5b. and terrors are in the way,
5c. And the almond tree wears blossoms,
5d. and the grasshopper drags itself along,
5e. and the caper-berry becomes inefficacious;
5f. Because the man is going to his everlasting home,
5g. and the mourners are going about in the street.

In 2b the word translated "after" (Hebrew ʾahar) has sometimes the secondary meaning "with."[1] In 3c according to some critics the clause "because they are few" should be translated "because they accomplish little." They point out that the verb is not in the Qal but rather in the Piʿel form.[2] In 4c the Hebrew reads "and he rises at the voice of the bird," a reading that makes no good sense.[3] One must conclude that the text is corrupt. Probably the most plausible emendation is *yiqmal* ("is thin") for *yāqûm l* ("he rises at"). The rendering of 4d is that of A. Bea.[4] The meaning of 5a may be that climbing is dreaded, or perhaps "that which is high" (lit. "from high") is the heavens. In 5c the translation "wears blossoms" is very doubtful. The verb—pointed as the imperfect of niphʿal from a root *nāʾar*—can mean "is despised," "is thrust aside." In 5e the word rendered "becomes inefficacious" also means "is broken." In both cases it is pointed as the imperfect of hophʿal (i.e. *tuphar*).

Generally the passage 2–5 is taken to be a picture of old age, but the individual clauses have received a variety of interpretations. The following is the exegesis most in favor with commentators:

2. Old age is compared to dark and wet winter weather; with advancing senility life loses its brightness, its charm.
3. Arms—or perhaps, ribs—("keepers of the house") tremble in old age; legs ("strong men") are bent; teeth ("grinders") cease to perform their ordinary work of masticating food; eyes ("those that look through the lattices") lose their sight.
4. The "doors in the street" are the ears closed in external sound, or—according to another view—the lips closed in toothless old age. The "mill-stone" is the mouth; the voice coming from the mouth is weak. 4c alludes to the piping voice of old age, and 4d to the fact that the old people sing no more. According to another explanation, however, 4cd mean that old people, because of the deafness of old age, no longer hear the song of the bird or the voices of the singers.

1. Cf. R. B. Y. Scott in *JTS* 50(1949), 178.
2. Cf. A. L. Williams, *Ecclesiastes,* Cambridge 1922, p. 143.
3. It cannot mean that an old man sleeps so badly that he rises at cock-crow, because old people generally do not get up early.
4. A. Bea, *Liber Ecclesiastae,* Romae 1950, p. 25.

5. Old people suffer from giddiness ("they fear that which is high"), and from timidity ("terrors are in the way"); their hair is white[5] ("the almond tree wears blossoms"); their gait is halting ("the grasshopper drags itself along"); their palate languid ("the caper-berry becomes inefficacious"—this fruit was a condiment).

In this interpretation of the whole passage the sense of verses 2–4 is the metaphorical sense, of 5ab the proper literal sense, of 5cd the metaphorical sense, and of 5efg the proper literal sense.

A recent commentator, Buzy,[6] unhesitatingly rejects the above in interpretation, namely, that verses 2–4 describe the failing members of the body, symbolically represented. He calls it the physiological—others call it the anatomical—interpretation. The exegesis of the passage which Buzy proposes may be summarized as follows:

2.   As in the former interpretation.
3ab.   Those courageous people who guard the homes of the rich, when they advance in years, experience the tremors of old age; those too who once were strong are bent in old age.
3c.   The reference is to the women of the household who grind the corn for the daily supply of bread, an irksome task which required strong arms. With old age these women are no longer equal to the work; they give up because they accomplish so little.
4a.   The doors are closed; the aged and infirm have no social contacts.
4b.   The upper mill-stone worked by a weary hand revolves slowly; the loss of energy is a feature of old age.
4cd.   Old people no longer pay attention to the song of the bird or the joyous ditties that once thrilled them.
5abcd.   As in the former interpretation.
5e.   Buzy here adopts the translation "the caper-berry is broken," and understands it to mean that the fruit when ripe splits open and lets the seed fall out. The allusion is to dissolution and death.

In Buzy's interpretation of the whole passage, therefore, verse 2 is to be taken in the metaphorical sense, 3–5b in the proper literal sense, 5cde in the metaphorical sense, and 5fg in the proper literal sense.

While Buzy's exegesis appears less forced and less fanciful than that generally accepted, the alternation of the metaphorical sense with the proper literal sense is strange and can scarcely be regarded as satisfactory. The view of a few earlier commentators[7] who held that the passage, or

---

5. W. M. Thomson in *The Land and the Book*, Thomas Nelson & Sons, 1913, p. 300 says, "The *point* of the figure is doubtless the fact that the *white* blossoms completely cover the whole tree, without any mixture of green leaves, for these do not appear until some time after."

6. In Pirot-Clamer, *La Sainte Bible*, vol. VI, Paris 1946, pp. 271ff.

7. Among them were F. Umbreit and C. Ginsburg; cf. C. H. H. Wright, *The Book of Koheleth*, London 1883, p. 249.

part of it, is a description of a thunder-storm appears to be along the right lines. While agreeing substantially with this view, one might venture to put forward an interpretation of some of the individual clauses which differs from theirs.[8]

It seems that what the Sacred Writer had in mind was the last moments of life and not the decay of old age. The words of 5fg imply this, viz "Because the man is going to his everlasting home, and the mourners are going about in the street." In verse 1 he bids man to remember his Creator in the days of his youth before old age comes, but in verses 2–5 he bids him to remember his Creator before *the hour of death* arrives. The author uses the imagery of a thunder-storm, a terrifying phenomenon in the East, in order to depict the fear, the gloom and desolation which grip the members of a household when one from among them is about to die or has just died. He describes facts literally, a raging storm and its wake of destruction, with the object of portraying the hour of death.

This then would appear to be the correct exegesis of the verses:

2. The storm breaks over an Eastern city; light is darkened; thick clouds pile up and obscure the sun.
3. Lightning flashes and thunder peals, sending terror into the hearts of all, of the police who guard the houses of the wealthy, of the strong men of the city (lit. 'the strong men bend themselves,' i.e. cower before the storm), of the women whose hands have forgotten their task of grinding, and into the darkened faces of those who peep timidly through their latticed windows.
4. Doors are shut against the wind and the rain, the sound of the millstone and the song of the bird are hardly heard; merry-makers are terrorized into silence.
5ab. Men fear the heavens out of which the storm is raging; there are terrors out of doors.
5cde. In the wake of the storm the earth lies battered and torn; the almond tree is thrust aside; the caper-shrub (not the berry) is broken; and even the least thing that moves, the grasshopper, has felt the power of the storm.

To repeat then, I believe that in Ecclesiastes 12:2–5 the inspired writer uses the imagery of a thunder-storm with the object of setting forth the fear, melancholy and desolation which grip a household upon which death has cast its shadow.

It may be, too, that 12:6 also is part of the storm allegory. The verse reads:

---

8. Ginsburg, for example, thought that 5de referred to certain kinds of food, once favorite dishes, which, by reason of the terror inspired by the storm, are no longer attractive.

Before the silver cord be snapped[9] *and the golden bowl be broken,*[10] *and the pitcher be smashed at the fountain and the wheel be broken into the cistern.*

All commentators[11] find here a series of metaphors portraying sudden death. It may be, however, that the sacred writer intended to continue the literal description of the destruction wrought by the storm.

9. Reading, with many modern scholars, *yinnāteq*.

10. Reading *w^etērōs*; cf. A. Bea, op. cit., p. 26.

11. Cf. e.g. *The Five Megilloth*, ed. A. Cohen. The Soncino Press 1946. The note on this verse reads (p. 188): "We have presented in highly figurative language a description of the body's dissolution."

32

AGING AND DEATH
IN QOHELETH 12

Michael V. Fox

E ccles. 12:1–8 is the most difficult passage in a difficult book. Con-tinuing the *carpe diem* theme begun in 11:7, Qohelet urges the reader to enjoy life before it is too late.[1] The nature of 12:2–5 in particular has been debated at length. These verses have almost always been read as an allego-ry representing the physical deterioration of aging, an interpretation in part val-id but in general inadequate. Even if this poem is an allegory entirely or in part, it communicates in other ways as well, and these have been largely ignored.

From the *Journal for the Study of the Old Testament* 42 (1988): 55–77. Reproduced by per-mission of Sheffield Academic Press.

1. The larger unit is 11:7–12:8, composed of two main sections: A. 11:7–10 (*carpe diem*) and B. 12:1–8 (*memento mori*). These two sections are linked syntactically in 12:1. The series of imperatives of section A continues in 12:1a. Then 12:1b begins a series of temporal clauses that describe aging and death (section B), all of which goes to motivate the advice of section A. *Hebel*-judgments in 11:8 and 10 demarcate the two segments of section A, and the phrase ʿad ʾăšer lōʾ subdivides B.

Eccles. 12:8 is the climax of the poem and the summary of the book's theme. The body of the poem, 12:1b–7, divides into three parts, unequal in length but unmistakably marked by the conjunction ʿad ʾăšer lōʾ: (a) 12:1b, (b) 12:2–5 and (c) 12:6–7.

This study will explore the interplay among literal, symbolic, and figurative dimensions of the poem's meaning, seeking to bring out scenes, connotations and implications that are accessible to the reader independently of the poem's possible allegorical significance.

12:1–8

(1) And remember your Creator[2] in the days of your youth—
    before the days of unpleasantness come,
    and years arrive of which you will say:
    "I take no pleasure in them";
(2) before the sun grows dark—
    with the light and the moon and the stars—
    and the clouds return after the rain;
(3) in the day when the keepers of the house tremble,
    and the powerful men writhe,
    and the grinding-maids are idle, for their numbers have
    dwindled,
    and the ladies looking through the lattices grow gloomy,[3]
(4) and the doors in the street are closed,
    as the sound of the mill fades low;
    and the bird begins to sing,
    and all the songstresses are bowed low
(5) and are also afraid of a height,
    and [scenes] of fright are along the way,
    while the almond tree blossoms,[4]
    and the <squill>[5] becomes laden,

---

2. Many commentators have found the reference to the Creator inappropriate here, for 12:1a requires a reference to a thought that will encourage one to enjoy life *prior* to old age and death, and a vague religious exhortation would not do that. Verse 1a cannot, however, be removed as a gloss (contrary to McNeile, Barton, et al.), because 12:1b cannot follow directly on 11:10b as a temporal clause, and if we begin a sentence with 12:1b, as Barton does, all of 12:1b–7 lacks a main clause. Various emendations have been suggested, but they are made unnecessary by the observation of Gilbert (1981:100) that in this context to think on one's creator is to think of death, for, as 12:7 says, the life-spirit must go back to the one who gave it. Gilbert believes that the sentence also implies a warning against sin, but that does not seem relevant to context. The only counsels that would be meaningful in 12:1a are advice to enjoy life (found in five other forms in 11:9–10) and advice to keep death in mind (as in 11:8b), and the latter is what is intended by the call to remember one's Creator.

3. Literally, "grow dark."

4. MT correctly points *wyn's* as NSS-hiphil.

5. Reading *ḥāṣāb* for MT *ḥgb*, following Ginsberg (p. 137) (the latter word is known from mishnaic Hebrew). The *ḥāṣāb*, sc., "sea onion," "squill," gives the appearance of dying in May, when it contracts into its bulb. With the increase of moisture in August, the bulb becomes laden (thus, *wᵉyistabbēl*) and quickly bursts into life again. This emendation is certainly less farfetched than the conjecture that the locust is an otherwise unknown, and rather weird, figure for the penis (Rashi, Ibn Ezra, *b. Shab.* 152a), the ankles (Targum), or the back of the pelvic cavity (Delitzsch, 1875; on the basis of a dubious Arabic etymology).

and the caperberry <buds[6]>—
        for a man is going to his eternal home,
        and the mourners are walking about in the street;
(6) before the silver cord snaps,
        and the golden bowl[7] is smashed,[8]
        and the jug breaks at the well,
        and the jar is smashed into the pit,
(7) and the soil returns to the earth as it was before,
        and the life-spirit returns to God, who gave it.
(8) Absurdity of absurdities, says the Qohelet,
        All is absurdity.[9]

Earlier Approaches to Interpretation

The allegorical interpretation of this poem, first found in *Qohelet Rabbah* and *b. Shabbat* 131b–132a, is still the dominant one. In this reading, each object mentioned in the poem is decoded as a part of the body, and the whole is taken as a description of the physical degeneration of aging. Allegorical decoding does (I will argue) have some validity in the explication of individual images, but the text as a whole largely resists this reading, and even in the interpretation of details the basis for an allegorical reading is not secure. It is mainly out of exegetical habit that we see the watchmen, for example, as the legs (or the arms), and the doors in the street as the lips (or the orifices, or the ears), and the stars as the pupils of the eyes (or the cheeks, or the five senses). The procrustean character of the allegorical interpretation may make it seem more effective than it really is. It is not difficult to connect almost any image[10] with something within the multifarious physical and psychological process of aging, and when this cannot be done, the interpreter is free to treat the image as literal or as a metaphor outside the allegorical frame. Difficulties in accommodating the text to the interpretation can be met by invoking the author's "Oriental richness of imagination and carelessness in exact use of metaphor" (Barton, p. 187). Yet even with all this hermeneutic flexibility, the allegorical interpretations leave much unexplained.[11]

6. Reading *wᵉtiprah* for MT *wtpr h-* (*h/h* haplography); Perles, 1895:30. *PRH* is parallel to *NṢṢ* in Cant. 7.13.

7. For *gagal* as 'pot' or the like see Dahood, 1952:216f.

8. Pointing *tērōṣ* (from *RṢṢ*), for MT *tārūṣ*. MT's pointing likely reflects an interpretation of *trṣ* as "run," though *RWṢ* is not used elsewhere of a fall.

9. I argue for translating *hebel* as "absurdity" rather than "vanity," "futility," etc. in Fox, 1986.

10. "Image" refers to any depiction of a sensory object (in this case, verbal) and to the mental replication of this depiction. Images may, but need not, function in metaphors (as vehicle *or* as referent), similes, symbols, or allegories.

11. Taylor (1874:51–63) summarizes various forms of the "anatomical" interpretation and shows that it can be maintained only by an exegesis too convoluted to be persuasive. His arguments are, I believe, basically valid. However, his insistence on "all or nothing," as if any variance from consistent anatomical figuration excludes the presence of any such figuration, seems to me extreme.

Some of the images of the poem may well be figurative representations of aging and death. But the poem as a whole is not an allegory. And it is certainly not *only* that. The "allegorical approach" has commonly treated the imagery as if it were a disguise covering the "true" meaning of the poem. The interpreter's task then becomes to strip off this disguise and triumphantly to reveal what lies hidden behind it. Once removed, the guise itself ceases to be of interest. The allegorical interpretation has invariably failed to recognize that the imagery, the surface of the poem, is what the author chooses to show us first and most clearly. Rather than thinking of imagery as an expendable outer garb, we should compare it to the visible surface of a painting. The imagery *is* the painting. We can discuss the painting's symbolism, emotive overtones, ideological message, and so on, but only as projections of the surface imagery, not as substitutes for it. To understand the poem we must first look carefully at the surface the author shows us.

Approaches other than the allegorical, most of them less persuasive, have been suggested. According to the literal interpretation of M. Gilbert (1981), vv. 3–4 describe the actual experience of the old: shaking, bending, blindness, obscurity, and isolation. But doors in the street would not actually close as one grows old, nor would milling cease as aged people became too few, for there would be others in the house.[12] Moreover, the phrasing of these verses implies that all this happens at once, whereas everyone in a town would not grow old simultaneously. O. Loretz (1964:189–93) understands 12:2–5a as an essentially literal description of a winter's day, which serves as a metaphor of old age. This is followed by the coming of spring (v. 5b), teaching that although plants may revive, man cannot. Although Loretz's understanding of v. 5b is, I believe, essentially correct, the events described earlier have nothing to do with winter. Winter, especially in Palestine, would not make men twist and tremble unless they were extraordinary cowards, nor would it cause the maids to halt their grinding, because preparation of bread is an endless chore. For similar reasons, I cannot accept C. D. Ginsburg's reading of the poem as a description of a gathering storm serving as a metaphor for the approach of death, or Leahy's interpretation of the poem as a depiction of fearful reactions to a thunderstorm, thereby representing the emotions in a household when someone dies (Leahy, 1954). The rain has stopped (v. 2b), and anyway a rainstorm is not *that* frightening. Moreover, the sun, moon, and stars would not be darkened all at once by a rainstorm.

J. F. A. Sawyer (1976) has offered a radical reinterpretation of 12:2–5. He accepts the presence of an allegory on aging in the *Massoretic* text of 12:2–5, but argues that the allegorizing elements are secondary accretions deriving

---

12. Gilbert (p. 104) regards *kî miʿēṭû* as an impersonal construction, "car on [sc. the aged] est trop peu nombreux." But this does not improve the logic of the sentence, since young people would always be taking their place.

from a very ancient interpretation of the text as allegorical. When these accretions are removed, he says, we find the figure of a ruined house representing the failure of human efforts. The poem envisages three situations that may interrupt the young man's progress towards achieving success and fulfillment (p. 523).

Sawyer's procedure is, however, circular, for the presumed accretions betray themselves only by their supposedly allegorical nature.[13] Various other emendations[14] and strained translations[15] are proposed for the sake of the presumed parable, not for independent textual-philological reasons. The reconstructed parable says: "Just as when an estate falls into disrepair (vv. 3a–4a), nature is indifferent (vv. 4a–5a), so too when a man dies (v. 5bα), life in his city goes on unchanged (v. 5bβ)" (my paraphrase). Even this tenuously reconstructed parable does not warn about unexpected disasters, but rather complains of nature's indifference. (In Sawyer's view, the parable also shows society's indifference.) Certainly the mourners going about their business does not demonstrate indifference; on the contrary, they are displaying at least a formalized concern for the dead man and doing what he presumably wanted. Furthermore, nature's and society's indifference to disaster would not be a reason to enjoy life while young.

H. Witzenrath (1979:46–50) interprets 12:3–4a as depicting the decay (*Verfall*) of a house, this process representing human ephemerality and death. She says that the images of these sentences (like the others in 12:2, 4–5aα, 6) describe the movement from a positive state (strength / activity / brightness / openness) to a negative one (weakness / inactivity / darkness / closure). As I will later argue, these images do indeed relate primarily to death, but not by depicting the dilapidation of a house, and not merely by suggesting a movement toward the "negative." First of all, only one of the images (the doors closed to the street) pertains to the house as such, whereas the house-body metaphor in the verses upon which Witzenrath bases her interpretation, Job 4:19 and Isa. 38:12, takes as its vehicle the image of a house or a tent, not a town or estate. Second, the images in Eccles. 12:3–4a do not suggest decay and dilapidation so much as pain and cessation of normal activity. The scene does not represent the experience of dying and death but rather other people's *response* to a death.

---

13. E.g. "*ḥšk* is perhaps more appropriate to the allegory than to the present interpretation" (ibid., p. 526); *kî miʿēṭû* in v. 3 "makes good sense only for the allegorizers" (and therefore should perhaps be omitted [p. 526]).

14. Including: *bayyôm* to *kayyôm* (3a), in order to "bring the parable into line with [various] quasi-proverbial allusions to Israel's history" (p. 529); *wᵉḥāšᵉkû* to *wᵉḥāsᵉkû* (3b), understood to mean "are held back," i.e. "appear [at the windows] no more" (pp. 526, 530); *wᵉyiššaḥû* to *wᵉyāśîḥû* (4b), translated "chattering" (mockingly) (p. 527); *kî* to *kēn* (5bα) (p. 530).

15. Including; "move," whence "leave" (sc. the house) for *yāzuʿû* (3a) (ibid., p. 525); "to be ruined in a court of law" for *hit ʿawwᵉtû* (3a) (p. 525); "so when a man goes" for *kēn* [thus he reads] *hōlēk hāʾādām* (5bβ) (p. 530).

No interpretation of this poem is entirely satisfactory; none (including the one I will offer) solves all the difficulties. The poem's obscurities are due in part to a number of philological-textual problems, in part to the fragmentary state of our knowledge of Israelite mourning customs and symbols, and in part to the poem's enigmatic character, which the abundance of unique or rare symbols suggests may be deliberate.

Three Types of Meaning

In spite of these difficulties, we can go a considerable way towards grasping the poem's significance. The poem retains its power even over those who do not understand it completely—and no one does. It is important to take stock of just how much the poem does communicate, even as it withholds the meaning of many details. We begin by looking at literal description. The powerful men are, first of all, powerful men; the women at the windows who "grow dark" are just that, and we should ask who they are and why they are bowing down and "growing dark." Then we ask what the imagery conveys apart from description. Imagery conveys moods as well as paraphrasable meanings, and these moods can often be described even where the meaning remains obscure.

This essay asks about three types of meaning in Eccles. 12:1–7: (a) the literal, (b) the symbolic, and (c) the figurative/allegorical. These meaning-types are not mutually exclusive. On the contrary, the figurative and the symbolic require a literal base line from which both types of the extended meaning may proceed. I will defer discussion of most exegetical and philological details to another publication,[16] because the main lines of my interpretation are largely independent of the details of exegesis and, I believe, are valid even if some of these must remain unexplained.

Literal Meaning

The literal meaning is the one given by a reading that attends to the things, actions, and events that the images depict. It is the meaning most adequately captured by paraphrase. A literal reading thinks of the images as phenomena we could actually see, were we present at the scene depicted. A movie showing the literal meaning of Jotham's allegory (Judg. 9:7–15), for example, would show trees discussing who will rule over them. Looking at Eccles. 12:1–7 that way, we ask: if we came into a village and saw the things this poem describes, what would we be observing?

Literal meaning may be conveyed in part by metaphor (vv. 2 and 7 are undoubtedly metaphorical). But in a literal reading, the metaphors aid in communicating the first level of meaning and are strictly subordinated to

---

16. *Qohelet and His Contradictions*, to be published by Almond Press. [This book was published in 1989.—Ed.]

it.[17] A literal reading does not assume the presence of a governing metaphor or look for a meaning conveyed by the images independently of the literal content.

Of the various literal interpretations that have been attempted, I am most persuaded by that of C. Taylor, *The Dirge of Coheleth*. He argues vigorously that 12:2–5 is a 'dirge describing the state of a household or community on an occasion of death and mourning' (pp. iii–iv). Although Taylor calls the poem a dirge, he seems to mean that it is a dirge-like description of a funeral. M. Anat (1970) goes further, maintaining that the poem is based on an actual dirge (*qînâ*), which he attempts to reconstruct by stripping away whatever does not fit his metrical scheme. In spite of his arbitrary methods and farfetched interpretations, Anat does show that some of the statements in this passage pertain to mourning. But the poem itself is not a dirge, for the purpose of a dirge is to bewail the loss of the deceased and to praise his virtues, and these themes are lacking in Eccles. 12.

We know very little about funerary laments in ancient Israel, but it is quite possible that some of the lines (e.g. vv. 3, 5aβb) are taken from actual dirges. Except for 2 Sam. 1:17–27 and 3:33f., all we know of dirges is at one remove.[18] The prophets almost certainly draw on existing *qînôt* either to create mocking laments (e.g. Isa. 14:4–20; Ezek. 26:17f.; 27:3b–10; 28:12–19), or to dramatize an impending national disaster by bewailing it or by quoting those destined to suffer it (e.g. Mic. 2:4). Lam. 1, 2, and 4 are communal laments (i.e. laments for a communal disaster). Lamentations 3 and 5 and several psalms are communal entreaties that include passages of lamentation (e.g. Pss. 44, 60, 74, 79, 80, 85). References to communal mourning include Amos 5:16; 2 Sam. 1:12; 1 Macc. 1:27; 9:41. But Eccles. 12:1–7 is not a dirge, for a dirge mourns the deceased rather than describing the funeral.

On behalf of the interpretation of 12:2–5 as depicting a funeral, we may consider that although Qohelet does urge enjoyment of life during one's youth, he does not show an obsession with physical decrepitude that would make him likely to conclude his teachings with a long threnody on the ailments of aging. He does, on the other hand, reveal an obsession with death, and his gaze most naturally returns to that subject as he brings his teachings to a close.

17. For example, the lamentation for the prince of Tyre in Ezek. 28 calls him a beautiful "seal" (read *ḥōtām*) in the garden of Eden (v. 2). This is a trope for beauty and contributes to the description of the first man in Eden. It remains within the bounds of the literal meaning of the allegory, which is the depiction of the first man in Eden as resplendent in wealth and beauty before being corrupted. Similarly, within a literal reading of Jotham's allegory, "shade" (Judg. 9:15) may be recognized as a metaphor for "protection" as well as a reference to actual blockage of sunlight.

18. Laments are quoted in rabbinic sources, e.g. *Sem.* 1.9; *b. B. Bat.* 91a–b; *b. Meg.* 6a; 28b; *b. Ber.* 6b; *b. Moʿed Q.* 25b.

The syntax of the passage supports the idea that 12:2–5 describes the time of death and mourning rather than the process of aging. Eccles. 12:3–5 is an extended temporal clause depicting the events that occur at the same time as "a man is going to his eternal home, and mourners are walking about in the street" (v. 5b). A man's going to his "eternal home" (v. 5bα) might be thought to mean that he is aging and heading to death, but the mourners' procession (v. 5bβ) can only signify the funeral, and thus v. 5b as well speaks of the procession to the grave.[19] Therefore all the events of vv. 3–5 happen at the time of an individual's death, not during the slow decline to death (though the blossoming, v. 5aβγ, continues beyond the funeral). Moreover, the darkening of the luminaries (v. 2) occurs "in the day when" (i.e. in the time when) the events of the long temporal clause (vv. 3–5) take place, not long before them.[20]

During the funeral, doors are closed and the mill grows silent (thus Anat, 1970:379). While Qohelet's description of the gloom a funeral casts on a village may be exaggerated, there is evidence to show that a passing cortege could bring activities temporarily to a halt. Josephus says that "all who pass by when a corpse is being buried must accompany the funeral and join in the lamentations" (*Contra Apionem*, 2.205). B. *Moꜥed Q.* 27b and *j. Bik* 65c (cf. *Shulḥan Arukh*, Y.D. 361, 4) speak of the obligation to rise and accompany a cortege for at least a symbolic four paces. From a time closer to Qohelet, Sira (7:34 and 38:16–17) shows that participation in a funeral was considered an important communal obligation.

The strength of Taylor's case lies in his attempt to grasp what is happening on the literal plane rather than jumping quickly, as most commentators do, to figurative meanings. He is, however, wrong in his insistent exclusion of all meaning other than the literal in vv. 3–5, for the literal meaning may well have a symbolic or figurative function. The funerary interpretation can, I believe, account for the passage as a whole better than can the figurative approach. Nevertheless, many gaps remain, and not all details accommodate themselves to the funeral-scene interpretation.

19. The coordinate clause, "and the mourners walk about in the street" (v. 5bβ) shows that v. 5bα refers not to the long process of aging but to an event occurring within a short period, the time it takes the mourners to go on their rounds. In other words, the clause signifies the dead man's procession to the grave. *hālak* is used of going from life to the underworld or to the grave in Eccles. 3:20; 9:10; Ps. 39:14; 1 Chron. 17:11; etc. The *kí* at the beginning of v. 5b may be understood as giving the reason for the entire complex of occurrences of vv. 3–5a, not specifically for the events of v. 5a.

20. *bayyôm še-* connects the events of v. 2 with those of vv. 3–5. The long temporal clause that it introduces must modify "the sun grows dark, etc." (and not "remember, etc." [1a]—for the remembering must take place before, not when, the events of vv. 3–5 occur). All of vv. 3–5 speaks of the same time (whether *yôm* means "day" or a less definite "time," the events are pictured as concurrent). That "day," as v. 5b shows, is the time of death, when the mourners go about in the streets and the village falls silent. Although the events described are concurrent, the processes they symbolize may not be.

The scene is one of communal mourning. The image of the mourners going about the streets is explicitly funerary, and several other images are probably taken from the same situation. On the first level, then, the scene describes what happens when one dies. The unit 11:7–12:7 as a whole says: enjoy yourself before your funeral; but it says this dramatically and memorably, while conveying the finality, bitterness, and absurdity of mortality. It does not matter if some details do not contribute directly to constructing the funeral scene, because there are unambiguous signs, above all the framework of temporal clauses, that indicate that the poem speaks of dying and death.

Qohelet leads us through a village, building the scene step by step but leaving many puzzles. What village is this? We may wonder if this is in some sense the "place," the state, we will come to when we grow old or when we die. We see sturdy men writhing.[21] What nameless dread terrifies them so? The grinding-maids, whatever else they represent, are first of all grinding-maids.[22] When they leave off from their work, one of the background sounds of everyday life stops, and the unwonted silence makes us aware of their earlier presence. Milling was a never-ending task, and in normal times its sound would drone on unabated. Hence its silencing would leave a disturbing void. The gloom of the ladies at the lattices darkens the mood of the village.[23] In the past their half-hidden presence, scarcely noticed, signaled human contact. They observed, noted, and registered the busy movements of everyday life. Now their faces

21. "The keepers of the house" may be servants, not watchmen. Taylor (pp. 8–9) notes that the term "keeper" is applied to various kinds of servants, not only to guards (2 Sam. 20:3 refers to ten concubines David left "to keep the house"). Taylor also suggests that ʾanšê heḥāyil, the "powerful men," are men of influence and position (compare the usage in Ruth 2:1 and 1 Chron. 9:13), in contrast to the servants or keepers of the house (ibid.).

22. The "grinding-maids," lit. "grinders" (fem.), are the maidservants, the counterparts of the men who keep the house. The "ladies looking through the lattices" are the well-to-do women, women of leisure, the counterparts of the "powerful men." If Taylor is right that ʾanšê ḥayil refers to influential, well-to-do men, the four types of people mentioned form an ABA′B′ pattern and together embrace the range of social classes in the village. A similar all-encompassing grouping appears in Isa. 24:2: "(Layman shall be like priest,) servant like his master, amid servant like her mistress."

23. "The ladies looking through," lit. "the lookers" (fem. pl.) grow dark: ḥāšᵉkû means "grow dark" in the sense of grow gloomy. ḤŠK alone is not elsewhere used in this sense, but the phrase ḥāšᵉkû ʿênênû, lit. "our eyes grew dark," means to become despondent, virtually blind with grief (Lam. 5:17). (In Ps. 69:24 the phrase teḥšaknāh ʿênêhem refers to literal blindness.) The metaphorical transfer from "dark" to "gloomy" is a natural one. This transfer is lexicalized in the synonymous QDR, which denotes the gloom of mourning; e.g. Jer. 8:21; 14:2; Job 5:11; and Ps. 38:7. In the last verse, emotional darkness (QDR) appears in conjunction with bowing (ŠḤḤ) and writhing (ʿWH); see above. On the literal level, then, the sentence means that the women of the village will grieve. If this image is also a figure for the eyes, it means that one loses eyesight with age. But the choice of ḤŠK instead of KHH implies that this is not merely a physiological process, but also an emotional one, namely the loss of joy. So whether the women's "darkening" is read literally or figuratively, it connotes grief.

grow dark. What grieves them? Doors are shut—against what?—and the sounds of daily life cease. Suddenly we realize that the background hum of human activity was reassuring, a constant reminder that we belong to the land of the living. Now it is gone. All we hear now is the indifferent chirp of the bird and the keening of the mourners; they alone are going about their business. Mourning women bow low.[24] Fear is all around.[25] Then: the budding, growing, blooming of plants.[26] But this rebirth is without cheer, because it mocks the finality of *our* end. For man there is the snapping of a cord, the plunge into the pit, the smashing of the vessel at the bottom.

Still leaving aside the symbolic significances—though these soon begin to intrude themselves into a literal reading—we may ask about the connotations of the imagery. The imagery of the poem, whatever its symbolic or figurative meaning, creates an atmosphere of pain, contortion, and constriction. It draws us into a world of decay, abandonment, dreary silence, and speechless grief, and makes us associate this atmosphere with aging and death—whose pain is heightened by contrast with the rejuvenation of nature.

The imagery is unsettling in an almost surrealistic way. The luminaries and light itself are extinguished. Clouds hang overhead. All is murky.[27] Then we encounter a succession of images of distortion and despair: trembling, writhing, cessation of activity, darkening, shutting, silence, bowing, fear. What do all these people see that so disconcerts them? For whom are they mourning

24. In accordance with a well-known use of *bēn/bat* as a noun of relation (BDB, p. 121b, [sn]8), *bᵉnôt haššîr* can mean "songstresses"; cf. Ugaritic *bnt hll*, lit. "the daughters of praise (songs)," which refers to the *krt*, the female singers. *bᵉnôt haššîr*, the songstresses, are probably mourning women, perhaps professionals, who sing their laments (note that in Amos 8:3, the songs of the palace have a mourning tone). In 2 Chron. 35:25, the "singers" (*šārîm*) and the "songstresses" (*šārôt*) speak "laments" (*qînôt*). The songstresses in Eccles. 12:4 are bowed down in the traditional posture of lamentation. Bowing low, sitting on the ground, and falling to the ground are expressions of mourning (see Gruber, 1980:460–79). Note in particular: "I went about as in mourning for a mother, I was bowed down (*šaḥōtî*) in gloom" (Ps. 35:14; see further Pss. 38:7; 107:39; Isa. 2:9; 5:15).

25. *Wᵉhathattîm badderek*, literally "And errors are along the way," probably refers to the emotions of those who observe the cortege passing (thus Anat, 1970:379). In other words, scenes of dismay accompany the procession.

26. The phrases in 12:5aβ have most often been interpreted symbolically, usually as sexual allusions (it is easy to see sexual implications in the most diverse images, even caperberries and locusts). They are more likely descriptions of nature which stand in *contrast* to man. Nature, but not man, is reborn in the spring (Hertzberg; Loretz, pp. 191–92). This thought is expressed in Job 14:7–10; "A tree has hope: if it is cut off, it will be renewed . . . But man dies and is helpless. A human expires and disappears."

27. The significance of the rain and of the cloud's returning after them is unclear. Clouds symbolize misery in Joel 2:2 and Zeph. 1:15. The cloud covering the sun is an eschatological image in Ezek. 32:7. But if the darkening in 12:2a refers to death, as comparison with 11:7 suggests, then the clouds may serve the depiction of the scene of gloom and despair rather than function as a figure for misery.

so intensely? The answer is inevitable (and now we move from literal to symbolic): they mourn for *you*, you to whom Qohelet addressed his advice and warnings; the "you" of v. 1. It is *your* fate that appalls them, for this, Qohelet says, is what awaits *you*. Your death is eclipsing their world, and you are present at the terrible scene.

Symbolism

Already we have seen that some features of the picture—still taken quite literally—disturb the mental construction of the funeral scene. These features show that this is no ordinary funeral. By diverting our attention from the mundane, they provoke a reading on another level, a symbolic reading.[28]

The distinction between symbolism and allegory (or figuration) is not an absolute one, but the terms are useful in discussing two perspectives on this poem. For present purposes, we can use Samuel Taylor Coleridge's classic definition of symbolism:

> . . . a symbol [in contrast to an allegory] . . . is characterized by a translucence of the Special in the Individual or of the General in the Especial or of the Universal in the General. Above all by the translucence of the Eternal through and in the Temporal. It always partakes of the Reality which it renders intelligible; and while it enunciates the whole, abides itself as a living part in that Unity, of which it is the representative (1832:40).

Coleridge is defining a particular type of symbolism, which we may designate "inherent symbolism,"[29] in which conception and embodiment are simultaneous and interpenetrating. Such symbols are characterized by an "immediate presentation of something not immediate," thus evoking an ineffable, "total organic response" (Mischel, 1952:72). Since the symbol carries with it an indefinite penumbra of connotations, paraphrase cannot exhaust its meaning, nor can a symbolic image be directly translated into an entity in another domain, as an allegorical-type figure can (e.g. grinding maids = teeth; thornbush = Abimelech). Rather, in a symbol we observe a reality thickened and clarified (e.g. Esther both *is* a Jew in the diaspora and symbolically *embodies* the experience of the Jewish people in the diaspora; Abel's murder *is* brotherly conflict and also *represents* all human strife). By this understanding of symbolism, how does the poem in Eccles. 12:1–7 communicate symbolically?

28. The following discussion of symbolism draws especially on Kurz, 1982:65–83.

29. Following Levin, 1956:15. "Symbolism" commonly refers to more kinds of signification than Coleridge's definition allows. Symbols may also be related to their referents by convention, prescription, or extrinsic association. Allegory, for its part, is a symbolic mode; see further Fletcher, 1964:14. In this discussion I am using "symbol" to refer to what Levin calls "inherent" or "natural" symbols.

The poem makes the reader see his death from another perspective, that of an outside observer. From this vantage point, he sees more than an ordinary death and burial. The poem depicts a community at mourning, but also something beyond that. (It is in this regard that Taylor's determined "literal rendering" of the poem as an ordinary funeral falls short.) After all, rarely does an individual's death cause communal grief so extreme and so pervasive. The sun, moon, and stars do not truly go dark when someone dies, and light itself, the primal light of creation, does not disappear. Nor does the return of actual clouds (a welcome phenomenon in Israel) cause consternation.

While the poem describes the death and funeral of an individual, some of its imagery concurrently suggests a disaster of cosmic magnitude. The universality of the darkness and the silence—encompassing everything from the stars to the mills, from the powerful men to the menials, from the rich women to the maids—is reminiscent of prophetic depictions of the national and universal desolation awaiting humanity and nature at the end of this age. Normal sounds are silenced and the land is blanketed in darkness and terror.[30]

> I will eliminate from them
> the voice of gladness and the voice of happiness,
> the voice of the groom and the voice of the bride,
> the sound of the millstones and the light of the candle.
> And all this land will become a desolate destruction (Jer. 25:10–11a).

> And I will cover . . . the heavens,
> and I will make their stars go dark.
> I will cover the sun with a cloud,
> and the moon will not shine its light.
> All the luminaries in the heavens
> I will blacken above you;
> and I will set darkness upon your land,
> says the Lord God (Ezek. 32:7–8).

The day of the Lord is

> a day of darkness and gloom,
> a day of cloud and mist . . .
> Before it peoples writhe,
> and all faces gather blackness . . .
> The sun and the moon go dark,
> and the stars withdraw their radiance (Joel 2:2a, 6, 10b).

---

30. The patristic commentator Gregory Thaumaturgus, in his *Metaphrasis,* apparently interprets Eccles. 12:1–6 as describing 'that great and terrible day of God' (quoted in Plumptre, 1881:90f.).

The cruel and wrathful day of the Lord will

> make the earth a desolation,
> and destroy sinners from upon it.
> For the stars of the heavens and their constellations
> will not shine their light:
> The sun will go dark when it arises,
> and the moon will not radiate its light (Isa. 13:9b–10).

Threat of darkness is a frequent prophetic topos; e.g. Isa. 5:30; 8:22; Amos 5:18–20; Zeph. 1:15. The extinguishing of light symbolizes the undoing of creation, the return to primeval darkness. The prophetic eschatology does not regard the day of the Lord truly as the annihilation of the universe,[31] but it does use hyperbolic, end-of-the-world images to suggest the extremity of that day's horror.

The prophet's eschatological symbolism draws upon imagery and possibly phraseology familiar from mourning practices, while applying the images and phrases to a personified city, land, or world: "The field is robbed, the land mourns" (Joel 1:10); "Shall the earth not quake for this, and all its inhabitants mourn?" (Amos 8:8); "The earth mourns and is withered; miserable, withered, is the land" (Isa. 24:4); "Her doors moan and mourn; wiped out, she sits on the ground" (Isa. 3:26); "For this the earth mourns, the heavens grow dark above" (Jer. 4:28); and many more like these.

The cessation of the daily chore of milling, restated in v. 4, epitomizes the disruption of ordinary activities. What has happened to the maids? In terms of the scene depicted, they may simply have stopped their chores and "become few" in number around the mill in order to join the mourning. But eschatological overtones call to mind the inactivity that follows depopulation. Prophetic eschatology speaks of the terrors of depopulation; e.g. "I will make man scarcer than fine gold, people than gold of Ophir" (Isa. 13:12). Depopulation will silence the millstones (Jer. 25:10, quoted above; cf. Rev. 18:22f.).

The emotional reaction of the denizens of the village in Eccles. 12 is also heightened beyond the formalized expressions of grief at a funeral. Everyone in the village seems not only to have joined in the formalized expressions of mourning, but to be smitten with terror and grief. Again their behavior recalls the horrified quaking and writhing common in eschatological scenes. The men in 12:3 tremble and twist just as people will do on the day of the Lord, when

---

31. See the definition and discussion of "eschatology" in Lindblom, 1952. Eschatology refers to visions of a new age in which the relations of history or the world are altered and conditions in general are radically changed (p. 81).

> . . . all hands will grow slack,
> and every human heart melt,
> and they will be terrified.
> Pangs and pains will seize them,
> they will writhe like a woman in labor (Isa. 13:7f.).

Their agony recalls that of the prophet, who says:

> Therefore my loins are full of trembling.
> I am seized with pangs,
> like the pangs of a woman in labor.
> I am too twisted [naᶜăwêtî] to hear,
> too terrified to look (Isa. 21:3).

The shaking and writhing of males is considered especially shocking (Jer. 30:6). The terror or grief—we cannot tell which—of the men in Qohelet's village suggests they have seen a disaster of high magnitude. And, in a sense, that is the case, because every individual is a microcosm and every death is a catastrophe; it is, in fact, the end of a world.

The light that is extinguished in 12:2 is the light that is sweet in 11:7, namely the light of life. Likewise the darkening of the light is the onset of the eternal darkness mentioned in 11:8. In one sense this is the extinction of an individual life; in another, the extinction of a universe. For the person who dies, the stars blink out, the sun goes dark (only the living "see the sun"), activities cease, and the world grows silent.

Both Qohelet and the prophets draw upon images of mourning and universal cataclysm. For the prophets, these images depict the disaster of a nation or the world at large. For Qohelet they represent the demise of the individual. Qohelet is shaping symbolism in a way contrary to its usual direction of signification. Symbolism usually views the general through the particular (Daniel representing the Jewish people in exile; a woman's mourning representing Jerusalem's; Jerusalem's mourning representing Israel's misery). Qohelet views the particular through the general, the small writ large.[32] He audaciously invokes images of general disaster to symbolize every death; more precisely—the death of you, the reader, to whom Qohelet is speaking when he addresses the youth, his ostensive audience.

The eschatological symbolism is manifest but restrained. Qohelet avoids heaping up pictures of natural upheaval and universal panic, slaughter, and destruc-

---

32. Many of John Donne's metaphors are of this sort, such as his description of his beloved as "my America, my new-found land," or his declaration: "She is all States, and all Princes, I" ('The Sun Rising'). For Donne and his contemporaries, such images were a deliberate expression of the concept of man as microcosm. "I am a little world made cunningly of elements," Donne wrote in *Holy Sonnets*, V.

tion. Such extremes would prevent the association of the imagery with the individual death. Still, Qohelet does choose imagery of a vast catastrophe to evoke a vision of death, that most ordinary of tragedies; and the angst he thereby reveals is not restricted to this poem. Throughout the book, Qohelet reveals an obsession with death unparalleled in biblical literature. There may be no explanation for this outside the author's personality; not every literary phenomenon has social or historical causes. But Qohelet's obsession with death intersects another of his peculiarities: he reveals no consciousness of himself as part of a nation or a community. All his values are solitary, measured by benefit or harm to the individual. This individualism imposes itself on his attitude toward death. Every death is an unmitigated loss, for its shock cannot be buffered by communal continuity.

Allegory and Figuration

It is doubtful that this poem, even as understood by the commentators who take the images as anatomical figures, would properly be classified as an allegory, as this term is commonly used in other areas of literary study. An allegory is an extended and complex image composed of an organized set of figures or tokens representing certain concepts, events, or entities in an extratextual reality. A succession of interrelated figures (related usually within a narrative structure) are subordinated to concepts or entities existing in a distinct domain of reality. An allegory should embrace an entire text or a relatively independent segment thereof, for the literal meaning must stand on its own (see Kurz, 1982:32f.). The interpretation of Eccles. 12 as an allegory of old age does not establish any cohesiveness among the figures themselves. Rather it treats them as independent figures drawn from disparate domains (houses, flora, fauna, people, luminaries, and more), each figure representing something in the external world. Some images are often left outside the "allegory" (see, for example, Gordis, p. 329).[33] Eccles. 12:1–8 lacks the degree of internal consistency necessary to give meaning and cogency to an allegory, especially one lacking an explanatory introduction or conclusion or other interpretive guides, such as a narrative context.

However, my concern here is not with the misapplication of a term but with the question of whether the poem is what its interpreters think it is. It is no refutation of an interpretation to claim that it is using a term in an eccentric fashion. Still, it is more accurate to refer to this approach as the "figurative interpretation" when it takes the poem as in the main a loose succession of figures, each representing a different symptom of aging. The attempt to explain the totality as a series of anatomical figures will be called the "allegorical interpretation."

---

33. Crenshaw (1986:10) says that because of the switches to and from literal imagery we should avoid the allegorical interpretation, but he does take most of the images as symbols of the aging process.

Whereas the symbolic meaning of an image extends the literal, the figurative meaning of an image replaces it through a series of equations: the thornbush = Abimelech, the vineyard = Israel (Isa. 5:1–6), (Orwell's) pigs = Bolsheviks, etc. As such, the contours of figurative meaning are more defined than the symbolic, the signifier (farm animals, etc.) and the signified (political parties, etc.) being kept in two distinct domains. A figurative reading calls for a decoding or a translation between these two domains. A figurative reading of Eccles. 12 translates the grinding maids into teeth, the women at the windows into eyes, and so on. Once the image is translated into referent, the figure is depleted of meaning, and interpretation can proceed without further reference to it.

There is, nevertheless, a certain rhetorical gain in figurative imagery, one inhering in the process of reading rather than in the results. That process, whatever answers it arrives at, requires the reader to scrutinize the individual images while simultaneously calling to mind the unhappy facts of aging and death. We discover for ourselves the truth of Qohelet's warning that misery lies ahead.

The possibility that Qohelet's poem includes several figures for aging mixed with literal statements is established by a Sumerian saying that does just that:

> My grain roasting fails,
> Now my youthful vigor, strength and personal god
>   have left my loins like an exhausted ass.
> My black mountain has produced white gypsum.
> My mother has brought in a man from the forest;
>   he gave me captivity.
> My mongoose which used to eat strong smelling things
>   does not stretch its neck towards beer and butter.
> My urine used to flow in a strong torrent,
>   but now you flee from my wind.
> My child whom I used to feed with butter and milk,
>   I can no more support it.
> And I have had to sell my little slave girl;
>   an evil demon makes me sick (Alster, 1975:93).

This text has two interpretive guides Qohelet's poem lacks; the first-person possessive, which directs us away from the literal plane (e.g. black mountains producing white gypsum) to something the speaker possesses (white hair); and a consistency in the domain of the signified—the difficulties of aging. Nevertheless, it does show that the objection occasionally made against the allegorical interpretation, namely that the figures are not coordinated and thus the poem is not allegorical,[34] has validity only as a comment on the term "allegorical." It does not preclude the possibility that some of the images are figures of aging.

---

34. E.g. Taylor claims that it is "scarcely possible to harmonize the various details on any rational plan. But assuredly, unless a consistent whole can be made out, there is but slight reason for granting the details of the interpretation" (1874:53).

A few of the images in Eccles. 12:2–8 lend themselves naturally to interpretation as figures for the infirmities of aging, though only two do so with much clarity. The women looking through the windows seem to represent eyes, because they are said to "look," and because *ḥāśak* is used elsewhere of eyes but not of people. The grinding-maids seem to represent the teeth, because milling is an obvious analogy to chewing, and because the maids are said to "grow few," a process more usual with teeth than with maids. Moreover the Hebrew terms used for both sets of women, literally "the lookers" (*hārōʾôt*) and "the grinders" (*haṭṭōḥănôt*), do not explicitly designate humans.[35] Another pair of images, the keepers of the house and the powerful men, accommodate themselves easily to a figurative interpretation as the arms and legs, though it is uncertain which is which.

Some of the images in Eccles. 12:2–6 are figures not of aging but of death. In v. 6 the smashing of the jug and jar into the cistern is undoubtedly figurative, though it is unclear whether the components of the image each have a specific referent, and also whether the images represent death or burial or both. Likewise, the darkening of the luminaries in v. 2 represents death figuratively. In any case, the images of vv. 2 and 6 are outside the description of aging, which is usually thought to be the point of the poem.

If the poem draws imagery from actual dirges, it may well have borrowed cryptic figures from them. Some biblical dirges are called *mešālîm* or speak of the dead figuratively: Isa. 14, called a *māšāl* in v. 4 (LXX *thrēnon*) speaks allegorically of Babylon as a divinity, Helel son of Dawn. Ezekiel's dirge (*qînâ*) over Tyre speaks of the prince of Tyre as the first man, who is in turn described figuratively as a precious seal (Ezek. 28:12–19). Num. 21:27–30 is a dirge over Moab spoken by *hammōšᵉlîm*, "the mashal makers," and *mešālîm* are said to require interpretation (Prov. 1:6). Some of the dirges recorded in the Talmud use images, some of them cryptic; e.g. "Our brothers are merchants, whose goods are examined at the customs house" (*b. Moᶜed Q*. 28b); "I have many coins, but no money changer to accept them" (*b. San*. 68a); "Borrow a Milesian robe for a free man who left no provision" (*b. Moᶜed Q*. 28b).[36] Some of

35. "Grinders" (*ṭoḥănôt*) is a natural trope for teeth, which do "grow few." It is, however, uncertain that *miᶜēṭû* does have that meaning.

Jenni (1968:52) explains *miᶜēṭû* as elliptical for "(ihre Zahl) verringern," though it seems like an unnecessary fiction to assume an ellipsis, as he does, when the fuller phrase (* *miᶜăṭû mispārām*) does not occur. More helpful is his claim that whereas the root in the qal, a conjugation frequently intransitive (*māᶜăṭû*), describes the process *in actu*, the piel intransitive is resultative: "weil ihrer wenig geworden sind" (ibid.). Ibn Ezra takes the verb as elliptical for *miᶜăṭû haṭṭᵉḥînâ* (or *miᶜăṭû ṭāḥōn*), "they do little grinding." But the verb he supplies is not clearly implicit in the preceding clause. Also the grinding-maids would not "cease" from their activity of grinding because of "grinding a little," whereas the diminution of their ranks might well bring the work to a halt, at least for much of the time.

36. Talmudic laments are collected, translated, and analyzed by Feldman, 1977:109–37.

the strange images in Qohelet's poem, such as the voice of the bird, the fear of the height (?), the terrors (obstacles?) in the path, and the almond, locust, and caperberry, may be figures whose meaning cannot be inferred from the passage itself.

The more images that can be identified with events in the process of aging, the closer the poem approaches allegory, but all the images besides those in vv. 3 and 6 resist such identification. The only way to establish further linkages is to ferret out analogous features, sometimes quite far-fetched ones, between images and referents, and this immediately leads into interpretive tangles. In v. 4a, for example, the "mill" is most naturally taken as something used by the grinding-maids mentioned in the preceding sentence. But if the latter are the teeth, the mill itself cannot be. And it is no help to take the "mill" as the mouth, because (1) the mouth does not grow silent in old age; and (2) if the "mill" is the mouth, the "doors" must be the lips ("doors" seem to represent lips in Job 41:6). But in what sense is the silencing of the mouth the *circumstance* of the lips' closing? And if the doors are figurative, what "street" are they on? Is that street different from the literal street in the next verse? The attempt to translate the other images in vv. 2, 4b, and 5 leads to similar blind alleys. The images that do work as figures do not add up to an allegory.

Information of the sort conveyed by allegorical-type figures (the eyes dim, the legs shake, the teeth fall out, and the like) is of marginal importance in this poem. First of all, the reader must *start* with the knowledge that the presumed figures communicate. We can know that the strong men's quaking represents the legs' shaking (if this is indeed so) only if we know that legs grow shaky with age. It cannot be the poem's goal to inform us of this. In any case, how great would our gain be if we knew for certain that Qohelet intended the powerful men to represent legs or the almond blossoms white hair? Not even the young need a sage to tell them that aging weakens the legs and grays the hair. But the poem's purpose is not to convey information; it is to create an attitude toward aging and, more importantly, death. A reader, especially a young one like the youth ostensibly addressed in this unit, may not be aware of the fear, loneliness, and nostalgia for an earlier reality irretrievably lost, which are the lot of many (and to some extent, perhaps all) of the aged, Qohelet undoubtedly among them. They might not know of the prospective mourning for a vanished existence. This awareness is gendered by the interaction of the literal and symbolic types of meaning.

I do not present this threefold interpretation as a "new reading" and certainly not as a novel decoding of hitherto hidden messages. This interpretation claims to give explicit (though not complete) formulation to the primary effects the poem is intended to have on the reader. An imaginative reading will, I believe, convey some sense of the pain and fear that hover over the scene and will connect that sense with thoughts of one's own death. Furthermore, because the entire scene is syntactically circumstantial to a main clause in the second person (12:1a), the scene must represent the fate of the reader. After all, Qohelet says quite clearly that this is what lies ahead for *you*. Moreover, the ancient reader would, I believe, discern a funeral scene in the description. Beyond that, the familiar eschatological symbolism associated with the scene would convey a sense of death as the undoing of a world, one's own very personal world. All these figures, symbols, allusions, and overtones are controlled by the culmination of the poem, with its unveiled, literal language (12:7–8), where we are reminded that all these images finally pertain to the individual's death, and that this event in itself means that "everything is absurd."

33

THE DIRGE OF COHELETH
IN ECCLESIASTES 12

C. Taylor

1. It has been noticed that the passage discussed falls naturally into three paragraphs, each commencing with ERE, and complete in itself. Considering the second paragraph, vv. 2–5, we may say that the literal rendering is *prima facie* the most natural: the words "for the man passeth to his eternal home, and the mourners go about in the street," suggest that the verses preceding describe the state of affairs while the mourners go about in the street. The man himself is addressed (v. 1) on the way in which his death will affect not only himself but others. Compare Ezek. 32:10; "Yea, I will make many people amazed at thee" &c.

2. The various classes are described as in a state of mental perturbation: there is a cessation of business and pleasure: the keepers of the house tremble (v. 2): they fear from on high (v. 5), &c. An impression may arise that some of the words used would better suit a time when calamity is impending than a time of mourning for the actual death of a great personage; and from this consideration perhaps the chief objection to the literal rendering will arise. But such passages as Ezekiel's description of the princes of the sea trembling as they mourn for Tyre, will go far to remove any objection of this nature:—

From C. Taylor, *The Dirge of Coheleth in Ecclesiastes XII* (Edinburgh: Williams and Norgate, 1874), 76–80.

"Then all the princes of the sea shall come down from their thrones, and lay away their robes, and put off their broidered garments: they shall clothe themselves with trembling; they shall sit upon the ground, and shall tremble every moment. And they shall take up a lamentation for thee, and say to thee, How art thou destroyed, &c" (Ezek. 26:16, 17).

In like manner the kings and merchants who mourn for Babylon are horror-stricken (Rev. 18:15); and this illustration is the more valuable because, as has been already remarked, the description from which it is taken coincides in several particulars with the dirge of Coheleth. In both alike the mill ceases to be heard: the unclean bird takes possession: the light of joy is quenched (Rev. 28:2, 22, 23). The Apocalyptic dirge is couched in the same strain as that of Coheleth, and differs from it chiefly in being applied to the case not of an individual but of a city.

3. There are some verbal coincidences which afford additional arguments for a literal rendering, and against the anatomical rendering. The mourners are said to go about the *street*, or ἀγορά (v. 5): the doors are closed to the *street* (v. 4). From this coincidence it may be assumed provisionally that "street" is literal in v. 4, as it is allowed to be in v. 5, until some reason has been assigned for taking the word literally in the one case and not literally in the other.

4. If "street" is literal in v. 4, it is only natural to assume that an actual "mill" is spoken of in the same context. This conclusion is confirmed by a further examination of the two verses; thus, in v. 5 the last clause is allowed to be literal, and it is also supposed that the opening words describe actual persons as awestricken. Add to this, that the intervening expressions, *almond, locust*, &c. are in themselves at least as naturally taken in a literal as in an anatomical sense, and there remains no valid reason for asserting that in their present context—viz. in a verse which begins and ends literally—they have any other than their natural meanings. Again, in v. 4, the "bird" is allowed to be literal, and some even of the anatomists take the parallel "daughters of song" literally. Thus throughout v. 4. 5 there is no place where it can be confidently affirmed that the literal rendering should be given up.

5. If the "mill" in v. 4 is literal, I think it sufficiently obvious that the "milleresses" in v. 3 are literal: the sound of the mill falls when the milleresses cease from work. It would follow that the remainder of v. 3 is literal. Perhaps the strongest point in the literal rendering is the interpretation of the first hemistich in verse 4 . . . ; and if it be granted that this is literal, there remains very little to be said for the anatomical theory as a whole.

6. The "house" in v. 3 must be, for all purposes of comparison, homogeneous with the "house of eternity" in v. 6. The latter is external to the man himself: hence we infer that the former is not the man himself or any part of him, but the mansion in which he lived.

7. The darkening of the sun &c. (v. 2) is clearly figurative. Between this and the allusion to literal mourners going about an actual street, there must some-

where be a point of transition from the figurative to the literal. As we have seen, it is very difficult to find such a point of transition anywhere after the commencement of v. 3, but on the other hand the expression "in the day when" might serve, and does elsewhere serve, as an indication that what follows is literal, and explanatory of the preceding general metaphor. Now not only is the darkening of the heavens a stereotyped figure of calamity in general, but it is also the practice of Biblical writers to pass from this general figure to matter-of-fact explanatory statements. To the numerous examples . . . one more may be added, in illustration of Coheleth's:

> Remember thy Creator
> Ere the sun and the moon be darkened
> In the day when the doors are shut to the street.

The passage runs as follows:

"Give glory to the *Lord* your God, before he cause darkness, and before your feet stumble upon the dark mountains, and while ye look for light, he turn it into the shadow of death, and make it gross darkness. But if ye will not hear it, my soul shall weep in secret places for your pride; and mine eye shall weep sore, and run down with tears, because the *Lord's* flock is carried away captive. Say unto the king and to the queen, Humble yourselves, sit down: for your principalities shall come down, even the crown of your glory. The cities of the south shall be shut up, and none shall open them: Judah shall be carried away captive all of it, it shall be wholly carried away captive" (Jer. 13:16–19).

8. As in Eccles. 2:4–9 the pleasure of possession is dwelt upon: "I made me great works; I builded me *houses* . . . I made me *gardens* . . . I got me servants and maidens, and had servants born in my house. . . . I got me men-singers and women-singers, and the delights of the sons of men, as musical instruments, and that of all sorts"; so in the passage under discussion we may see contrasted with this the gloom cast over a great house, with gardens, &c. when the life of its owner has passed away. It is not that the house is dilapidated, but that it is desolated, *the man*, now reduced to the level of ordinary mortals, leaves it for another: "when he dieth he shall carry nothing away: his glory shall not descend after him" (Ps. 49:17).

It is unnecessary to add anything to what has been already said on the details of the literal rendering. It certainly gives a consistent picture, and so far has the advantage over the anatomical rendering; which again, if it cannot claim consistency, has little else to rest upon. It is remarkable that the latter should so long have held its ground in spite of its grotesque repulsiveness and defiance of analogy, when the mention of the mourners who go about in the street suggests with the utmost plainness that the preceding verses are of the nature of a literal dirge.

SELECT BIBLIOGRAPHY

Books

Barton, George A. *A Critical and Exegetical Commentary on the Book of Ecclesiastes.* International Critical Commentary. Edinburgh: T. & T. Clark, 1908.

Bridges, Charles. *Ecclesiastes.* 1860. Reprint, Carlisle, Penn.: Banner of Truth Trust, 1961.

Crenshaw, James L. *Ecclesiastes: A Commentary.* Philadelphia: Westminster, 1987.

Davidson, Robert. *Ecclesiastes and the Song of Solomon.* Philadelphia: Westminster, 1986.

Delitzsch, Franz. *Biblical Commentary on the Song of Songs and Ecclesiastes.* Translated by M. G. Easton. 1891. Reprint. Grand Rapids: Eerdmans, 1950.

Eaton, Michael A. *Ecclesiastes.* Tyndale Old Testament Commentaries. Downers Grove, Ill.: InterVarsity, 1983.

Fox, Michael V. *Qohelet and His Contradictions.* Sheffield: Almond, 1989.

Garrett, Duane A. *Proverbs, Ecclesiastes, Song of Songs.* New American Commentary. Nashville: Broadman, 1993.

Ginsberg, H. L. *Studies in Koheleth.* New York: Jewish Theological Seminary of America, 1950.

Ginsburg, Christian D. *The Song of Songs and Coheleth.* 1861. Reprint, New York: KTAV, 1970.

Goldberg, Louis. *Ecclesiastes.* Bible Study Commentary. Grand Rapids: Zondervan, 1983.

Good, Edwin M. *Irony in the Old Testament.* Philadelphia: Westminster, 1965. Chapter 6, "Qoheleth: The Limits of Wisdom."

Gordis, Robert. *Koheleth—The Man and His World: A Study of Ecclesiastes.* 3d ed. New York: Schocken, 1968.

———. *Poets, Prophets, and Sages.* Bloomington, Ind.: Indiana University Press, 1971. Chapter 14, "The Wisdom of Koheleth."

Hubbard, David Allan. *Beyond Futility.* Grand Rapids: Eerdmans, 1976.

———. *Ecclesiastes, Song of Solomon.* Communicator's Commentary. Dallas: Word, 1991.

Kaiser, Walter C., Jr. *Ecclesiastes: Total Life.* Chicago: Moody, 1979.

Kidner, Derek. *The Message of Ecclesiastes.* Downers Grove, Ill.: InterVarsity, 1976.

Leupold, H. C. *Exposition of Ecclesiastes.* Grand Rapids: Baker, 1966.

Loader, J. A. *Ecclesiastes: A Practical Commentary.* Grand Rapids: Eerdmans, 1986.

———. *Polar Structure in the Book of Qohelet.* New York: Walter de Gruyter, 1979.

Murphy, Roland E. *Ecclesiastes.* Word Biblical Commentary. Dallas: Word, 1992.

Ogden, Graham S. *Qoheleth.* Sheffield: JSOT Press, 1987.

Scott, R. B. Y. *Proverbs, Ecclesiastes.* Anchor Bible. Garden City, N.Y.: Doubleday, 1965.

Swindoll, Charles R. *Living on the Ragged Edge.* Waco: Word, 1985.

Whitby, Charles F. *Koheleth: His Language and Thought.* New York: Walter de Gruyter, 1979.

Articles and Essays

Archer, Gleason L. "The Linguistic Evidence for the Date of 'Ecclesiastes.'" *Journal of the Evangelical Theological Society* 12 (Summer 1969): 167–81.

Brindle, Wayne A. "Righteousness and Wickedness in Ecclesiastes 7:15–18." *Andrews University Seminary Studies* 23 (Autumn 1985): 243–57.

Bruns, J. Edgar. "The Imagery of Ecclesiastes 12:6a." *Journal of Biblical Literature* 84 (1965): 428–30.

Caneday, Ardel B. "Qoheleth: Enigmatic Pessimist or Godly Sage?" *Grace Theological Journal* 7 (1986): 21–56.

Castellino, George R. "Qohelet and His Wisdom." *Catholic Biblical Quarterly* 30 (1968): 15–28.

Davis, Barry C. "Ecclesiastes 12:1–8—Death: An Impetus for Life." *Bibliotheca Sacra* 148 (July–September 1991): 298–318.

Forman, Charles C. "Koheleth's Use of Genesis." *Journal of Semitic Studies* 5 (1960): 1256–63.

Fox, Michael V. "Aging and Death in Qohelet 12." *Journal for the Study of the Old Testament* 42 (1988): 55–77.

———. "The Meaning of *Hebel* for Qoheleth." *Journal of Biblical Literature* 105 (1986): 409–27.

Fredericks, Daniel C. "Chiasm and Parallel Structure in Qoheleth 5:9–6:9." *Journal of Biblical Literature* 108 (1989): 17–35.

Garrett, Duane A. "Ecclesiastes 7:25–29 and the Feminist Hermeneutic." *Criswell Theological Review* 2 (1988): 309–21.

Ginsberg, H. L. "The Quintessence of Koheleth." In *Biblical and Other Studies*, edited by Alexander Altmann. Cambridge: Harvard University Press, 1963.

———. "The Structure and Contents of the Book of Koheleth." In *Wisdom in Israel and in the Ancient Near East*, edited by Martin Noth and D. Winton Thomas. Leiden: Brill, 1955.

Glenn, Donald A. "Ecclesiastes." In *The Bible Knowledge Commentary, Old Testament*, edited by John F. Walvoord and Roy B. Zuck. Wheaton, Ill.: Victor, 1985.

Good, Edwin M. "The Unfilled Sea: Style and Meaning in Ecclesiastes 1:2–11." In *Israelite Wisdom: Theological and Literary Essays in Honor of Samuel Terrien*, edited by John G. Gammie et al. Missoula, Mont.: Scholars, 1978.

Harris, R. Laird. "Ecclesiastes: Solomon—the Divine Philosopher." *Covenant Seminary Review* 7 (Spring–Fall 1981): 115–19.

Johnston, Robert K. "'Confessions of a Workaholic': A Reappraisal of Qoheleth." *Catholic Biblical Quarterly* 38 (January 1976): 14–28.

Kaiser, Walter C., Jr. "Integrating Wisdom Theology into Old Testament Theology: Ecclesiastes 3:10–15." In *A Tribute to Gleason Archer*, edited by Walter C. Kaiser, Jr., and Ronald F. Youngblood. Chicago: Moody, 1986.

Lohfink, Norbert. "Qoheleth 5:17–19." *Catholic Biblical Quarterly* 52 (1990): 625–35.

Mitchell, Hinckley G. "'Work' in Ecclesiastes." *Journal of Biblical Literature* 32 (1913): 123–38.

Murphy, Roland E. "A Form-Critical Consideration of Ecclesiastes VII." *Society of Biblical Literature Abstracts and Seminar Papers*. Missoula, Mont.: Society of Biblical Literature, 1974.

———. "Ecclesiastes (Qoheleth)." In *Wisdom Literature*. The Forms of the Old Testament Literature, vol. 13. Grand Rapids: Eerdmans, 1981.

Ogden, Graham S. "Qoheleth IX:1–16." *Vetus Testamentum* 32 (April 1982): 158–69.

———. "Qoheleth IX 17–X 20: Variations on the Theme of Wisdom's Strength and Vulnerability." *Vetus Testamentum* 30 (1980): 27–37.

———. "Qoheleth XI 1–6." *Vetus Testamentum* 33 (1983): 222–30.

———. "'Vanity' It Certainly Is Not." *Bible Translator* 38 (July 1987): 301–7.

———. "The "Better" –Proverb *(Tôb-Spruch)*, Rhetorical Criticism and Qoheleth." *Journal of Biblical Literature* 96 (1977): 489–505.

Osborn, Noel D. "A Guide for Balanced Living: An Exegetical Study of Ecclesiastes 7:1–14." *Bible Translator* 21 (October 1970): 185–96.

Polk, Timothy. "The Wisdom of Irony: A Study of *Hebel* and Its Relation to Joy and the Fear of God in Ecclesiastes." *Studia Biblica et Theologica* 6 (1976): 3–17.

Rainey, A. F. "A Study of Ecclesiastes." *Concordia Theological Monthly* 35 (1964): 149–57.

Sawyer, John F. A. "The Ruined House in Ecclesiastes 12: A Reconstruction of the Original Parable." *Journal of Biblical Literature* 94 (December 1975): 519–31.

Shank, H. Carl. "Qoheleth's World and Life View as Seen in His Recurring Phrases." *Westminster Theological Journal* 37 (Fall 1974): 57–73.

"The Scope and Plan of the Book of Ecclesiastes." *Princeton Review* 29 (July 1857): 419–40.

Whybray, R. N. "Qoheleth, Preacher of Joy." *Journal for the Study of the Old Testament* 23 (1982): 87–98.

Williams, Jerry G. "What Does It Profit A Man?' The Wisdom of Koheleth." *Judaism* 20 (1971): 179–93. Reprinted in *Studies in Ancient Israelite Wisdom,* compiled by James L. Crenshaw. New York: KTAV, 1976.

Wright, Addison G. "Additional Numerical Patterns in Qoheleth." *Catholic Biblical Quarterly* 45 (January 1983): 32–43.

———. "The Riddle of the Sphinx: The Structure of the Book of Qoheleth." *Catholic Biblical Quarterly* 30 (1968): 313–34.

Wright, J. Stafford. "Ecclesiastes." In *The Expositor's Bible Commentary,* vol. 5. Grand Rapids: Zondervan, 1991.

———. "The Interpretation of Ecclesiastes." *Evangelical Quarterly* 18 (1946): 18–34. Reprinted in *Classical Evangelical Essays in Old Testament Interpretation,* compiled by Walter C. Kaiser, Jr. Grand Rapids: Baker, 1972.

Wyngaarden, Martin F. "The Interpretation of Ecclesiastes." *Calvin Forum* 20 (1953–55): 157–60.

Youngblood, Ronald F. "Qoheleth's 'Dark House' (Eccl. 12:5)." *Journal of the Evangelical Theological Society* 29 (December 1986): 397–410.

Zimmerman, Frank. "The Aramaic Provenance of Qohelet." *Jewish Quarterly Review* 36 (1945): 17–45.

———. "The Question of Hebrew in Qohelet." *Jewish Quarterly Review* 40 (1949): 79–102.

Zuck, Roy B. "God and Man in Ecclesiastes." *Bibliotheca Sacra* 148 (January–March 1991): 46–56.

INDEX OF SUBJECTS

INDEX OF SCRIPTURE

417